T0323973

Measuring Human Capital

Measuring Human Capital

EDITED BY

BARBARA FRAUMENI
Central University of Finance and Economics, Beijing, China

ACADEMIC PRESS
An imprint of Elsevier

ELSEVIER

Academic Press is an imprint of Elsevier
125 London Wall, London EC2Y 5AS, United Kingdom
525 B Street, Suite 1650, San Diego, CA 92101, United States
50 Hampshire Street, 5th Floor, Cambridge, MA 02139, United States
The Boulevard, Langford Lane, Kidlington, Oxford OX5 1GB, United Kingdom

Notices
Knowledge and best practice in this field are constantly changing. As new research and experience broaden our
understanding, changes in research methods, professional practices, or medical treatment may become
necessary.

Practitioners and researchers must always rely on their own experience and knowledge in evaluating and using
any information, methods, compounds, or experiments described herein. In using such information or
methods they should be mindful of their own safety and the safety of others, including parties for whom they
have a professional responsibility.

To the fullest extent of the law, neither the Publisher nor the authors, contributors, or editors, assume
any liability for any injury and/or damage to persons or property as a matter of products liability, negligence or
otherwise, or from any use or operation of any methods, products, instructions, or ideas contained in the
material herein.

Library of Congress Cataloging-in-Publication Data
A catalog record for this book is available from the Library of Congress

British Library Cataloguing-in-Publication Data
A catalogue record for this book is available from the British Library

ISBN 978-0-12-819057-9

For information on all Academic Press publications
visit our website at https://www.elsevier.com/books-and-journals

Publisher: Brian Romer
Editorial Project Manager: Lena Sparks
Production Project Manager: Kiruthika Govindaraju
Cover Designer: Alan Studholme

Typeset by SPi Global, India

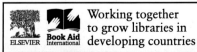

Working together
to grow libraries in
developing countries

www.elsevier.com • www.bookaid.org

Contents

PART I
INTRODUCTION

INTRODUCTION, *ix*
Gang Liu, Barbara M. Fraumeni

PART II
MAJOR MEASURES OF HUMAN CAPITAL

SECTION II.A
MONETARY MEASURES

1   **The Impact of Air Pollution on Human Capital Wealth,** *1*
Glenn-Marie Lange, Shun Chonabayashi, Kenan Karakülah, Esther Naikal
1.1 Introduction, *1*
    1.1.1 National Wealth and the Importance of Human Capital for Development, 1
    1.1.2 Human Capital in National Wealth Accounts, 2
    1.1.3 Threats to Human Capital: Air Pollution and Human Health, 4
    1.1.4 Outline of This Chapter, 4
1.2 Data and Methods for Measuring the Impact of Air Pollution on Human Capital, *4*
    1.2.1 Measuring Human Capital Wealth in the Wealth of Nations: Conceptual Approach, 5
    1.2.2 Estimating the Impact of Air Pollution, 7
1.3 Results, *8*
1.4 Next Steps for Human Capital and Air Pollution, *17*
Appendix 1.1 Global Wealth Accounts, 1995–2014, *22*
Appendix 1.2 Methodology for Calculating Human Capital Wealth, *24*
Appendix 1.3 Estimates of Human Capital and Wealth for 2014 With Impacts of No Premature Deaths From Air Pollution, *38*
References, *38*

2   **Global Human Capital: View From Inclusive Wealth,** *39*
Moinul Islam, Shunsuke Managi
2.1 Introduction, *39*
2.2 Methodology, *40*
2.3 Results and Discussion, *41*
    2.3.1 Progress of Nations' Human Capital, 41
    2.3.2 Discussion, 42
2.4 Conclusion and Policy Recommendation, *52*
Annex, *52*
References, *53*

SECTION II.B
INDEXES

3   **The World Bank Human Capital Index,** *55*
Paul Corral, Nicola Dehnen, Ritika D'Souza, Roberta Gatti, Aart Kraay
3.1 Introduction, *55*
3.2 Methodology of the World Bank Human Capital Index, *56*
    3.2.1 Components of the Human Capital Index, 56
    3.2.2 Aggregation Methodology, 57
    3.2.3 Connecting the HCI to Future Income, Growth, and Poverty Reduction, 59
3.3 The Human Capital Index 2020 Update, *60*
    3.3.1 HCI 2020—Index Components, 60
    3.3.2 HCI 2020—Results, 64
    3.3.3 HCI Measures of Gender Gaps in Education, 68
3.4 Discussion, *71*
    3.4.1 Limitations of the HCI, 71
    3.4.2 The Role of Country Rankings, 71
    3.4.3 Comparison With Other Measures of Human Capital and Development, 72
    3.4.4 Subnational Disaggregation of the HCI, 75
    3.4.5 The Utilization-Adjusted Human Capital Index (UHCI), 76
3.5 The Measurement Agenda Ahead, *77*
References, *79*

4   Human Development: A Perspective on Metrics, *83*
Pedro Conceição, Milorad Kovacevic, Tanni Mukhopadhyay
4.1 Introduction, *83*
4.2 Human Development and the Capabilities Approach, *84*
  4.2.1 The Distinction Between Means and Ends, 85
  4.2.2 Challenges for the Capabilities Approach, 86
4.3 Measurement Framework of Human Development, *86*
4.4 Simplicity of the HDI and Related Criticisms, *88*
4.5 Choice of Indicators for the Human Development Index, *89*
  4.5.1 Health Indicator, 92
  4.5.2 Education Indicators, 92
  4.5.3 Indicator of Standard of Living, 94
4.6 Functional Form of the HDI, *94*
  4.6.1 Functional Transformation of Income, 95
  4.6.2 Scaling (Normalization) of Indicators, 97
  4.6.3 Weighting, 103
  4.6.4 Aggregation, 105
4.7 Summary of the Critiques and a Debate About the Switch to the Geometric Mean, *106*
4.8 Country Ranking and Classification by HDI, *108*
4.9 Data Issues and Perspectives, *109*
4.10 Conclusion, *110*
References, *111*
Further Reading, *115*

5   Summary of Lim, S. S., et al., "Measuring human capital: A systematic analysis of 195 countries and territories, 1990–2016", *117*
Barbara M. Fraumeni, Gang Liu
5.1 Methods, *117*
  5.1.1 Educational Attainment, 118
  5.1.2 Learning, 118
  5.1.3 Functional Health Status, 118
  5.1.4 Survival, 118
  5.1.5 Uncertainty Analysis, 118
  5.1.6 Association Between Expected Human Capital and Gross Domestic Product (GDP), 119
  5.1.7 Overall Index of Expected Human Capital, 119
5.2 Results, *119*
5.3 Discussion, *122*
References, *123*

6   Summary of World Economic Forum, "The Global Human Capital Report 2017—Preparing people for the future of work", *125*
Barbara M. Fraumeni, Gang Liu
6.1 Capacity, *126*
6.2 Deployment, *127*
6.3 Development, *128*
6.4 Know-How, *130*
6.5 Overall Human Capital Index, *130*
  6.5.1 East Asia and the Pacific, 131
  6.5.2 Eastern Europe and Central Asia, 131
  6.5.3 Latin America and the Caribbean, 131
  6.5.4 Middle East and North Africa, 132
  6.5.5 North America, 132
  6.5.6 South Asia, 132
  6.5.7 Sub-Saharan Africa, 132
  6.5.8 Western Europe, 133
6.6 Income (Gross National Income per Capita), *133*
6.7 Brief Summary of Human Capital Components in Other Recent WEF Reports, *134*
  6.7.1 The Global Competitiveness Report 2019, 134
  6.7.2 Global Gender Gap Report 2020, 136
6.8 Conclusion of the WEF 2017 Human Capital Report, *137*
References, *137*

PART III
COUNTRY STUDIES

7   Human Capital of Mainland China, Hong Kong and Taiwan, 1997–2018, *139*
Xianfang Xiong, Xing Chen, Yuzhe Ning, Haizheng Li, Belton M. Fleisher
7.1 Introduction, *139*
7.2 Human Capital Measurements, *140*
7.3 Labor Force Composition and Age Structure, *141*

7.3.1 Labor Force Definition and Size, 141
7.3.2 Labor Force Aging, 142
7.4 Overview of the Education Systems, *143*
7.4.1 Education Systems in Mainland China, 143
7.4.2 Education Systems in Hong Kong, 144
7.4.3 Education Systems in Taiwan, 144
7.5 Education-Based Human Capital Measures, *145*
7.6 Jorgenson-Fraumeni Measure of Human Capital, *148*
7.6.1 Estimating Individual Labor Earnings, 148
7.6.2 Estimating Lifetime Income, 149
7.6.3 Total Human Capital, 149
7.6.4 Human Capital per Capita, 153
7.7 Human Capital, GDP and Physical Capital, *156*
7.8 Human Capital Development and Population Dividends, *159*
7.8.1 Education and Age Structure of Labor Force, 160
7.8.2 Labor Force Composition and Human Capital Stock, 160
7.8.3 Human Capital Reserve and Population Dividend Sustainability, 162
7.9 Conclusion, *164*
Acknowledgment, *165*
References, *165*

8 Accumulation of Human and Market Capital in the United States: The Long View, 1948–2013, *167*

Barbara M. Fraumeni, Michael S. Christian, Jon D. Samuels

8.1 Human Capital Methodology, *168*
8.2 Factors Impacting on Human and Market Capital, *170*
8.3 Overview of the Accounts, *173*
8.4 Analysis of the Accounts in Nominal Dollars, *176*
8.4.1 Expanded Production and Factor Outlay, 176
8.4.2 Expanded Private National Labor and Gross Private National Property Income, 178
8.4.3 Expanded Gross Private National Consumer Expenditures, 180
8.4.4 Expanded Gross Private National Capital Saving, 182
8.4.5 Expanded Wealth, 184
8.5 Analysis of Contributions and Rates of Growths, *184*
8.5.1 Contributions to Expanded Gross Private Domestic Product and Economic Growth and Rates of Growth, 184
8.5.2 Contributions to Expanded Gross Private National Saving and Rates of Growth, 188
8.5.3 Contributions to Expanded Private National Expenditure and Income and Rates of Growth, 189
8.5.4 Contributions to Expanded Private National Wealth and Rates of Growth, 190
8.6 Conclusion, *191*
Appendix, *192*
References, *196*

INDEX, *199*

Introduction

GANG LIU[a,*] • BARBARA M. FRAUMENI[b,c,d,e,f]
[a]Statistics Norway, Oslo, Norway, [b]Central University of Finance and Economics, Beijing, China,
[c]University of Southern Maine, Portland, ME, United States, [d]National Bureau of Economic Research,
Cambridge, MA, United States, [e]IZA Institute for Labor Economics, Bonn, Germany, [f]Hunan University,
Changsha, China
[*]Corresponding author: gang.liu@ssb.no

Human capital can be regarded as "the knowledge, skills, competencies and attributes embodied in individuals that facilitate the creation of personal, social and economic well-being" (OECD, 2001). The notion of human capital being equally essential as conventional tangible capital can at least be traced back to Adam Smith's work in the 18th century (Smith, 1776), but it was not widely recognized until around the mid-twentieth century, when economists began to use it to investigate income and growth differentials (e.g., Friedman and Kuznets, 1945; Mincer, 1958, 1962; Schultz, 1961, 1962; Becker, 1962, 1964).

In the 1980s and 1990s, human capital regained its importance both within the neoclassical growth accounting framework (e.g., Jorgenson and Fraumeni, 1989, 1992a,b) and through the endogenous growth models (e.g., Romer, 1986; Lucas Jr., 1988; Mankiw et al., 1992). It was also employed regularly in the development accounting works (e.g., Klenow and Rodriguez-Clare, 1997; Hall and Jones, 1999).

Measures of human capital can serve many purposes as human capital is a key indicator of the current and future potential of a country and its individuals. In most countries, human capital is the largest form of wealth. In others where natural resources are the largest form of wealth, human capital is often a growing source of wealth (Lange et al., 2018; Managi and Kumar, 2018). Countries with a relatively young population can have significant advantages over countries with older populations over the longer term. Within the context of sustainable development, human capital measures can be used to gauge how well a country is managing its total

national wealth, with the purpose of assessing its long-term sustainability (e.g., UNECE, 2009). There are both monetary and nonmonetary, including subjective, ramifications of the level of human capital (Dolan et al., 2008). Most recently, human capital is frequently applied to inform "beyond GDP" discussions, since its distribution across households and individuals and the noneconomic benefits due to its investment are among the crucial determinants of people's "quality of life" and well-being (e.g., Stiglitz et al., 2010; OECD, 2011, 2013, 2015, 2017).

This book is about measuring human capital. Currently existed human capital measures can be divided into two broad categories: the indicators-based and the monetary measures.[a] Except for the Introduction chapter, all the other eight chapters collected in the book reflect just this division, with four chapters applying the indicators-based approach, while the other four using monetary measures. The monetary measures emphasize demographics such as age and education with underlying gender break-outs, as well as income, while the indicators-based measures have a wide-array of types of components in addition such as health, standard of living, deployment, and know-how.

Another distinct feature of the book is its global perspective, with six chapters focusing directly on large-scale projects for international human capital comparisons that have been undertaken by several international

---

[a]For an earlier overview of the different measures of human capital within and across the two broad categories, please refer to e.g., Liu and Fraumeni (2016).

organizations and/or universities. Each covers at least 130 countries. While the other two chapters are single-country studies, the two countries, respectively addressed, are the United States and China, nowadays the two of the three largest economies in the world.

With various human capital measures being discussed, the book does not take the stand that there exists one specific measure that should be used under any circumstances; rather, it is intended to serve as one of the valuable resources for statisticians, researchers, analysts, policy-makers, and government officials in searching for comparable information, so as to make their own decisions on what human capital measures are best suitable for their purpose.

In the following, a brief description of different methodologies applied in the projects for human capital comparisons is provided. However, readers are strongly encouraged to read each and every individual chapter in the book in order to have a more comprehensive and deeper understanding of why and how the different detailed methodologies were implemented in practice. A simple comparison of the results is then discussed, with the purpose of giving a flavor of taste of the rich information that can be drawn from these studies.

I.1. MONETARY MEASURES PROJECTS

The first two chapters are excellent examples of comparing human capital across countries by applying the monetary measures. In both examples, human capital is measured together with nonhuman capital (such as conventional fixed capital and natural capital) within a consistent framework of comprehensive wealth accounting, with the goal being to help governments plan for a more sustainable economic future.

Chapter 1 is based on the World Bank's latest wealth accounts that cover the period 1995–2014 for 141 countries (Lange et al., 2018). Plenty of data from the accounts, including country human capital measures in constant 2014 US$, was presented in the 2018 report: *The Changing Wealth of Nations 2018: Building a Sustainable Future* (CWON hereafter).

In the World Bank's previous works, human capital was not measured explicitly but included in a residual resulting from deducting produced capital, natural capital, and net foreign assets from total national wealth that was calculated as the present value of future consumption (World Bank, 2006, 2011). Although a large part of this residual could be attributed to human capital (e.g., Ferreira and Hamilton, 2010; Hamilton and Liu, 2014), the nonexplicit measure of human capital makes it difficult for policy-making.

Human capital in the new CWON wealth accounts was measured by applying the well-known Jorgenson-Fraumeni lifetime income approach (Jorgenson and Fraumeni, 1989, 1992a,b), based on a unique database developed by the World Bank, the International Income Distribution Database, which contains more than 1500 household surveys. When a household survey is not available for any country for a given year, previous or later surveys that are controlled by country-wide totals for the nonsurvey years are then used as the basis for these years.

First, for each country and year covered by the CWON project, wage profiles by age, education, and gender were derived by applying the estimated parameters from Mincer equations (Montenegro and Patrinos, 2014, 2016). Then, the estimated wage profiles were benchmarked to the total employment and the compensation of employees that are drawn from UN, ILO databases, the Penn World Table (Feenstra et al., 2015), and other sources.

For an individual in the working age population (aged 15–65), the lifetime income is calculated as

$$h_{a,e} = p_{a,e}^m w_{a,e}^m + \left(1 - r_{a,e}^{e+1}\right) * \varphi * v_{a+1} * h_{a+1,e} + r_{a,e}^{e+1} * \varphi * v_{a+1} * h_{a+1,e+1}, \tag{I.1}$$

where

$h_{a,e}$ = lifetime income for an individual with age of a and education of e;

$p_{a,e}^m$ = probability to be employed;

$w_{a,e}^m$ = received compensation of employees when employed;

$r_{a,e}^{e+1}$ = school enrolment rate for taking one more year's education from education of e to one-year higher level of $e+1$ (assuming equal to 0 for those aged 25–65);

φ = adjustment factor[b];

v_{a+1} = survival rate (probability of surviving one more year).

Eq. (I.1) indicates that the lifetime income of an individual is estimated as the sum of two parts: the first part is the current labor income, adjusted by the probability of being employed ($p_{a,e}^m w_{a,e}^m$); the second part is the expected lifetime income in the next year, which can be elaborated on as the following: in the next year, the individual will be confronted to two courses of action: the first is to continue to work (holding the same education level as before) and earn income of $\varphi * v_{a+1} * h_{a+1,e}$,

---

[b]The adjustment factor (φ) is defined in terms of the real rate of labor income growth (g) and a discount rate (σ), i.e., $\varphi = (1+g)/(1+\sigma)$.

with the probability of $(1 - r_{a,e}^{e+1})$; the second is to take one more year education and (after finishing) to receive income as $\varphi * v_{a+1} * h_{a+1, \, e+1}$, with the probability of $r_{a,e}^{e+1}$.

Chapter 2 describes outcomes from the biennial *Inclusive Wealth Report* (IWR hereafter), the latest of which was published in 2018, with annual data (in 2005 PPP US$) covering the period 1990–2014 for 140 countries (Managi and Kumar, 2018). The IWR project has built up its comprehensive wealth accounting by following a framework developed by Arrow et al. (2012, 2013) and Klenow and Rodriguez-Clare (1997).[c]

Within this framework, for each country and year, human capital per capita due to education is measured as

$$h_E = \left(e^{\rho E} * P_{5+E} * \int_0^T w(\tau)e^{-\delta\tau}d\tau \right) / P \qquad \text{(I.2)}$$

where

h_E = human capital per capita with the average years of total schooling E;

ρ = rate of return on education (assumed to be 8.5%);

P_{5+E} = population who has had education equal to or greater than E;

w = average compensation to employees;

T = expected working years;

δ = discount rate (assumed to be 8.5%);

P = total population.

Eq. (I.2) shows that human capital per capita is calculated as the total human capital divided by total population, while the former is measured as a multiplication of one unit of human capital ($e^{\rho E}$), the corresponding population (P_{5+E}), and the shadow price of one unit of human capital ($\int_0^T w(\tau)e^{-\delta\tau}d\tau$). E is the average years of school completed by the population. The shadow price is calculated by the present value of lifetime income, which is proxied by that of the average compensation to employees (w) over the expected working years (T).

Note that both the CWON and IWR projects make the estimates of human capital per capita, indicated by Eqs. (I.1) and (I.2), respectively. However, the CWON project makes use of household surveys data, which offer detailed information at disaggregated level, while the IWR project does not depend on such detailed survey data and, therefore, is less data demanding. The IWR project computes human capital for the whole population, while CWON estimates human capital for those who earn labor income. The IWR project uses a snapshot of the average level of education for the country as a whole, while CWON allows for additional education of individuals over their lifetime because of the more extensive data base it has.

Monetary measures are being considered as a basis for incorporating human capital into expanded accounts of the System of National Accounts (SNA) (Sub-group on Well-being and Sustainability, 2021).[d]

I.2. INDICATORS-BASED MEASURES PROJECTS

Four chapters collected in the book (Chapters 3–6) focus on several outstanding examples of comparing country human capital in the world by using the indicators-based measures, i.e., by constructing various composite indexes for human capital.

Chapter 3 is about the World Bank's Human Capital Index (WB HCI hereafter) (see IBRD and World Bank, 2018). Chapter 4 presents the United Nation's Human Development Index (UN HDI hereafter) published in the Human Development Report that has been issued by the United Nations Development Programme (UNDP) since 1990 (see, e.g., UNDP, 2019). Chapter 5 is about another large-scale human capital measurement project carried out by the Institute for Health Metrics and Evaluation (IHME) at University of Washington in the US (see Lim et al., 2018). The construction methodology for a human capital index (IHME HCI hereafter) and the results from the project are summarized and discussed briefly in the chapter.

Table I.1 lists a number of selected characteristics among the above-mentioned three human capital indexes compiled internationally. As shown, the WB HCI and the IHME HCI are built upon two basic dimensions: education and health, because the two indexes focus on how human capital can be expected to enhance productivity through these two most important investment channels.

In addition to education and health, the UNDP HDI has one more dimension in its index construction: standard of living, which is represented by the indicator of gross national income per capita in a country.

---

[c]The 2018 IWR project calculated two different versions of wealth: conventional and frontier, the latter including health capital as a component of human capital wealth. In this book, conventional wealth is described and used in comparisons as it is most similar in coverage to the World Bank CWON monetary measure (Lange et al., 2018).

---

[d]Two possible approaches to integrating human capital into the SNA have been developed (Liu, 2015; chapter 6 of UNECE, 2016).

TABLE I.1

Comparison of selected characteristics among different human capital indexes.

	WB HCI	IHME HCI	UN HDI
Latest publication date	2018	2018	2019
Coverage (year)	2018	1990–2016	1990–2018
Coverage (country/economy)	157	195	189
Coverage (gender)	Both	Both	Both
Definition of index	The amount of human capital a child born in 2018 can expect to acquire by age 18	Expected years lived from age 20 to 64 years, adjusted for educational attainment, learning, and functional health status	A summary measure of achievements in three key dimensions of human development: a long and healthy life, access to knowledge, and a decent standard of living
Value range of index	[0–1]	[0–45]	[0–1]
Components of Index			
1. *Education*			
Quantity of education	Expected years by age 18 of those who start preschool earliest at age 4; range = [0–14]	Average years of completed schooling, by 5-year age groups, from 5 to 24; range = [0–18]	Expected years with range = [0–18] Mean years with range = [0–15]
Quality of education	Harmonized average test score (out of a benchmark score of 625)	Harmonized average test score, relative to highest national average score, by 5-year age groups, from 5 to 19, scaled [0–1]	
2. *Health*			
Health indicators (adults)	Share of 15-year-olds who survive until age 60	Expected years lived from age 20 to 64; Prevalence of health conditions linked to productivity/learning: anemia, cognitive impairment, hearing loss, vision loss, infectious diseases, by 5-year age groups, from age 20 to 64, scaled [0–1]	Life expectancy; range = [20–85]
Health indicators (children)	Stunting and mortality rates among children under age 5	Stunting and wasting rates among children under age 5	
3. *Standard of living*			Ln (Gross National Income per capita in 2011 PPP $); range = [ln(100)-ln(75,000)]
Data sources	Various UN databases; UNICEF-WHO-World Bank Joint database; Data provided by World Bank staff; Student achievement tests from 162 economies in Patrinos and Angrist (2018)	Global Burden of Diseases, Injuries, and Risk Factors Study 2016; 2522 censuses and household surveys from 194 countries; 1894 student achievement tests from 132 countries and 163 subnational locations	ICF Macro Demographic and Health Surveys; Various databases from UN, World Bank, IMF and OECD; Barro and Lee (2018)

Source: IBRD and World Bank (2018); Lim et al. (2018); UNDP (2019).

The reason is that the UN HDI aims to illustrate the current state of development of a country/economy.

Both the WB HCI and IHME HCI have indicators for addressing the quality of education, while these are missing in the UN HDI. In terms of heath indicators, the IHME HCI has much richer information that are drawn from a unique and profoundly comprehensive database: The Global Burden of Diseases, Injuries, and Risk Factors Study 2016 (Murray et al., 2017).

Besides the differences and similarities as listed in Table I.1, how the human capital index is practically constructed also differs across projects. The composite index of the WB HCI is compiled as follows:

$$WB\,HCI = \frac{P}{P^*} * e^{\emptyset(S_{NG}-S^*)} * e^{\gamma(Z_{NG}-Z^*)} \tag{I.3}$$

where

P = probability that a child born today survives;

P^* = benchmark of complete survival, equal to 1;

$\emptyset$ = increase in productivity per additional year of school, equal to 8%;

S_{NG} = expected future education;

S^* = benchmark of complete quality-adjusted schooling, equal to 14 years;

γ = estimated return to productivity per unit increase in each health indicator (0.65 for adult survival rate and 0.35 for not-stunted rate);

Z_{NG} = expected future health;

Z^* = benchmark of complete health, equal to 1.

In Eq. (I.3), the WB HCI index measures the human capital of the next generation, which is the amount of human capital that a child born today can expect to achieve in view of the risks of poor health and poor education currently prevailing in the country where that child lives. Therefore, the WB HCI is designed to highlight how investments that improve health and education outcomes today will affect the productivity of future generations of workers. In addition, it is a measure of productivity relative to the benchmark of full health and complete education, an ideal scenario.

The composite index of the IHME HCI is compiled as follows:

$$IHME\,HCI = \left(\frac{\sum_{x=20}^{64} nL_{xt}FH_{xt}}{l_0}\right) * \left(\frac{\sum_{x=5}^{24} Edu_{xt}Learn_{xt}}{18}\right) \tag{I.4}$$

where

nL_{xt} = expected years lived in age group x for year t;

FH_{xt} = functional health status in age group x in year t, transformed to a 0 to 1 scale;

l_0 = starting birth cohort;

Edu_{xt} = years of education attained during age group x for year t;

$Learn_{xt}$ = average standardized test score in age group x for year t, transformed to a 0 to 1 scale.

Eq. (I.4) gives an index measure of expected human capital for each birth cohort, which is calculated as the expected years lived from age 20 to 64 years and adjusted for educational attainment, learning or education quality, and functional health status using rates specific to each time period, age, and sex for all countries covered by the project. The functional health status combines seven health status outcomes into a single measure using principal components analysis.

It is worth mentioning that uncertainty analysis was undertaken in both the IHME HCI and the WB HCI projects and the corresponding estimated uncertainty in the measure of human capital are reported.

The composite index of the UNDP HDI is compiled as the geometric mean of normalized indices for each of the three dimensions: Health, Education, and Income.

$$UN\,HDI = (I_{Health} * I_{Education} * I_{Income})^{1/3} \tag{I.5}$$

where I_{Health}, $I_{Education}$, and I_{Income} are three normalized dimensional indexes and each of them, with defined minimum and maximum values, is calculated as

$$Dimension\,index = \frac{actual\,value - minimum\,value}{maximum\,value - minimum\,value} \tag{I.6}$$

As shown in Eq. (I.5), the three dimensions of health, education, and income are equally weighted. On the one hand, such a construction reflects that the UN HDI focuses on the snapshot illustration of the current state of development of a country/economy, in which all the three dimensions are considered equally important.

On the other hand, the UN HDI is distinctively different from the WB HCI and IHME HCI, because the latter two place their focuses on the extent to which education and health can impact on the potential productivity largely as a means, while the UN HDI treat education and health not only as a means but also as an end-in-itself.

It is worth noting that there also exist a variety of UN HDI by taking inequality, gender, and poverty into considerations, such as the Inequality-adjusted Human Development Index (IHDI), Gender Development Index (GDI), Gender Inequality Index (GII), and Multidimensional Poverty Index (MPI). In addition, there are also five Human Development Dashboards which extend to address environmental and socioeconomic sustainability (see UNDP, 2019).

As the last one among four chapters in the book applying indicators-based human capital measures, Chapter 6 presents a summary of another Global Human Capital Index which has been constructed by the World Economic Forum since 2015 (WEF GHCI hereafter). The latest data based on updated methodologies was published in *The Global Human Capital Report 2017*, covering 130 countries/economies for 2017 (World Economic Forum, 2017).

The WEF GHCI assesses the degree to which countries have optimized their human capital for the benefit of their economies and of individuals themselves. By emphasizing both employment and education, it provides a means of measuring a country's human capital—both current and expected—across its population. Moreover, it measures the quantifiable elements of countries' talent resources holistically according to individuals' ability to acquire, develop and deploy skills throughout their working life rather than simply during the formative years. Thus, it treats human capital as a dynamic rather than fixed concept.

In addition, the WEF GHCI has a number of subcomponents dependent upon the WEF's Executive Opinion Survey and membership information from LinkedIn. Another unique feature of the WEF GHCI project is that it measures the skill diversity of recent tertiary graduates with a Herfindahl–Hirschman Index (HHI) of concentration among the broad fields of study.[e]

The composite index of the WEF GHCI is compiled based on four dimensions, for each of them, there is a subindex. The four dimensions are Capacity, Deployment, Development, and Know-how. Each corresponding subindex is constructed by using a number of indicators and following basically the same formula as shown in Eq. (I.6). The four thematic subindexes are weighted equally in the aggregate overall GHCI, while the age-group specific data within these subindexes is weighted by population (see World Economic Forum, 2017).

Essentially, the WEF GHCI shares a common feature with the WB HCI, the IHME HCI, and the UN HDI in that the WEF GHCI holds all countries to the same standard, measuring countries' "distance to the ideal" state, or gap in human capital optimization. To arrive at this score, the Index examines each indicator in relation to a meaningful maximum value that represents "the ideal". Every indicator's score is a function of the country's "distance from the ideal" for the specific dimension measured.

I.3. COMPARISON OF HUMAN CAPITAL ESTIMATES AMONG PROJECTS

It is interesting and informative to make some comparisons based on the results from the above-mentioned different human capital projects, both in terms of either the monetary or the index measures and of the rankings thereof. Such comparisons can be implemented by means of correlation analysis which shows whether these measures tend to change together, if yes, to what extent.[f]

To serve the purpose, two frequently applied correlation measures, describing both the strength and the direction of the relationship, will be applied here. One is the Pearson correlation,[g] and the other is the Spearman correlation.[h] Both the Pearson and Spearman correlation coefficients have the value range from -1 to $+1$.

Since the available projects that have been discussed in this book have different country and year coverage, the comparison will be undertaken between each two of them, based on mutually the same selected countries and in the same, or the closest year.

The first comparison is between the two monetary measures covered in this book, i.e., human capital per capita measure by the World Bank's CWON project compared with that by the IWR project in year 2014. If the comparison was done with total human capital for each country, the rankings could differ as the proportion of the population working can differ by country. CWON estimates the human capital of the working population only, while IWR estimates the human capital of the total adult population. Among the 123 countries compared, the Slovak Republic is the outlier. With the Slovak Republic included, the

---

[e]The Herfindahl–Hirschman Index (HHI) is a commonly accepted measure of market concentration and is often used to determine market competitiveness. In the WEF GHCI project, the HHI is applied for measuring the concentration of the distribution of graduates among various disciplines (World Economic Forum, 2017).

[f]Another way that the various measures could be compared is to track changes in the measures over time.

[g]The Pearson correlation evaluates the *linear* relationship between two continuous variables. A relationship is linear when a change in one variable is associated with a proportional change in the other variable.

[h]The Spearman correlation evaluates the *monotonic* relationship between two continuous or ordinal variables. In a monotonic relationship, the variables tend to change together, but not necessarily at a constant rate. The Spearman correlation coefficient is based on the ranked values for each variable rather than the raw data.

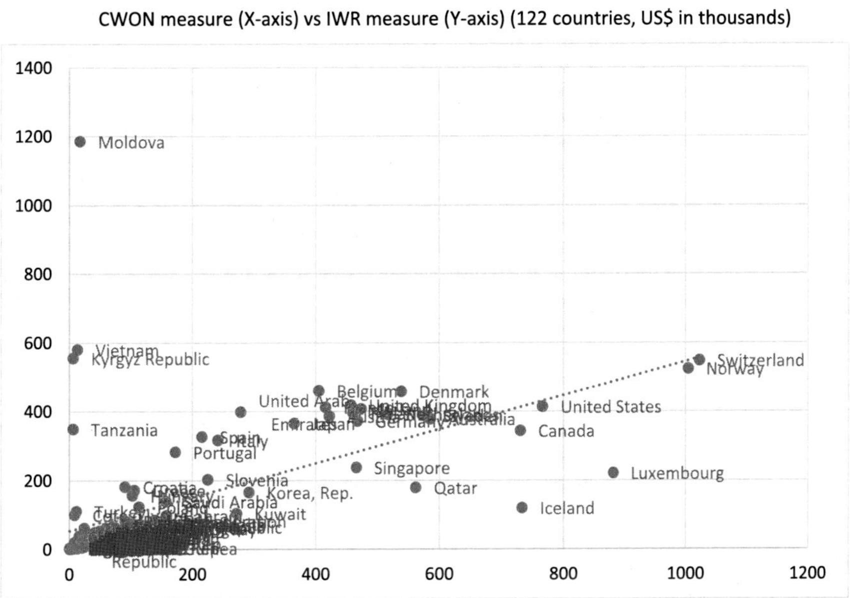

CWON measure (X-axis) vs IWR measure (Y-axis) (122 countries, US$ in thousands)

FIG. I.1 Comparison of human capital per capita measure between CWON (2014) and IWR (2014). Note: Pearson correlation = 0.60. (Source: Authors' own calculations.)

calculated Pearson correlation is 0.15, albeit positive, but a low value.

Fig. I.1 demonstrates the relationship of the human capital per capita measure between the CWON and the IWR project for 122 countries when the Slovak Republic is removed from the comparison. As visualized, the CWON human capita per capita measures for the majority of the countries covered are higher than their corresponding IWR measures. Moldova is an outlier among the countries shown. Further, without the Slovak Republic, the calculated Pearson correlation has increased substantially from 0.15 to 0.60.

Fig. I.2 displays the relationship based on the rankings of the two monetary human capital per capita measures from the CWON and IWR projects. The calculated Spearman correlation, also based on 122 countries, is 0.81, which means that there is a high positive correlation between the two rankings, despite the existence of several outliers, such as Moldova, Vietnam, Kyrgyz Republic, Tanzania, Turkey, and Cote d'Ivoire. In addition to the Slovak Republic, all these countries just mentioned have much higher rankings of human capital per capita in the CWON project than in the IWR project, which merits further investigations.[i]

Note that although the comparison as shown in Figs. I.1 and I.2 is carried out based on the same (122) countries and for the same year (2014), the human capital per capita is measured in constant 2014 US$ by means of the market exchange rates in the CWON project, while it is measured in 2005 US$ by using the Purchasing Power Parity (PPP) exchange rates in the IWR project. As a result, the differences between the two monetary measures come from at least two sources: one is the choice of the base year, i.e., 2014 vs. 2005, and the other is the choice of exchange rates, i.e., market exchange rates vs. PPPs. Therefore, if all these issues are taken into consideration and are addressed properly, the comparison results could have been different.[i]

In this Introduction, two human capital measures by applying the indicators-based approach, i.e., the WB HCI and the IHME HCI, are selected for presenting the visual relationship between the two human capital index measures. Figs. I.3 and I.4 are based on these two index measures and on the rankings thereof, respectively. As shown, both the calculated Pearson and

---

[i]Since the value of ranking is given according to the descending order of country human capital per capita, a country with lower value in ranking has actually higher ranking status.

[i]There are some differences in the 2014 rankings of these countries in GDP per capita, constant 2010 US dollars used by CWON versus GDP per capita, PPP, constant 2011 international dollars (PPPs) used by IWR.

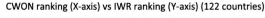

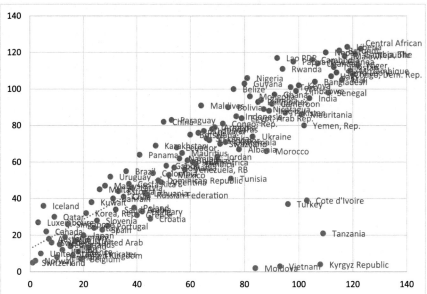

FIG. I.2 Comparison of human capital per capita ranking between CWON (2014) and IWR (2014). Note: Spearman correlation = 0.81. (Source: Authors' own calculations.)

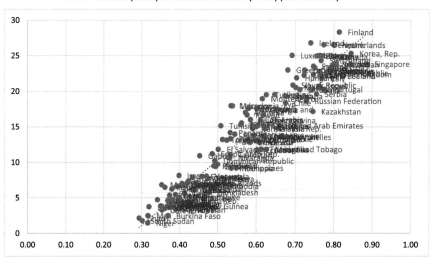

FIG. I.3 Comparison of human capital index measure between WB HCI (2018) and IHME HCI (2014). Note: Pearson correlation = 0.95. (Source: Authors' own calculations.)

Spearman correlations are as high as 0.95, based on the selected 151 countries/economies.

In Table I.2, both the Pearson and Spearman correlations among the two monetary and the four indicators-based measures are reported with each other. Note that for data used by the WB HCI, 2018 is the only year available. As for the WEF GHCI, data for 2017 is used. There exist data for 2015; however, the estimating method was quite different from the latest one as applied by the WEF GHCI for 2017.

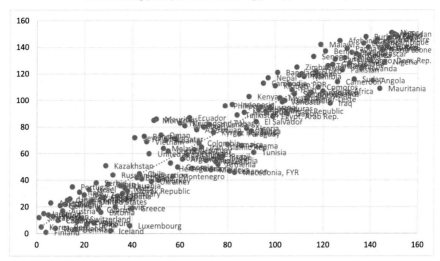

FIG. I.4 Comparison of human capital index ranking between WB HCI (2018) and IHME HCI (2014). Note: Spearman correlation = 0.95. (Source: Authors' own calculations.)

TABLE I.2
Correlation of human capital estimates among international projects in 2014.

Pearson/Spearman correlation	CWON	IWR	WB HCI	IHME HCI	UN HDI	WEF GHCI
CWON	–	0.60/0.81 (122)	0.67/0.85 (131)	0.69/0.86 (140)	0.67/0.94 (139)	0.66/0.80 (117)
IWR		–	0.55/0.78 (129)	0.37/0.79 (139)	0.27/0.80 (138)	0.53/0.70 (123)
WB HCI			–	0.95/0.95 (151)	0.94/0.95 (153)	0.89/0.91 (125)
IHME HCI				–	0.93/0.94 (183)	0.86/0.88 (130)
UN HDI					–	0.85/0.87 (129)
WEF GHCI						–

Source: Authors' own calculations.
Notes: 1. Data used by WB HCI and WEF GHCI are for 2018 and 2017, respectively; 2. The number of selected countries/economies for each comparison is in parenthesis.

As shown in Table I.2, the positive correlations are found among different measures of human capital discussed in this book, both in terms of the measures and of the rankings. The range of the calculated Pearson correlation is between 0.27 and 0.95 with the mean equal to 0.70, while the range of the calculated Spearman correlation is between 0.70 and 0.95 with the mean equal to 0.86.

The ranking correlation (indicated by the Spearman correlation) is not lower than the corresponding level correlation (indicated by the Pearson correlation), with only one exception where the former is slightly lower than the latter between the WB HCI and the IHME HCI. This finding indicates that policy-makings related to human capital based on the rankings might be more suggestive than those based on pure level or index measures.

As also shown in Table I.2, the correlations within the indicators-based measures are higher than within the monetary measures. All the correlations are higher between the CWON measure, than between the IWR measure, and any of the indicators-based measures. In addition, the correlations are higher between each of the WB HCI, the IHME HCI, and the UN HDI, than between the WEF GHCI and the CWON measure. Moreover, among the indicators-based measures, the correlations between each pair of the WB HCI, the IHME HCI, and the UN HDI are higher than between any of the first three indexes and the WEF GHCI.

I.4. SINGLE-COUNTRY STUDIES

Finally, the last two chapters in the book present two single-country studies, respectively. Chapter 7 is about human capital measurement in China. In the chapter, a detailed introduction and analysis of human capital in Mainland China, Hong Kong, and Taiwan are provided. Comparisons are made of human capital stock, trends, and dynamics based on different measures of human capital, including traditional education-based indexes and the Jorgenson-Fraumeni lifetime income measures. In addition, given the drastic disparities in economic development in Mainland China, two most advanced cities, Beijing and Shanghai, are selected to compare with Hong Kong and Taiwan. Discussions are given covering the years starting from 1997 when Hong Kong returned to China, to 2018. Moreover, the impact of human capital growth on population aging and population dividends is also discussed in the chapter.

Chapter 8 presents the latest human capital estimates for the United States. In this chapter, human capital measured by using the Jorgenson-Fraumeni approach is integrated into the national income accounting system, which improves our understanding of the economic growth across time and within some specific periods in the US. For instance, the growth would have been reduced during the 1995–2000 economic boom period, while tempered in the 2007–2009 recession period, if human capital investment was taken into consideration. Over the longer period, first the post-World War baby boom and then the substantial increase in education led to higher economic growth than otherwise expected. However, as the pace of increase in education slowed and the workforce aged toward the end of the period, human capital induced growth was reduced accordingly.

As editor of this book, I, Barbara Fraumeni, was assisted in the review of the introduction and the chapters by Wulong Gu from Statistics Canada and Gang Liu from Statistics Norway. I thank Gu for reviewing the introduction and Liu for reviewing Chapters 1, 7, and 8.

REFERENCES

Arrow, K.J., et al., 2012. Sustainability and the measurement of wealth. Environ. Dev. Econ. 17 (3), 317–353.

Arrow, K.J., et al., 2013. Sustainability and the measurement of wealth: further reflections. Environ. Dev. Econ. 18 (4), 504–516.

Barro, R.J., Lee, J.-W., 2018. Dataset of Educational Attainment, February 2016 Revision. www.barrolee.com. (Accessed 15 June 2019).

Becker, G.S., 1962. Investment in human capital: a theoretical analysis. J. Polit. Econ. 70 (5, Part 2, Supplement), 9–49.

Becker, G.S., 1964. Human Capital: A Theoretical and Empirical Analysis, with Special Reference to Education. Columbia University Press, New York, NY.

Dolan, P., et al., 2008. Do we really know what makes us happy? A review of the economic literature on the factors associated with subjective wellbeing. J. Econ. Psychol. 29, 94–122.

Feenstra, et al., 2015. The next generation of the Penn world table. Am. Econ. Rev. 105 (10), 3150–3182.

Ferreira, S., Hamilton, K., 2010. Comprehensive wealth, intangible capital, and development. In: Policy Research Working Paper 5452. The World Bank, Washington, DC.

Friedman, M., Kuznets, S.S., 1945. Income from Independent Professional Practice. NBER, New York, NY.

Hall, R., Jones, C., 1999. Why do some countries produce so much more output per worker than others? Q. J. Econ. 114 (1), 83–116.

Hamilton, K., Liu, G., 2014. Human capital, tangible wealth, and the intangible capital residual. Oxf. Rev. Econ. Policy 30 (1), 70–91.

IBRD (International Bank for Reconstruction and Development), World Bank, 2018. The Human Capital Project. The World Bank, Washington, DC.

Jorgenson, D.W., Fraumeni, B.M., 1989. The accumulation of human and non-human capital, 1948-1984. In: Lipsey, R. E., Tice, H.S. (Eds.), The Measurement of Savings, Investment, and Wealth. NBER, The University of Chicago Press, Chicago, pp. 227–282.

Jorgenson, D.W., Fraumeni, B.M., 1992a. The output of education sector. In: Griliches, Z., et al. (Eds.), Output Measurement in the Service Sectors. NBER, The University of Chicago Press, Chicago, pp. 303–341.

Jorgenson, D.W., Fraumeni, B.M., 1992b. Investment in education and U.S. economic growth. Scand. J. Econ. 94 (Supplement), 51–70.

Klenow, P., Rodriguez-Clare, A., 1997. The Neoclassical Revolution in Growth Economics: Has It Gone Too Far? NBER Macroeconomics Annual. NBER, The University of Chicago Press, Chicago, pp. 73–103.

Lange, G.-M., et al. (Eds.), 2018. The Changing Wealth of Nations 2018: Building a Sustainable Future. The World Bank, Washington, DC.

Lim, S.S., et al., 2018. Measuring human capital: a systematic analysis of 195 countries and territories, 1990–2016. Lancet 392 (October 6), 1217–1234.

Liu, G., 2015. A stylized satellite account for human capital. In: Statistics Norway Discussion Paper No. 816, August.

Liu, G., Fraumeni, B.M., 2016. Human capital measurement: country experiences and international initiatives. In: Jorgenson, D.W., et al. (Eds.), The World Economy - Growth or Stagnation? Cambridge University Press, Cambridge, UK.

Lucas Jr., R.E., 1988. On the mechanics of economic development. J. Monet. Econ. 22 (1), 3–42.

Managi, S., Kumar, P. (Eds.), 2018. Inclusive Wealth Report 2018: Measuring Progress Towards Sustainability. UNEP and Kyushu University Urban Institute, Routledge, London and New York.

Mankiw, N.G., et al., 1992. A contribution to the empirics of growth. Q. J. Econ. 107 (2), 408–437.

Mincer, J., 1958. Investment in human capital and personal income distribution. J. Polit. Econ. 66 (4), 281–302.

Mincer, J., 1962. On-the-job training: costs, returns and some implications. J. Polit. Econ. 70 (5, part 2), 50–79.

Montenegro, C.E., Patrinos, H., 2014. Comparable estimates of returns to schooling around the world. In: Policy Research Paper 7020. World Bank, Washington, DC.

Montenegro, C.E., Patrinos, H., 2016. A Data Set of Comparable Estimates of the Private Rate of Return to Schooling Around the World, 1970–2014. Unpublished, World Bank, Washington, DC.

Murray, C.J.L., et al., 2017. Global, regional, and national under-5 mortality, adult mortality, age-specific mortality, and life expectancy, 1970–2016: a systematic analysis for the global burden of disease study 2016. Lancet 390, 1084–1150.

OECD, 2001. The Well-Being of Nations: The Role of Human and Social Capital. OECD Publishing, Paris, France.

OECD, 2011, 2013, 2015, 2017. How's Life? Measuring Well-Being. OECD Publishing, Paris, https://doi.org/10.1787/9789264121164-en.

Patrinos, H.A., Angrist, N., 2018. A global dataset on education quality: A review and an update (1965–2018). In: World Bank Policy Research Working Paper 8592. World Bank, Washington, DC.

Romer, P.M., 1986. Increasing returns and long-run growth. J. Polit. Econ. 94, 1002–1037.

Schultz, T.W., 1961. Investment in human capital. Am. Econ. Rev. 51 (1), 1–17.

Schultz, T.W., 1962. Reflections on investment in man. J. Polit. Econ. 70 (5, Part 2, Supplement), 1–8.

Smith, A., 1776. An Inquiry into the Nature and Causes of the Wealth of Nations. Book 2. W. Strahan & T. Cadell, London, UK.

Stiglitz, J.E., et al., 2010. Mismeasuring Our Lives: Why GDP Doesn't Add Up. New Press, New York, NY and London, UK.

Sub-group on Well-being and Sustainability, Area Group on Labour, Human Capital, and Education. 2021. Guidance note on labour, human capital and education. Prepared for the 15th Meeting of the Advisory Expert Group on National Accounts, April 6-8, 2021, January.

UNDP, 2019. Human Development Report 2019 - Beyond Income, Beyond Averages, Beyond Today: Inequalities in Human Development in the 21st Century. United Nations Development Programme, New York, NY.

UNECE, 2009. Measuring Sustainable Development, Report of the Joint UNECE/OECD/Eurostat Working Group on Statistics for Sustainable Development (WGSSD). United Nations, New York, NY and Geneva, Switzerland.

UNECE, 2016. Guide on Measuring Human Capital. United Nations, New York, NY and Geneva, Switzerland.

World Bank, 2006. Where Is the Wealth of Nations? The World Bank, Washington, DC.

World Bank, 2011. The Changing Wealth of Nations: Measuring Sustainable Development in the New Millennium. The World Bank, Washington, DC.

World Economic Forum, 2017. The Global Human Capital Report 2017 - Preparing People for the Future of Work. https://www.weforum.org/.

CHAPTER 1

The Impact of Air Pollution on Human Capital Wealth

GLENN-MARIE LANGE • SHUN CHONABAYASHI •
KENAN KARAKÜLAH • ESTHER NAIKAL
World Bank, Washington, DC, United States

1.1 INTRODUCTION

1.1.1 National Wealth and the Importance of Human Capital for Development

National income and well-being are underpinned by a country's wealth—measured comprehensively in this chapter to include produced capital, natural capital, human capital, and net foreign assets. Sustained long-term economic growth requires investment and management of this broad portfolio of assets. Although a macroeconomic indicator such as gross domestic product (GDP) provides an important measure of economic progress, it measures only income and production and does not reflect changes in the underlying asset base. Used alone, GDP may provide misleading signals about the health of an economy, the efficiency of asset utilization, and the sustainability of development. GDP does not reflect depreciation and depletion of assets, whether investment and accumulation of wealth are keeping pace with population growth or whether the mix of assets is consistent with a country's development goals. GDP indicates whether an economy is growing; wealth indicates the prospects for maintaining economic growth over the long term. Economic performance is best evaluated by monitoring both GDP growth and wealth.

Nobel Laureate Joseph Stiglitz observed that a business is always evaluated by both its income statement and its balance sheet (assets and liabilities, or wealth). Similarly, a prospective homeowner can obtain a mortgage only by demonstrating both her income and net assets—income in any given year can always be made to look good by selling off assets, but liquidating assets undermines the ability to generate income in the future; the true picture of economic health requires looking at both income and wealth. The economic performance of countries, however, is only evaluated based on national income; wealth has typically been ignored.

To fill this gap, the World Bank initiated a program two decades ago to measure national wealth and changes in wealth to monitor long-term economic well-being and guide the development process through the lens of a country's portfolio of assets. The first report, Where is the Wealth of Nations? Measuring Capital for the 21st Century (2006) provided a "proof of concept" that demonstrated that wealth accounts could be constructed for a large number of countries. The second edition, The Changing Wealth of Nations: Measuring Sustainable Development in the New Millennium (2011), provided a time-series of wealth accounts for 140 countries over 10 years that allowed us to examine the dynamic relationship between development and wealth. The third edition, The Changing Wealth of Nations 2018: Building a Sustainable Future (2018), included, for the first time, an explicit measure of countries' human capital, disaggregated by gender and including the self-employed. Previous wealth accounts, the World Bank's Human Capital Project, and extensive research have shown that the accumulation of human capital has been a key factor in economic growth, sustainable development, and poverty reduction. Building on these three reports, the current edition, The Changing Wealth of Nations 2021: Managing Assets for the Future,

Measuring Human Capital. https://doi.org/10.1016/B978-0-12-819057-9.00003-2

will be released in 2021 with detailed wealth accounts for 146 countries over the period 1995 to 2018.

The goal of the wealth accounting initiative is to broaden the measures economists, policy makers, the private sector, and civil society use to assess economic progress. Without a forward-looking indicator, it is difficult to conclude that we can accurately measure economic progress. Wealth, by its nature, concerns the future—the flow of income that each asset can generate over its lifetime. Measuring changes in wealth permits us to monitor the sustainability of development, an urgent concern today for all countries. GDP indicates whether a country's income is growing; wealth indicates the prospects for maintaining that income and its growth over the long term. They are complementary indicators; economic performance is best evaluated by monitoring the growth of both GDP and wealth.

1.1.2 Human Capital in National Wealth Accounts

Human capital wealth in the World Bank's Changing Wealth of Nations (CWON) is defined as the discounted value of future earnings for a country's labor force, following the Jorgenson and Fraumeni lifetime earnings approach (Jorgenson and Fraumeni, 1989, 1992a,b). In other words, human capital wealth is considered to be an asset that generates a stream of future economic benefits (earnings). This approach fits well with the concept of asset value found in national accounts and the approach used for valuing other assets in the wealth accounts. The Jorgenson-Fraumeni approach has been implemented by many countries, although there is no decision at this time for including human capital in national balance sheets defined by the System of Nations Accounts.

This concept of human capital wealth differs from that of human development or human capabilities. A good education has an intrinsic value apart from the fact that it helps workers be better paid. Good health also is beneficial in itself, independent of its impact on production and wages. These important benefits are acknowledged, but they are not part of this measure of human capital. Human capital in CWON complements the other major initiative on human capital by the World Bank, the Human Capital Index (https://www.worldbank.org/en/publication/human-capital), which is discussed in another chapter of this book. CWON takes a purely monetary approach to human capital and its growth over time, while the Human Capital Index compiles observable physical indicators related to human capital like health and educational attainment.

The work on human capital in previous volumes of CWON demonstrated the critical role of human capital for long term development. Not only is human capital the largest asset globally (64% in 2014, the latest year currently available), but it is also a critical asset for development. While human capital accounts for only 41% of national wealth in low-income countries, it constitutes 70% of national wealth in high-income OECD countries, and it is growing faster than any other asset (Figs. 1.1 and 1.2). Total national wealth accounts by income group are provided in Appendix 1.3; the full dataset for wealth accounts, methodology, and publications can be found on https://datacatalog.worldbank.org/dataset/wealth-accounting.

From 1995 to 2014, growth of human capital was quite high, well over 100%, across all income groups except high-income OECD (Fig. 1.3). Adjusting for population growth, the per capita gains are much lower

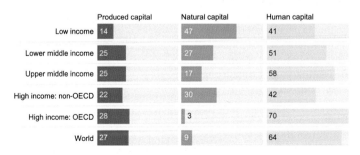

Note: Net Foreign assets, which can be either positive or negative, comprise a very small share of national wealth and are omitted here.
Source: Data from https://datacatalog.worldbank.org/dataset/wealth-accounting

FIG. 1.1 Economic Development and the Composition of Wealth (%), 2014. Note: Net Foreign assets, which can be either positive or negative, comprise a very small share of national wealth and are omitted here. (Source: Data from https://datacatalog.worldbank.org/dataset/wealth-accounting.)

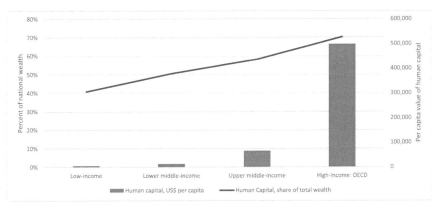

Source: Data from https://datacatalog.worldbank.org/dataset/wealth-accounting

FIG. 1.2 Human capital, percent share of national wealth and US$ per person, 2014. ((Source: Data from https://datacatalog.worldbank.org/dataset/wealth-accounting.)

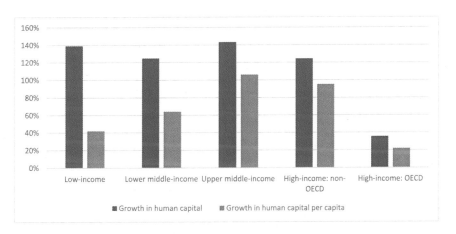

Source: Data from https://datacatalog.worldbank.org/dataset/wealth-accounting

FIG. 1.3 Growth of human capital between 1995 and 2014, percent. (Source: Data from https://datacatalog.worldbank.org/dataset/wealth-accounting.)

though still impressive, particularly in low-income countries (down from 142% to 39%) and lower-middle income countries (down from 125% to 64%). The growth rates for human capital wealth per capita tend to be higher in countries at lower or middle levels of economic development than in high-income countries. This would be akin to the convergence often observed in GDP per capita, but in this case the convergence is evident for human capital wealth per capita. The fact that growth rates are higher at lower levels of human capital wealth per capita appears even more clearly when looking at data for individual countries,

as opposed to the data for income groups, which tend to give greater weight to larger countries. However, several factors should be taken into account in explaining these trends. Low-income countries that start with the lowest human capital in 1995 build human capital more slowly than middle-income countries. This is partly the result of high population growth rates that dilute the growth of per capita human capital. At the other end, the relatively slow growth of per capita human capital in high-income countries reflects a combination of the aging of the population and slow wage growth over the period.

1.1.3 Threats to Human Capital: Air Pollution and Human Health

Given the importance of human capital for development, it is critical to identify any obstacles to building human capital. A major challenge includes threats to human health, which can result in both premature mortality and productivity losses due to nonfatal illness and disability, reducing human capital. Air pollution is a major threat in many developing countries and was the 5th leading cause of mortality globally in 2015 (Fig. 1.4). Recent evidence suggests that air pollution may worsen the impact of COVID-19, increasing the number of deaths than might have occurred if skies were pollution free (Mani and Yamada, 2020).

Sources of air pollution are usually characterized as either ambient or "outdoor" pollution from sources such as fossil fuel combustion and indoor pollution from sources like cooking with biomass. Drawing on previous work for the World Bank's Adjusted Net Savings indicator (Cropper and Khanna, 2014; Narain and Sall, 2016; Sall and Narain, 2018), we extend that work to estimate the impact of both ambient and indoor air pollution on premature mortality and its impact on human capital. Due to a lack of comprehensive global data, we are not able to quantify the impacts of productivity losses at this time.

1.1.4 Outline of This Chapter

We begin the next section of this chapter by explaining the conceptual approach to measuring human capital and how we implement the Jorgenson-Fraumeni measure, focusing on key data sources and critical assumptions made for these estimations. We then discuss the methods and data for estimating the impact of air pollution on human capital. A more detailed explanation of the methods and data sources used for human capital estimates are given in Appendix 1.2. Results are then presented, comparing human capital under current levels of air pollution to the potential value of human capital possible if pollution were low enough to have no impact on mortality rates. We highlight the most vulnerable countries, as well as those that have made the most progress from 1995 to 2014 in reducing the impact of air pollution. This is followed by a concluding section that focuses on our new work to extend and improve the human capital accounts.

1.2 DATA AND METHODS FOR MEASURING THE IMPACT OF AIR POLLUTION ON HUMAN CAPITAL

In this section, we start with an explanation of the approach to measuring human capital and then discuss how the impact of air pollution on human capital is estimated.

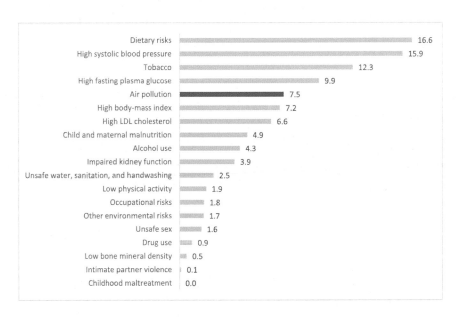

Source: Data from Global Burden of Disease Study 2017

FIG. 1.4 Percent of total deaths globally in 2017 (by cause of death). (Source: Data from Global Burden of Disease Study 2017.)

1.2.1 Measuring Human Capital Wealth in the Wealth of Nations: Conceptual Approach

The CWON human capital accounts use the Jorgenson-Fraumeni lifetime earnings approach, which requires estimation of the present value of future labor earnings. Although this definition of human capital wealth is conceptually simple, a number of steps must be undertaken to build the accounts from survey data. Those steps and some of the important choices involved in the empirical estimations are described below, with a more detailed methodology described in Appendix 1.2.

Briefly, the expected lifetime income of a representative individual consists of the current labor income, obtained from household surveys, and the expected lifetime income in the next years until leaving the labor force. The CWON human capital accounts include only persons between the ages of 15 and 65, although in some countries people younger than 15 work and those over 65 continue to work. The current labor income is adjusted by the probabilities of being employed, and the lifetime income in the next year is adjusted by a discount factor and the corresponding survival rate. In addition, for an individual aged 15–24, there are two courses of action: (1) holding the same education level and continue to work or (2) leaving the labor force to take an additional year of education and earning income after completing education. The lifetime income profiles for a representative individual are multiplied by the corresponding number of people in a country to calculate national human capital stock by age, gender, and education. Aggregating across these groups generates an estimate of the total monetary value of the human capital stock for each country for a given year.

Earnings Profiles from Household Surveys

Individuals are characterized by age, gender, and level of education. Household surveys are used to construct a set of matrices that capture (1) the probability that individuals are working depending on their age, gender, and years of education; and (2) their likely earnings when working, again, by age, gender, and years of schooling. Matrices are calculated separately for men and women.

The estimates of the likelihood of working are based on observed values in the available household and labor force surveys for the various countries. Following Montenegro et al. (2016), the estimates of likely earnings are based on Mincerian wage regressions. The regressions enable us to compute expected earnings for workers throughout their working lives, taking into account gender, education, and assumed experience (computed on the basis of age and the number of years

of education completed). Expected earnings are computed for all individuals in the surveys from age 15 to 65 years, noting that some individuals may go to school beyond age 15 years (for the purpose of these estimations until age 24 years). The analysis also takes into account the life expectancy of the labor force. In countries with high life expectancy, workers are expected to work until age 65 years, but in other countries, they may not be able to.

Until recently, estimating wage regressions and the discounted value of future wages for the labor force for a large number of countries was not feasible because of a lack of standardized household survey data with which to make the estimations in a systematic way.[a] Our estimates utilize the World Bank's International Income Distribution Database[b] of household and labor force surveys. The database provides access to surveys for over 150 countries and more than 25 years (Montenegro and Hirn, 2009). The surveys are used to estimate both the likelihood of participation in the labor force by age, sex, and years of education and expected earnings, again by age, sex, and education level.

Adjustments to Align with National Accounts Data

The household surveys used for the computation of the earnings profiles—as well as the probability of working—are designed to be nationally representative. The surveys are in many cases of good quality, but may not be that accurate in all countries, especially some low- and middle-income countries with limited resources. The extensive resources required for such surveys means that they are not conducted frequently outside of high-income countries. Results from the surveys, in principle, should be fairly similar to estimates of the Compensation of Employees reported in the System of National Accounts (EC (European Commission), 2009). However, survey results may diverge from the System of National Accounts for several reasons. Therefore, adjustments

---

[a]An exception was an OECD study which estimated human capital for 15 OECD and one non-OECD countries (Liu, 2011).

[b]The World Bank's International Income Distribution Database (I2D2) is a global database of more than 2000 household surveys from around the world, spanning several decades. I2D2 was started in 2006 by the World Development Report (WDR) on Gender and Equality. It has since been maintained by the Development Economics Vice Presidency at the World Bank. It is a major effort to harmonize the surveys for analysis of poverty, education, and inequality issues. I2D2 has continually added surveys to the database, and the information has been used by many global practices across the World Bank.

described below are made to the earnings profiles in order to scale up from survey to national level.

First, to ensure consistency of the earning profiles from the surveys with published data from the System of National Accounts, earnings estimates from the surveys are adjusted to reflect the share of labor earnings in GDP, Compensation of Employees. Compensation of Employees includes the economic value of benefits, such as housing, pensions, or health insurance, in addition to wages, but the household surveys typically report only the wages received, thus underestimating total compensation. In some countries, additional benefits can be substantial. Total earnings derived from the survey, and the resultant human capital, are expected to be too low in comparison with those based on the share of labor earnings in GDP because they do not include benefits. This is addressed by using Compensation of Employees as a control total to scale up earnings profiles from the surveys.

Accounting for the Human Capital of the Self-Employed

The other major adjustment concerns the self-employed. The economic role of the self-employed can be especially important in many low- and middle-income countries where subsistence agriculture and informal economy are very common. However, the earnings of the self-employed are not well represented in the national accounts of many countries because, with few exceptions, Compensation of Employees includes only workers who are formally employed. The earnings of the self-employed are included as part of another category, mixed income, which is the total income earned by self-employed workers. Therefore, it is a combination of capital and labor income. In addition, earnings of the self-employed workers may also be poorly represented in household surveys.

Correcting this omission requires i) identifying the earnings in mixed income that can be attributed to the self-employed and ii) distinguishing the labor component of such earnings from returns to other factors of production, which are all combined. For human capital estimates, only the labor portion from the earnings of the self-employed should be included. The Penn World Table database (Feenstra et al., 2015) has made estimates of the labor component of the earnings of the self-employed, which we add to Compensation of Employees to produce the control total for total labor earnings that is used to scale up survey-derived earnings profiles by age, sex, and years of education. This approach implicitly assumes that the demographic and earnings profiles of the self-employed are the same as employee workers in formal labor markets. Although we know that is unlikely in many countries, there is insufficient data with global coverage to refine treatment of the self-employed at this time.

Adjustments to Align with National Population Data

To scale up from survey to national level human capital accounts, the estimations of expected lifetime earnings rely on two sets of demographic variables: population data by age and gender, and mortality rates by age and gender (so that the expected years of work can be adjusted, accounting for the fact that some workers will die before age 65 years). The demographic profiles obtained from the surveys may be inconsistent with official population data for some countries. For example, although surveys are designed to be nationally representative because of limited sample sizes for some categories of individuals, household surveys may not precisely estimate the distribution of the population by age and sex nor life expectancy. For those in the 15-to-24 year age group, the probability of being in school also has to be taken into account. To ensure that human capital estimates are appropriate, data from the surveys are adjusted to population estimates from the United Nations Population Division.

Choice of Discount Rate

Those familiar with present value computations recognize that the choice of discount rate can make a major difference in the estimates. A higher discount rate will generate lower values for human capital wealth, whereas a lower discount rate will lead to higher estimates of human capital wealth.

Human capital is calculated under the assumption that labor earnings grow at a constant rate g (owing to increases in efficiency) and are discounted at rate r. The discount rate used for all the CWON asset valuation estimates is 4% per year. Due to a lack of data about country-specific wage growth, the same wage growth rate was applied in all countries, 2.5% per year. We recognize that wage growth rates can vary a great deal across countries and the next report, Changing Wealth of Nations 2021, use differentiated wage growth rates in order to better estimate the variation of human capital among countries.

Coverage of Household Surveys and Gap Filling

Data from the System of National Accounts are available for all countries on a yearly basis, but data from household surveys are not. Although upper-middle-income and high-income countries may have annual surveys (or in some countries quarterly surveys), low-income and lower-middle-income countries often conduct labor or household surveys with detailed information on earnings less frequently, in some countries with 10 or more years between surveys. The latest household survey is used for estimates in subsequent years, until a new survey is available. This choice means that estimates from the latest available survey are carried forward in time, but still with adjustments based on data from the national accounts for the share of labor earnings in GDP.

In a handful of cases, estimates of labor earnings obtained from household surveys seemed to be off by a wide margin. In those few cases, interpolations were used instead. Finally, for countries from the Gulf Cooperation Council (Bahrain, Kuwait, Oman, Qatar, Saudi Arabia, and the United Arab Emirates), because no household survey data were publicly available,[c] estimates of human capital wealth per capita were based instead on a simple estimation taking into account the countries' GDP per capita, labor share in GDP, and education level.

1.2.2 Estimating the Impact of Air Pollution

The effects of air pollution on human capital are wide-ranging, from deaths due to carbon monoxide poisoning and respiratory and heart related health problems stemming from pollution exposure to reduced labor productivity due to worsening cognitive performance. Sources of air pollution include both indoor pollution from burning solid fuels in homes and ambient or outdoor pollution, which has many sources. Even though the deaths stemming from air pollution are observable, it is difficult to measure the effects of air pollution on productivity. First, precisely quantifying the effect of air pollution on cognitive performance is difficult. In addition, the literature documenting the effects of air pollution on human productivity is limited. Therefore, the calculations in this chapter reflect only the direct effect of air pollution on premature mortality due to limited data on productivity impacts.

In addition, deaths caused by air pollution can take place in different time periods depending on the form and impact of air pollution. While an intense carbon monoxide intake could cause a sudden death, persistent exposure to low levels of carbon monoxide could cause death in months or years. However, the available global data do not include sufficient information about the duration of exposure to air pollution before death so as to include this effect.

As described in Section 1.2.1, the lifetime income approach developed by Jorgenson and Fraumeni is applied to measure human capital. A critical parameter in the calculations is the survival rate by age and gender, that is, how many individuals do not continue work due to mortality. The survival rates combine all causes of mortality, including premature mortality from air pollution. To estimate the impact of air pollution on human capital wealth, we adjust the survival rate to exclude the premature deaths due to air pollution, and recalculate human capital. We then compare human capital *without* air pollution impact to estimates of human capital that include such deaths. The difference between the two is the hypothetical estimate of the impact of air pollution on human capital wealth.

To implement this approach, information from the Global Burden of Disease is used to disaggregate the mortality rates by cause of death and adjust the resulting survival rates. The Global Burden of Disease Study database includes global, regional, and national age–sex-specific mortality for 282 causes of death in 195 countries and territories for the period of 1980–2017 (Global Burden of Disease Collaborative Network, 2016). Deaths are considered as air pollution related if they are associated with any of air pollution risk factors in the Global Burden of Disease Study data, including household air pollution from solid fuels, ambient particulate matter pollution, and ambient ozone pollution. The following section presents the results.

The Differential Effect of Air Pollution by Age and Impact on Human Capital

While there can be a great deal of variation by region, air pollution has the greatest impact on premature mortality on adults (15–64 years) and the elderly (65+ years), except in Sub-Saharan Africa where the young (under 15 years) are strongly impacted (Fig. 1.5). Depending on the region, the elderly population account from 35%–70% of annual deaths from air pollution. These most vulnerable age groups are not included in the CWON human capital accounts, which estimate human capital for the age group 15 to 65 years of age. This results in a lower estimate of total human capital and of the loss of human capital due to air pollution. Although it is not clear how exact this omission is impacting human capital estimates, human capital for those under 15 would be heavily discounted because many young people do not join the labor force until later. At the other end of the demographic profile, the human capital of those over

---

[c]Surveys have been made available for the Gulf Cooperation Council countries for CWON 2021.

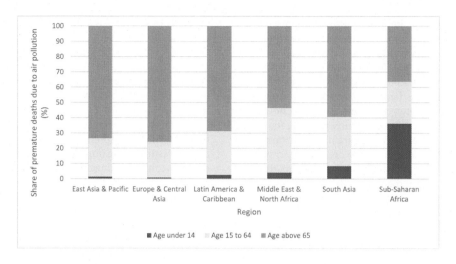

Source: Data from Global Burden of Disease Study 2017

FIG. 1.5 Premature mortality from air pollution by age group across geographic region, 2017 (percent of total air pollution deaths). (Source: Data from Global Burden of Disease Study 2017.)

65 will not be very large because of fewer years remaining of labor force participation.

1.3 RESULTS

The global total number of deaths associated with ambient particulate matter pollution decreased from 1990 to 2017 while that of household air pollution from solid fuels increased during the same period (Fig. 1.6). As a result, the total air pollution mortality did not change much over the last two decades.

Access to clean fuels and technologies for cooking can be considered as one of the key factors that contributed to the household air pollution mortality decline for the last two decades (Fig. 1.7). High-income countries already achieved almost 100% access to clean fuels and technologies while low-income and middle-income countries have been still improving it. We also observe

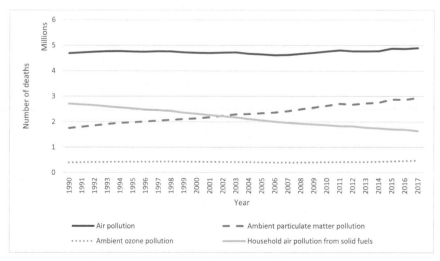

Source: Data from Global Burden of Disease 2017

FIG. 1.6 Global air pollution related deaths by risk factor. (Source: Data from Global Burden of Disease 2017.)

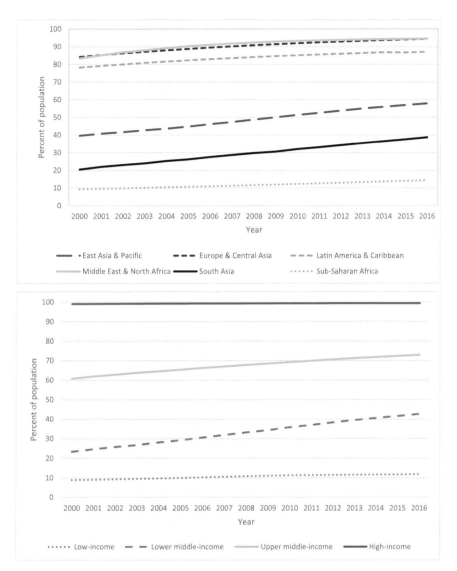

Source: Authors, using data from World Bank. Accessible at:
<https://data.worldbank.org/indicator/EG.CFT.ACCS.ZS>

FIG. 1.7 Access to clean fuels and technologies for cooking by income group and region. (Source: Authors, using data from World Bank. Accessible at: https://data.worldbank.org/indicator/EG.CFT.ACCS.ZS.)

regional differences in the access to clean fuels and technologies. In 2016, more than 85% of population in Europe & Central Asia, Latin America & Caribbean, and Middle East & North Africa regions has the access to clean fuels and technologies while East Asia & Pacific, South Asia, and Sub-Saharan Africa regions have the access rate of 58%, 39%, and 14%, respectively. People in developing countries, particularly in the regions with the low access rate of clean energy, still have high

dependence on solid fuels and risks of exposure to indoor air pollution.

All estimates of human capital and wealth with the hypothetical impact of premature deaths due to air pollution by economy and aggregate averages (i.e., income group, geographic region, region with only low- and middle-income economies) in 2014 U.S. dollars at market exchange rates are reported in Appendix 1.3. A loss of human capital due to premature deaths attributable to air pollution is clearly observed. Globally, in 2014, the loss of human capital wealth and total wealth due to premature deaths attributable to air pollution was 0.66% and 0.16%, respectively, which is equivalent of an increase of about 1.2 trillion in constant 2014 U.S. dollars at market exchange rates. This effect has a decreasing trend in both percentage and level terms from 1995 to 2014.

We also find positive effects of reducing air pollution on human capital in every region, but the magnitude of the impact is heterogeneous across regions. South Asia, Middle East and North Africa, and Sub-Saharan Africa have a relatively large loss in 2014 human capital of 1.72%, 1.16%, and 0.97%, respectively, while other regions have a smaller loss (Fig. 1.8). We observe a similar trend in the impact on wealth. At the income group

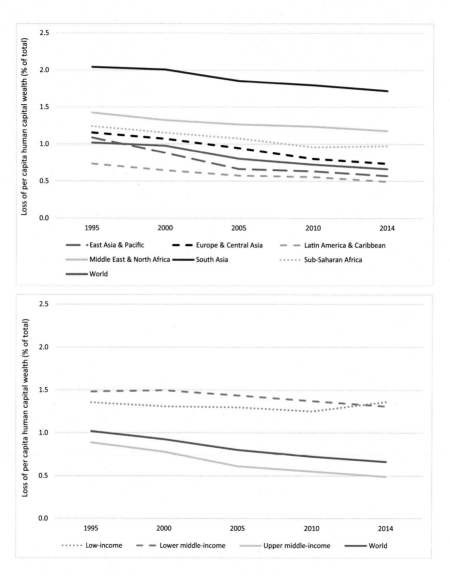

Note: All numbers are percent changes in per-capita human capital with the hypothetical value of human capital

FIG. 1.8 Loss of per capita human capital wealth due to premature deaths attributable to air pollution. Note: All numbers are percent changes in per capita human capital with the hypothetical value of human capital if there were no premature deaths from exposure to air pollution.

level, the impact is higher in low-income and lower-middle-income countries, compared with upper-middle-income and high-income countries.

Conversely, these trends in the level-term at the regional and income group levels are decreasing with exception of Latin America and Caribbean (Fig. 1.9), which is due to the following reasons. First, human capital increased in each region and income group over the period of 1995 to 2014. Second, given that the global total number of air pollution related premature deaths did not change much from 1995 to 2014, the human capital increase due to the hypothetical decrease in air pollution related mortality became relatively smaller as total human capital increased.

It is worth noting that our measures of human capital losses only include by design those between the ages of 15 and 65, as discussed in the previous section. For this reason, premature mortality attributable to air pollution for this age group drives the results presented in this section and needs to be carefully examined. In this spirit, we compare composition of air pollution related deaths by age group at the regional and income group levels. About 20% to 40% of the air pollution related mortality is for ages 15–64. This ratio for each region and income group constantly increased during the last two decades while there was heterogeneity in magnitude.

At the regional level, we find the total number of deaths attributable to air pollution for ages 15–64

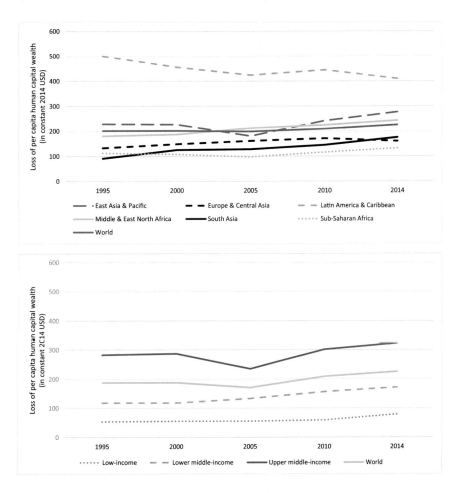

Note: All numbers are changes in per capita human capital in constant 2014 USD with the hypothetical value of

FIG. 1.9 Loss of per capita human capital wealth due to premature deaths attributable to air pollution. Note: All numbers are changes in per capita human capital in constant 2014 USD with the hypothetical value of human capital if there were no premature deaths from exposure to air pollution.

increased in all regions from 1990 to 2017 with exception of Europe & Central Asia (Figs. 1.10 and 1.11). At the income group level, we observe a couple of notable trends. First, the total number of deaths attributable to air pollution for ages 15–64 in both low-income and lower-middle-income groups increased while that in the upper-middle-income group decreased (Figs. 1.12 and 1.13). Second, the number of deaths associated with household air pollution from solid fuels in the low-income group increased while that in both lower-middle-income and upper-middle-income groups

decreased. These trends indicate the followings. First, the mortality associated with both ambient particulate matter pollution and household air pollution from solid fuels significantly increases as low-income economies grow to lower-middle-income economies. Second, as lower-middle-income economies grow to upper-middle-income economies, the mortality associated with household air pollution declines, which also leads the overall air pollution related mortality to decline.

We take a closer look at 15 countries with the least impacts of reducing air pollution mortality on 2014

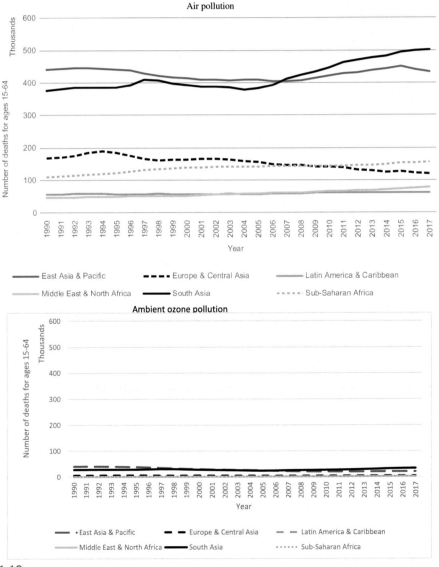

FIG. 1.10

(Continued)

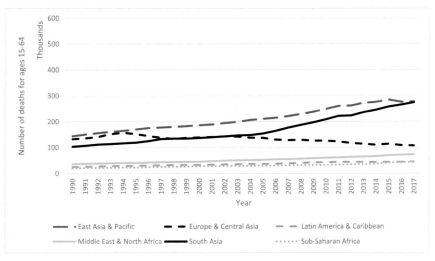

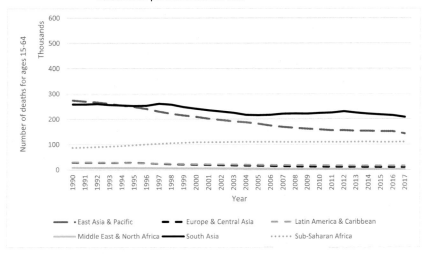

Source: Data from Global Burden of Disease Study 2017

FIG. 1.10,   **CONT'D** Air pollution related deaths for ages 15–64 by region. (Source: Data from Global Burden of Disease Study 2017.)

human capital (Fig. 1.14). These countries have a decreasing trend in the percent change of the loss of human capital for the period of 1995 to 2014. For example, Panama, Costa Rica, and Maldives have the lowest losses of human capital wealth in 2014, 0.27%, 0.23%, and 0.20%, respectively. We find these three countries had lower mortality rates of all types of air pollution than the global average rate in 2014 (Fig. 1.15). It is worth noting that Maldives significantly decreased the mortality rate associated with household air pollution over the last two decades, which makes the country to have one of the least impacts of reducing air pollution on 2014 human capital wealth.

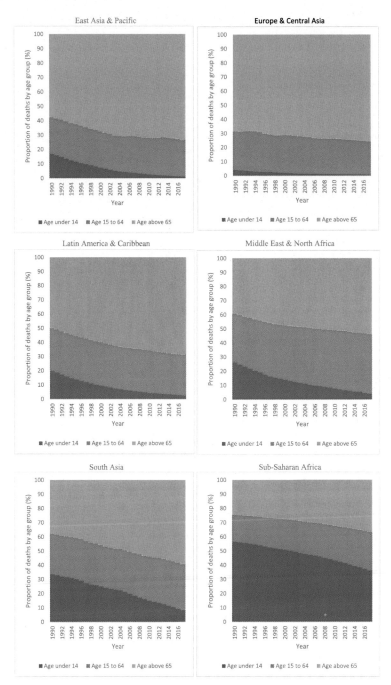

FIG. 1.11 Age group composition of air pollution related deaths by region. (Source: Data from Global Burden of Disease Study 2017.)

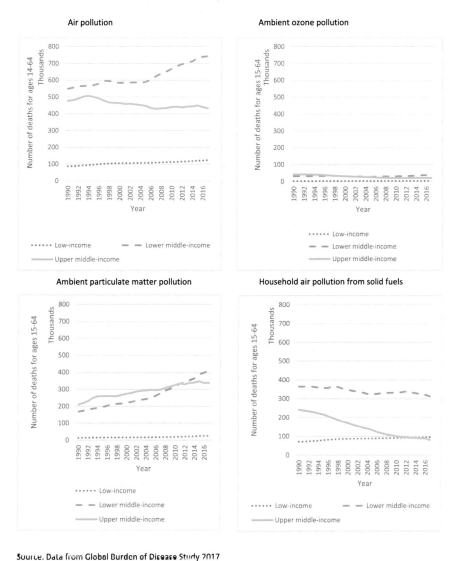

Source. Data from Global Burden of Disease Study 2017

FIG. 1.12 Air pollution related deaths for ages 15–64 by income group. (Source: Data from Global Burden of Disease Study 2017.)

Contrastingly, we observe both increasing and decreasing trends of the loss in human capital for 15 countries with the largest impacts of reducing premature mortality attributable to air pollution on 2014 human capital (Fig. 1.16). For instance, Papua New Guinea, Solomon Islands, and Yemen have the largest losses of human capital wealth in 2014, 3.4%, 3.1%, and 2.3%, respectively. We also observe that these three countries had a decreasing trend in the historical air pollution related mortality rate as well as higher mortality rates associated with outdoor air pollution and household

air pollution from solid fuels than the global averages during the last two decades (Fig. 1.17). Furthermore, the household air pollution mortality rate is higher than that of either ambient particulate matter or ambient ozone pollution and is a driving factor of the overall magnitude of air pollution related mortality rates in these three countries. For such economies, reducing household air pollution would be an effective way to decrease air pollution related mortality and thus increase human capital.

We analyze the premature mortality attributable to air pollution at the age group level to further examine the

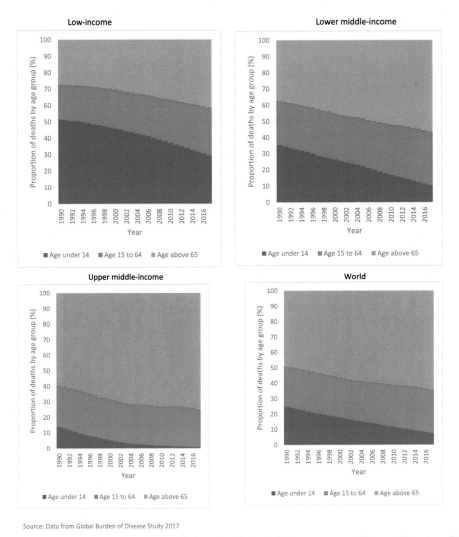

Source: Data from Global Burden of Disease Study 2017

FIG. 1.13 Age group composition of air pollution related deaths by income group. (Source: Data from Global Burden of Disease Study 2017.)

results for the age group of 15–64, which is particularly relevant for our study. A proportion of premature deaths attributable to air pollution for ages 15–64 in the above-mentioned 15 least impacted countries from reducing air pollution related deaths is 24.5% on average and lower than that in the 15 most impacted countries by 7.8% (Fig. 1.18). Furthermore, the average mortality rate for ages 15–64 in the least impacted countries for 2014 is 24.5 deaths per 100,000 people while that in the most impacted countries is 37.2 deaths per 100,000 people. These figures indicate the most impacted countries have more severe air pollution related mortality, particularly for the age group of 15–64.

Finally, we focus the analysis on two large developing economies, namely, China and India. It is interesting to compare results for these countries as China has a much smaller percentage loss of human capital due to premature deaths from exposure to air pollution than India does. Both countries have a similar historical trend in the overall air pollution mortality rate, which is a slight decline above the global average from 1995 to 2014 (Fig. 1.19). However, composition of the air pollution related deaths differs between the two countries. India has a lower mortality rate from ambient particulate matter and ozone pollution and a higher mortality rate from household air pollution than

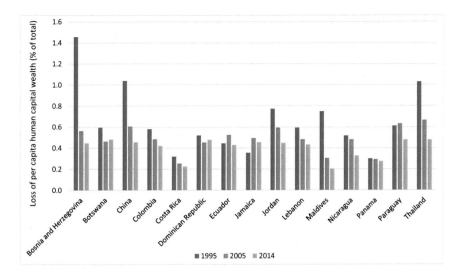

Note: all numbers are percent changes in per-capita human capital with the hypothetical value of human capital if there were no premature deaths from exposure to air pollution.

FIG. 1.14 Countries with the least impacts of reducing air pollution mortality on per capita human capital. Note: All numbers are percent changes in per capita human capital with the hypothetical value of human capital if there were no premature deaths from exposure to air pollution.

China does. As also observed in other lower-middle-income countries, abating household air pollution would be an effective way for India to decrease the overall air pollution related mortality and decrease associated human capital losses.

In summary, the analysis of the countries with the least and largest impacts of reducing air pollution mortality on human capital in this section provides a few insights. First, the countries with the largest impacts are either low-income or lower-middle-income economies while the countries with the least impacts are mostly upper-middle-income economies. This finding is consistent with the labor income losses due to air pollution reported by Sall and Narain (2018). Second, reducing air pollution mortality in countries with a lower air pollution mortality rate leads to a smaller increase in human capital than that with countries with a higher air pollution mortality rate. Third, air pollution related mortality for all age groups, particularly for the age group of 15–64, is more severe in the most impacted countries than in the least impacted countries.

1.4 NEXT STEPS FOR HUMAN CAPITAL AND AIR POLLUTION

The air pollution impacts discussed here are based on the first attempt to provide global estimates of human capital using survey data to implement the Jorgenson-Fraumeni lifetime earnings approach. CWON demonstrates the critical role of human capital for development and the importance of addressing factors, like air pollution, that create obstacles to building human capital. Our estimates seek to make explicit the impact of air pollution on human capital through premature mortality, hence more amenable to targeted interventions to reduce air pollution.

These human capital estimates and the impact of air pollution are viewed as a 'work in progress" of the ongoing CWON initiative. As the first attempt to make these estimates, there are many limitations and shortcomings, which will be addressed in future editions of CWON. The work on human capital and all other components of CWON is constrained by certain data requirements: data for compiling the accounts must provide global coverage (for a minimum of 100 countries), support an annual time series for each country from 1995 with regular updates, and, for the most part, data must be publicly available. In future, we will both improve the underlying human capital accounts and explore new applications of the accounts. Some of the priority areas for improvement include:

1. Improving the quality of human capital accounts and the impact of air pollution

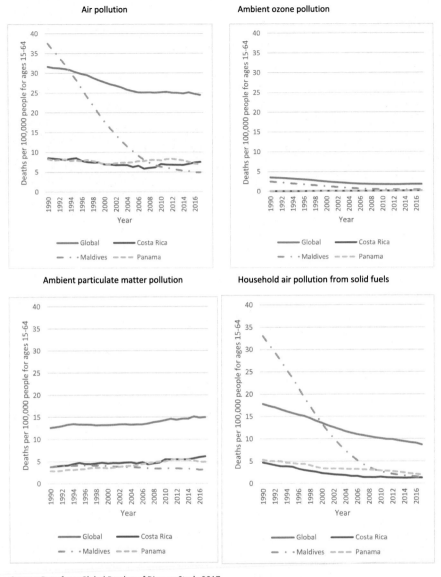

Source: Data from Global Burden of Disease Study 2017

FIG. 1.15 Historical air pollution in countries with the least impact of reducing premature mortality attributable to air pollution. (Source: Data from Global Burden of Disease Study 2017.)

- *Greater country coverage and survey coverage*: In order to solve some of the data problems, we will take advantage of the growing number of surveys in I2D2. More countries will be included and the number of surveys for the recent years will be increased for some countries supporting a longer time series for some countries in the next volume of CWON. In addition, quality

checks on the survey data have been conducted since the publishing of the current report and will help identify questionable surveys.

- *Country-specific wage growth rates*: The current assumption of a uniform wage growth rate across all countries will be replaced by country-specific wage growth rates estimated by the World Bank's macroeconomic forecasting unit.

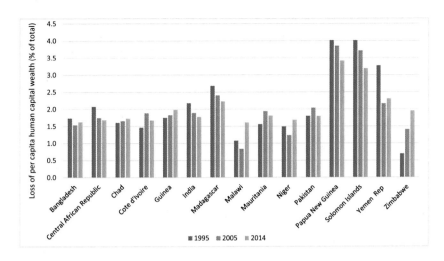

Note: all numbers are percent changes in per-capita human capital with the hypothetical value of human capital if there were no premature deaths from exposure to air pollution.

FIG. 1.16 Countries with the largest impacts of reducing air pollution mortality on per capita human capital. Note: All numbers are percent changes in per capita human capital with the hypothetical value of human capital if there were no premature deaths from exposure to air pollution.

- *Impact of air pollution on productivity*: Current estimates include only premature mortality but not morbidity, which results in productivity losses. Future work will draw on new efforts to estimate the indirect effects of air pollution on human capital wealth, lost productivity.
- *Subnational spatial distribution*: The concentration of air pollution and impact on human capital can vary enormously within a single country. Impacts that appear small at the national level may hide very large impacts at specific subnational locations. Development of spatially explicit estimates at the subnational level will greatly improve the design of solutions.

2. Analytical work based on human capital accounts
   - *Impact of external shocks and 'green swans'*: The World Bank's CWON defines human capital wealth as the discounted value of future earnings, following the Jorgensen and Fraumeni lifetime earnings approach. We seek a measure of wealth that informs us about likely future well-being. This methodology essentially assumes that GDP is relatively stable over the long term, and in fact growing at a moderate rate over the course of a working life (as much as 50 years). For most countries in most years, this has seemed a reasonable

assumption. But for countries that have recently experienced a natural disaster or a war, this assumption does not hold, and human capital estimates would need to build on an assumed recovery path for the economy.

Furthermore, in the age of climate change, this assumption seems increasingly unreasonable. In a recent report from the Bank for International Settlements and the Banque du France (Bolton et al., 2020), the potential impacts of climate change are introduced as green swans: events that are i) rare and unexpected, hence outside regular expectations; ii) with the potential for extreme or wide-ranging impacts; that, iii), can only be explained after the fact, not on the basis of past experience and probability distributions. The report by the Bank for International Settlements highlighted the importance of considering the risk of such events in asset valuation. The recent COVID-19 virus pandemic illustrates that green swans are not limited to climate change effects, but may arise from a wide range of sources. In the new analysis of human capital for CWON 2021, we compare human capital using pre- and post-COVID estimates of country wage growth profiles, to estimate losses due to COVID.

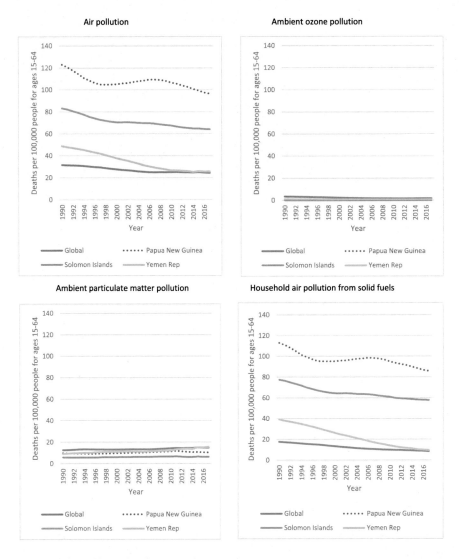

Source: Data from Global Burden of Disease Study 2017

FIG. 1.17 Historical air pollution in countries with the largest impacts of reducing air pollution. (Source: Data from Global Burden of Disease Study 2017.)

While revised growth rates are the immediate impact of disruptive events like COVID, there are longer term impacts as well. Of particular importance is the long-term impact of disruption of education on the accumulation of human capital by young people. This effect will be considered in future editions of CWON.

- *Cross-country comparisons of human capital*: Comparisons of human capital and the impacts of air pollution across countries are estimated using market exchange rates. However, the purchasing power of

one U.S. dollar varies enormously across countries. Purchasing power parity prices (PPP) have been developed to adjust for these differences, hence, provide a better indicator of how material well-being varies across countries than market exchange rates can provide. The next CWON will include human capital measured in both market exchange rates and purchasing power parity prices.

- *Treatment of migrant labor*: A further issue to be considered in comparing countries is better

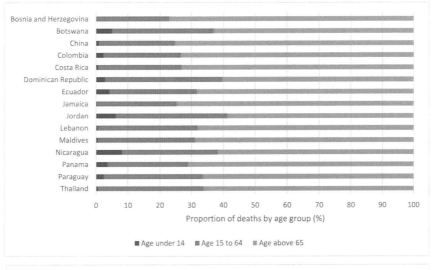

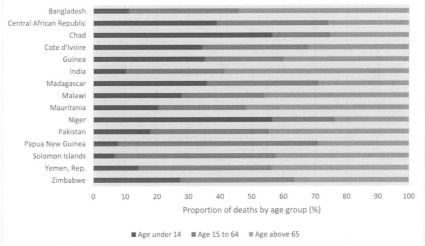

Source. Data from Global Burden of Disease Study 2017

FIG. 1.18 Age group composition of 2014 air pollution related deaths in countries with the least (top figure) and largest (bottom figure) impacts of reducing air pollution mortality on 2014 human capital. (Source: Data from Global Burden of Disease Study 2017.)

understanding of migrant labor in human capital. Many high-income oil producers in the Middle East, for example, import a great deal of labor, from unskilled domestic workers to highly skilled professionals like doctors and engineers. Many of the migrants come from lower-income countries like India, Bangladesh, and the Philippines. In high-income countries as well, migrant workers of all skill levels constitute an important part of the labor force.

For highly skilled workers from low- or middle-income countries, the value of their human capital can increase tremendously simply through migration, not the accumulation of skills, experience, and expertise. And the country that supplied the training may lose that human capital as workers migrate. Better understanding of migration and the ensuing impact on a country's human capital will improve the comparison of human capital across countries.

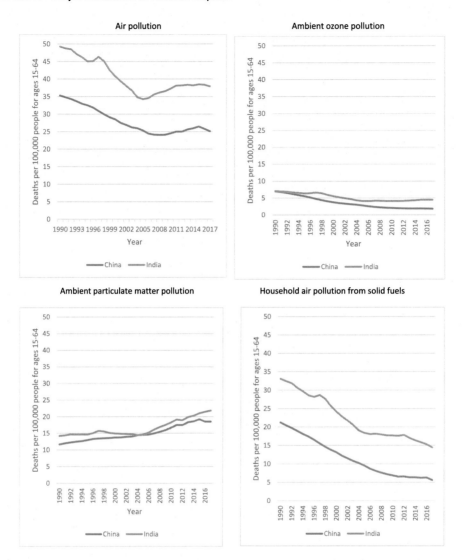

Source: Data from Global Burden of Disease Study 2017

FIG. 1.19 Comparison of the historical air pollution related mortality rates in China and India. (Source: Data from Global Burden of Disease Study 2017.)

APPENDIX 1.1 GLOBAL WEALTH ACCOUNTS, 1995–2014

In 2014, global wealth stood at $1143 trillion (Table A1.1). This figure represents an increase in total wealth of 66% over 20 years—an average annual growth rate of 2.7%. Human capital turns out to be the most important component of wealth, even though its share in total wealth decreased from 69% in 1995 to 64% in 2014. Human capital wealth reached $737 trillion in

2014, an increase of 55% since 1995—an average annual growth rate of 2.3%.

While Table A1.1 presents the global wealth figures in total terms, the following section focuses on measures in per capita terms to control for population growth.

Globally, total wealth stood at $168,580 per person in 2014 versus $128,929 in 1995. Human capital wealth stood at $108,654 per person in 2014 versus $88,874 in 1995 (Table A1.2). With an average annual growth rate

TABLE A1.1
Global wealth, by type of asset, 1995 and 2014.

	1995		2014	
	Billion US$	Share of total (%)	Billion US$	Share of total (%)
Produced capital	164,781	24	303,548	26
Natural capital	52,457	8	107,427	9
Forests and protected areas	14,515	2	18,290	2
Agricultural land	25,859	4	39,890	3
Energy resources (fossil fuels)	11,087	2	39,094	3
Metals and minerals	99,7	<1	10,154	1
Human capital	475,594	69	736,854	64
Net foreign assets	−2890	<1	−4581	<1
Total wealth	689,942	100	1,143,249	100

Note: Figures are in constant 2014 US dollars at market exchange rates.
Source: Data from https://datacatalog.worldbank.org/dataset/wealth-accounting.

TABLE A1.2
Trends in wealth per capita, by level of development, 1995–2014.

	1995	2000	2005	2010	2014	Annual growth (%)
World						
Total wealth per capita (US$)	128,929	138,064	145,891	158,363	168,580	1.42%
Human capital per capita (US$)	88,874	96,478	97,707	102,170	108,654	1.06%
Human capital as share of total (%)	69%	70%	67%	65%	64%	
Low-income countries						
Total wealth per capita (US$)	11,601	10,435	10,240	11,802	13,629	0.85%
Human capital per capita (US$)	3921	4016	4046	4447	5564	1.86%
Human capital as share of total (%)	34%	38%	40%	38%	41%	
Lower-middle-income countries						
Total wealth per capita (US$)	17,718	16,745	19,426	23,675	25,948	2.03%
Human capital per capita (US$)	7992	7917	9301	11,421	13,117	2.64%
Human capital as share of total (%)	45%	47%	48%	48%	51%	
Upper-middle-income countries						
Total wealth per capita (US$)	51,142	57,623	66,224	93,811	112,798	4.25%
Human capital per capita (US$)	31,906	36,716	38,526	54,740	65,742	3.88%
Human capital as share of total (%)	62%	64%	58%	58%	58%	
High-income non-OECD countries						
Total wealth per capita (US$)	163,827	163,232	194,243	241,224	264,998	2.56%
Human capital per capita (US$)	57,319	67,122	79,265	103,229	111,793	3.58%
Human capital as share of total (%)	35%	41%	41%	43%	42%	

Continued

TABLE A1.2
Trends in wealth per capita, by level of development, 1995–2014—cont'd

	1995	2000	2005	2010	2014	Annual growth (%)
High-income OECD countries						
Total wealth per capita (US$)	547,419	614,791	653,078	672,866	708,389	1.37%
Human capital per capita (US$)	408,992	458,949	472,722	471,270	498,399	1.05%
Human capital as share of total (%)	75%	75%	72%	70%	70%	

Note: Figures are in constant 2014 US dollars at market exchange rates.
Source: Data from https://datacatalog.worldbank.org/dataset/wealth-accounting.

of 1.0% over the past two decades, human capital wealth per capita increased by 22%, versus 31% for total wealth per capita. The decline in the share of human capital wealth in global wealth has not occurred in all countries, only in comparatively richer countries, primarily due to the aging of the working age population and slow wage growth.

In Table A1.2, aggregate data are provided globally as well as for groups of countries according to their level of economic development. Five groups of countries are considered: low income, lower-middle income, upper-middle income, high-income non-OECD, and high-income OECD. Inequality in human capital wealth as well as total wealth is high. In high-income OECD countries, total wealth per capita is greater than $700,000, and human capital wealth alone is at close to $500,000 per person. This is not far from 100 times more than the levels observed in low-income countries, where human capital wealth is an estimated $5564 per person.

At the global level, the dynamics of human capital wealth accumulation are driven primarily by shifts taking place in OECD and upper-middle-income countries because those countries account for 87% of global wealth (65% for the OECD, and 22% for upper-middle-income countries). The proportions are even larger for human capital wealth. In these countries, the share of human capital wealth in total wealth is falling. Recall from the methodology section that the estimates of human capital wealth are anchored in the share of labor earnings in GDP. For some time, labor earnings as a share of GDP have declined in OECD countries because of technological change, stagnating wages, and in many countries a reduction in the share of the population in the labor force, due in part to aging.

By contrast, the share of human capital wealth in total wealth is rapidly increasing in low-income and lower-middle-income countries. This share increased from 34% to 41% over two decades in low-income countries and from 45% to 51% in lower-middle-income countries. Many of these countries are experiencing a demographic transition and are reaping the benefits of the demographic dividend as population growth rates are declining and the population is becoming better educated. We thus have diverging trends for poorer and richer countries in the increasing or decreasing role played by human capital over time. However, overall it is clear that as countries achieve higher levels of economic development, human capital wealth clearly dominates, whereas at lower levels of economic development, produced and natural capital (not shown in Table A1.2) tend to be larger.

APPENDIX 1.2 METHODOLOGY FOR CALCULATING HUMAN CAPITAL WEALTH

This section explains how the lifetime income approach developed by Jorgenson and Fraumeni (1989, 1992a,b) was implemented to estimate human capital wealth for the Changing Wealth of Nations 2018. According to this approach, human capital wealth is estimated as the total present value of the expected future labor income that could be generated over the lifetime of women and men currently living in a country.

The implementation of the lifetime income approach requires data by age and gender about population, employment and labor force participation, education, earnings profiles, and survival rates. The data sources for each variable are included in Table A1.3. The estimation is carried out in seven steps described below.

(In the equations below, country and gender dimensions of variables are omitted for ease of presentation.)

Step 1: Estimating the earnings regressions. The World Bank's International Income Distribution Database (I2D2), a unique database of more than 2000 household surveys maintained by the World Bank, is used to construct a database containing information on the number of people, their age, gender, earnings,

TABLE A1.3
Data sources for human capital wealth calculations.

Indicator/variable	Data sources	Notes
Annual earnings	International Income Distribution Database (I2D2)	Annual earnings are calculated utilizing the Mincerian regression results. The (relative) earnings profile by age, education and gender are derived for each country/year given the corresponding data availability
Education attainment	International Income Distribution Database (I2D2)	Years of education by age and gender are derived for each country/year
Employment rates	International Income Distribution Database (I2D2)	The employment rate and self-employment rate by age, gender and education level are calculated for each country/year. These rates have to be calculated by the employed (or self-employed) persons divided by the whole population that includes the employed, self-employed, unemployed, and the people out of the labor force
School enrolment rates	International Income Distribution Database (I2D2)	Whether an individual by age, gender, education is enrolled in school or not; used for the probability of remaining employed in future years
Employment	International Labor Organization	The ILO employment data are used as control totals for scaling up employment from the I2D2 database. ILO employment data are also used for filling data gaps when necessary
Compensation of employees, GDP	United Nations National Accounts database	The Compensation of Employees data are used as input to control totals for scaling up annual earnings estimates from the I2D2 database and for filling the data gaps. In addition, the GDP data are used for expressing variables as a percent of GDP
Labor share of earnings of the self-employed	Penn World Table database	Penn World Table estimates of the labor component of the earnings of the self-employed out of total earnings of the self-employed. Used as input to control total, Total labor earnings
Total labor earnings	United Nations National Accounts database and Penn World Table database	Compensation of Employees + Labor earnings of the self-employed. This combined Labor earnings estimate is used as control total for scaling up earnings estimates from I2D2 to national level
Population	United Nation's World Population Prospects	By sex and age groups. The distribution of workers from the I2D2 database is scaled up using the population data
Survival rates	Global Burden of Disease Study from the Institute for Health Metrics and Evaluation	Survival rates are calculated utilizing the death rates obtained from the Global Burden of Disease Study (GBD). The GBD database includes global, regional, and national age-sex-specific mortality for 282 causes of death in 195 countries and territories

educational attainment, school enrolment rates, and employment rates. This database is used to estimate the Mincerian coefficients. The Mincerian wage regressions are estimated as

$$Ln(w_i) = \alpha + \beta_1 e_i + \beta_2 X_i + \beta_3 X_i^2 + \mu_i \qquad \text{(A1.1)}$$

where $Ln(w_i)$ is the natural log of earnings for the individual i, e_i is years of schooling (from 0 to 24), X_i is labor market working experience (estimated as AGE_i (from age 15 to 64) - e_i - 6), X_i^2 is working experience-squared, and μ_i is a random disturbance term reflecting unobserved abilities. The coefficient β_1 measures the return to an extra year of schooling as the coefficients β_2 and β_3 measure the return to working experience. Since working experience shows a decreasing marginal return, in general, the coefficient β_3 is expected to be a negative value. The constant, α, measures the average log earnings of individuals with zero years of schooling and working experience. Eq. (A1.1) is estimated for each economy for each survey year for male and female separately.

Even though the I2D2 includes number of years of schooling for most countries, some countries have data on levels of education instead of number of years of schooling. Therefore, a conversion is needed to estimate the Mincerian coefficients. In this case, including the levels of education as dummy variables in the Mincerian equation, the Mincerian coefficients are estimated for each level of education. For example, if a country's schooling data are represented as primary, secondary, and tertiary, the Eq. (A1.1) is converted to the following form:

$$Ln(w_i) = \alpha + \beta_{1p}e_{ip} + \beta_{1s}e_{is} + \beta_{1t}e_{it} + \beta_2 X_i + \beta_3 X_i^2 + \mu_i \quad \text{(A1.2)}$$

where the subscripts p, s, and t represent the levels of education (i.e., primary, secondary, and tertiary). Hence, the private rate of return to different levels of schooling (r) can be derived from the following equations:

$$r_p = \beta_{1p}S_p \quad \text{(A1.3)}$$

$$r_s = \left(\beta_{1s} - \beta_{1p}\right)/(S_s - S_p) \quad \text{(A1.4)}$$

$$r_t = (\beta_{1t} - \beta_{1s})/(S_t - S_s) \quad \text{(A1.5)}$$

where S_p, S_s, and S_t stand for the total number of years of schooling for each successive level.

Wages/earnings profile by age, education, and gender, $AIN_{s,a,e}$, can be readily derived for each economy/year using the following equation:

$$AIN_{s,a,e} = \exp\left(\alpha + \beta_1 e + (\beta_2 + \beta_3 X_{s,a,e})X_{s,a,e}\right) \quad \text{(A1.6)}$$

Based on the results of the Mincerian regressions, a matrix of expected earnings, H, is constructed. Each cell in the matrix accounts for labor earnings of the population of age a, gender s, and education level e. If $n_{s,a,e}$ is the number of workers of age a, gender s, and years of schooling e, each cell in the matrix is defined as

$$H_{s,a,e} = n_{s,a,e} \cdot AIN_{s,a,e} \quad \text{(A1.7)}$$

Step 2: Scaling up earnings and estimating labor earnings of the self-employed

For the calculation of human capital, total earnings should include not only wages but also the value of any additional benefits provided to employees, such

as social security payments, health insurance, housing, or other benefits in cash or in-kind. The earnings profiles from the surveys represent an underestimate of total earnings because they include only wages and do not include any additional benefits. To adjust for this underestimate, we use the Compensation of Employees from the System of National Accounts to benchmark survey earnings profiles. In this approach, the relative wages from the surveys matter rather than the absolute level values.

However, there is one more step needed to include all human capital. Total labor income consists of two components: the incomes of the employed and the self-employed. The earnings of the employed workers are included in the SNA under Compensation of Employees. The earnings of the self-employed are included in the SNA under Mixed Income or a more general category, Gross Operating Surplus, which includes all incomes not accruing to employees, mostly returns to capital and natural resources. The estimation of each component and how they are used to benchmark survey earnings profiles is discussed in this section.

Earnings of employees.

The household surveys used for the computation of the earnings profiles—as well as the probability of working—are nationally representative. The surveys are in most cases of good quality, but they may still generate estimates that are not consistent with Compensation of Employees in the System of National Accounts (SNA, EC et al. 2009). Compensation of Employees includes the economic value of benefits, such as housing or health insurance, in addition to wages, but household surveys typically report only the wages received, thus underestimating total compensation. In some countries, additional benefits, in cash or in-kind, can be substantial. Total earnings from the survey, and the resultant human capital, are expected to be too low in comparison with the share of labor earnings in GDP because they do not include other benefits. This is addressed by using Compensation of Employees as part of the control total to scale up earnings profiles from the surveys.

Estimating the labor income of the self-employed.

The economic role of the self-employed can be especially important in many low- and middle-income countries where subsistence agriculture and informal economy are very common. However, the earnings of the self-employed are not well represented in the national accounts of many countries because, with few exceptions, Compensation of Employees includes only workers who are formally employed. The earnings of the self-employed are included as part of another category, Mixed Income or Gross Operating Surplus, which also includes income accruing to produced capital and natural resources (resource rents). Earnings of the self-employed workers may also be poorly represented in household surveys.

Correcting this omission requires (i) identifying the earnings that can be attributed to the self-employed and (ii) distinguishing the labor component of earnings from returns to other factors of production, which are all combined. For human capital estimates, only the labor portion from the earnings of the self-employed should be included. The Penn World Table database has made estimates of the labor component of the income of the self-employed (Feenstra et al., 2015), which is described below.

For the purpose of disaggregating the earnings by employment, we used the shares of labor income of employees and self-employed from the Penn World Table data on total compensation of labor except for China where its income group average was used.[d] The Penn World Table (PWT) data on total compensation of labor construct a 'best estimate" labor share based on four options for adjustment, discussed below, to estimate the shares of labor income of employees and self-employed.

The first two adjustment estimation methods proposed by PWT are used for countries that report mixed income as a separate income category in national accounts, roughly 60 countries. Mixed income isolates total income earned by self-employed workers from resource rents and returns to produced capital by other producers. Mixed income combines both capital and labor income accruing to the self-employed, and can be considered as an upper bound to the amount of labor income earned by the self-employed. The two adjustment methods are as follows:

(1) All mixed income is allocated to labor assuming self-employed workers only use labor input.
(2) Half of the mixed income is allocated to labor assuming self-employed workers use labor and capital in the same proportion.

The third adjustment method assumes the self-employed earn the same average wage as employees. However, this method has some drawbacks for countries where the share of employees in the labor force is low. Assuming self-employed earn the same average wage as employees will overstate the labor income of the self-employed in those countries. In particular, in most low-income countries agriculture employs about half of the self-employed. This leads to the fourth

adjustment method, which is based on the share of agriculture in GDP. Total value added in agriculture is considered a good enough proxy for the labor earnings of the self-employed.

As explained all four methods have some drawbacks, and therefore, the Penn World Table data on total compensation of labor construct a best estimate labor share. Adjustments based on mixed income are applied where available since the mixed income captures the income of self-employed. The second adjustment method is preferable since the first adjustment method assumes no use of produced capital by the self-employed. The third and fourth adjustment methods are used if there is no mixed income data and the share of labor compensation of employees is below 0.7.

Total labor earnings.

The Penn World Table database has made estimates of the labor component of the earnings of the self-employed, which we add to Compensation of Employees to produce the control total for total labor earnings to scale up survey-derived earnings profiles by age, gender, and years of education. This approach implicitly assumes that the demographic and earnings profiles of the self-employed are the same as employee workers in formal labor markets. Although we know that is unlikely, there is insufficient data with global coverage to refine treatment of the self-employed at this time.

The total labor compensation (W) consists of two parts: (comp_employ) + (comp_self). By using the PWT data, it can be calculated as the following:

$$W = comp_{employ} + comp_{self} = LABSH * GDP \quad \text{(A1.8)}$$
$$comp_{employ} = LABSH_{employ} * GDP \quad \text{(A1.9)}$$
$$comp_{self} = LABSH_{self} * GDP \quad \text{(A1.10)}$$

where $LABSH$,[e] $LABSH_{employ}$, and $LABSH_{self}$ represent the total labor share (including both employees and the self-employed), labor share of employees and self-employed, respectively. Therefore, $comp_{employ}$ and $comp_{employ}$ stand for total compensation of employees and self-employed, respectively.

We also assume that the annual labor income ($AIN_{s,a,e}$) is the same for both employees and the self-

---

[d]Official data on labor income for China includes income of both employed and self-employed workers.

[e]The LABSH variable in the PWT is expressed as a share of GDP at basic prices. Therefore, when incorporated in the human capital wealth calculations, LABSH is multiplied by an adjustment factor, reflecting the ratio of GDP at basic prices to GDP at market prices. Thus, the resulting LABSH is expressed as a share of GDP at market prices and used accordingly in Eqs. (A1.8)–(A1.10).

employed and is estimated by using information for employees in the I2D2 database (Eq. A1.6). Then the following adjustment can be made:

$$\sum_{s,a,e} \left[\overline{AIN}_{s,a,e} * n_{s,a,e} \right] = W, \qquad \text{(A1.11)}$$

where $n_{s,a,e}$, as before, includes the number of people for both employees and the self-employed, and $\overline{AIN}_{s,a,e}$ is the after-adjustment annual income. $\overline{AIN}_{s,a,e}$ is estimated as follows:

$$\overline{AIN}_{s,a,e} = \frac{W}{\sum_{s,a,e} [AIN_{s,a,e} * n_{s,a,e}]} * AIN_{s,a,e} \qquad \text{(A1.12)}$$

After the lifetime income ($h_{s,a,e}$) for each cell (by gender s, age a, and education e) has been derived (as described in the step 6), one can apply the I2D2 sample share of the self-employed to the corresponding population data to generate the human capital for the self-employed.

In other words, the human capital for total employed (employees + self-employed) is calculated first by using the adjusted annual income profiles as shown in Eq. (A1.12). Then among the calculated total human capital, the part contributed by the self-employed can be separately estimated.

Step 3: Filling the data gaps. Since the estimations rely on labor force and household surveys, it is important to have at least one survey for each year and each country. Unfortunately, this is not the case for most countries. Moreover, some countries have only one survey for the entire period. Therefore, filling the data gaps is a crucial step for the human capital wealth calculations. Even though the current method for filling the gap has some drawbacks, it is useful.

To fill the data gaps, we hold the estimated Mincer parameters, the I2D2 sample employment and enrollment rates for the survey year as constant until the next available survey year, and use control totals for earnings for each of the intervening years to generate the human capital estimates for the years between two survey years. For example, if there exists only one survey for a country, parameters of this one survey are used for the entire period. If there exist three surveys (e.g., 1995, 2000, and 2010) for the period of 1990–2014, the parameters of year 1995 are used for the period of 1990–1999, the parameters of year 2000 is used for the period of 2000–2009, and the parameters of year 2010 is used for the period 2010 and onwards.

Obviously, there are significant problems associated with this method. First, an occasional jump occurs between human capital estimates from a non-survey year to a survey year. For example, if there are surveys for 1995 and 2010, all the data gaps until 2009 are filled

TABLE A1.4
Countries and number of I2D2 surveys.

Survey count	# of countries
1	34
2	19
3	14
4	7
5	9
6	9
8	11
9	20
11–15	13
16–23	11
Total	147

with the parameters of the 1995 survey. So, a jump could occur between human capital estimates of 2009 to 2010. In addition, if there is only one survey, all the period must be estimated with one survey data and this does not allow policymakers to see the effects of policy changes if any (Table A1.4).

Step 4: Scaling up the employment and population. Since the survey data do not capture the whole population, the data from the surveys are adjusted to population estimates from the United Nations to ensure that estimates are adequate.

If $n_{s,a,e}$ $n_{s,a,e}$ is the number of workers of age a, gender s and years of schooling e, and P is the total number of population of a country received from the United Nation's World Population Prospects, the scale parameter a is calculated as

$$\alpha = \frac{P}{\sum\limits_{s,a,e} [n_{s,a,e}]} \qquad \text{(A1.13)}$$

Thus, the scaled number of workers of age a, gender s, and years of schooling e, $N_{s,a,e}$, is calculated as.

$$N_{s,a,e} = \alpha * [n_{s,a,e}] \qquad \text{(A1.14)}$$

Step 5: Survival rates for each country. Survival rates utilize death rates obtained from the Global Burden of Disease Study (GBD)[f]. The GBD database includes global,

---

[f]The Global Burden of Disease Study 2013 database is used for the human capital wealth calculations of the Changing Wealth of Nations (2018) report. The Global Burden of Disease Study 2019 database is going to be used for the human capital wealth calculations of the next volume of the report.

regional, and national age-sex-specific mortality for 282 causes of death in 195 countries and territories for the period of 1980–2017. Survival rates are calculated as

$$v_{a+1} = 1 - death_a \qquad \text{(A1.15)}$$

where v_{a+1} is the probability of surviving one more year at age a, and $death_a$ is the death rate at age a. The Eq. (A1.15) is calculated for each country for each survey year for male and female separately.

Step 6: Calculating the lifetime income. The project distinguishes between two stages in the lifecycle of an individual of working age: ages 15–24 and ages 25–65. The main assumption here is that the ones aged 15–24 have the possibility to receive further education while the ones aged 25–65 are assumed to have no such possibility. Based on this assumption, the lifetime labor income of an individual is calculated as

- Persons aged 25–65

$$h_{s,a,e} = p^m_{s,a,e} w^m_{s,a,e} + p^s_{s,a,e} w^s_{s,a,e} + d * v_{s,a+1} * h_{s,a+1,e} \qquad \text{(A1.16)}$$

- Persons aged 15–24

$$h_{s,a,e} = p^m_{s,a,e} w^m_{s,a,e} + p^s_{s,a,e} w^s_{s,a,e} + \left(1 - r^{e+1}_{s,a,e}\right) * d * v_{s,a+1} * h_{s,a+1,e}$$

$$+ r^{e+1}_{s,a,e} * d * v_{s,a+1} * h_{s,a+1,e+1} \qquad \text{(A1.17)}$$

where $h_{s,a,e}$ is the present value of the lifetime income for an individual with age of a, gender s, and education of e, $p^m_{s,a,e}$ is the probability to be employed, $w^m_{s,a,e}$ is the received compensation of employees when employed, $p^s_{s,a,e}$ is the probability to be self-employed, $w^s_{s,a,e}$ is the received compensation of employees when self-employed, $r^{e+1}_{s,a,e}$ is the school enrolment rate for taking one more year's education from education of e to one-year higher level of $e+1$, d is the discount factor and v_{a+1} is the probability of surviving one more year.

Eqs. (A1.16) and (A1.17) suggest that the lifetime income of a representative individual consists of the current labor income and the lifetime income in the next year. The current labor income is adjusted by the probabilities of being either employed or self-employed and the lifetime income in the next year is adjusted by a discount factor and the corresponding survival rate. In addition, for an individual aged 15–24, there are two courses of action: first holding the same education level and continue to work and second taking one more year education and earn income after completing the education.

The probabilities of being either employed ($p^m_{s,a,e}$) or self-employed ($p^s_{s,a,e}$) can be approximated by the employment rate or self-employment rate for people with age of a, gender s, and education of e. Note that

these rates have to be calculated by the employed (or self-employed) persons divided by the whole population that includes the employed, self-employed, unemployed, and the people out of the labor force. The sample ratio from the I2D2 database is used for the ratios.

The empirical implementation of Eqs. (A1.16) and (A1.17) is based on backwards recursion. This suggests that the lifetime labor income of a representative individual aged 65 is zero since it is presumed that there is no working life after the age 65. Therefore, the lifetime labor income of a person aged 64 is her current labor income. Likewise, the lifetime labor income of a representative individual aged 63 is sum of her current labor income and the present value of the lifetime labor income of a person aged 64. Hence, the present value of the lifetime income matrix is created for an economy by applying the backward recursion to the Eqs. (A1.16) and (A1.17).

In addition, the Eqs. (A1.16) and (A1.17) include a strong assumption about the growth rate of labor earnings. It is assumed that labor earnings grow at a constant rate g, 2.46% per year and are discounted at rate r, 4% per year, the rate used to discount all CWON assets. This assumption is somewhat arbitrary and is a drawback of the methodology. In the next volume of the Wealth of Nations report, country-specific wage growth rates will be used.

Step 7: Generating the lifetime income for all people in an economy. The calculations from step one to step six generate the lifetime income profiles for a representative individual cross-classified by age, gender, and education. The lifetime income profiles for a representative individual are multiplied by the corresponding number of people in a country, and therefore, the human capital stock by age, gender, and education is calculated. Summing up the stocks of human capital across all classified categories generates the estimate of the aggregate value of the human capital stock for each country.

$$HC = \sum_{s,a,e} [h_{s,a,e}] * pop_{s,a,e} \qquad \text{(A1.18)}$$

where HC is the human capital stock, $h_{s,a,e}$ is the present value of the lifetime income for an individual with age of a, gender s, and education of e, and $pop_{s,a,e}$ is the population of age a, gender s, and education level e.

Since no household survey data are publicly available for countries from the Gulf Cooperation Council (Bahrain, Kuwait, Oman, Qatar, Saudi Arabia, and the United Arab Emirates), estimates of human capital wealth per capita is calculated using a simple estimation taking into account the countries' GDP per capita, labor share in GDP, and education level.

TABLE A1.5
Estimates of human capital wealth and total wealth for 2014 with impacts of no premature deaths from air pollution.

GLOBAL RESULTS:

Year	Original human capital	New human capital	Change in human capital	Percent change in human capital (%)	Original total wealth	New total wealth	Percent change in total wealth (%)	Original human capital shares of wealth (%)	New human capital shares of wealth (%)	Change in human capital shares of wealth (%)	Population
2014	33,974	34,199	225.3	0.66	60,296	60,521	0.37	56.3	56.5	0.16	5,348,499,089
2010	28,894	29,103	209.1	0.72	51,883	52,092	0.40	55.7	55.9	0.18	5,075,277,902
2005	21,345	21,516	171.2	0.80	38,608	38,779	0.44	55.3	55.5	0.20	4,752,000,400
2000	20,305	20,493	187.9	0.93	34,164	34,352	0.55	59.4	59.7	0.22	4,430,093,557
1995	18,437	18,625	188.0	1.02	32,105	32,293	0.59	57.4	57.7	0.25	4,093,482,958

REGIONAL RESULTS:

Region	Year	Original human capital	New human capital	Change in human capital	Percent change in human capital (%)	Original total wealth	New total wealth	Percent change in total wealth (%)	Original human capital shares of wealth (%)	New human capital shares of wealth (%)	Change in human capital shares of wealth (%)	Population
East Asia & Pacific	2014	53,387	53,664	276.9	0.52	91,581	91,858	0.30	58.3	58.4	0.13	1,939,183,399
Europe & Central Asia	2014	23,404	23,564	159.8	0.68	66,983	67,143	0.24	34.9	35.1	0.15	204,833,399
Latin America & Caribbean	2014	83,142	83,552	409.5	0.49	133,614	134,024	0.31	62.2	62.3	0.12	513,384,647
Middle East & North Africa	2014	19,478	19,708	229.3	1.18	48,862	49,091	0.47	39.9	40.1	0.28	209,992,349
South Asia	2014	9393	9554	161.3	1.72	18,400	18,561	0.88	51.1	51.5	0.43	1,688,760,066
Sub-Saharan Africa	2014	13,566	13,699	132.2	0.97	26,820	26,952	0.49	50.6	50.8	0.24	792,345,229
East Asia & Pacific	2010	41,612	41,854	242.0	0.58	71,423	71,665	0.34	58.3	58.4	0.14	1,884,811,533
Europe & Central Asia	2010	20,998	21,156	157.1	0.75	62,447	62,604	0.25	33.6	33.8	0.17	197,777,065
Latin America & Caribbean	2010	79,882	80,326	444.5	0.56	128,859	129,303	0.34	62.0	62.1	0.13	489,996,217
Middle East & North Africa	2010	18,159	18,384	224.6	1.24	46,854	47,079	0.48	38.8	39.0	0.29	190,933,925

South Asia	2010	8033	8177	144.2	1.80	15,710	15,854	0.92	51.1	51.6	0.44	1,600,007,109
Sub-Saharan Africa	2010	12,083	12,193	115.9	0.96	26,876	26,992	0.43	45.0	45.2	0.24	711,752,053
East Asia & Pacific	2005	25,086	25,252	166.6	0.66	44,097	44,263	0.38	56.9	57.1	0.16	1,818,316,001
Europe & Central Asia	2005	17,024	17,185	160.8	0.94	52,054	52,215	0.31	32.7	32.9	0.21	192,231,489
Latin America & Caribbean	2005	73,937	74,361	423.9	0.57	116,989	117,413	0.36	63.2	63.3	0.13	459,433,316
Middle East & North Africa	2005	15,679	15,878	198.6	1.27	34,773	34,971	0.57	45.1	45.4	0.31	173,050,421
South Asia	2005	6885	7012	127.7	1.85	12,511	12,639	1.02	55.0	55.5	0.45	1,485,813,502
Sub-Saharan Africa	2005	9036	9134	97.4	1.08	23,944	24,042	0.41	37.7	38.0	0.25	623,155,671
East Asia & Pacific	2000	24,193	24,407	213.4	0.88	37,507	37,721	0.57	64.5	64.7	0.20	1,741,587,257
Europe & Central Asia	2000	13,940	14,075	134.7	0.97	44,981	45,116	0.30	31.0	31.2	0.21	189,111,930
Latin America & Caribbean	2000	70,745	71,201	455.9	0.64	108,250	108,706	0.42	65.4	65.5	0.15	428,091,446
Middle East & North Africa	2000	14,133	14,320	187.0	1.32	27,169	27,356	0.69	52.0	52.3	0.33	157,080,038
South Asia	2000	5541	5652	111.2	2.01	10,523	10,634	1.06	52.7	53.1	0.50	1,365,693,443
Sub-Saharan Africa	2000	9313	9420	107.5	1.15	22,866	22,973	0.47	40.7	41.0	0.28	548,529,443
East Asia & Pacific	1995	20,771	20,986	215.2	1.04	31,261	31,476	0.69	66.4	66.7	0.23	1,646,560,957
Europe & Central Asia	1995	12,026	12,158	132.6	1.10	49,057	49,190	0.27	24.5	24.7	0.20	187,320,930
Latin America & Caribbean	1995	68,255	68,755	500.4	0.73	108,167	108,667	0.46	63.1	63.3	0.17	394,410,651
Middle East & North Africa	1995	12,669	12,849	180.5	1.42	25,033	25,214	0.72	50.6	51.0	0.35	142,208,934
South Asia	1995	4454	4545	91.0	2.04	9251	9342	0.98	48.1	48.7	0.50	1,241,622,404
Sub-Saharan Africa	1995	9898	10,001	112.6	1.14	27,113	27,226	0.42	36.5	36.8	0.26	481,359,082

Continued

TABLE A1.5

Estimates of human capital wealth and total wealth for 2014 with impacts of no premature deaths from air pollution—cont'd

INCOME GROUP RESULTS:

Income group	Year	Original human capital	New human capital	Change in human capital	Percent change in human capital (%)	Original total wealth	New total wealth	Percent change in total wealth (%)	Original human capital shares of wealth (%)	New human capital shares of wealth (%)	Change in human capital shares of wealth (%)	Population
Low-income	2014	5940	6019	78.9	1.33	13,857	13,936	0.57	42.9	43.2	0.32	450,508,094
Lower-middle-income	2014	13,114	13,286	171.8	1.31	25,940	26,112	0.66	50.6	50.9	0.33	2,721,103,779
Upper-middle-income	2014	65,850	66,172	322.5	0.49	112,850	113,173	0.29	58.4	58.5	0.12	2,176,887,216
Low-income	2010	4713	4772	59.1	1.25	12,257	12,316	0.48	38.4	38.7	0.30	404,459,906
Lower-middle-income	2010	11,417	11,574	156.6	1.37	23,664	23,820	0.66	48.2	48.6	0.34	2,561,108,098
Upper-middle-income	2010	54,747	55,048	301.5	0.55	93,738	94,039	0.32	58.4	58.5	0.13	2,109,709,898
Low-income	2005	4271	4326	55.5	1.30	10,517	10,573	0.53	40.6	40.9	0.31	353,458,297
Lower-middle-income	2005	9292	9426	133.5	1.44	19,403	19,537	0.69	47.9	48.2	0.36	2,368,501,025
Upper-middle-income	2005	38,379	38,614	235.2	0.61	65,906	66,141	0.36	58.2	58.4	0.15	2,030,041,078
Low-income	2000	4238	4293	55.5	1.31	10,244	10,300	0.54	41.4	41.7	0.32	309,523,485
Lower-middle-income	2000	7908	8027	118.4	1.50	16,724	16,842	0.71	47.3	47.7	0.37	2,177,493,267
Upper-middle-income	2000	36,756	37,043	286.9	0.78	57,519	57,806	0.50	63.9	64.1	0.18	1,943,076,805
Low-income	1995	3959	4012	53.7	1.36	10,552	10,606	0.51	37.5	37.8	0.32	269,522,324
Lower-middle-income	1995	7990	8108	118.4	1.48	17,713	17,831	0.67	45.1	45.5	0.36	1,987,030,016
Upper-middle-income	1995	31,862	32,144	282.9	0.89	50,836	51,118	0.56	62.7	62.9	0.21	1,836,930,618

Economy	Original human capital	New human capital	Percent change in human capital (%)	Original total wealth	New total wealth	Percent change in total wealth (%)	Original human capital shares of wealth	New human capital shares of wealth	Change in human capital shares of wealth (%)	Population
Albania	22,818	22,957	0.61	53,107	53,246	0.26	42.97	43.11	0.15	2,893,654
Argentina	71,429	71,752	0.45	126,516	126,839	0.26	56.46	56.57	0.11	42,980,026
Armenia	27,329	27,579	0.91	52,894	53,143	0.47	51.67	51.90	0.23	3,006,154
Australia	585,737	586,365	0.11	1,046,785	1,047,413	0.06	55.96	55.98	0.03	23,460,694
Austria	421,846	422,663	0.19	694,616	695,433	0.12	60.73	60.78	0.05	8,541,575
Azerbaijan	11,961	12,053	0.77	85,341	85,433	0.11	14.02	14.11	0.09	9,535,079
Bangladesh	7170	7286	1.63	12,714	12,831	0.92	56.39	56.79	0.40	159,077,513
Belarus	49,004	49,382	0.77	99,685	100,064	0.38	49.16	49.35	0.19	9,474,511
Belgium	404,997	405,849	0.21	645,969	646,821	0.13	62.70	62.75	0.05	11,231,213
Belize	23,989	24,126	0.57	58,872	59,009	0.23	40.75	40.88	0.14	351,706
Bolivia	24,805	24,979	0.70	49,235	49,409	0.35	50.38	50.56	0.17	10,561,887
Bosnia and Herzegovina	20,243	20,333	0.45	40,486	40,576	0.22	50.00	50.11	0.11	3,817,554
Botswana	47,087	47,314	0.48	95,797	96,024	0.24	49.15	49.27	0.12	2,219,937
Brazil	123,696	124,304	0.49	188,883	189,490	0.32	65.49	65.60	0.11	206,077,898
Bulgaria	47,593	47,878	0.60	81,878	82,163	0.35	58.13	58.27	0.15	7,223,938
Burkina Faso	4970	5032	1.25	12,323	12,385	0.50	40.33	40.63	0.30	17,589,198
Burundi	4496	4552	1.25	7579	7635	0.74	59.32	59.62	0.30	10,816,860
Cambodia	7337	7430	1.25	16,933	17,025	0.54	43.33	43.64	0.31	15,328,136
Cameroon	14,414	14,592	1.23	31,398	31,576	0.57	45.91	46.21	0.30	22,773,014
Canada	730,832	731,994	0.16	1,016,593	1,017,756	0.11	71.89	71.92	0.03	35,544,564
Central African Republic	846	860	1.69	21,055	21,070	0.07	4.02	4.08	0.07	4,804,316
Chad	9099	9256	1.73	20,077	20,234	0.78	45.32	45.75	0.42	13,587,053
Chile	139,512	140,014	0.36	237,713	238,215	0.21	58.69	58.78	0.09	17,762,647
China	63,369	63,657	0.46	108,172	108,460	0.27	58.58	58.69	0.11	1,364,270,000
Colombia	87,674	88,042	0.42	129,289	129,657	0.28	67.81	67.90	0.09	47,791,393
Comoros	3402	3454	1.52	8836	8887	0.59	38.51	38.86	0.36	769,991

Continued

TABLE A1.5
Estimates of human capital wealth and total wealth for 2014 with impacts of no premature deaths from air pollution—cont'd

2014 COUNTRY RESULTS:

Economy	Original human capital	New human capital	Percent change in human capital (%)	Original total wealth	New total wealth	Percent change in total wealth (%)	Original human capital shares of wealth	New human capital shares of wealth	Change in human capital shares of wealth (%)	Population
Congo, Rep.	25,906	26,256	1.35	68,779	69,129	0.51	37.67	37.98	0.32	4,504,962
Costa Rica	122,640	122,917	0.23	166,985	167,262	0.17	73.44	73.49	0.04	4,757,606
Cote d'Ivoire	8986	9137	1.68	24,485	24,635	0.61	36.70	37.09	0.39	22,157,107
Croatia	90,549	90,887	0.37	147,545	147,883	0.23	61.37	61.46	0.09	4238,389
Denmark	538,947	539,932	0.18	854,331	855,315	0.12	63.08	63.13	0.04	5,643,475
Djibouti	12,097	12,184	0.72	22,914	23,000	0.38	52.79	52.97	0.18	876,174
Dominican Republic	73,055	73,404	0.48	97,257	97,606	0.36	75.12	75.20	0.09	10,405,943
Ecuador	52,696	52,922	0.43	102,451	102,677	0.22	51.44	51.54	0.11	15,902,916
Egypt, Arab Rep.	22,591	22,936	1.53	38,470	38,815	0.90	58.72	59.09	0.37	89,579,670
El Salvador	31,951	32,129	0.56	44,131	44,309	0.40	72.40	72.51	0.11	6,107,706
Estonia	155,041	155,356	0.20	258,903	259,218	0.12	59.88	59.93	0.05	1,314,545
Ethiopia	6723	6814	1.35	13,125	13,216	0.69	51.22	51.56	0.34	96,958,732
Finland	460,082	460,584	0.11	726,422	726,924	0.07	63.34	63.36	0.03	5,461,512
France	415,851	416,653	0.19	641,707	642,510	0.13	64.80	64.85	0.04	66,268,972
Gabon	62,233	63,075	1.35	199,901	200,744	0.42	31.13	31.42	0.29	1,687,673
Gambia, The	2745	2778	1.19	5208	5240	0.63	52.71	53.01	0.29	1,928,201
Georgia	21,251	21,504	1.19	44,327	44,581	0.57	47.94	48.24	0.30	3,727,000
Germany	467,668	468,782	0.24	729,064	730,177	0.15	64.15	64.20	0.05	80,982,500
Ghana	13,853	14,026	1.25	25,044	25,217	0.69	55.31	55.62	0.31	26,786,598
Greece	105,663	105,995	0.31	227,925	228,257	0.15	46.36	46.44	0.08	10,892,413
Guatemala	25,450	25,629	0.70	43,140	43,319	0.42	58.99	59.16	0.17	16,015,494
Guinea	621	633	1.98	8943	8955	0.14	6.94	7.07	0.13	12,275,527
Guyana	21,801	22,014	0.98	69,971	70,184	0.30	31.16	31.37	0.21	763,893
Haiti	6135	6211	1.25	15,040	15,117	0.51	40.79	41.09	0.30	10,572,029

Honduras	27,372	27,573	0.73	44,778	44,979	0.45	61.13	61.30	0.17	7,961,680
Hungary	102,557	103,076	0.51	165,519	166,037	0.31	61.96	62.08	0.12	9,866,468
Iceland	733,612	734,643	0.14	825,857	826,888	0.12	88.83	88.84	0.01	327,386
India	8755	8911	1.78	18,211	18,367	0.85	48.08	48.52	0.44	1,295,291,543
Indonesia	23,701	23,917	0.91	46,919	47,134	0.46	50.52	50.74	0.23	254,454,778
Iraq	15,473	15,589	0.75	101,705	101,820	0.11	15.21	15.31	0.10	35,273,293
Ireland	473,656	474,501	0.18	627,256	628,101	0.13	75.51	75.55	0.03	4,617,225
Italy	241,350	241,832	0.20	427,466	427,948	0.11	56.46	56.51	0.05	60,789,140
Jamaica	41,884	42,074	0.45	71,766	71,956	0.27	58.36	58.47	0.11	2,783,301
Japan	365,157	366,032	0.24	571,927	572,801	0.15	63.85	63.90	0.06	127,131,800
Jordan	27,312	27,435	0.45	49,287	49,409	0.25	55.41	55.53	0.11	7,416,083
Kazakhstan	76,617	77,209	0.77	180,911	181,503	0.33	42.35	42.54	0.19	17,289,224
Kenya	9556	9635	0.83	19,412	19,491	0.41	49.23	49.43	0.21	44,863,583
Korea, Rep.	291,748	292,707	0.33	424,052	425,011	0.23	68.80	68.87	0.07	50,423,955
Kyrgyz Republic	6729	6787	0.86	24,429	24,487	0.24	27.54	27.72	0.17	5,835,500
Lao PDR	13,762	13,956	1.40	39,307	39,500	0.49	35.01	35.33	0.32	6,689,300
Latvia	113,472	113,901	0.38	236,906	237,336	0.18	47.90	47.99	0.09	1,993,782
Lebanon	42,153	42,335	0.43	65,148	65,330	0.28	64.70	64.80	0.10	5,612,096
Liberia	3636	3678	1.16	10,227	10,269	0.41	35.55	35.81	0.26	4,396,554
Lithuania	100,081	100,488	0.41	169,046	169,453	0.24	59.20	59.30	0.10	2,932,367
Luxembourg	881,629	882,910	0.15	1,288,607	1,289,888	0.10	68.42	68.45	0.03	556,319
Macedonia, FYR	24,770	24,894	0.50	52,210	52,334	0.24	47.44	47.57	0.12	2,075,625
Madagascar	3784	3868	2.22	9237	9321	0.91	40.97	41.50	0.53	23,571,713
Malawi	4003	4068	1.61	10,442	10,507	0.62	38.34	38.72	0.38	16,695,253
Malaysia	180,729	182,122	0.77	239,203	240,596	0.58	75.55	75.70	0.14	29,901,997
Maldives	33,905	33,974	0.20	44,991	45,060	0.15	75.36	75.40	0.04	401,000
Mali	4334	4391	1.33	17,165	17,223	0.34	25.25	25.50	0.25	17,086,022
Malta	218,865	219,311	0.20	303,804	304,250	0.15	72.04	72.08	0.04	427,364
Mauritania	9368	9538	1.81	29,380	29,549	0.58	31.89	32.28	0.39	3,969,625
Mauritius	51,520	51,842	0.63	97,018	97,341	0.33	53.10	53.26	0.16	1,260,934
Mexico	59,334	59,650	0.53	110,471	110,788	0.29	53.71	53.84	0.13	125,385,833

Continued

Estimates of human capital wealth and total wealth for 2014 with impacts of no premature deaths from air pollution—cont'd

2014 COUNTRY RESULTS:

Economy	Original human capital	New human capital	Percent change in human capital (%)	Original total wealth	New total wealth	Percent change in total wealth (%)	Original human capital shares of wealth	New human capital shares of wealth	Change in human capital shares of wealth (%)	Population
Moldova	17,852	17,939	0.49	35,380	35,467	0.25	50.46	50.58	0.12	3,556,397
Mongolia	20,635	20,873	1.15	79,004	79,241	0.30	26.12	26.34	0.22	2,909,871
Morocco	16,490	16,612	0.74	40,488	40,610	0.30	40.73	40.91	0.18	33,921,203
Mozambique	3486	3529	1.22	7718	7760	0.55	45.17	45.47	0.30	27,216,276
Namibia	52,458	52,956	0.95	84,398	84,896	0.59	62.16	62.38	0.22	2,402,858
Nepal	6402	6471	1.08	14,368	14,437	0.48	44.55	44.82	0.26	28,174,724
Netherlands	516,543	517,710	0.23	792,396	793,563	0.15	65.19	65.24	0.05	16,865,008
Nicaragua	16,698	16,752	0.33	37,084	37,138	0.15	45.03	45.11	0.08	6,013,913
Niger	1041	1059	1.69	11,623	11,640	0.15	8.96	9.10	0.14	19,113,728
Nigeria	20,934	21,098	0.78	37,408	37,571	0.44	55.96	56.15	0.19	177,475,986
Norway	1,004,649	1,006,132	0.15	1,671,756	1,673,239	0.09	60.10	60.13	0.04	5,137,232
Pakistan	13,587	13,831	1.80	22,182	22,426	1.10	61.25	61.67	0.42	185,044,286
Panama	102,886	103,169	0.27	136,125	136,408	0.21	75.58	75.63	0.05	3,867,535
Papua New Guinea	11,071	11,449	3.42	50,489	50,868	0.75	21.93	22.51	0.58	7,463,577
Paraguay	54,026	54,285	0.48	85,575	85,834	0.30	63.13	63.24	0.11	6,552,518
Peru	39,502	39,729	0.58	81,931	82,159	0.28	48.21	48.36	0.14	30,973,148
Philippines	17,790	18,024	1.31	30,823	31,057	0.76	57.72	58.03	0.32	99,138,690
Poland	113,406	113,886	0.42	154,932	155,412	0.31	73.20	73.28	0.08	38,011,735
Portugal	172,163	172,463	0.17	274,453	274,754	0.11	62.73	62.77	0.04	10,401,062
Russian Federation	90,812	91,254	0.49	188,715	189,156	0.23	48.12	48.24	0.12	143,819,666
Rwanda	13,649	13,796	1.08	21,619	21,766	0.68	63.13	63.38	0.25	11,341,544
Senegal	6260	6359	1.58	13,085	13,184	0.76	47.84	48.23	0.39	14,672,557
Sierra Leone	4529	4600	1.57	14,742	14,813	0.48	30.72	31.05	0.33	6,315,627
Singapore	466,119	467,439	0.28	775,196	776,515	0.17	60.13	60.20	0.07	5,469,724

Slovak Republic	147,386	147,925	0.37	213,211	213,751	0.25	69.13	69.20	0.08	5,418,649
Slovenia	225,046	225,513	0.21	351,776	352,244	0.13	63.97	64.02	0.05	2,061,980
Solomon Islands	15,327	15,817	3.19	31,245	31,734	1.57	49.06	49.84	0.79	572,171
South Africa	44,921	45,246	0.72	77,348	77,673	0.42	58.08	58.25	0.18	54,146,735
Spain	215,593	215,993	0.19	342,470	342,871	0.12	62.95	63.00	0.04	46,480,882
Sri Lanka	32,410	32,671	0.80	44,970	45,231	0.58	72.07	72.23	0.16	20,771,000
Suriname	30,782	30,962	0.59	161,690	161,870	0.11	19.04	19.13	0.09	538,248
Swaziland	26,811	27,094	1.06	52,670	52,953	0.54	50.90	51.17	0.26	1,269,112
Sweden	576,521	577,145	0.11	886,129	886,753	0.07	65.06	65.09	0.02	9,696,110
Switzerland	1,022,950	1,024,74C	0.18	1,466,757	1,468,555	0.12	69.74	69.78	0.04	8,188,649
Tajikistan	5015	5073	1.16	42,286	42,344	0.14	11.86	11.98	0.12	8,295,840
Tanzania	6706	6777	1.06	17,451	17,522	0.41	38.43	38.68	0.25	51,822,621
Thailand	33,573	33,733	0.48	62,599	62,759	0.26	53.63	53.75	0.12	67,725,979
Togo	11,869	12,032	1.37	18,924	19,086	0.86	62.72	63.04	0.32	7,115,163
Tunisia	24,796	24,942	0.59	45,150	45,297	0.32	54.92	55.06	0.15	11,130,154
Turkey	12,081	12,145	0.53	45,998	46,062	0.14	26.26	26.37	0.10	77,523,788
Turkmenistan	47,510	47,882	0.78	146,831	147,204	0.25	32.36	32.53	0.17	5,307,188
Uganda	6889	6963	1.07	13,732	13,806	0.54	50.17	50.44	0.27	37,782,971
Ukraine	18,952	19,067	0.61	56,053	56,168	0.21	33.81	33.95	0.14	45,271,947
United Kingdom	457,223	458,136	0.20	647,694	648,607	0.14	70.59	70.63	0.04	64,613,160
United States	766,470	768,735	0.30	983,280	985,544	0.23	77.95	78.00	0.05	318,907,401
Uruguay	171,310	171,841	0.31	254,601	255,132	0.21	67.29	67.35	0.07	3,419,516
Venezuela, RB	49,332	49,565	0.47	162,560	162,793	0.14	30.35	30.45	0.10	30,693,827
Vietnam	13,740	13,807	0.49	27,368	27,435	0.24	50.21	50.33	0.12	90,728,900
Yemen, Rep.	9002	9209	2.30	22,909	23,116	0.90	39.29	39.84	0.54	26,183,676
Zambia	17,549	17,782	1.32	40,965	41,198	0.57	42.84	43.16	0.32	15,721,343
Zimbabwe	9877	10,070	1.95	18,958	19,150	1.02	52.10	52.58	0.48	15,245,855

Incorporating the Air Pollution into the Human Capital Wealth Calculations

While calculating the impact of air pollution on human capital wealth, the effect of air pollution on deaths is taken into consideration in this study due to some practical purposes. Reducing air pollution will have some positive effects on labor productivity, thanks to improved public health, but measuring this effect needs significant focus. In addition, the effect of air pollution on death rates occurs by time, and it changes by the level of air pollution. So, it may take shorter or longer depending on the causes of the pollution. However, the death rates in the Global Burden of Disease Study are the snapshot of a year. Therefore, this study focuses on the effects of air pollution on human capital wealth through the impact on death rates.

To that end, survival rates play a crucial role. Survival rates are calculated utilizing the death rates obtained from the Global Burden of Disease Study. To reflect the effect of air pollution, deaths stemming from air pollution are excluded in the calculation of death rates. Once the number of deaths caused by air pollution is excluded from the total number of deaths, the change in the death rates improve the survival rates. The survival rates are calculated as

$$v_{a+1}^{base} = 1 - death_a^{all\ causes} \qquad \text{(A1.19)}$$

$$v_{a+1}^{air\ pollution} = 1 - death_a^{excl.air\ pollution} \qquad \text{(A1.20)}$$

Differentiating the survival rates, the human capital wealth calculation steps are applied. The difference between the human capital wealth with air pollution and without air pollution is calculated for each country and in each year.

$$\Delta HC = HC_{no\ air\ pollution} - HC_{with\ air\ pollution} \qquad \text{(A1.21)}$$

APPENDIX 1.3 ESTIMATES OF HUMAN CAPITAL AND WEALTH FOR 2014 WITH IMPACTS OF NO PREMATURE DEATHS FROM AIR POLLUTION

Table A1.5 shows estimates of per capita human capital and wealth for 2014 by economy and aggregate averages (income group, geographic region, region with only low- and middle-income economies). Estimates are in 2014 U.S. dollars at market exchange rates. New estimates include the hypothetical value of human capital wealth and total wealth if there were no premature deaths from air pollution.

REFERENCES

Bolton, P., et al., 2020. The Green Swan: Central Banking and Financial Stability in the Age of Climate Change. Bank for International Settlements, Geneva, Switzerland.

Cropper, M., Khanna, S., 2014. How Should the World Bank Estimate Air Pollution Damages? Discussion Paper No. 14-30, Resources for the Future, Washington, D.C.

EC (European Commission), et al., 2009. System of National Accounts 2008. United Nations, New York, NY.

Feenstra, R.C., et al., 2015. The next generation of the Penn world table. Am. Econ. Rev. 105 (10), 3150–3182.

Global Burden of Disease Collaborative Network, 2016. Global Burden of Disease Study, 2013 (GBD 2013). Institute for Health Metrics and Evaluation (IHME), Seattle, WA.

Jorgenson, D.W., Fraumeni, B.M., 1989. The accumulation of human and nonhuman capital, 1948–1984. In: Lipsey, R. E., Tice, H.S. (Eds.), The Measurement of Savings, Investment, and Wealth. The University of Chicago Press, Chicago, IL, pp. 227–282.

Jorgenson, D.W., Fraumeni, B.M., 1992a. The output of education sector. In: Griliches, Z. (Ed.), Output Measurement in the Service Sectors. The University of Chicago Press, Chicago, IL, pp. 303–341.

Jorgenson, D.W., Fraumeni, B.M., 1992b. Investment in education and U.S. economic growth. Scand. J. Econ. 94 (Supplement), S51–S70.

Liu, G., 2011. Measuring the Stock of Human Capital for Comparative Analysis: An Application of the Lifetime Income Approach to Selected Countries, OECD Statistics Working Papers, No. 2011/06. OECD Publishing, Paris, France, https://doi.org/10.1787/5kg3h0jnn9r5-en.

Mani, M., Yamada, T., 2020. Is Air Pollution Aggravating Covid-19 in South Asia? https://blogs.worldbank.org/endpovertyinsouthasia/air-pollution-aggravating-covid-19-south-asia#:~:text=Despite%20the%20welcome%20respite%2C%20air,and%201.53%20years%20in%20India.

Montenegro, C.E., Hirn, M., 2009. A New Disaggregated Set of Labor Market Indicators Using Standardized Household Surveys from around the World. World Bank, Washington, DC.

Montenegro, C.E., Patrinos, H.A., 2016. A Data Set of Comparable Estimates of the Private Rate of Return to Schooling around the World, 1970–2014. Unpublished, World Bank, Washington, DC.

Narain, U., Sall, C., 2016. Methodology for Valuing the Health Impacts of Air Pollution: Discussion of Challenges and Proposed Solutions. World Bank, Washington, DC.

Sall, C., Narain, U., 2018. Air pollution: impact on human capital and wealth. In: Lange, G.M., et al. (Eds.), The Changing Wealth of Nations 2018: Building a Sustainable Future. World Bank, Washington, DC.

CHAPTER 2

Global Human Capital: View From Inclusive Wealth

MOINUL ISLAM[a,b,c,*] • SHUNSUKE MANAGI[a,d]

[a]Urban Institute, Kyushu University, Fukuoka, Japan, [b]School of Economics and Management, Kochi University of Technology, Kochi City, Japan, [c]Research Institute for Future Design, Kochi University of Technology, Kochi City, Japan, [d]Faculty of Engineering, Kyushu University, Fukuoka, Japan
*Corresponding author: moinul.eco@gmail.com

2.1. INTRODUCTION

Human capital is a key component of the productive base; it is education that develops the human capital resources for the economy and the society. Education improves human skills, norms, behaviors, and productivity and leads to the upgrading of a society's living standard. Economists consider education as a consumer as well as a capital good, the latter which is used as an input for the production of other goods and services. Human capital represents the investment of nations on education to enhance the economic growth. The importance of investing in human capital is unavoidable for sustainable development.

Years of schooling has been considered as a good proxy of human capital for long time. A country, which increases the average years of proper schooling by several years significantly, improves its human capital. However, the investment of education, which repays individuals by improving the employment opportunity, greater economic activity, and growth, will be beneficial. Education can enhance both economic and noneconomic benefits through the improvement of health, nutrition, self-satisfaction, and so on.

Generally, well-educated persons have lower mortality rates; also, child mortality in an educated family is low (Kc and Lentzner, 2010). Women with better education have fewer children as they can easily access birth control facilities (Bongaarts, 2010). It is not hard to assume that education enhances motivation to lead a better life by improving the socioeconomic conditions. Human capital usually captures both the education and health of individuals. Many studies primarily focus on the education because it can be measured more consistently across countries.

Total years of schooling are globally considered as an important input to the human capital calculation. Many countries are focusing on this human capital to evaluate the sustainable development of nations. Especially for the densely populated developing countries, education improvement will increase the level of knowledge as well as the total wealth of these countries. The Inclusive Wealth Report 2018 (Managi and Kumar, 2018), 2014 (UNU-IHDP and UNEP, 2014), and 2012 (UNU-IHDP and UNEP, 2012) have identified the significantly higher contribution of human capital to total wealth compared to other forms of capital.

Education matters greatly for almost every single stage of human development, social welfare, happiness, and economic progress. There are several key indicators, which lead to capturing these conditions. There is a reason to assume that the Human Development Index (HDI), genuine savings, gross domestic product (GDP), and happiness index are relevant to the human capital of nations. However, the statistical evidence has been rather weak and sometimes ambiguous.

Human capital is playing an important role in economic growth and sustainable development. There are several methodological improvements to measure the stock of human capital. For instance, costs, income, education, and health are considered in concurrent literature as a base to measure the human capital. Table 2.1 summarizes the literatures that use different approaches to evaluate the human capital of regions and nations. We can notice that there are three different types of approaches to calculate the human capital, (a) cost, (b) income, and (c) education. The cost-based approach provides an estimate of the resources invested in the education and other human capital-related sectors, which is used for cost-benefit analyses. Jorgenson and Fraumeni (1989, 1992) develop a very comprehensive method of human capital measurement using the income-based approach. They suggest a new system of human capital accounts by including both market and nonmarket economic activities. In the education-based

Measuring Human Capital. https://doi.org/10.1016/B978-0-12-819057-9.00006-8

TABLE 2.1
Selected human capital literature.

Author	Year	Countries	Method	Important information
Psacharopoulos and Arriagada (1986)	1960–1983	99 nations	Education-stock induced method	Labor force is considered as human capital
Jorgenson and Fraumeni (1989, 1992)	1947–1986	United States	Jorgenson and Fraumeni method	The stock of human capital increased, almost double from 1949 to 1984
Macklem (1997)	1963–1994	Canada	Macroeconomic (income-based) method	Human wealth sharply increases from 1963 to 1973. Afterward, it decreases until 1980. Subsequently, it increases through the end of the study period
Laroche and Mérette (2000)	1976–1996	Canada	Koman and Marin's method	Using average years of schooling as the human capital measure concludes that per capita human capital increases by 15%
Jeong (2002)		45 poor and rich nations	Mulligan and Sala-i-Martin's method	The richest countries have 2.2–2.8 times more human capital than the poor countries
Wei (2004)	1981–2001	Australia	Jorgenson and Fraumeni method	The stock of human capital in Australia increased by 75% over the period
Barro and Lee (2001, 2013)	1960–2000	142 nations	Education-stock induced method	Population aged 15 and over are considered as human capital
Nehru et al. (1995)	1960–1987	85 nations	Education-stock induced method	Population aged 15–64 are considered as human capital
de la Fuente and Doménech (2006)	1960–1990	21 OECD nations	Education-stock induced method	Population aged 25 and over are considered as human capital
Cohen and Soto (2007)	1960–2010	95 nations	Education-stock induced method	Population aged 15–64 are considered as human capital
Krueger and Lindahl (2001)	1990	34 nations	Education-stock induced method	Labor force is considered human capital

approaches, educational achievements are considered as proxies for, but not direct measures of, human capital.

The rest of this chapter is organized as follows. In Section 2.2, we discuss the methodology behind human capital is laid out. Section 2.3 presents central results from human capital calculations and discusses the comparative statistics with other welfare indicators. Section 2.4 concludes with potential directions to improve the human capital calculation.

2.2. METHODOLOGY

Three capital assets of nations, human capital, produced capital, and natural capital, are the components of the inclusive wealth. The Inclusive Wealth Reports (Managi and Kumar, 2018; UNU-IHDP and UNEP,

2012, 2014) contributed to the development of a standard measure of the capital of nations by country in different time series. In these reports, inclusive wealth is represented by the shadow price of each asset; this price is considered as the weight in the metric. Among three types of capitals, human capital is the most important contributor to inclusive wealth in most countries. In this chapter, we focus on human capital in detail.

We calculate the value of human capital based on a method proposed by Arrow et al. (2012) and Klenow and Rodriguez-Clare (1997). In the calculation, education is represented by the average years of total schooling per person; the data are from Barro and Lee (2013). They have used a combination of cost, income, and education-based methods to develop a dataset on educational attainment for countries over a 5-year period.

Using this data, we calculate the shadow price of per unit human capital from the present value of the average labor payment and the expected life's working period.

Education pays off later in life as raised lifetime income and well-being, both at personal and aggregate levels. In line with the literature on human capital and for practical reasons, we focus on the return on formal education, but this does not mean that other nonformal education (e.g., early childhood education, vocational training) does not contribute to wealth. We estimate the value of human capital from a production function with human capital as the output, with education levels as the important factor, using an income approach. In contrast, some other estimates focus on the input side of the production function, typically by looking at educational expenditure, using a cost approach.

We estimate the value of human capital based on the idea that educational attainment yields return to human capital. Educational attainment is proxied by the average years of total schooling per person, A. The rate of return on education is assumed to be constant at $\rho = 8.5\%$. This is multiplied by the population who has had education, P_{5+edu}. Thus, the stock of human capital is

$$H = e^{\rho A} * P_{5+edu}$$

Regarding the shadow price of one unit of human capital, it is calculated by the present value of lifetime income, which is proxied by the average compensation to employees, w, per unit of human capital times the expected working years, T. Here, δ is the time discount rate, also set to be constant at 8.5%. This brings us to the following formula:

$$p_H(t) = \int_0^{T(t)} w(\tau) e^{-\delta \tau} d\tau$$

To create the dataset of human capital of 140 countries, we use the information from various data sources. Table 2.2 summarizes the dataset we have used for calculation.

The methodological soundness and availability of the data contribute to increase the acceptance of "years of schooling" as a key indicator of human capital. For global level analysis and to identify the comparative progress of nations in the context of human capital, "years of schooling" is considered as a proxy of human capital stock in literatures. However, this variable also misses some important features of human capital, for instance, work experience, informal education, training, and so on. In addition, quality of schooling is overlooked, which is often considered as more important than the quantity of schooling.

TABLE 2.2
Data sources and assumptions for the calculation of human capital.

Variables	Data sources/assumptions
Educational attainment, A	Barro and Lee dataset (Barro and Lee, 2013)
Population P by age, gender, time	United Nations Population Division (2016)
Market rate of interest, ρ	Klenow and Rodriguez-Clare (1997)
Discount rate, δ	It is assumed a rate of 8.5%
Employment	International Labour Organization (2015); Conference Board (2016)
Compensation of employees	United Nations Statistical Division (2016); OECD (2016); Feenstra et al. (2013); Lenzen et al. (2013); Conference Board (2016)

2.3. RESULTS AND DISCUSSION

2.3.1. Progress of Nations' Human Capital

In our study period, the growth of global human capital is increasing continuously since 1992. Fig. 2.1 shows the positive growth of human capital per capita. Per capita GDP growth has been positive in most years, although the enormous financial crisis caused a drop of GDP in 2008. However, the growth rate of GDP per capita is much higher compared to the growth of human capital per capita. For instance, compared to the base year 1991, the GDP per capita growth is 74% in 2014, while the human capital per capita growth is only 28%.

Education is the contributor to human capital, and countries can increase their human capital score by increasing their investment in education. Education also uplifts the productivity of the individuals. Thus, investment in education provides a high rate of return to the inclusive wealth of countries, both directly through accumulating human capital and enhancing total factor productivity.

However, how can we boost investment in education? Many possibilities come to mind, from physical infrastructure (school building, toilets) to consumables (textbook, uniform, nutritious meal) and to human capital (quantity and quality of teachers, class size). All of them can potentially be the source of the low average years of schooling shown in Fig. 2.2.

Fig. 2.3 shows the human capital share, annually averaged for 1990–2014 for the whole world. It demonstrates that human capital accounts for the lion's share

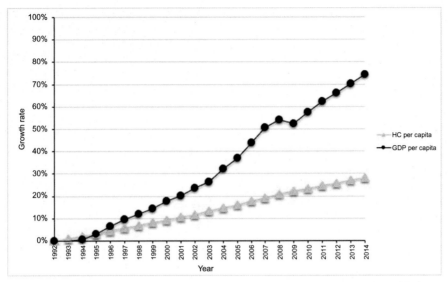

FIG. 2.1 GDP per capita vs. human capital (HC) per capita growth from 1992 to 2014.

in many countries. The percentage of human capital in total wealth is high in Europe, USA, India, and Japan. There are, however, several exceptions in the less developed world. As of 2014, it was still less than 20% in Belize, Bolivia, Guyana, the Central African Republic, Laos, Liberia, Mongolia, Papua New Guinea, and Tanzania.

Fig. 2.4 shows that countries with high shares of human capital are likely to have a low share of natural capital (the total value of natural resources). The higher the share of natural capital is, the lower the share of human capital tends to be. However, this amount is the global aggregate, and a closer look is always warranted. In particular, the share of natural capital has little to do with the advancement of the economy in question. After all, it is the change in combined wealth that counts.

In Fig. 2.5, we plot the growth rate of human capital from 1990 to 2014. Human capital has grown by more than 2%, with several exceptions. Notable exceptions include several former Soviet republics, such as Ukraine, Russia, Kazakhstan, Lithuania, and the Republic of Moldova, the populations, and, thus, human capital of which have decreased in the latest quarter century. This increase in human capital indicates the growing effort of the governments to improve the level of education globally. For instance, oil-rich gulf countries (Bahrain, the United Arab Emirates, and Qatar) have significant growth in human capital. Developed countries are experiencing higher human capital compared to developing/less developed countries. Switzerland, Norway, Belgium, Denmark, United Kingdom, United States of America, France, and Ireland are the top countries where the human capital per capita is more than $400,000 in 2014. Population burden and the comparatively less investment in the education sector cause the lower human capital in developing countries overall.

2.3.2. Discussion

In this section, we compare our results, based on conventional calculations, with the past performances of other well-known indices. GDP per capita is the most popular index to date for monitoring the progress of nations. For our comparison, we exhibit inclusive wealth per capita, both before and after adjustments, because they differ greatly.

GDP has been criticized for sending an incorrect message regarding the sustainability of social well-being. Its growth can differ from our human capital per capita, as shown in Fig. 2.6. Countries in Quadrant I, which form the majority, have experienced both the positive growth of GDP and human capital on per capita terms. This finding is understandable to a certain extent since portions of GDP are directed toward investment in physical assets.

Since its launch in early 1990s, the HDI has also been widely cited as an index for tracking the development of nations. What about the correlation of human capital and another index of development, HDI? Fig. 2.7 shows that there is an apparent relationship between the

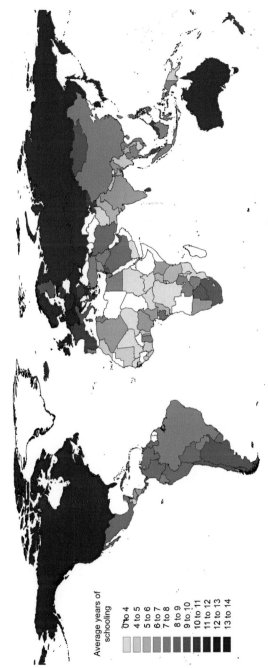

FIG. 2.2 Average year of schooling in 2010. (Source: Barro-Lee dataset—Barro, R.J., Lee, J.W., 2013. A new data set of educational attainment in the world, 1950–2010. J. Dev. Econ. 104, 184–198.)

Average years of schooling

0 to 4
4 to 5
5 to 6
6 to 7
7 to 8
8 to 9
9 to 10
10 to 11
11 to 12
12 to 13
13 to 14

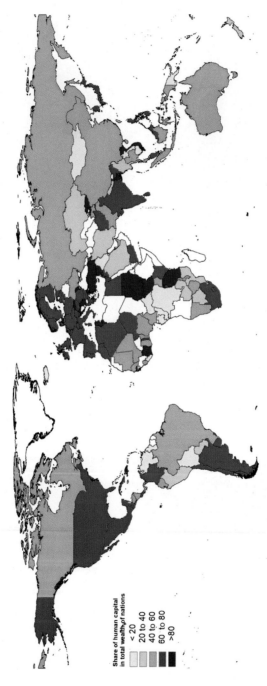

Share of human capital
in total wealth of nations

< 20
20 to 40
40 to 60
60 to 80
>80

FIG. 2.3 Share of human capital in total wealth of nations in 2014.

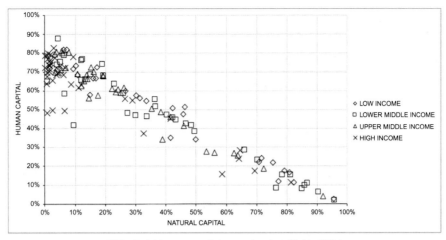

FIG. 2.4 Human capital vs. natural capital in 2014.

two indices; the correlation is high at 0.72. Like the previous case, most of the countries in Quadrant I have experienced both the positive growth of HDI and human capital on per capita terms.

Happiness, or more generally subjective well-being, has gained attention recently, shedding light on the other side of social well-being, rather than our determinant-based indicator of social well-being. As depicted in Fig. 2.8, there seems to be almost no correlation between happiness and human capital, at least in our studied sample. Note that the vertical axis represents the status of happiness, instead of the growth rate of happiness. For some income categories, a slightly negative relationship even can be detected.

Finally, we discuss the World Bank's genuine savings, formally adjusted net savings, which keeps track of savings (and dissaving) in produced, human, and natural capital. Human capital is recorded as the change in inputs (i.e., education expenditure) instead of outputs (i.e., return on education). Fig. 2.9 shows the relationship between genuine savings and human capital per capita. Several low-income countries experience negative growth of genuine savings along with the low progress in human capital growth over the year 1990–2014.

The human capital calculation cannot capture the child labor and other market imperfection problems simultaneously. Fig. 2.10 shows the percentage of children (7–14 years) employed in the labor market; apparently, most of the African nations and certain Asian and Latin American countries have alarming percentages of child labor. Understanding the reasons for low years of schooling and the economics of child labor can improve the education condition in low-income

countries. These child labor problems should be examined to improve the human capital investment.

What about the wealth composition across the whole world? Fig. 2.11 indicates that, on average, human capital is responsible for more than half of inclusive wealth, followed by natural capital, with approximately one quarter of total wealth. Produced capital accounts for the smallest share of inclusive wealth, less than one fifth of total wealth worldwide. Note, however, that this figure is aggregated both over time and worldwide. In Fig. 2.12, instead of calculating the average of the shares, we first aggregate each capital for a specific year for the whole world to compute each capital share in the right panel. This amount is further averaged for the whole period in the pie chart. According to this calculation, human capital contributes 65% of the total wealth.

This apparent tradeoff between produced and natural capital tempts us to assert that natural capital is being depleted and converted into human capital. Our approximation suggests that, if one starts from the state of natural capital being 100% of wealth, a 20% decrease in natural capital would translate into a 15% increase in human capital, which would be reminiscent of the well-known Hartwick rule, which says that rents of depleted natural capital should be invested into other forms of capital to maintain future consumption and well-being (Dixit et al., 1980; Hartwick, 1977).

In other words, the way that capital assets are substituted for each other differs from country to country according to their historical paths. Moreover, it is important to remember that this result does not suggest any causation; it could be that, in theory, nations can invest into natural capital, resulting in a lower share of human capital.

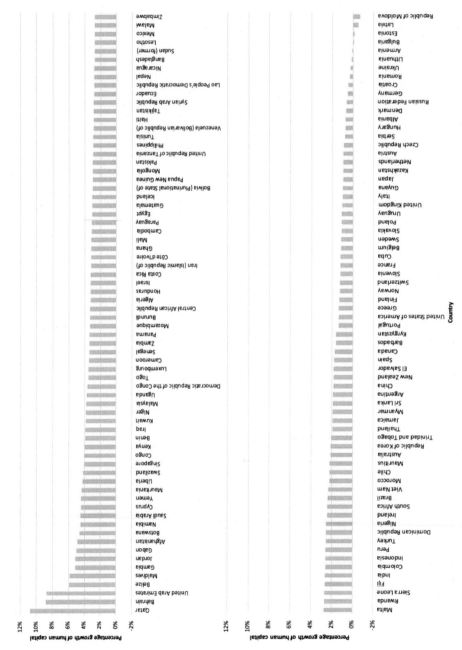

FIG. 2.5 Percentage growth of human capital from 1990 to 2014.

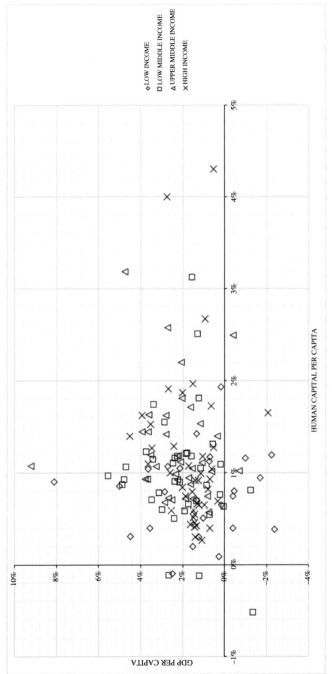

FIG. 2.6 Relationship between the growth of GDP per capita and human capital per capita.

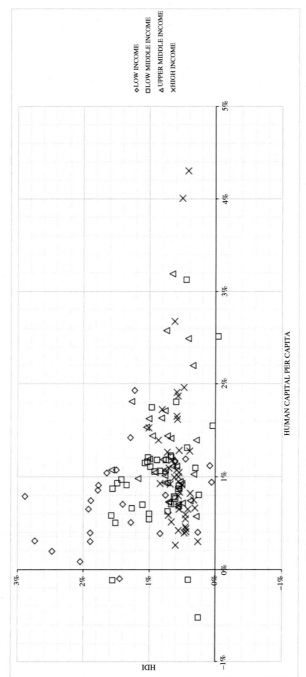

FIG. 2.7 Relationship between the growth of HDI per capita and human capital per capita.

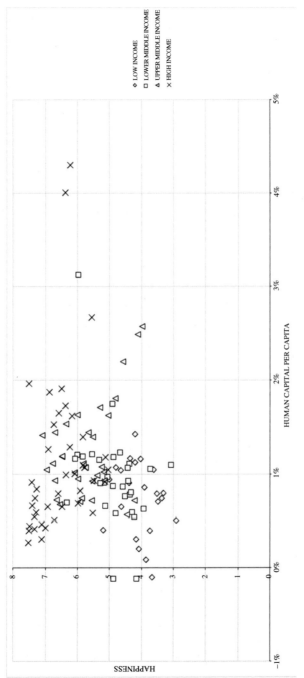

FIG. 2.8 Relationship between happiness index and the growth of human capital per capita.

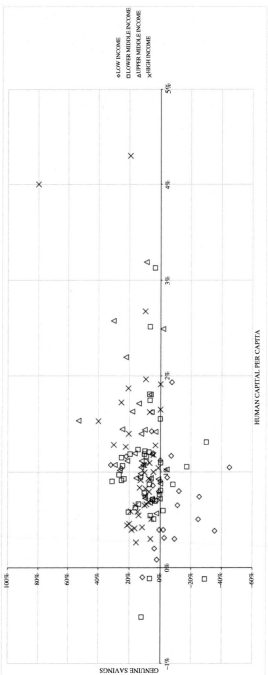

FIG. 2.9 Relationship between the growth of genuine savings and human capital per capita.

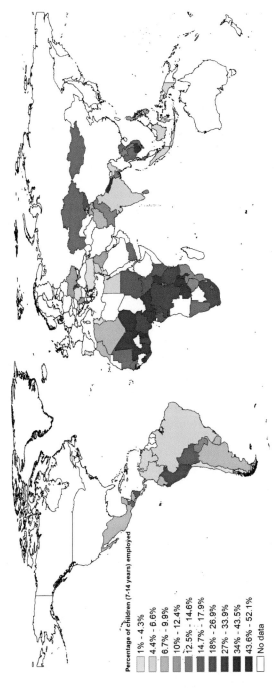

Percentage of children (7-14 years) employed

1% – 4.3%
4.4% – 6.6%
6.7% – 9.9%
10% – 12.4%
12.5% – 14.6%
14.7% – 17.9%
18% – 26.9%
27% – 33.9%
34% – 43.5%
43.6% – 52.1%
No data

FIG. 2.10 Percentage of children (7–14 years) employed in labor. (Source: World Development Indicators (WDI), World Bank.)

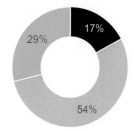

- Productive Capital - Human Capital - Natural Capital

FIG. 2.11 Global aggregate wealth composition, mean 1990–2014 and over time.

- Produced Capital - Human Capital - Natural Capital

FIG. 2.12 Global aggregate wealth composition, mean 1990–2014 and over countries.

2.4. CONCLUSION AND POLICY RECOMMENDATION

The country-level analysis of human capital indicates that to achieve long-term growth and sustainability, economies requires a much deeper human capital perspective. There is clear evidence that the development of a country is not explained by GDP growth alone but is clearly impacted by the level of investments in education. Countries with high HDI and better GDP in terms of per-capita income are not always among the top human capital nations. Different forms of capital can be substitutes or complements, and the degree of substitutability or complementarity should be analyzed.

Our findings clearly show a slow progress of human capital, compared to GDP, which is a clear indication of less focus on human development than economic advancement. Education is certainly important for economic progress in developing and developed nations, while developing countries have comparatively less focus in this issue. Investment in education, especially in developing countries, will benefit labor income and ensure the optimization of human capital. In addition, schooling enrollments for younger cohorts in developing countries are increasing over the past years. So, there is potential to invest and subsidize the education of this young cohort. This will be a sustainable strategy to achieve success on human capital development.

We focus on the quantitative side of educational attainment, in terms of the average years of total schooling. Human capital accumulated due to education will be different if the quality of education varies. The data on education driven productivity are not available and limiting the analysis. We noticed that the income loss due to the burden of diseases and the labor income of unpaid work force are some valuable information to incorporate in future release of human capital data. These are some of the limitations of this study. More

detailed estimates of human capital stock will be useful, and doing this is currently in process.

Future economic development needs more highly educated people. Our data analysis shows that the returns to the investments in education are significantly valuable for national wealth. As a result, more investments in higher education in South Asia and the Sub-Saharan Africa regions are, therefore, rewarding. Female education is another import part of the development of these regions as there is a significant share of uneducated female individuals in these societies who are not engaging them into economic activities. Mothers' education also has impact on kids' enrollments in educational institutes as well as family health. Along with economic growth, education attainment and guided human capital can ensure the sustainable development of nations.

Our human capital valuation has certain limitations. The estimates in this study are very conservative. It should also be remembered that education is often involved with significant health impacts, which are not considered in the study because of lack of data. Similarly, the child labor has a lot of unaccounted effects on education and they are not properly reflected in human capital; thus, these values are to be viewed as conservative.

ANNEX

Africa	Asia	Europe
Eastern Africa	*Eastern Asia*	*Eastern Europe*
Burundi	China	Bulgaria
Kenya	Japan	Czech Republic
Malawi	Mongolia	Hungary
Mauritius	Republic of Korea	Poland
Mozambique	*South-Central Asia*	Republic of Moldova

Rwanda	Afghanistan	Romania	Nigeria	Turkey	Switzerland
Uganda	Bangladesh	Russian Federation	Senegal	United Arab Emirates	
United Republic of Tanzania	India	Slovakia	Sierra Leone	Yemen	
Zambia	Iran (Islamic Republic of)	Ukraine	**Latin America and Caribbean**	**Northern America**	**Oceania**
Zimbabwe	Kazakhstan	*Northern Europe*	*Caribbean*	*Northern America*	*Australia/New Zealand*
Middle Africa	Kyrgyzstan	Denmark	Barbados	Canada	Australia
Cameroon	Maldives	Estonia	Cuba	United States of America	New Zealand
Central African Republic	Nepal	Finland	Dominican Republic		*Melanesia*
Congo	Pakistan	Iceland	Haiti		Fiji
Democratic Republic of the Congo	Sri Lanka	Ireland	Jamaica		Papua New Guinea
Gabon	Tajikistan	Latvia	Trinidad and Tobago		
Northern Africa	*South-Eastern Asia*	Lithuania	*Central America*		
Algeria	Cambodia	Norway	Belize		
Egypt	Indonesia	Sweden	Costa Rica		
Morocco	Laos	United Kingdom	El Salvador		
Sudan (former)	Malaysia	*Southern Europe*	Guatemala		
Tunisia	Myanmar	Albania	Honduras		
Southern Africa	Philippines	Croatia	Mexico		
Botswana	Singapore	Greece	Nicaragua		
Lesotho	Thailand	Italy	Panama		
Namibia	Vietnam	Malta	*South America*		
South Africa	*Western Asia*	Portugal	Argentina		
Swaziland	Armenia	Serbia	Bolivia		
Western Africa	Bahrain	Slovenia	Brazil		
Benin	Cyprus	Spain	Chile		
Côte d'Ivoire	Iraq	*Western Europe*	Colombia		
Gambia	Israel	Austria	Ecuador		
Ghana	Jordan	Belgium	Guyana		
Liberia	Kuwait	France	Paraguay		
Mali	Qatar	Germany	Peru		
Mauritania	Saudi Arabia	Luxembourg	Uruguay		
Niger	Syrian Arab Republic	Netherlands	Venezuela		

REFERENCES

Arrow, K.J., et al., 2012. Sustainability and the measurement of wealth. Environ. Dev. Econ. 17, 317–353. https://doi.org/10.1017/s1355770x12000137.

Barro, R.J., Lee, J., 2001. International data on educational attainment: updates and implications. Oxf. Econ. Pap. 53, 541–563.

Barro, R.J., Lee, J.W., 2013. A new data set of educational attainment in the world, 1950–2010. J. Dev. Econ. 104, 184–198.

Bongaarts, J., 2010. The causes of educational differences in fertility in sub-Saharan Africa. Vienna Yearb. Popul. Res. 8, 31–50.

Cohen, D., Soto, M., 2007. Growth and human capital: good data, good results. J. Econ. Growth 12, 51–76. https://doi.org/10.1007/s10887-007-9011-5.

Conference Board, 2016. Total Economy Database™ (Adjusted Version).

de la Fuente, A., Doménech, R., 2006. Human capital in growth regressions: how much difference does data quality make? J. Eur. Econ. Assoc. 4, 1–36. https://doi.org/10.1162/jeea.2006.4.1.1.

Dixit, A., et al., 1980. On Hartwick's rule for regular maximin paths of capital accumulation and resource depletion. Rev. Econ. Stud. 47, 551–556.

Feenstra, R.C., et al., 2013. Penn world table version 8.0. In: The Next Generation of the Penn World Table. Available: www.ggdc.net/pwt.

Hartwick, J.M., 1977. Intergenerational equity and the investing of rents from exhaustible resources. Am. Econ. Rev. 67, 972–974.

International Labour Organization, 2015. Key Indicators of the Labour Market (KILM) Database.

Jeong, B., 2002. Measurement and human capital input across countries: a method based on the laborer's income. J. Dev. Econ. 67, 333–349. https://doi.org/10.1016/S0304-3878 (01)00194-8.

Jorgenson, D.W., Fraumeni, B.M., 1989. The accumulation of human and nonhuman capital, 1948–1984. In: Lipsey, R.E., Tice, H.S. (Eds.), The Measurement of Savings, Investment and Wealth. Palgrave Macmillan, London.

Jorgenson, D.W., Fraumeni, B.M., 1992. The output of the education sector. In: Output Measurement in the Service Sectors. University of Chicago Press, pp. 303–341.

Kc, S., Lentzner, H., 2010. The effect of education on adult mortality and disability: a global perspective. Vienna Yearb. Popul. Res. 8, 201–235.

Klenow, P.J., Rodriguez-Clare, A., 1997. The neoclassical revival in growth economics: has it gone too far? NBER Macroecon. Annu. 12, 73–103.

Krueger, A.B., Lindahl, M., 2001. Education for growth: why and for whom? J. Econ. Lit. 39, 1101–1136. https://doi.org/10.1257/jel.39.4.1101.

Laroche, M., Mérette, M., 2000. Measuring Human Capital in Canada. Department of Finance Canada.

Lenzen, M., et al., 2013. Building Eora: a global multi-region input–output database at high country and sector resolution. Econ. Syst. Res. 25, 20–49.

Macklem, R.T., 1997. Aggregate wealth in Canada. Can. J. Econ., 152–168.

Managi, S., Kumar, P., 2018. Inclusive Wealth Report 2018: Measuring Progress Towards Sustainability. Routledge, New York, USA.

Nehru, V., et al., 1995. A new database on human capital stock in developing and industrial countries: sources, methodology, and results. J. Dev. Econ. 46, 379–401. https://doi.org/10.1016/0304-3878(94)00054-G.

OECD, 2016. OECD National Accounts.

Psacharopoulos, G., Arriagada, A.M., 1986. The educational composition of the labour force: an international comparison. Int. Labour Rev. 125, 561.

United Nations Population Division, 2016. World Population Prospects: The 2017 Revision.

United Nations Statistical Division, 2016. National Accounts Estimates of Main Aggregates.

UNU-IHDP and UNEP, 2012. Inclusive Wealth Report 2012: Measuring Progress Toward Sustainability. New York Cambridge Univ. Press.

UNU-IHDP and UNEP, 2014. Inclusive Wealth Report 2014: Measuring Progress Toward Sustainability. New York Cambridge Univ. Press.

Wei, H., 2004. Measuring the stock of human capital for Australia. In: Working Papers in Econometrics and Applied Statistics: No 2004/1. Australian Bureau of Statistics. Cat. No. 1351.0.55.001.

CHAPTER 3

The World Bank Human Capital Index ☆

PAUL CORRAL[a] • NICOLA DEHNEN[a] • RITIKA D'SOUZA[a] • ROBERTA GATTI[b] • AART KRAAY[c]

[a]Office of the Chief Economist for Human Development, The World Bank, Washington, DC, United States, [b]Chief Economist for the Middle East and North Africa Region, The World Bank, Washington, DC, United States, [c]Deputy Chief Economist and Director of Development Policy, The World Bank Group, Washington, DC, United States

3.1 INTRODUCTION

Investments in human capital deliver substantial economic returns in the long term. However, the benefits of these investments often take time to materialize and are not always very visible to voters. This is one reason why policymakers may not sufficiently prioritize programs to support human capital formation. In 2018, the World Bank launched the Human Capital Project, a global effort to promote human capital development as a core element of strategies to increase productivity and growth across the world's economies. At the center of this effort is the Human Capital Index (HCI). The aim of the index is to increase the salience of the economic costs and long-term consequences arising from under-investment in the health and education of the young.

The HCI measures the human capital that a child born today can expect to attain by age 18, given the risks of poor health and poor education that prevail in the country where she lives. The HCI follows the trajectory from birth to adulthood of a child born today. In the poorest countries in the world, there is a significant risk that the child does not survive to her fifth birthday. Even if she does reach school age, there is a further risk that she does not

start school, let alone complete the full cycle of 14 years of school from preschool to grade 12 that is the norm in rich countries. The time she does spend in school may translate unevenly into learning, depending on the quality of the teachers and schools she experiences. When she reaches age 18, she carries with her the lasting effects of poor health and nutrition in childhood that limit her physical and cognitive abilities as an adult.

The HCI quantitatively illustrates the key stages in this trajectory and their consequences for the productivity of the next generation of workers. The HCI consists of three components: (1) survival, measured as the probability of survival to age 5; (2) school, which combines a measure of the number of years of school a child born today can expect to attain given prevailing enrollment rates with a measure of the quality of education based on international student achievement tests; and (3) health, which uses childhood stunting rates and adult survival rates as proxies for the overall health environment.

The health and education components of human capital all have intrinsic value that is undeniably important but difficult to quantify. This in turn makes it challenging to combine the different components into a single index. Rather than relying on ad hoc aggregation with arbitrary weights, the HCI uses techniques from the literature on development accounting to convert measures of health and education into contributions to worker productivity, relative to a benchmark of complete education and full health.[a] In the case of survival,

---

☆This chapter draws heavily on several recent World Bank publications and reports coauthored by the authors of this chapter in the course of their work developing and implementing the HCI. References to the corresponding publications and reports are noted at the beginning of each section of this chapter. The authors are grateful to the many colleagues in the World Bank and beyond who have supported and contributed to the development, update, and extensions of the HCI. The views expressed here are the authors', and do not reflect those of the World Bank, its Executive Directors, or the countries they represent.

[a]For interested readers, more comprehensive reviews of the development accounting literature in general can be found in Caselli (2005) and Hsieh and Klenow (2010). Bleakley (2010) and Weil (2014) provide reviews focusing on health, and Rossi (2018) provides a recent review focusing on human capital.

Measuring Human Capital. https://doi.org/10.1016/B978-0-12-819057-9.00001-9

the relative productivity interpretation is very stark, since children who do not survive childhood never become productive adults. The contributions of education and health to productivity are calibrated using microeconometric estimates of the labor market returns to education and health. The resulting HCI ranges from zero to one, and a value of x means that a child born today can expect to be only $x \times 100\%$ as productive as a future worker as she would be had she received complete education and full health.

The HCI is intended primarily as a tool to communicate to policymakers in a simple way the likely future economic consequences of shortfalls in education and health among the young. Consequently, its design has been guided by a number of criteria: a focus on salient outcomes, a coherent aggregation strategy across its different components, and broad cross-country coverage of directly measured data. An outcome-based rather than inputs-based index is more likely to center the conversation on what matters—results—and to provide incentives for countries not only to invest more but also to invest better. Conversely, an index measuring spending on health, education, or social protection would only capture dollars spent on specific sectors and not whether spending led to better outcomes. The need to produce a salient metric that is responsive to policy action in the short to medium term has oriented the choice of components toward measuring the human capital of the next generation rather than measuring the stock of human capital of the current workforce, which largely is the result of policy choices made decades ago when the current workforce was of school age. As a result of the focus on widely measured outcomes that are salient to policymakers, the index is, unavoidably, a simplification that does not capture all the elements of human capital.

The HCI illustrates for countries how insufficient investment in the human capital of citizens translates into lower worker productivity and stifles economic growth. This is particularly relevant for lower-income countries with poor human capital outcomes that face decisions about how to allocate limited resources across competing development priorities. It is also relevant for countries at the higher end of the income distribution that may have impressive outcomes in some components like child survival, but are further away from the frontier when it comes to the quality of education or adult survival rates. Further, while the HCI reports national averages, it also provides countries with a methodology that can be applied to examine within-country gaps in human capital, identifying groups (within even high-income countries) that require more targeted investment. By bringing data

on human capital outcomes into the spotlight, the index also spurs improvements in data collection and measurement.

This chapter provides an introduction to the HCI, including its methodology, results, limitations, and extensions. Section 3.2 outlines the methodology of the index. Section 3.3 presents the 2020 update of the HCI, covering 174 economies. Section 3.4 covers several issues related to the HCI, including its limitations, the role of rankings, comparisons with other measures, and extensions. Section 3.5 concludes with a discussion of the measurement agenda ahead and how the HCI serves as a useful tool and conversation starter toward improved measurement, better policies, and ultimately better human capital outcomes.

3.2 METHODOLOGY OF THE WORLD BANK HUMAN CAPITAL INDEX[b]

The HCI is designed to highlight how improvements in current health and education outcomes among children shape the productivity of the next generation of workers. It brings together measures of different dimensions of human capital: health (child and adult survival, stunting) and education (expected years of school and international test scores). Using estimates of the economic returns to education and health, the components are combined into an index that captures the expected productivity of a child born today as a future worker, relative to a benchmark of complete education and full health. This section provides a summary of the methodology of the HCI.

3.2.1 Components of the Human Capital Index

The HCI illustrates the key stages in a child's human capital trajectory from birth to adulthood and their consequences for the productivity of the next generation of workers, with three components:

Component 1: Survival. This component of the index reflects the unfortunate reality that not all children born today will survive until the age when the process of human capital accumulation through formal education begins. It is measured using the under-5 mortality rate, with survival to age 5 as the complement of the under-5 mortality rate.

Component 2: School. This component of the index combines information on the quantity and quality of

---

[b]This section draws on Kraay (2018) and the technical appendix on the HCI in World Bank (2018).

education. The *quantity* of education is measured as the number of years of school a child can expect to obtain by age 18 given the prevailing pattern of enrollment rates. The maximum possible value is 14 years, corresponding to the maximum number of years of school obtained as of her 18th birthday by a child who starts preschool at age 4. In the data, expected years of school range from around 4 to close to 14 years. The *quality* of education reflects work at the World Bank to harmonize test scores from major international student achievement testing programs into a measure of harmonized test scores (HTS).[c] HTS are measured in units of the Trends in International Mathematics and Science Study (TIMSS) testing program and range from around 300 to around 600 across countries. Test scores are used to convert expected years of school into learning-adjusted years of school. Learning-adjusted years of school are obtained by multiplying expected years of school by the ratio of test scores to 625, corresponding to the TIMSS benchmark of advanced achievement.[d] For example, if expected years of school in a country is 10 and the average test score is 400, then the country has $10 \times (400/625) = 6.4$ learning-adjusted years of school. The distance between 10 and 6.4 represents a learning gap equivalent to 3.6 years of school.

Component 3: Health. There is no single broadly accepted, directly measured, and widely available summary measure of health that can be used in the same way that years of school is used as a standard measure of educational attainment. Instead, two proxies for the overall health environment are used. First, adult survival rates (measured as the share of 15-year-olds who survive until age 60) serve as a proxy for the range of nonfatal health outcomes that a child born today would experience as an adult if current conditions prevail into the future. Second, healthy growth among children under age 5 is measured as the complement of the stunting rate, i.e. one minus the share of children under 5 who are below a defined threshold (usually two standard deviations below the WHO's Child Growth Standards Median) height for age. Stunting serves as an indicator for the prenatal, infant, and early childhood health environment, summarizing the risks to good health that children born today are likely to experience in their early years, with important consequences for health and well-being in adulthood.

Section 3.3.1 provides a more detailed discussion of the data sources for the components of the HCI and describes patterns in the data across countries observed in the data for the 2020 edition of the HCI.

3.2.2 Aggregation Methodology

The components of the HCI are combined into a single index by first converting them into contributions to productivity.[e] Multiplying component contributions to productivity gives the overall HCI, a summary measure of how productive children born today will be as members of the workforce in the future. HCI is measured in units of productivity relative to a benchmark corresponding to complete education and full health.

In the case of survival, the relative productivity interpretation is stark: children who do not survive childhood never become productive adults. As a result, expected productivity as a future worker of a child born today is reduced by a factor equal to the survival rate, relative to the benchmark where all children survive.

In the case of education, the relative productivity interpretation is anchored in the large empirical literature measuring the returns to education at the individual level. A rough consensus from this literature is that an additional year of school raises earnings by about 8%. This evidence can be used to convert differences in learning-adjusted years of school across countries into differences in worker productivity. For example, compared with a benchmark where all children obtain a full 14 years of school by age 18, a child who obtains only 9 years of education can expect to be 40% less productive as an adult (a gap of 5 years of education, multiplied by 8% per year).

In the case of health, the relative productivity interpretation is based on the empirical literature measuring the economic returns to better health at the individual level. The key challenge in this literature is that there is no unique directly measured summary indicator of the various aspects of health that matter for productivity. This microeconometric literature often uses proxy indicators for health, such as adult height. This is because adult height can be measured directly and reflects the accumulation of shocks to health through childhood and adolescence. A rough consensus drawn from this literature is that an improvement in health associated with a 1-cm increase in adult height raises productivity by 3.4%.

---

[c]The methodology for harmonizing test scores is detailed in Altinok et al. (2018) and Patrinos and Angrist (2018).

[d]This methodology was introduced by the World Bank (2018) and is elaborated on in Angrist et al. (2019).

[e]This approach is anchored in the literature on development accounting (for example, Caselli, 2005; Hsieh and Klenow, 2010), and closely follows Weil (2007). Galasso et al. (2016) apply a similar framework to measure the costs of stunting.

Converting this evidence on the returns to one proxy for health (adult height) into the other proxies for health used in the HCI (stunting and adult survival) requires information on the relationships between these different proxies[f]: For stunting, there is a direct relationship between stunting in childhood and future adult height because growth deficits in childhood persist to a large extent into adulthood, together with the associated health and cognitive deficits. Available evidence suggests that an improvement in health that reduces stunting by 10.2 percentage points will lead to increased average adult height of about 1 cm and, thus, an improvement in worker productivity of 3.5%. For adult survival, the empirical evidence suggests that, if overall health improves, both adult height and adult survival rates increase in such a way that adult height rises by 1.9 cm for every 10 percentage point improvement in adult survival. This implies that an improvement in health that leads to an increase in adult survival rates of 10 percentage points is associated with an improvement in worker productivity of $1.9 \times 3.4\%$, or 6.5%.

To calculate the HCI, The estimated contributions of health to worker productivity based on these two alternative proxies are averaged together (if both are available) and are used individually (if only one of the two is available). The contribution of health to productivity is expressed relative to the benchmark of full health, defined as the absence of stunting, and a 100% adult survival rate. For example, compared with a benchmark of no stunting, in a country where the stunting rate is 30%, poor health reduces worker productivity by $30 \times 0.34\%$ or 10%. Similarly, compared with the benchmark of 100% adult survival, poor health reduces worker productivity by $30 \times 0.65\%$ or 19.5% in a country where the adult survival rate is 70%.

The overall HCI is constructed by multiplying the contributions of survival, school, and health to relative productivity, as follows:

$$HCI = Survival \times School \times Health \qquad (3.1)$$

with the three components defined as

$$Survival \equiv \frac{1 - Under\ 5\ Mortality\ Rate}{1} \qquad (3.2)$$

$$School \equiv e^{\phi\left(Expected\ Years\ of\ School \times \frac{Harmonized\ Test\ Score}{625} - 14\right)} \qquad (3.3)$$

$$Health \equiv e^{\left(\gamma_{ASR} \times (Adult\ Survival\ Rate - 1) + \gamma_{Stunting} \times (Not\ Stunted\ Rate - 1)\right)/2} \qquad (3.4)$$

---

[f]For details, see Weil (2007) and Kraay (2018), section A2, and accompanying references.

The components of the index are expressed here as contributions to productivity relative to the benchmark of complete high-quality education and full health. The parameter $\phi = 0.08$ measures the returns to an additional year of school. The parameters $\gamma_{ASR} = 0.65$ and $\gamma_{Stunting} = 0.35$ measure the improvements in productivity associated with an improvement in health, using adult survival and stunting as proxies for health. The benchmark of complete high-quality education corresponds to 14 years of school and a harmonized test score of 625. The benchmark of full health corresponds to 100% child and adult survival and a stunting rate of 0%.

These parameters serve as weights in the construction of the HCI. The weights are the same across countries, so that cross-country differences in the HCI reflect only cross-country differences in the component variables. This facilitates the interpretation of the index. This is also a pragmatic choice because estimating country-specific returns to education and health for all countries included in the HCI is not feasible.

As reported in Figure 3.1, child survival rates range from around 90% in the highest-mortality countries to near 100% in the lowest-mortality countries. This implies a loss of future productivity of 10% relative to the benchmark of no mortality. Learning-adjusted years of school range from around 3 years to close to 14 years. This gap in learning-adjusted years of school implies a gap in productivity relative to the benchmark of complete education of $e^{\phi(3-14)} = e^{0.08(-11)} = 0.4$, that is, the productivity of a future worker in countries with the lowest years of learning-adjusted school is only 40% of what it would be under the benchmark of complete education. For health, adult survival rates range from 60% to 95%, while the share of children not stunted ranges from around 60% to over 95%. Using adult survival rates indicates a gap in productivity of $e^{\gamma_{ASR}(0.6-1)} = e^{0.65(-0.4)} = 0.77$. Thus, based on adult survival rates as a proxy for health, the productivity of a future worker is only 77% of what it would be under the benchmark of full health. Using the share of children not stunted leads to a gap in productivity of $e^{\gamma_{Stunting}(0.6-1)} = e^{0.35(-0.4)} = 0.87$. The productivity of a future worker using the stunting-based proxy for health is therefore only 87% of what it would be under the benchmark of full health.

The Human Capital Index uses the returns to education and health to convert the education and health indicators into differences in worker productivity across countries. The higher the returns, the larger the resulting worker productivity differences. The size of the returns also influences the relative contributions of education and health to the overall index. For example, if the returns to education are high, while the returns to health are low, then cross-country differences in education will account for a larger portion of cross-country differences in the index. Although varying the assumptions about the returns to education and health will affect the relative positions of countries on the index, in practice, these changes are small because the health and education indicators are strongly correlated across countries.[g]

3.2.3 Connecting the HCI to Future Income, Growth, and Poverty Reduction

A country's HCI score can be used to measure not just the expected productivity as a future worker of a child born today, but also to develop scenarios for future GDP per capita. Specifically, the HCI can be connected to future aggregate income levels and growth following the logic of the development accounting literature. This literature typically adopts a simple Cobb-Douglas form for the aggregate production function, as follows:

$$y = A k_p^\alpha k_h^{1-\alpha}, \tag{3.5}$$

where y is GDP per worker; k_p and k_h are the stocks of physical and human capital per worker; A is total factor productivity; and α is the output elasticity of physical capital. To analyze how changes in human capital may affect income in the long run, it is useful to rewrite the production function as follows:

$$y = \left(\frac{k_p}{y}\right)^{\frac{\alpha}{1-\alpha}} A^{\frac{1}{1-\alpha}} k_h \tag{3.6}$$

In this formulation, GDP per worker is proportional to the human capital stock per worker, holding constant the level of total factor productivity and the ratio of physical capital to output, $\frac{k_p}{y}$. This formulation can be used to answer the question, "By how much does an increase in human capital raise output per worker in the long run after taking into account the increase in physical capital that is likely to be induced by the increase in human capital?" Eq. (3.6) shows the answer: output per worker increases equiproportionately to human capital per worker, that is, a doubling of human capital per worker will lead to a doubling of output per worker in the long run.

Linking this framework to the HCI requires a few additional steps. First, assume that the stock of human capital per worker that enters the production function, k_h, is equal to the human capital of the average worker. Second, the human capital of the next generation, as measured in the HCI, and the human capital stock that enters the production function need to be linked. This

can be done by considering different scenarios. Imagine first a status quo scenario in which the expected years of learning-adjusted school and health as measured in the HCI today persist into the future. Over time, new entrants to the workforce with status quo health and education will replace current members of the workforce until eventually the entire workforce of the future has the expected years of learning-adjusted school and health captured in the current human capital index. Let $k_{h,\ NG} = e^{\phi s_{NG} + \gamma z_{NG}}$ denote the future human capital stock in this baseline scenario, where s_{NG} represents the number of learning-adjusted years of school of the next generation of workers, and γz_{NG} is shorthand notation for the contribution of the two health indicators to productivity in the HCI in Eq. (3.4). Contrast this with a scenario in which the entire future workforce benefits from complete education and enjoys full health, resulting in a higher human capital stock, $k_h^* = e^{\phi s^* + \gamma z^*}$, where s^* represents the benchmark of 14 years of high-quality school, and z^* represents the benchmark of complete health.

Assuming that total factor productivity and the physical capital-to-output ratio are the same in the two scenarios, the eventual steady-state GDP per worker in the two scenarios is as follows:

$$\frac{y}{y^*} = \frac{k_{h,NG}}{k_h^*} = e^{\phi(s_{NG} - s^*) + \gamma(z_{NG} - z^*)} \tag{3.7}$$

This expression is the same as the human capital index in Eqs. (3.1)–(3.4) except for the term corresponding to survival to age 5 (because children who do not survive do not become part of the future workforce). This creates a close link between the human capital index and potential future growth. Disregarding the contribution of the survival probability to the HCI, Eq. (3.7) shows that a country with an HCI equal to x could achieve GDP per worker that would be $1/x$ times higher in the future if citizens enjoy complete education and full health (corresponding to $x = 1$). For example, a country such as Morocco with an HCI 2020 value of around 0.5 could, in the long run, have future GDP per worker in this scenario of complete education and full health that is $\frac{1}{0.5} = 2$ times higher than GDP per worker in the status quo scenario. What this means in terms of average annual growth rates depends on how long the long run is. For example, under the assumption that it takes 50 years for these scenarios to materialize, then a doubling of future per capita income relative to the status quo corresponds to roughly 1.4 percentage points of additional growth per year.

The calibrated relationship between the HCI and future income described above is simple because it

---

[g]For more details, see Kraay (2018), section A4.

focuses only on steady-state comparisons. In related work, Collin and Weil (2018) elaborate on this by developing a calibrated growth model that traces out the dynamics of adjustment to the steady state. They use this model to trace out trajectories for per capita GDP and poverty measures for individual countries and global aggregates under alternative assumptions for the future path of human capital. They also calculate the equivalent increase in investment rates in physical capital that would be required to deliver the same rises in output associated with improvements in human capital.

The calibrations of these transitional dynamics are based on assumptions of how fast countries are moving to the HCI "frontier," i.e., what the HCI would be if those entering the workforce had full health and complete education. These assumptions are anchored in past performance, where they find that the median country reduces that gap by 5% every 5 years. For the more successful group of countries (75th percentile), the gap closes at a rate of 11% every 5 years, which corresponds roughly to rates of progress in countries such as Poland, Ecuador, and Albania.

Collin and Weil (2018) analyze what would happen if countries (i) continued to close the gap at this "typical" rate of 5% per 5 years or (ii) at an "ambitious" rate of 11% every 5 years. They use an economic simulation model to estimate income and poverty in these scenarios over the next 35 years, relative to a baseline in which the gap never changes. In the typical scenario, estimated global GDP per capita would be 6 percentage points higher by 2050 than in the baseline. In the ambitious scenario, estimated GDP per capita would be 12.2 percentage points higher globally, and 24.2 percentage points higher in low and lower-middle income countries than it would have been under the baseline scenario. In the ambitious scenario, estimated global poverty in 2050 would be nearly half as low as in the baseline, with the benefits concentrated in low and middle-income countries. To realize the same value of income gains as investments in human capital in this ambitious scenario, the simulation model projected that investment rates in physical capital would have to increase by 5.5% of GDP in low and lower-middle income countries.

The economic benefits from investing in human capital of new generations of children materialize slowly. Even in the ambitious scenario, global poverty in 2030 would be reduced by less than 1 percentage point relative to the baseline. This reflects the reality that building human capital takes time. For instance, most children who benefit from better health and education today will just begin entering the workforce by 2030.

However, better policies can increase the returns to investments in human capital and investments that target the poorest, especially early in life when the returns are often the highest, can have large effects on poverty reduction.[h]

3.3 THE HUMAN CAPITAL INDEX 2020 UPDATE

This section describes in detail the results of the 2020 edition of the HCI, which was released in September 2020.[i] The HCI covers 174 countries, adding 17 new countries relative to the inaugural 2018 edition of the index, based on data available as of March 2020. Computed using data collected before COVID-19 hit on a global scale, the Human Capital Index 2020 provides a useful pre-COVID benchmark to track the evolution of human capital and its key components in the wake of the pandemic. The HCI and component data are available at www.worldbank.org/en/publication/human-capital.

3.3.1 HCI 2020—Index Components

The components of the Human Capital Index 2020 are built using publicly available official data, primarily from administrative sources.

Child survival

The probability of survival to age 5 is calculated as the complement of the under-5 mortality rate. The under-5 mortality rate is the probability of a child born in a specified year dying before reaching the age of 5 if subject to current age-specific mortality rates. Under-5 mortality rates are calculated by the United Nations Interagency Group for Child Mortality Estimation (IGME) based on mortality as recorded in household surveys and vital registries. For the 2020 edition of the HCI, under-5 mortality rates come from the September 2019 update of the IGME estimates and are available at the Child Mortality Estimates website.[j]

Expected years of school

The expected years of school (EYS) component of the HCI captures the number of years of school a child born today can expect to obtain by age 18, given the prevailing pattern of enrollment rates in her country. Conceptually, EYS is the sum of enrollment rates by age from ages 4 to 17. Because age-specific enrollment rates are

---

[h]See Elango et al. (2015).
[i]This section draws heavily on World Bank (2020), chapter 1.
[j]http://www.childmortality.org/.

neither broadly nor systematically available for a large cross-section of countries, data on enrollment rates by level of school are used to approximate enrollment rates in different age brackets. Preprimary enrollment rates approximate the enrollment rates for 4- and 5-year-olds, primary enrollment rates approximate the rates for 6- to 11-year-olds, lower-secondary rates approximate for 12- to 14-year-olds, and upper secondary rates approximate for 15- to 17-year-olds. Cross-country differences in school starting ages and the duration of the various levels of school imply that these will only be approximations of the number of years of school a child can expect to complete by age 18. Enrollment rates as close as possible to 2020 for each school level and for different enrollment rate types are obtained from the UNESCO Institute for Statistics (UIS).[k] UIS data were then complemented with inputs from World Bank country teams working to validate the data and provide more recent values when available.[l]

Harmonized test scores

The data on learning come from a large-scale effort to harmonize international student achievement tests from several multicountry testing programs, the Global Dataset on Education Quality. A detailed description of the test score harmonization methodology is provided in Patrinos and Angrist (2018), and the HCI draws on an updated version of this dataset as of January 2020 as described in Angrist et al. (2019). The dataset harmonizes scores from three major international testing programs: Trends in International Mathematics and Science Study (TIMSS), Progress in International Reading Literacy Study (PIRLS), and the Programme for International Student Assessment (PISA).[m] It further includes four major regional testing programs: the Southern and Eastern Africa Consortium for Monitoring Educational Quality (SACMEQ), the Programme for the Analysis of Education Systems (PASEC), the Latin American Laboratory for Assessment of the Quality of Education (LLECE), and the Pacific Island Learning and Numeracy Assessment (PILNA). It also incorporates Early Grade Reading Assessments (EGRAs) coordinated by the United States Agency for International Development. The dataset covers 184 countries with data points

between 2000 and 2019, covering 99% of the world's population. The test scores from these different programs are harmonized into TIMSS units, and range from around 300 to 600 across countries, with a score of 400 corresponding to "minimum proficiency" and a score of 625 corresponding to "advanced attainment."

Fraction of children under 5 not stunted

The fraction of children under 5 not stunted is calculated as the complement of the under-5 stunting rate. The stunting rate is defined as the share of children under the age of 5 whose height is more than two reference standard deviations below the reference median for their ages. The reference median and standard deviations are set by the World Health Organization (WHO) for normal healthy child development.[n] Child-level stunting prevalence is averaged across the relevant 0–5 age range to arrive at an overall under-5 stunting rate. The stunting rate is used as one of two proxies for the overall health environment, in addition to the adult survival rate, in countries where stunting data are available. Stunting rates for the 2020 update of the HCI come from the March 2020 update of the Joint Malnutrition Estimates (JME) database, available at the UNICEF website.[o]

Adult survival rates

The adult survival rate is calculated as the complement of the mortality rate for 15- to 60-year-olds. The mortality rate for 15- to 60-year-olds is the probability of a 15-year-old dying before reaching the age of 60 if subject to current age-specific mortality rates. Adult mortality rates for the 2020 update of the HCI come from the 2019 update of the United Nations Population Division (UNPD) World Population Prospects estimates.[p]

---

[k]http://data.uis.unesco.org/.

[l]For the 2020 update, this resulted in refinements and updates of the UIS-reported data for more than 50 countries.

[m]In addition to the core PISA test, the dataset includes observations from the PISA for Development testing program (PISA-D). PISA-D test scores are used in the HCI only for Panama and Bhutan.

[n]World Health Organization (2009).

[o]UNICEF/WHO/The World Bank Group Joint Child Malnutrition Estimates: Levels and Trends in Child Malnutrition: Key Findings of the 2020 Edition. https://www.who.int/publications-detail/jme-2020-edition. This data is supplemented by information provided by World Bank country teams for five countries.

[p]United Nations Population Division, https://population.un.org/wpp/. Since UNPD does not report adult mortality rates for countries with less than 90,000 inhabitants, data from the UNPD are supplemented with adult mortality rates from the Global Burden of Disease (GBD) project at the Institute of Health Metrics and Evaluation (IHME) available at http://www.healthdata.org/results/data-visualizations for Dominica and the Marshall Islands. Data for Nauru, Palau, San Marino, St. Kitts and Nevis, and Tuvalu come from the World Health Organization (WHO) https://data.un.org/.

Index components across countries

Fig. 3.1 provides an overview of the components of the 2020 HCI. All five components of the index increase with income, though at a different pace. Child survival rates range from 0.998 (2 deaths per 1000 live births) in the richest countries to around 0.880 (120 deaths per 1000 live births) in the poorest countries, reflecting the disproportionate burden of child mortality that low-income countries continue to face. Child survival rates also vary significantly by region, with economies in the Europe and Central Asia region bunched at the top of the distribution and the lowest rates in Sub-Saharan Africa, in countries like Chad, Nigeria, and Sierra Leone. However, in a number of economies in Sub-Saharan Africa, including Burundi, Malawi, or Rwanda, child survival rates are significantly higher than their level of GDP would predict.

While internationally comparable stunting measures are primarily collected in low- and middle-income countries, the share of stunted children decreases as countries get richer. However, income and stunting rates do not always go in lockstep. In countries such as Papua New Guinea, Timor-Leste, and Guatemala, more than 45% of children are stunted. On the other end of the spectrum are economies like Samoa, Tonga, Moldova, or West Bank and Gaza, where the stunting rate is below 10%, and significantly lower than their level of GDP would predict. The same heterogeneity is true across socioeconomic groups within countries.[q] For example, in countries such as Burundi, Niger, and Tanzania, the gap in stunting rates between the first and the fourth socioeconomic quintiles is smaller than the gap between stunting rates in the fourth and fifth quintiles (the richest households).[r]

The second proxy for health—adult survival—is lowest in Lesotho, Eswatini, and the Central African Republic, where the chances of surviving from age 15 to age 60 are at 60% or lower. This is in contrast to the richest countries where 95% of 15year-olds can expect to survive until age 60. As with the other indicators, there is considerable variation around this relationship, with countries such as Morocco and Tajikistan having higher adult survival rates than might be expected given their income levels, while the opposite is true for countries such as South Africa and Namibia.

The quantity of schooling—as measured by Expected Years of School (EYS)—increases as countries get richer. High-income countries are clustered at the top of the distribution and low-income countries are at the bottom of the distribution. However, in economies like Malawi, Zimbabwe, Nepal, or the Kyrgyz Republic, expected years of school are higher than their level of GDP would predict, reflecting the progress these countries were able to make in improving access to schooling (Fig. 3.1). Outliers where the quantity of schooling is about 2.5–5.3 years below what their level of GDP would predict include economies such as Iraq, Mali, and Liberia, which are characterized by varying levels of institutional fragility and conflict.

The quality of schooling—as measured by harmonized test scores (HTS)—increases with income as well. The HTS ranges from a score of around 300 in the poorest countries to a score of around 575 in the richest countries (Fig. 3.1). To interpret the units of the HTS, recall that 400 corresponds to the benchmark of "minimum proficiency" in TIMSS at the student level, while 625 corresponds to "advanced attainment." Accounting for the level of GDP, economies such as Vietnam, Ukraine, and Uzbekistan, as well as Kenya and Cambodia, performed particularly well in learning. Vietnam reaches an HTS of 519, a level similar to countries like Sweden, the Netherlands, and New Zealand, which are significantly richer.[s] Economies where learning is below what their income per capita would predict include high-income countries such as Kuwait, Saudi Arabia, and Qatar. Their relatively disappointing performance in learning may result in part from a traditional emphasis on investing in school infrastructure rather than other factors that are also necessary to improve educational outcomes. These include governance and accountability, effective monitoring mechanisms, information sharing with parents and students, and school systems geared toward inclusive learning.[t] Education systems in these countries may also be reacting to the pull from labor markets, where pervasive informality generates low returns to schooling, and the lure of public employment puts more emphasis on diplomas than on skills.[u] As a consequence, learning lags behind the progress that countries in this region have achieved in access to schooling and gender parity.

---

[s]Note that Vietnam enters the HCI 2020 with its 2015 PISA score, since 2018 PISA scores are not reported for the country. While Vietnam participated in the 2018 round of PISA using paper-based instruments, the OECD's country note states that the international comparability of the country's performance in reading, mathematics, and science could not be fully ensured (OECD (Organisation for Economic Co-operation and Development), 2019).

[t]Galal et al. (2008).

[u]World Bank (2013) and El-Kogali and Krafft (2020).

---

[q]de Onis and Branca (2016).

[r]World Bank (2019).

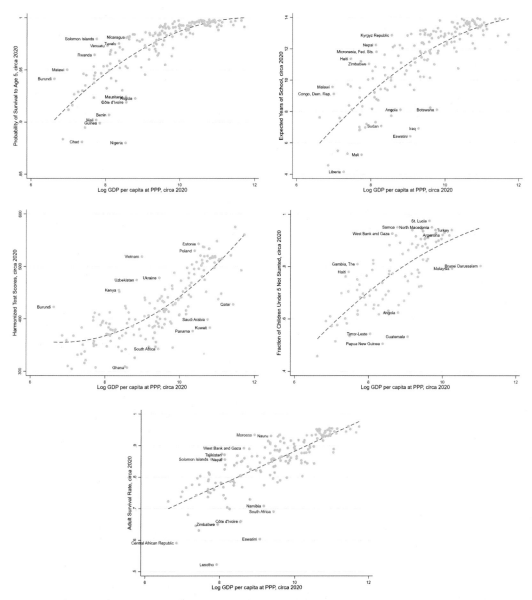

FIG. 3.1 Human Capital Index 2020—Index Components. The figure reports the most recent cross-section of 174 economies for the five HCI components (child survival, expected years of school, harmonized test scores, fraction of children under 5 not stunted, and adult survival), as used to calculate the 2020 HCI. Each panel plots the country-level averages for each component on the y-axis and GDP per capita in PPP on the x-axis. The *dashed line* illustrates the fitted regression line between GDP per capita and the respective component. *Scatter points* above (below) the fitted regression line illustrate economies that perform higher (lower) in the outcome variable than their level of GDP would predict. Countries above the 95th and below the 5th percentile in distance to the fitted regression line are labeled. (From: World Bank, 2020. The Human Capital Index 2020 Update: Human Capital in the Time of COVID-19. World Bank, Washington, DC.)

3.3.2 HCI 2020—Results

The HCI 2020 scores are reported in Table 3.1. HCI scores by country are sorted from the lowest to the highest value. Globally, a child born today would expect to achieve on average only 56% of her full productivity as a future worker. This is before accounting for any impact that may have resulted from the COVID-19 pandemic. Clearly, there is considerable heterogeneity around the 56% figure. In the poorest countries in the world, a child born today will grow up to be only 30% as productive as

TABLE 3.1
The Human Capital Index (HCI), 2020.

Economy	Lower Bound	Value	Upper Bound	Economy	Lower Bound	Value	Upper Bound	Economy	Lower Bound	Value	Upper Bound
Central African Republic	0.26	0.29	0.32	India	0.49	0.49	0.50	Mauritius	0.60	0.62	0.64
Chad	0.28	0.30	0.32	Egypt, Arab Rep.	0.48	0.49	0.51	Uzbekistan	0.60	0.62	0.64
South Sudan	0.27	0.31	0.33	Guyana	0.48	0.50	0.51	Brunei Darussalam	0.62	0.63	0.63
Niger	0.29	0.32	0.33	Panama	0.49	0.50	0.51	Kazakhstan	0.62	0.63	0.63
Mali	0.31	0.32	0.33	Dominican Republic	0.49	0.50	0.52	Costa Rica	0.62	0.63	0.64
Liberia	0.30	0.32	0.33	Morocco	0.49	0.50	0.51	Ukraine	0.62	0.63	0.64
Nigeria	0.33	0.36	0.38	Tajikistan	0.48	0.50	0.53	Seychelles	0.61	0.63	0.66
Mozambique	0.34	0.36	0.38	Nepal	0.49	0.50	0.52	Montenegro	0.62	0.63	0.64
Angola	0.33	0.36	0.39	Micronesia, Fed. Sts.	0.47	0.51	0.53	Albania	0.62	0.63	0.64
Sierra Leone	0.35	0.36	0.38	Nicaragua	0.50	0.51	0.52	Qatar	0.63	0.64	0.64
Congo, Dem. Rep.	0.34	0.37	0.38	Nauru	0.49	0.51	0.53	Turkey	0.64	0.65	0.66
Guinea	0.35	0.37	0.39	Fiji	0.50	0.51	0.52	Chile	0.64	0.65	0.66
Eswatini	0.35	0.37	0.39	Lebanon	0.50	0.52	0.52	Bahrain	0.64	0.65	0.66
Yemen, Rep.	0.35	0.37	0.39	Philippines	0.50	0.52	0.53	China	0.64	0.65	0.67
Sudan	0.36	0.38	0.39	Tunisia	0.51	0.52	0.52	Slovak Republic	0.66	0.66	0.67
Rwanda	0.36	0.38	0.39	Paraguay	0.51	0.53	0.54	United Arab Emirates	0.66	0.67	0.68
Côte d'Ivoire	0.36	0.38	0.40	Tonga	0.51	0.53	0.55	Serbia	0.67	0.68	0.69
Mauritania	0.35	0.38	0.41	St. Vincent and the Grenadines	0.52	0.53	0.54	Russian Federation	0.67	0.68	0.69
Ethiopia	0.37	0.38	0.39	Algeria	0.53	0.53	0.54	Hungary	0.67	0.68	0.69
Burkina Faso	0.36	0.38	0.40	Jamaica	0.52	0.53	0.55	Luxembourg	0.68	0.69	0.69
Uganda	0.37	0.38	0.40	Indonesia	0.53	0.54	0.55	Vietnam	0.67	0.69	0.71
Burundi	0.36	0.39	0.41	Dominica	0.53	0.54	0.56	Greece	0.68	0.69	0.70
Tanzania	0.38	0.39	0.40	El Salvador	0.53	0.55	0.56	Belarus	0.69	0.70	0.71
Madagascar	0.37	0.39	0.41	Kenya	0.53	0.55	0.56	United States	0.69	0.70	0.71
Zambia	0.38	0.40	0.41	Samoa	0.54	0.55	0.56	Lithuania	0.70	0.71	0.72
Cameroon	0.38	0.40	0.42	Brazil	0.55	0.55	0.56	Latvia	0.69	0.71	0.72
Afghanistan	0.39	0.40	0.41	Jordan	0.54	0.55	0.56	Malta	0.70	0.71	0.72
Benin	0.38	0.40	0.42	North Macedonia	0.55	0.56	0.56	Croatia	0.70	0.71	0.72
Lesotho	0.38	0.40	0.42	Kuwait	0.55	0.56	0.57	Italy	0.72	0.73	0.74
Comoros	0.36	0.40	0.43	Grenada	0.55	0.57	0.58	Spain	0.72	0.73	0.73
Pakistan	0.39	0.41	0.42	Kosovo	0.56	0.57	0.57	Israel	0.72	0.73	0.74
Iraq	0.40	0.41	0.41	Georgia	0.56	0.57	0.58	Iceland	0.74	0.75	0.75
Malawi	0.40	0.41	0.43	Saudi Arabia	0.56	0.58	0.59	Austria	0.74	0.75	0.76
Botswana	0.39	0.41	0.43	Azerbaijan	0.56	0.58	0.59	Germany	0.74	0.75	0.76
Congo, Rep.	0.39	0.42	0.44	Armenia	0.57	0.58	0.59	Czech Republic	0.74	0.75	0.76
Solomon Islands	0.41	0.42	0.43	Bosnia and Herzegovina	0.57	0.58	0.59	Poland	0.74	0.75	0.76
Senegal	0.40	0.42	0.43	West Bank and Gaza	0.57	0.58	0.59	Denmark	0.75	0.76	0.76
Gambia, The	0.39	0.42	0.44	Moldova	0.57	0.58	0.59	Cyprus	0.75	0.76	0.76
Marshall Islands	0.40	0.42	0.44	Romania	0.57	0.58	0.60	Switzerland	0.75	0.76	0.77
South Africa	0.41	0.43	0.44	St. Kitts and Nevis	0.57	0.59	0.60	Belgium	0.75	0.76	0.77
Papua New Guinea	0.41	0.43	0.44	Palau	0.57	0.59	0.61	France	0.75	0.76	0.77
Togo	0.41	0.43	0.45	Iran, Islamic Rep.	0.58	0.59	0.60	Portugal	0.76	0.77	0.78
Namibia	0.42	0.45	0.47	Ecuador	0.59	0.59	0.60	Australia	0.76	0.77	0.78
Haiti	0.43	0.45	0.46	Antigua and Barbuda	0.58	0.60	0.60	Norway	0.76	0.77	0.78
Tuvalu	0.43	0.45	0.46	Kyrgyz Republic	0.59	0.60	0.61	Slovenia	0.77	0.77	0.78
Ghana	0.44	0.45	0.46	Sri Lanka	0.59	0.60	0.60	New Zealand	0.77	0.78	0.78
Timor-Leste	0.43	0.45	0.47	Uruguay	0.59	0.60	0.61	Estonia	0.77	0.78	0.79
Vanuatu	0.44	0.45	0.47	Argentina	0.59	0.60	0.61	United Kingdom	0.77	0.78	0.79
Lao PDR	0.44	0.46	0.47	St. Lucia	0.59	0.60	0.62	Netherlands	0.78	0.79	0.80
Gabon	0.43	0.46	0.48	Trinidad and Tobago	0.57	0.60	0.62	Ireland	0.78	0.79	0.80
Guatemala	0.45	0.46	0.47	Colombia	0.59	0.60	0.62	Sweden	0.79	0.80	0.81
Bangladesh	0.46	0.46	0.47	Peru	0.59	0.61	0.62	Macao SAR, China	0.79	0.80	0.80
Zimbabwe	0.44	0.47	0.49	Oman	0.60	0.61	0.62	Finland	0.79	0.80	0.80
Bhutan	0.45	0.48	0.50	Thailand	0.60	0.61	0.62	Canada	0.79	0.80	0.81
Myanmar	0.46	0.48	0.49	Malaysia	0.60	0.61	0.62	Korea, Rep.	0.79	0.80	0.81
Honduras	0.47	0.48	0.49	Mexico	0.60	0.61	0.62	Japan	0.80	0.80	0.81
Cambodia	0.47	0.49	0.51	Bulgaria	0.60	0.61	0.62	Hong Kong SAR, China	0.80	0.81	0.82
Kiribati	0.46	0.49	0.52	Mongolia	0.60	0.61	0.63	Singapore	0.87	0.88	0.89

HCI < 0.40   0.40 ≤ HCI < 0.50   0.50 ≤ HCI < 0.60   0.60 ≤ HCI < 0.70   0.70 ≤ HCI < 0.80   0.80 ≤ HCI

(Reproduced from World Bank, 2020. The Human Capital Index 2020 Update: Human Capital in the Time of COVID-19. World Bank, Washington, DC.)

Notes: The Human Capital Index (HCI) ranges between 0 and 1. The index is measured in terms of the productivity of the next generation of workers relative to the benchmark of complete education and full health. An economy in which a child born today can expect to achieve complete education and full health will score a value of 1 on the index. Lower and upper bounds indicate the range of uncertainty around the value of the HCI for each economy.

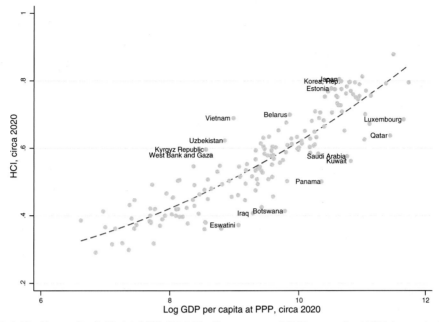

FIG. 3.2 The Human Capital Index (HCI), 2020. The figure uses real GDP per capita at PPP, in constant 2011 US$, for most recently available data as of 2019. Per capita GDP data for South Sudan are not available. The figure plots the country-level HCI on the *y*-axis and GDP per capita in PPP on the *x*-axis. The *dashed line* illustrates the fitted regression line between GDP per capita and the HCI 2020. *Scatter points* above (below) the fitted regression line illustrate economies that perform higher (lower) in the HCI than their level of GDP would predict. Countries above the 95th and below the 5th percentile in distance to the regression fitted line are labeled. (From: World Bank, 2020. The Human Capital Index 2020 Update: Human Capital in the Time of COVID-19. World Bank, Washington, DC for HCI data and World Development Indicators and Penn World Tables 9.1 for per capita GDP data.)

she could be, while in the richest countries the corresponding figure is 80% or more.[v]

All the components of the HCI are measured with some error, and this uncertainty naturally has implications for the precision of the overall HCI. To capture this imprecision, the HCI estimates for each country are accompanied by upper and lower bounds (Table 3.1). These bounds are constructed by recalculating the HCI using lower- and upper-bound estimates of the components of the HCI. They are a tool to highlight to users that the estimated HCI values for all countries are subject to uncertainty. In cases where these intervals overlap for two countries, the differences in the HCI estimates for these two countries should not be overinterpreted

because they are small relative to the uncertainty around the value of the index itself. This is intended to help move the discussion away from rankings and small differences between countries, and instead to focus on the level of the HCI of each country and what this implies for the productivity of its future workers.

Fig. 3.2 plots the HCI 2020 on the vertical axis against log GDP per capita at PPP on the horizontal axis and shows a strongly increasing pattern. While the correlation between the HCI and GDP per capita is high, some economies perform significantly better than their income levels might suggest. These include Estonia, Kyrgyz Republic, Vietnam, and West Bank and Gaza. Conversely, in a number of countries, human capital is lower than per capita income would suggest. Among these are a few resource-rich countries such as Saudi Arabia, Kuwait, or Qatar, where human capital has not yet matched the potential that one would envisage given their level of development. These country-level disparities are mirrored in regional disparities (Table 3.2). For example, a child in Sub-Saharan Africa can expect

---

[v]There is also significant heterogeneity in HCI scores across groups *within* countries. Analytical work disaggregating the HCI by quintiles of socioeconomic status (SES) finds that roughly one-third of the total variation in human capital outcomes is due to variation across SES quintiles within countries (D'Souza et al., 2019; see also section 4.4).

TABLE 3.2
Human Capital Index 2020, averages by World Bank region.

Indicator	East Asia & Pacific	Europe & Central Asia	Latin America & Caribbean	Middle East & North Africa	North America	South Asia	Sub-Saharan Africa
HCI Component 1: Survival							
Probability of Survival to Age 5	0.98	0.99	0.98	0.98	0.99	0.96	0.93
HCI Component 2: School							
Expected Years of School	11.9	13.1	12.1	11.6	13.3	10.8	8.3
Harmonized Test Scores	432	479	405	407	523	374	374
HCI Component 3: Health							
Survival Rate from Age 15 to 60	0.86	0.90	0.86	0.91	0.91	0.84	0.74
Fraction of Children Under 5 Not Stunted	0.76	0.90	0.85	0.82	–	0.69	0.69
Human Capital Index (HCI) 2020	**0.59**	**0.69**	**0.56**	**0.57**	**0.75**	**0.48**	**0.40**

(*From*: World Bank, 2020. The Human Capital Index 2020 Update: Human Capital in the Time of COVID-19. World Bank, Washington, DC.)
Notes: The table reports averages of the index components and the overall Human Capital Index (HCI) by World Bank Group regions. –, not available.

to be only 58% as productive as a future worker as a child in Europe and Central Asia.

The correlation between poverty and low HCI scores is also high. The world's extreme poor (those living on less than the World Bank's international poverty line of $1.90 per day) are disproportionately found in countries with the lowest HCI. Thirty percent of the world's extreme poor reside in the 10 countries with the lowest HCI values, although these 10 countries are home to only 5% of the total global population (Fig. 3.3). Moreover, 80% of the world's extreme poor reside in countries with an HCI under 0.5. If prosperity is to be shared, growth must be inclusive for those at the bottom of the distribution, and inclusive growth necessitates strong investments in human capital.

Which components of the HCI contribute most to cross-country differences in the HCI? A simple decomposition exercise can help to account for these differences in the HCI across country income groups.[w] Consider the HCI difference between the typical low-income and high-income country, which is about 0.33 (Fig. 3.4). Of these 33 HCI points, almost 25 are accounted for by the differences in expected years of school and harmonized test scores. Overall, differences in the quality and quantity of schooling account for the largest share of index differences across country income groups, ranging from 65% to 85%.

There is also considerable heterogeneity within country income groups, and the difference in HCI

between the country with the lowest and the country with the highest HCI in each income group rivals the differences between income groups and, in some cases, exceeds it. For example, the difference in the HCI between the top and bottom performers among high-income economies is roughly 0.38, or 38 HCI points. This compares with a difference of 33 points between the average HCI values of high- and low-income countries. Overall, both within and across all groups, education still accounts for the largest share of the differences observed between top and bottom performers (Fig. 3.5).

However, education accounts for a smaller share as one moves down income groups, falling from roughly 90% among high-income to 60% among low-income economies. In contrast, differences in child survival rates account for less of the difference in HCI scores among high-income countries, largely because countries in this group are close to universal child survival. The same is true for the health component, with stunting and adult survival taken together for easy comparison. Health differences explain a lower share of HCI differences as one moves from low- to higher-income countries, since health outcomes tend to be uniformly better as countries get richer.[x] These results reflect the fact that, within high-income groups, values for health and survival components in most countries are close to the frontier, whereas there is still considerable variation in test scores across countries.

---

[w]The decomposition of the group averages is obtained via a Shapley decomposition. For an application, see Azevedo et al. (2013).

[x]Among upper-middle-income economies, the health component value of the bottom performer is higher than that of the top performer, and thus it accounts for a negative share of the difference.

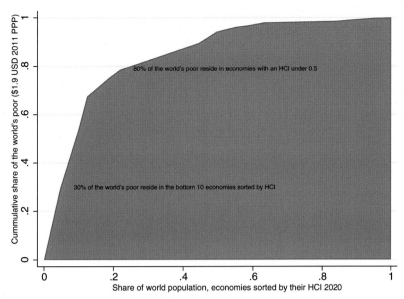

FIG. 3.3 Concentration of the extreme poor in economies sorted by their Human Capital Index. The *horizontal axis* represents the share of the global population accounted for by the countries sorted by their HCI value. *HCI*, Human Capital Index; *PPP*, purchasing power parity. (From: World Bank, 2020. The Human Capital Index 2020 Update: Human Capital in the Time of COVID-19. World Bank, Washington, DC and Corral, P., et al., 2020. Fragility and Conflict: On the Front Lines of the Fight Against Poverty, February 27, World Bank, Washington, DC.)

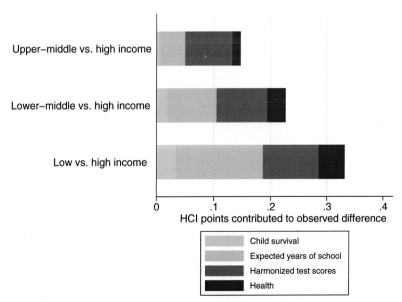

FIG. 3.4 Decomposition of observed mean HCI differences between selected country income groups. The figure plots the contribution to observed HCI differences between income groups. (From: World Bank, 2020. The Human Capital Index 2020 Update: Human Capital in the Time of COVID-19. World Bank, Washington, DC.)

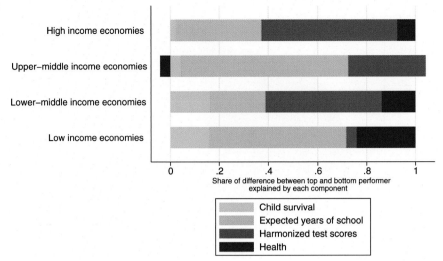

FIG. 3.5 Differences between the top and bottom HCI performers within each country income group. The figure plots the share of the observed HCI differences between selected economies by component. Comparison economies for the high-income group are Singapore and Panama; for the upper-middle-income group Belarus and Iraq; for lower-middle-income economies Nigeria and Vietnam; and for low-income economies Central African Republic and Tajikistan. (From: World Bank, 2020. The Human Capital Index 2020 Update: Human Capital in the Time of COVID-19. World Bank, Washington, DC.)

3.3.3 HCI Measures of Gender Gaps in Education[y]

Globally, the average HCI is slightly higher for girls (0.59) than for boys (0.56).[z] This pattern can be observed across all HCI components (Fig. 3.6). Although the gap between boys and girls has closed in these early-life outcomes, boys and girls both remain far from the frontier of complete education and full health. The gap in human capital compared to full potential far exceeds any gender gap in HCI in most economies. Boys and girls are, respectively, 2.6 and 2.5 years of schooling away from completing upper-secondary education. Large shares of boys and girls are stunted—24% and 21%, respectively. Far too many boys and girls do not survive beyond their fifth birthday—2.8% and 2.4%, respectively. Conditional on making it to age 15, only 83% of boys and 89% of girls are expected to survive to age 60.

The gender gap in the HCI varies quite widely across economies, with a difference in the score between boys and girls ranging from a low of −0.043 in Afghanistan to

a high of 0.096 in Lithuania (Fig. 3.7). Overall, girls are outperforming boys in 140 of the 153 economies for which sex-disaggregated data are available.

Gender gaps in EYS and HTSs show similar patterns. The gender gap in EYS favors boys in just 46 economies (30% of all economies with a sex-disaggregated HCI, Fig. 3.7). In learning outcomes, boys are favored in 31 economies (20%). The top-five economies where girls outperform boys in learning outcomes are Nauru, Qatar, Oman, Bahrain, and Samoa, three of which are in the Middle East and North Africa region. Conversely, 6 in 10 economies where boys have higher learning outcomes than girls are in Sub-Saharan Africa. In high- and middle-income economies, girls outperform boys in enrollment and learning outcomes (Bossavie and Kanninen, 2018). For example, in Guyana, girls are expected to complete one-fifth of a year more schooling than boys, with 5% higher learning outcomes. This reverse gap in enrollment begins in lower-secondary education and widens in upper-secondary, where girls are 11% more likely to be enrolled than boys.

In survival and health outcomes, girls are generally better off than boys. Girls have higher adult survival rates in all of the 153 economies for which sex disaggregation is available in the HCI 2020. In all but two economies—India and Tonga—child survival rates are

---

[y]This subsection draws on World Bank (2020), chapter 1, including contributions by Daniel Halim.

[z]This difference is statistically significant at the 5% level.

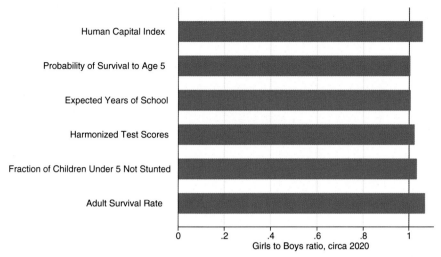

FIG. 3.6 Sex-disaggregated Human Capital Index and its components. The *vertical line* indicates gender parity for each component. Simple averages are computed without population weights. (From: World Bank, 2020. The Human Capital Index 2020 Update: Human Capital in the Time of COVID-19. World Bank, Washington, DC.)

higher for girls than for boys. Meanwhile, girls are more likely to be stunted than boys in just 5 of 85 economies: Bhutan, Iraq, Kazakhstan, Moldova, and Tunisia.[aa]

Overall, out of the 13 economies where boys have a higher HCI score than girls, 8 are in Sub-Saharan Africa, 2 in South Asia, 1 is in the East Asia and Pacific region, 1 is in Latin America and the Caribbean, and 1 is in the Middle East and North Africa region. Seven of those economies are low-income, 5 are lower-middle-income, and 1 is upper-middle-income. In all 13 economies, EYS for boys are higher than for girls, ranging from a quarter year in Peru to almost three full years in Afghanistan. On average, boys have a 10-percentage-point higher likelihood of completing primary education, a 12-percentage-point higher likelihood of completing lower-secondary education, and a 13-percentage-point higher likelihood of completing upper-secondary education. Boys also have better learning outcomes than girls in 9 of these 13 economies. In Chad and Guinea, this difference reaches more than 14% in favor of boys.

Human capital accumulation is a complex process. This complexity is especially clear when looking at the HCI to understand gender gaps. Women, girls, men, and boys face different challenges at different stages of the life cycle. The HCI focuses on specific life-cycle stages in which girls have slight biological advantages over

boys in child and adult survival rates (Crimmins et al., 2019; United Nations, 2011). As with any indicator, the components of the index are not perfect proxies of human capital and try to balance accuracy and data availability. For example, the index does not capture gender bias in terms of sex-selective abortions (Bongaarts and Guilmoto).[ab] Moreover, health is proxied by adult mortality rates, but some evidence shows that, although women live longer than men, they are not necessarily in better health (Bora and Saikia, 2018; Guerra et al., 2008). As a measure of the human capital potential of children today, the index does not capture gender gaps in human capital among the current population of adults. These caveats are important backdrops to any analysis of gender gaps using the HCI.

Finally, the HCI implicitly assumes that a child born today will have opportunities in the labor market to use her human capital potential to generate income, when, in fact, female labor participation rates, globally, are 27 percentage points lower than male labor participation rates.[ac] Section 3.4.5 on human capital utilization delves

---

[aa]Stunting rates are calculated using survey data, and differences in average rates between girls and boys may not be statistically significant.

[ab]The number of "missing women" was estimated to be 126 million in 2010 (Bongaarts and Guilmoto, 2015). This term refers to the deficit of females relative to males, compared to the figures that would have been observed had all female fetuses been allowed to be born.

[ac]Data from ILOSTAT, the International Labour Organization's labor statistics database. Retrieved from World Bank Gender Data Portal, https://datatopics.worldbank.org/gender/.

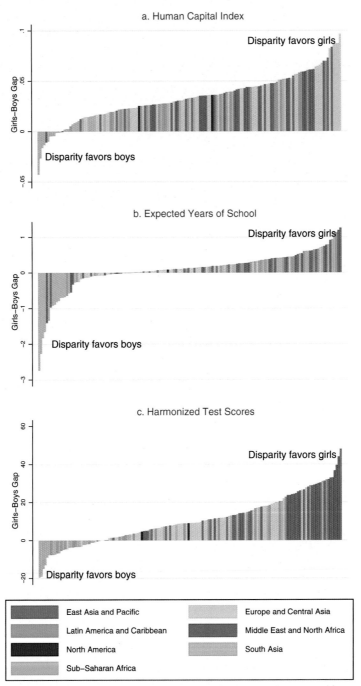

FIG. 3.7 Global variations in gender gaps, Human Capital Index and education components. The *x*-axis show economies ranked by girls-to-boys gap in the variable in question. (From: World Bank, 2020. The Human Capital Index 2020 Update: Human Capital in the Time of COVID-19. World Bank, Washington, DC.)

into this disparity, by proposing an adjustment of the HCI that captures labor market outcomes. These outcomes reflect one of many ways human capital is utilized to improve well-being and overall economic development. Equal access to education and health is far from realized. Despite progress, girls continue to face greater challenges. Child marriage, household responsibilities, teenage pregnancies, and gender-based violence in schools pose challenges to keeping girls enrolled, especially, but not only, in low-income settings.

3.4 DISCUSSION

3.4.1 Limitations of the HCI[ad]

The HCI was constructed with a view to galvanize investments in human capital globally by drawing attention to the critical contributions health and education make to individual productivity and, in turn, to the economic growth of countries. Like all cross-country benchmarking exercises, however, the HCI has limitations.

Components of the HCI such as stunting and test scores are measured only infrequently in some countries, and not at all in others. Others like child and adult survival rates are imprecisely estimated in countries where vital registries are incomplete or nonexistent. Data on enrollment rates needed to estimate expected school years often have many gaps and are reported with significant lags. As a result, the HCI for a country may rely on measures that are somewhat dated that do not reflect the most up-to-date state of human capital in a country.

The test score harmonization exercise draws on test scores come from different international testing programs and converts these into common units. However, the age of test takers and the subjects covered vary across testing programs. As a result, harmonized scores may reflect differences in sampling and cohorts participating in tests (Liu and Steiner-Khamsi, 2020). Moreover, test scores may not accurately reflect the quality of the whole education system in a country, to the extent that tests-takers are not representative of the population of all students. Reliable measures of the quality of tertiary education do not yet exist, despite the importance of higher education for human capital in a rapidly changing world. The index also does not explicitly capture other important aspects of human capital, such as non-cognitive skills, although they may contribute directly

and indirectly to human capital formation (see, for example, Lundberg, 2017).

One objective of the HCI is to call attention to these data shortcomings, and to spur action to remedy them. Improving data will take time. In the interim, and recognizing these limitations, the HCI should be interpreted with caution. The HCI provides rough estimates of how current education and health will shape the productivity of future workers, and not a finely graduated measurement of small differences between countries.

Naturally, since the HCI captures outcomes, it is not a checklist of policy actions, and the right type and scale of interventions to build human capital will be different in different countries. Although the HCI combines education and health into a single measure, it is too blunt a tool to inform the cost-effectiveness of policy interventions in these areas—which should instead be assessed based on careful cost-benefit analysis and impact assessments of specific programs. Since the HCI uses common estimates of the economic returns to health and education for all countries, it does not capture cross-country differences in how well countries are able to productively deploy the human capital they have. Finally, the HCI is not a measure of welfare, nor is it a summary of the intrinsic values of health and education—rather it is simply a measure of the contribution of current health and education outcomes to the productivity of future workers.

3.4.2 The Role of Country Rankings[ae]

Many cross-country measurement exercises place considerable emphasis on how countries rank relative to one another—which country is first, and which is last, and who is ahead of whom. While cross-country rankings can doubtlessly spur healthy competition, there are several reasons why the HCI does not emphasize rankings but rather focuses on its meaningful measurement of future worker productivity as a means to benchmark cross-country comparisons.

First, and most important, there is no need to focus on country ranks because the index itself is expressed in units that are meaningful. Because the HCI is measured in terms of the productivity of the next generation of workers relative to the benchmark of complete education and full health, the units of the index have a natural interpretation: a value of 0.50 for a country means that the productivity as a future worker of a child born in a

---

[ad]This section draws on World Bank (2018), section 5 of the technical appendix on the HCI methodology.

[ae]This section draws on World Bank (2020), section 1.6.

given year in that country is only half of what it could be under the benchmark. Rankings place an inordinately large focus on the fact that a country with an HCI of 0.51 (such as Fiji) is ahead of a country with an HCI of 0.50 (such as Morocco). However, this interpretation misses the more critical issue, which is that in both Fiji and Morocco, children born today will grow up with half their human capital potential unfulfilled. This is vastly more important than whether one country is "ahead of" another.

Second, rankings artificially inflate small differences in HCI scores. For example, there are eight countries clustered between HCI scores of 0.60 and 0.61, so if one of those countries at 0.60 improves by just 0.01, it would move up eight places in the ranking. By contrast, there are just two countries between 0.70 and 0.71, and so if one of those two countries were to improve its score by 0.01, it would only move up one rank.[af]

Third, comparing rankings over time suppresses information on the absolute gains and losses countries have made on the HCI. The HCI has also been calculated for 2010 to enable comparisons over the past decade, for a subset of 103 countries for which comparable data are available. Consider, for example, the comparison of HCI 2020 and HCI 2010, which is graphed in the left panel of Fig. 3.8. Most countries have improved their human capital outcomes, reflected by the fact that they are above the 45-degree line in the figure. Rankings cannot convey these absolute gains (or losses), because they only present the positions of countries relative to each other. This is illustrated in the right panel of Fig. 3.8, which plots the same information for 2020 versus 2010 but in rank terms. Even countries that have made gains in human capital accumulation may fall below the 45-degree line simply because of their position relative to other countries. In addition, points in the right panel are more spread out compared with those on the left, illustrating how ranks artificially magnify small changes.

3.4.3 Comparison With Other Measures of Human Capital and Development[ag]

The HCI is one of several measures that aim to highlight the importance of human capital to growth and development. This section briefly highlights key methodological differences between the HCI and three other closely related cross-country measures of human capital or human development: (1) the Human Development Index (HDI) constructed by the United Nations Development Programme, (2) the human capital index constructed by the Institute for Health Metrics and Evaluation (IHME) as described in Lim et al. (2018) and referred to here as the IHME Index (IHMEI), and (3) the measure of the monetary value of human capital in the World Bank's Changing Wealth of Nations (CWON) report, described in Lange et al. (2018).

The HDI and IHMEI are similar to the HCI in the sense that they are composite indicators that combine measures of health and education into a single summary index. The HDI is a geometric average of (a) the logarithm of Gross National Income per capita, (b) life expectancy at birth, and (c) and average of expected future years of school and average years of educational attainment of the adult population. Each of the components is expressed as a fraction of a corresponding benchmark value, and so the overall HDI can be interpreted as measuring average distance from these benchmark values. The IHMEI is a measure of expected years lived between age 20 and 64, adjusted for educational attainment, learning, and functional health status proxied using estimates of the prevalence of seven different health conditions. The adjustment factors are expressed as ratios of the education, learning, and health measures relative to the corresponding best possible values, and then life expectancy is discounted by the product of these ratios.

Since measures of health and education tend to increase strongly with per capita income, it is not very surprising that the HCI, HDI and IHMEI are positively correlated with each other and with per capita income. Using data from the 2018 edition of the HCI, and in the set of 153 countries where all three measures are available, the correlations of the HCI, HDI, and IHMEI with log real GDP per capita are 0.86, 0.95, and 0.87, respectively, while the pairwise correlation between (a) the HCI and HDI is 0.94, (b) the HCI and IHMEI is 0.95, and (c) the HDI and IHMEI is 0.94. These very high positive correlations, however, obscure conceptual differences in their components, how they are measured, and how they are combined into the overall index.

[af]This problem is amplified by the fact that the components of the HCI are measured with some error, and this uncertainty naturally has implications for the precision of the overall HCI. To capture this imprecision, the HCI estimates for each country are accompanied by upper and lower bounds that reflect the uncertainty in the measurement of HCI components. In cases where these intervals overlap for two countries, this indicates that the differences in the HCI estimates for these two countries should not be overinterpreted because they are small relative to the uncertainty around the value of the index itself. Rankings further amplify these minor differences.

[ag]This section draws on Kraay (2019), section 7, Andrews and Kraay (2018), and Collin et al. (2018).

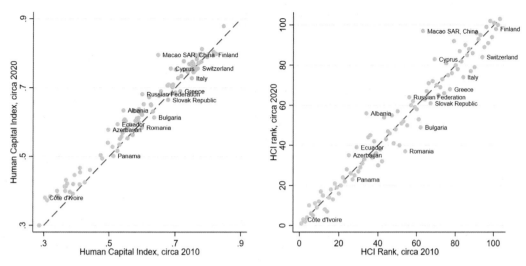

FIG. 3.8 Rankings do not communicate real changes in the HCI. (From: World Bank, 2020. The Human Capital Index 2020 Update: Human Capital in the Time of COVID-19. World Bank, Washington, DC.)

The components of the indices are well-described in the documentation of the respective measures. Differences between them can be briefly summarized as follows. The main differences between the HDI and HCI components are that (a) the HDI includes per capita income as one of its components while the HCI does not; (b) the HDI includes a measure of average educational attainment of the entire workforce while the HCI includes only a forward-looking measure of expected years of school; (c) the HCI adjusts educational attainment for quality using data from international testing programs while the HDI does not; and (d) the HCI includes stunting and adult survival rates as proxies for health, while the HDI uses life expectancy at birth. Distinctions between the components of the IHMEI and the HCI are less pronounced. Both indexes contain measures of survival, the quantity and quality of education, and health. The main difference in the components is that the IHMEI contains a larger number of health indicators.

The more interesting differences between the HCI, HDI, and IHMEI concern how the components are measured and how they are aggregated. On the measurement front, a distinguishing feature of the IHMEI is its use of heavily imputed health and education data, taken from the Global Burden of Disease project and related work at IHME. This project takes data from existing surveys and studies that report information on specific health and education outcomes for a particular age/sex/location/period. It then uses statistical modeling techniques to extrapolate to other age/sex/location/period cells for

which direct measurement is not available. The details of the extrapolation methodology vary from indicator to indicator, but typically extrapolations are based on (a) trends in the actual data, (b) estimated relationships with a limited number of more widely available covariates of the indicator of interest, such as per capita income, and (c) outcomes in geographically nearby locations. Large-scale imputation allows the IHMEI to cover 195 countries with annual data between 1990 and 2016.[ah] However, gaps in the underlying directly measured data are substantial. For example, the IHMEI data on learning is based on largely the same set of international testing data used in Patrinos and Angrist (2018). This implies that only about 20% of country-year observations on learning in IHMEI correspond to a year in which a test was actually taken, and for 65 countries in the IHMEI no directly measured testing data at all is used. Instead, the missing data are extrapolated across countries and within countries over time using estimates of educational attainment as a covariate.

While data extrapolation is a valuable tool to address data gaps, the use of extrapolated data has implications for analysis and policy dialogue. On the analytical front, one concern is the extent to which patterns in imputed data are driven by patterns in the underlying covariates

---

[ah]The extensive coverage of the IHME database can doubtless be very useful. The HCI uses adult survival rates from the IHME database for two countries (Dominica and the Marshall Islands) that are not reported by the UNPD because they have less than 90,000 inhabitants.

used in the imputation model rather than actual relationships in the unobserved missing data. For example, some of the health indicators used in the IHMEI are imputed across countries and over time using models that include income as a covariate. In this case, the strong positive correlations between changes in log per capita income and changes in the IHMEI reported in Lim et al. (2018) may be difficult to interpret since they reflect a combination of the actual relationship between changes in human capital and growth, and relationships driven by the fact that some of the components of IHMEI are imputed using income and other covariates that move with income.[ai]

The use of imputed data may also have implications for policy engagement. At a basic level, the apparent pervasiveness of imputed data on outcomes of interest could dull incentives to invest in the hard work of direct measurement of the actual outcomes. Imputation may also create perverse incentives for policy effort. For example, in a growing economy, policymakers can spuriously take credit for improvements in health and education outcomes that are imputed based on covariates that improve with per capita income, even if there are no actual improvements in the outcomes themselves. Similarly, knowledge of the imputation technology can distort incentives toward improving the covariates in the imputation model rather than the outcome itself. For example, as noted above, data on the quality of education, i.e., test scores, in IHMEI is imputed using data on the quantity of education, i.e., average attainment. With such imputed data, improvements in quantity will be rewarded as improvements in quality even if the latter did not happen, and this in turn may undermine incentives to improve quality. Until major investments in direct measurement of health and education quality are made, striking an appropriate balance between the obvious appeal of imputed data and these potential shortcomings is likely to continue to be a challenge for efforts to measure human capital across countries.

Turning to aggregation methods, the HCI is anchored in the development accounting literature and is measured in units of productivity that are calibrated based on microeconometric evidence on the returns to education and health. The HDI is intended to summarize average achievement across its three dimensions, which it interprets as measures of the "capabilities" of members of society. However, Ravallion (2011) notes that the use of a geometric average implies tradeoffs across components of the HDI that are difficult to rationalize from a welfare standpoint. The IHMEI is described as a measure of human capital. However, unlike the HCI, the IHMEI aggregation method does not reflect available evidence on the magnitude of contributions of health and education to worker productivity, clouding the interpretation of the units of the IHMEI. Consider, for example, functional health, which in the IHMEI is measured using the first principal component of the prevalence of seven health conditions, each rescaled to run from zero to one. The resulting health indicator runs from 0.36 in the least healthy country to 0.90 in the healthiest country. Since these components enter the IHMEI multiplicatively, this means that human capital as measured by IHMEI is $\frac{0.90}{0.36} = 2.5$ times higher in the country with the best health outcomes, holding constant the other components of the index. The magnitude of this difference is difficult to reconcile with the more modest contribution of cross-country differences in health to human capital differences across countries in the HCI, which imply that better health improves productivity by a factor of only about 20%, consistent with available microeconometric evidence in which the HCI is anchored. In fact, to rationalize the 2.5-fold differences in human capital associated with health differences across countries in the IHMEI requires an assumed return to health that is four times as large as is suggested by microeconometric evidence discussed in Section 3.2.[aj]

Finally, the HCI is conceptually closely related to measures of the monetary value of human capital based on the present value of future earnings of individuals such as those in CWON. This is because of the close link between the aggregation method of the HCI and the microeconometric literature on the labor market returns to education and health. To see this, suppose that log wages of individual i at some future time t are given

---

[ai]This problem of extrapolated data analysis uncovering patterns attributable to the extrapolation model rather than actual patterns in the data is not inevitable. There is a well-developed statistical literature on the analysis of imputed data that proposes techniques to avoid these difficulties (see, for example, Rubin, 1996). The basic idea is to generate multiple versions of the imputed dataset, and then average estimates of relationships of interest across these multiple datasets, including variation across datasets in the measures of uncertainty of these estimates.

[aj]To see this, consider the contribution of health to productivity, using adult survival rates (ASR) as the proxy for health. In the HCI this is calibrated as $e^{\gamma_{ASR} \times (ASR-1)}$ where γ_{ASR} measures the increase in productivity associated with an improvement in health that raises adult survival rates. ASR ranges from 0.60 to 0.95 across countries in the HCI. To convert this difference into a productivity difference of 2.5 requires $\gamma_{ASR} = \frac{\ln(2.5)}{0.35} = 2.6$, which is four times larger than the value used in the HCI.

by a health-augmented Mincer equation like $lnw_{it} = \phi s_i + \gamma z_i + g_i t$, where g_i represents future trend growth in wages for the individual. Treating the unskilled wage as the numeraire, human capital measured as the present value of future wages is simply $\frac{h_i}{\delta - g_i}$, where δ represents the discount rate, and $h_i = e^{\phi s_i + \gamma z_i}$ is a measure of the human capital of an individual. Measures of human capital along these lines have a long history (see, for example, Jorgenson and Fraumeni, 1989) and are extensively discussed in the context of satellite national accounts in UN (2016). In addition to CWON, measures of human capital along these lines in a cross-country setting have been developed since 2012 in the United Nations University "Inclusive Wealth Index" study (UNU, 2012).

One incremental difficulty in constructing these measures is coming up with plausible measures of future earnings growth, g_i. Because the difference between the growth rate and the discount rate is small and enters in the denominator of this measure, small changes in assumed growth rates are magnified into large changes in measured human capital. For example, if the discount rate is 5%, changing the assumed growth rate from 3% to 4% per year has the effect of doubling measured human capital. In practice, CWON calculates the financial value of human capital by taking aggregate labor income from the national accounts and applying a common difference between the discount rate and the growth rate of $\delta - g_i = 0.015$ for all countries. This means that measured human capital roughly[ak] is a fixed multiple of aggregate labor income from the national accounts. Since the variation in labor income shares in GDP is small relative to the variation in GDP per capita across countries, the CWON measure is strongly correlated with GDP per capita across countries.

3.4.4 Subnational Disaggregation of the HCI[al]

The HCI provides an international metric to benchmark important components of human capital across countries. While comparisons of national averages are important, they often mask significant differences across groups within the country that policymakers must address if they hope to realize the full potential of their citizens. A subnational disaggregation of HCI components and the overall index can shed light on inequities in health and education outcomes across space. It can

prove a powerful tool for targeting policy since, in many cases, returns to investing in the human capital of disadvantaged groups are the highest. It could also allow policy makers to identify and learn from subnational units that have been making more effective investments in human capital. The HCI methodology can be applied to calculate scores at any subnational level of interest, provided representative data are available for that level.

The HCI can also be disaggregated by socioeconomic status (SES) to shed light on these inequalities between the richest and poorest households within a country. Socioeconomic inequality in the distribution of human capital can reflect the presence of financial and access barriers to investing in human capital and can itself affect the human capital of the next generation. D'Souza et al. (2019) use comparable cross-country data from Demographic and Health Surveys (DHS) and Multiple Indicator Cluster Surveys (MICS), and student-level data from the Global Dataset on Education Quality to calculate an HCI disaggregated by quintiles of SES for 50 countries.

The DHS and MICS contain information on household characteristics and asset ownership that can be used to create a wealth index consistently across countries. Similarly, for testing data, Abdul-Hamid and Iqbal (2019) develop proxies for the SES of the households in which each student resides based on data collected by the testing program on the home possessions of students, as well as parental education and occupation. When combining survey data with data from testing programs, the analysis must align data from DHS-MICS surveys with test score data to account for the fact that the positions of students in the SES distribution in the test score data cover only the households of children who are attending school (because the harmonized test scores are measured using school-based tests), while the DHS-MICS data cover all households, including those in which children do not attend school.[am]

[ak]The CWON calculation also takes into account differences in life expectancy, employment rates, and current and expected future educational attainment across countries when calculating the present value of labor income.

[al]This section draws on the introduction to World Bank (2019) and D'Souza (2019).

[am]Consider, for example, a country where the test scores are taken from the Programme for International Student Assessment (PISA), which is administered to 15-year-olds. Enrollment rates for 15-year-olds by SES quintile in the DHS-MICS are used to calculate the fraction of students attending school associated with each SES quintile in the DHS-MICS. For instance, if students in the bottom SES quintile are more likely to drop out of school, then students in the bottom quintile might, for example, represent only 15% of test takers even though they account for 20% of households. In this case, the average harmonized test score for the poorest 15% of test-takers (according to the SES-HCI in the test score data) is assigned to the households in the poorest quintile in the DHS-MICS. A similar approach is applied for each quintile to arrive at average harmonized test scores for each DHS-MICS quintile.

The disaggregation of the HCI by SES quintile reveals gaps in human capital outcomes across SES quintiles within countries to be large. Pooling all SES quintiles in all countries, roughly one-third of the total variation in human capital outcomes is due to variation across SES quintiles within countries. Further, human capital outcomes increase with income across countries at roughly the same rate as they do within countries across SES quintiles. This indicates that the sharing of income-related human capital risks is on average no better within countries (where in principle social protection programs might mitigate these risks) than it is between countries at different income levels.

While the global HCI draws on cross-country datasets that report national averages, countries are likely to have disaggregated data for HCI components for different geographic regions or administrative units. There is growing consensus among economists that place-based policies should be tailored around the skills of the people who live in the places. For example, the benefits that a community obtains from major infrastructure relative to a targeted welfare program or research and development incentives depend on the skills of the residents.[an] Geographically disaggregated measures of human capital can provide a useful lens to identify areas where governments can target their resources most effectively to invest in the human capital of the young.

A challenge that countries are likely to face when undertaking the spatial disaggregation of the HCI is producing harmonized test scores in TIMSS-equivalent units. On occasion, the international and regional student achievement testing programs (ISATs and RSATs), respectively, that the HCI relies on are representative at the subnational level. In this case, countries can apply the exchange rate employed by the Global Dataset on Education Quality for its own harmonization exercise to calculate harmonized test scores at the subnational level. However, ISATs and RSATs that make up the HTS database are not always representative at the subnational unit of interest. In this case, countries have rescaled test scores from their national assessments to TIMSS-equivalent units.[ao]

As an example, the World Bank country team in Pakistan used data from an ASER 2018 assessment to produce HCI scores at the province level.[ap] The team estimated a proficiency score for each student, based on the reading test information available (Urdu/Sindhi/Pashto and English) and standardized these test scores for the country at a mean of 500, with a standard deviation of 100. The country-level means of ASER were then linked to EGRA (the testing program used for Pakistan in the global HTS dataset), through the provinces that have administered both assessments (Azad Jammu and Kashmir, Balochistan, Federally Administered Tribal Areas, Gilgit-Baltistan, Islamabad Capital Territory, Khyber Pakhtunkhwa, and Sindh). This was done by estimating an exchange rate between tests, assuming that the distributions for these provinces have the same mean for EGRA and ASER (the value of 339, which was estimated for the original HCI). Finally, this exchange rate was applied to the entire dataset, producing provincial level estimates of learning outcomes.

3.4.5 The Utilization-Adjusted Human Capital Index (UHCI)[aq]

The HCI measures the expected productivity as a future worker of a child born today. However, the HCI does not consider whether a child born today will be employed in the future, or the type of job she will have and whether it will fully use her skills and cognitive abilities. To address these limitations of the HCI, the Utilization-Adjusted Human Capital Index (UHCI) adjusts the HCI to reflect the level of underutilization of human capital (Pennings, 2020).

The "basic" UHCI adjusts the HCI downward by the employment rate, i.e., it is the employment to working age population ratio[ar] times the HCI. The simplicity of

---

the rescaled national assessment to the country-level HTS score as reported in the HCI country data file to calculate subnational scores. In the absence of formal linking items, both approaches are reasonable approximations to convert national assessment scores to HTS units. The advantage of the first method is that it preserves the standard deviation across subnational units of the national assessment, while the advantage of the second method is that it is conceptually closer to how assessments are linked cross-nationally in the HTS database.

[ap]ASER is a household survey in both rural and urban communities, although for the 2018 wave, only rural data has been made available. The survey instrument contains a basic learning assessment in the language of the parental home, in mathematics and English.

[aq]This section is based on Pennings (2020).

[ar]The data on employment come from the ILO and the World Bank's JOIN database.

[an]Austin et al. (2018); Hendrickson et al. (2018).

[ao]Test scores from a national assessment can be converted into HTS units in two ways. The first is to rescale the national assessment to have the same mean and standard deviation of the ISAT/RSAT. The HTS exchange rate can then be applied to convert these rescaled scores to HTS units. The alternative approach is to rescale the national assessment to have a mean of 500 and standard deviation of 100, and then use the ratio of the mean of

this basic extension of the HCI is appealing, and it represents the long-run increase in productivity that workers get from their human capital, on the assumption that current employment ratios prevail into the future.

A variant on this is the "full" UHCI that takes into account the fact that workers may end up in jobs where they do not use their full human capital. The full UHCI reflects the income gains from matching workers to jobs where they can make the most of their human capital. Pennings (2020) defines the types of jobs where returns to human capital can be increased as "better employment,"[as] defined as nonagricultural employment. The better employment rate (BER) is calculated as the ratio of better employment to the working-age population.

The resulting "full" UHCI is a weighted average of the HCI and a theoretical minimum HCI that is roughly equal to 0.2 and is constant across countries. The weight assigned to the HCI is the better employment rate (since people in better employment can use their human capital), while the weight assigned to the minimum HCI is the complement of the better employment rate (since people in these jobs typically are not able to use their full human capital), i.e.,

$$full\ UHCI = BER \times HCI + (1 - BER) \times minimum\ HCI \quad (3.8)$$

The full UHCI has lower country coverage than the basic UHCI since it requires more granular data on types of employment. However, it provides a measure that takes into account the fact that many of those who find employment may be employed in jobs that do not maximize the returns to their accumulated human capital. A key finding is that both variants of the UHCI tend to be lower than the HCI in countries where female labor force participation is low. These results suggest the need for targeted policy that facilitates women's participation in the labor market, including safe transport, pay transparency, affordable childcare options, parental leave policies and flexible work options.

3.5 THE MEASUREMENT AGENDA AHEAD[at]

The HCI, and the broader Human Capital Project of which it is a part, is built around the idea that better measurement and transparent information can be transformational in safeguarding and strengthening human capital. By generating a shared understanding among diverse actors, measurement can shine a light on constraints that limit progress in human capital. Through this process, effective measurement can facilitate political consensus based on facts and muster support for reforms, help target interventions to those most in need, and provide feedback to guide course corrections as implementation moves forward.

Since its launch in 2018, the HCI has alerted countries to critical gaps in the human capital of their citizens. For example, despite impressive progress in sustaining high growth and improving human capital outcomes over the last few decades, Rwanda was in the bottom quartile of HCI scores in the first release of the index in 2018 with a score of 0.37. The country's weak HCI performance was driven by low quality of education and a relatively high stunting rate. Subsequently, policymakers in the country identified low human capital as one of the key structural bottlenecks to achieving Rwanda's inclusive growth and poverty reduction agenda. Rwanda's renewed commitment to accelerate human capital development was highlighted when it became one of the first countries to join the World Bank's Human Capital Project (HCP)—a growing global network of 78 countries that focuses on more and better investments in people for greater equity and growth. The country is now undertaking an ambitious multisectoral program of policy and institutional reform to build and protect human capital.

The HCI has proved a useful tool for policy dialogue, in large part because it incorporates measures of human capital that are easily recognizable, consistently measured across the world, and salient to policymakers. While there are multiple aspects of human capital that can be measured in sophisticated ways, the relatively straightforward components of the HCI provide a snapshot of some of the most vital aspects of human capital accumulation. It is worth noting that even these fundamental components included in the index suffer from significant data gaps and quality issues. For example, child and adult survival rates are based on data on birth and death rates by age group. These data are primarily sourced from national vital registries that are mandated to record births and deaths. Vital statistics are essential to the measurement of demographic indicators like life expectancy and to identifying health priorities for the population, and can also help target health interventions and monitor their progress. However, the coverage of vital registries varies widely; only 68% of countries register at least

---

[as]Pennings (2020) notes that this is not a value judgment on the type of work done, but it is meant to capture the type of employment that is relatively rare in poorer economies and thus linked to higher productivity.

[at]This section draws heavily on World Bank (2020), chapter 5.

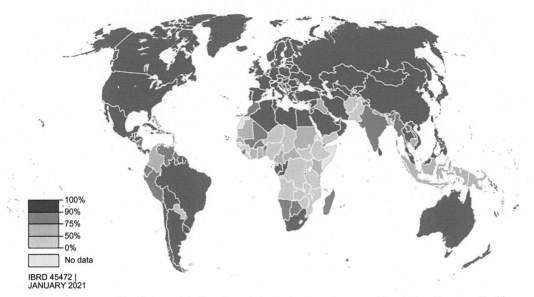

100%
90%
75%
50%
0%
No data

IBRD 45472 |
JANUARY 2021

FIG. 3.9 Coverage of live births registration. Boundaries and names shown, and the designations used in this map do not imply official endorsement or acceptance by the United Nations or the World Bank. (From: United Nations Statistics Division.)

90% of births occurred (see Fig. 3.9) and only 55% of countries cover at least 90% of deaths. Birth registration has increased by only 7 percentage points (from 58% to 65%) in the past decade,[au] and in Sub-Saharan Africa, only eight countries have coverage of 80% or more for under-5 birth registration.[av]

There are similar gaps in the timely measurement of stunting, a key indicator for the prenatal, infant, and early childhood health environments. The JME database that collates and reports global stunting data reports data for 152 countries, of which 33 have data that are more than 5 years old. In 10 countries, the most recent survey is over 10 years old.

Gaps also remain in education data. The expected years of school measure is based on enrollment data that national governments provide to the UIS. Of the 174 countries that form part of the HCI 2020 sample, 22 countries rely on primary enrollment data that come from 2015 or earlier. Since primary enrollment data are typically the most consistently reported, the issue of data freshness is of even greater concern for other levels of school. There are also significant gaps in time series data on enrollment

rates. Of the 103 countries included in the 2010 HCI sample, 22 countries were missing primary enrollment rates for 2010 and could only be included in the sample by applying average growth rates to older enrollment data. Data gaps are more numerous at other levels of schooling—over 30 countries were missing secondary-level enrollment data for 2010 and 42 countries were missing these data at the preprimary level.

Finally, the latest update to the Global Dataset on Education Quality that produces the harmonized test scores covers 98.7% of the school-age population. However, of the 174 countries appearing in the HCI, 13 rely on test score data from Early Grade Reading Assessments (EGRAs) that are not representative at the national level. In terms of timeliness, 65 countries (roughly 37% of the sample) rely on test score data that are from 2015 or earlier.

There are also significant gaps in sex-disaggregated data across HCI components. The JME reports disaggregated stunting data for only 56% of the 887 surveys that are part of the database. While sex-disaggregated enrollment rates are reasonably complete at the primary level, they are missing at the lower secondary level for 29 of the 174 countries that are part of the HCI 2020 sample. Sixteen countries in this sample are also missing disaggregated test score data. As a result of these gaps, 21 of

[au]UNICEF (2013).

[av]UNSD (2014).

the 174 countries in the 2020 sample do not have sex-disaggregated HCI scores. These gaps in disaggregated data span all regions[aw] and income groups.[ax]

High-quality data collection can doubtlessly be a costly undertaking, but countries can also explore more cost-effective ways of monitoring the health and education outcomes of their citizens. For instance, instead of bearing the costs of participating in an international assessment like PISA or TIMSS, countries can augment regularly conducted national assessments with short modules of globally benchmarked and validated items to construct globally comparable measures of education quality.[ay] While there is no comprehensive bank of globally benchmarked items, there are items from international assessments that can be incorporated into national assessments as "linking items." These linking items provide commonality with international assessments, enabling learning outcomes to be placed on a global scale.[az] For instance, Uzbekistan conducted its first ever nationally representative and internationally comparable assessment (using TIMSS linking items) for grade 5 students in Mathematics with World Bank support in 2019. The data from these tests are now part of the country's 2020 HCI score.

In addition to highlighting gaps in data on fundamental measures of human capital, the HCI also seeks to draw attention to other aspects of human capital where data remain sparse or nonexistent. For example, despite growing evidence on the links between skills developed in childhood to lifelong cognitive, physical, and socioemotional development; very few countries systematically measure skills in early years. Similarly, measuring skills—cognitive and noncognitive—among adolescents and adults is still rare in most countries.

A related question is understanding the "production function" of health and education outcomes. Beyond the diagnostic that data on outcomes can provide, policymakers need information on interventions that can successfully build human capital both in the short and long term. For example, there is well-established evidence that conditional cash transfers (CCTs) have improved a variety of health and education outcomes within a few years of program inception. However, there is relatively little evidence on whether and how the increased time spent in school under the CCT led to better learning outcomes and improved labor market opportunities. Projects should be prepared to monitor a wide variety of potential outcomes, including educational attainment, socioeconomic changes and health indicators. Similarly, long-term evidence on the efficacy of some types of interventions often relies on findings from small pilots that were not followed by country-wide scale-up and questions therefore remain about the generalizability of promising findings.

The HCI and the HCP illustrate the importance and effectiveness of using data to drive policy dialogue. At the same time, the index has highlighted gaps in our ability to measure human capital and our understanding of how it is accumulated over the life cycle, as well as the interventions that can support this accumulation. Advancing this unrealized measurement agenda requires purposeful investments. In turn, funding measurement is a way to increase the efficiency and impact of future policy action across multiple domains. By supporting the political economy of reform processes and guiding policy choices toward (cost) effective solutions, better measurement and data use are investments that pay off.

[aw]Thirteen of the 21 countries missing a sex-disaggregated HCI score are from Sub-Saharan Africa; 2 each from East Asia and the Pacific, Latin America and the Caribbean and South Asia; and 1 each from the Middle East and North Africa and Europe and Central Asia.

[ax]Three of the 21 countries missing a sex-disaggregated HCI score are high income countries, 4 are upper-middle income, 7 are lower-middle income, and 6 are low-income.

[ay]Birdsall et al. (2016) and UNESCO (2018).

[az]Kolen and Brennan (2004).

REFERENCES

Abdul-Hamid, H., Iqbal, S.A., 2019. Inequity in Education: Trends and Lessons From 140 Countries. In progress.

Altinok, N., et al., 2018. Global data set on education quality (1965–2015). In: Policy Research Working Paper 8314. World Bank, Washington, DC.

Andrews, K., Kraay, A., 2018. Comparing the World Bank and IHME human capital indexes. In: Internal World Bank note. unpublished.

Angrist, N., et al., 2019. Measuring human capital. In: World Bank Policy Research Working Paper 8742. World Bank, Washington, DC.

Austin, B.A., et al., 2018. Jobs for the heartland: place-based policies in 21st century America. In: NBER Working Paper 24548. National Bureau of Economic Research, Cambridge, MA.

Azevedo, J.P., et al., 2013. Decomposing the recent inequality decline in Latin America. In: World Bank Policy Research Working Paper 6715. World Bank, Washington, DC.

Birdsall, N., et al., 2016. Learning data for better policy: a global agenda. In: Center for Global Development Policy Paper 096. Center for Global Development Policy, Washington, DC.

Bleakley, H., 2010. Health, human capital, and development. Annu. Rev. Econ. 2, 283–310.

Bongaarts, J., and C. Guilmoto. 2015. "How Many More Missing Women? Excess Female Mortality and Prenatal Sex Selection, 1970–2050." *Population and Development Review* 41 (2): 241–69.

Bora, J.K., Saikia, N., 2018. Neonatal and under-five mortality rate in Indian districts with reference to sustainable development goal 3: an analysis of the National Family Health Survey of India (NFHS), 2015–2016. PLoS One 13 (7), e0201125.

Bossavie, L., Kanninen, O., 2018. What explains the gender gap reversal in educational attainment? In: Policy Research Working Paper 8303. World Bank, Washington, DC.

Caselli, F., 2005. Accounting for cross-country income differences. In: Aghion, P., Dulauf, S. (Eds.), Handbook of Economic Growth, first ed. vol. 1B. North-Holland, Amsterdam, Netherlands, pp. 679–741.

Collin, M., Weil, D., 2018. The effect of increasing human capital investment on economic growth and poverty: a simulation exercise. In: Policy Research Working Paper 8590. World Bank, Washington, DC.

Collin, M., et al., 2018. Comparing the human capital index and the human development index. In: Internal World Bank Note. unpublished.

Crimmins, E., et al., 2019. Differences between men and women in mortality and the health dimensions of the morbidity process. Clin. Chem. 65 (1), 135–145.

de Onis, M., Branca, F., 2016. Childhood stunting: a global perspective. Matern. Child Nutr. 12 (Suppl. 1), 12–26.

D'Souza, R., 2019. Guide to calculating a subnational human capital index. In: Internal World Bank Note. unpublished.

D'Souza, R., et al., 2019. A socioeconomic disaggregation of the World Bank human capital index. In: Policy Research Working Paper 9020. World Bank, Washington, DC.

Elango, S., et al., 2015. Early childhood education. In: Moffitt, R.A. (Ed.), Economics of Means-Tested Transfer Programs in the United States. Vol. 2. National Bureau of Economic Research, Cambridge, MA, pp. 235–297.

El-Kogali, S., Krafft, C., 2020. Expectations and Aspirations: A New Framework for Education in the Middle East and North Africa. World Bank, Washington, DC.

Galal, A.M., et al., 2008. The road not traveled: education reform in the Middle East and North Africa. In: MENA Development Report. World Bank, Washington, DC.

Galasso, E., Wagstaff, A., Naudeau, S., Shekar, M., 2016. The economic costs of stunting and how to reduce them. In: Policy Research Note 5 (March). World Bank, Washington, DC.

Guerra, R.O., et al., 2008. Life course, gender and ethnic inequalities in functional disability in a Brazilian urban elderly population. Aging Clin. Exp. Res. 20 (1), 53–61.

Hendrickson, C., et al., 2018. Countering the geography of discontent: strategies for left-behind places. In: Brookings Report (November). Brookings Institution, Washington, DC.

Hsieh, C.T., Klenow, P., 2010. Development accounting. Am. Econ. J. Macroecon. 2 (1), 207–223.

Jorgenson, D.W., Fraumeni, B.M., 1989. The accumulation of human and nonhuman capital, 1948-1984. In: Lipsey, R. E., Tice, H.S. (Eds.), The Measurement of Savings, Investment and Wealth. University of Chicago Press, Chicago, IL, pp. 227–282.

Kolen, M.J., Brennan, R.L., 2004. Test Equating, Scaling, and Linking: Methods and Practices, second ed. Springer-Verlag, New York, NY.

Kraay, A., 2018. Methodology for a World Bank human capital index. In: Policy Research Working Paper 8593. World Bank, Washington, DC.

Kraay, A., 2019. The World Bank human capital index: a guide. World Bank Res. Obs. 34 (1), 1–33.

Lange, G.M., et al. (Eds.), 2018. The Changing Wealth of Nations 2018: Building a Sustainable Future. World Bank, Washington, DC.

Lim, S.S., et al., 2018. Measuring human capital: a systematic analysis of 195 countries and territories, 1990–2016. Lancet 392, 1217–1234.

Liu, J., Steiner-Khamsi, G., 2020. Human capital index and the hidden penalty for non-participation in ILSAs. Int. J. Educ. Dev. 73, 102149.

Lundberg, S., 2017. Noncognitive skills as human capital. In: Hulten, C.R., Ramey, V.A. (Eds.), Education, Skills, and Technical Change: Implications for Future US GDP Growth. Studies in Income and Wealth, vol. 77. National Bureau of Economic Research, University of Chicago Press, Chicago, IL, pp. 219–243.

OECD (Organisation for Economic Co-operation and Development), 2019. Viet Nam country note—PISA 2018 results. In: Programme for International Student Assessment (PISA). OECD, Paris, France.

Patrinos, H.A., Angrist, N., 2018. Global dataset on education quality: a review and update (2000–2017). In: Policy Research Working Paper 8592. World Bank, Washington, DC.

Pennings, S., 2020. The utilization-adjusted human capital index. In: Policy Research Working Paper 9375. World Bank, Washington, DC.

Ravallion, M., 2011. Mashup indices of development. World Bank Res. Obs. 27, 1–32.

Rossi, F., 2018. Human Capital and Macroeconomic Development: A Review of the Evidence. Manuscript, Johns Hopkins School of Advanced International Studies, Washington, DC.

Rubin, D., 1996. Multiple imputation after 18+ years. J. Am. Stat. Assoc. 91 (434), 473–489.

UNESCO, 2018. TCG4 Measurement Strategies. UNESCO Institute for Statistics, Montreal, Canada.

UNICEF, 2013. A Passport to Protection: A Guide to Birth Registration Programming. UNICEF, New York, NY.

United Nations, 2011. Sex Differentials in Childhood Mortality. Department of Economic and Social Affairs, Population Division, United Nations, New York, NY.

United Nations Statistics Division (UNSD), 2014. Coverage of Birth and Death Registration. UNSD, New York, NY. http://unstats.un.org/unsd/demographic/CRVS/CR_coverage.htm.

United Nations University, 2012. International Human Dimensions Programme on Global Environmental Change. In: Inclusive Wealth Report: Measuring Progress Towards Sustainability. Cambridge University Press, Cambridge, UK.

Weil, D., 2007. Accounting for the effect of health on economic growth. Q. J. Econ. 122 (3), 1265–1306.

Weil, D., 2014. Health and economic growth. In: Aghion, P., Durlauf, S. (Eds.), Handbook of Economic Growth. vol. 2B. Elsevier, North Holland, Amsterdam, Netherlands, pp. 623–682.

World Bank, 2013. Jobs for Shared Prosperity: Time for Action in the Middle East and North Africa. World Bank, Washington, DC.

World Bank, 2018. The Human Capital Project. World Bank, Washington, DC.

World Bank, 2019. Insights From Disaggregating the Human Capital Index. World Bank, Washington, DC.

World Bank, 2020. The Human Capital Index 2020 Update: Human Capital in the Time of COVID-19. World Bank, Washington, DC.

World Health Organization, 2009. The WHO Multicentre Growth Reference Study (MGRS). World Health Organization, Geneva, Switzerland.

CHAPTER 4

Human Development: A Perspective on Metrics

PEDRO CONCEIÇÃO* • MILORAD KOVACEVIC • TANNI MUKHOPADHYAY

United Nations Development Programme, New York, NY, United States
*Corresponding author: Pedro.Conceicao@undp.org

4.1 INTRODUCTION

Development debates in the aftermath of the World War II were marked in part by a divide between economic, social, and cultural rights, on the one hand, and civil and political freedoms, on the other. Policy choices were often seen in light of perceived choices to be made between these two sets of rights.[a] It was in this context that emerged concerns over meeting basic needs, for which rising levels of income and equitable growth were seen as necessary, but not necessarily sufficient. Economic growth alone, even when equitable, did not ensure access to education, healthcare, or even rapid reductions in poverty. A fundamental claim of the basic needs approach was that the poor not only need a monetary income but also some very basic goods and services such as clean water, enough food, health services, and education.[b]

This claim was in part driven by the aspiration to realize economic and social rights and was therefore not based on the recognition of the importance of healthy and educated people as "factors of production," which has been part of economic growth models since the 1960s. Both the basic needs and the instrumental value of investing in health and education had been part of development cooperation policy from the 1970s, but were overshadowed by concerns with macroeconomic stability and "getting the prices right" favored by the international financial institutions in the 1980s. The human development approach, proposed by Mahbub Ul Haq and informed by work on welfare economics and social choice by Amartya Sen, recasts the goal of development by emphasizing people's substantive freedoms, in the sense of ensuring they have the capabilities to lead a life they value and have reason to value. As such, substantive freedom depends not just on people's rights and liberties, but on their abilities and characteristics and the economic, social and natural environment around them. Amartya Sen argued that the HDRs presentation of an alternative to the monoconcentration of utility (and its "younger brother," real income) for the evaluation of wellbeing and development was key for the success of the HDRs. The genius of Mahbub Ul Haq, Sen argued, was to confederate "large armies of discontent" with the single-minded focus on income, and to put forward a "broad and permissive framework for social evaluation" open to multiple concerns—a framework that allows "to have many different things as being simultaneously valuable."[c]

The Human Development Index (HDI) is a basic multidimensional metric to track this broader notion of progress. It was introduced to account for a basic set of capabilities: longevity, education, and "command over resources to enjoy a decent standard of living."[d] Proxied by income per person, this third component of the HDI was to be interpreted "strictly as residual catch-all, to reflect something of other basic capabilities not already incorporated in the measures of longevity and education."[e] Thus, while the indicators for health and education reflected directly capabilities, income is included as something with instrumental value, as a "causal antecedent for basic human capabilities" to account for other "basic concerns that have to be captured in an accounting of elementary capabilities,"[f] which could include freedom from hunger, having a shelter, mobility, or Adam Smith's notion that "the clothing and other resources on needs "to appear in public without shame" depends on what other people

---

[c]This paragraph is based on Sen (2000), with direct quotations from this work. See also Stewart et al. (2018).

[d]UNDP, (1990), p. 1.

[e]Anand and Sen (2000b), p. 86.

[f]Anand and Sen (2000b), p. 86.

---

[a]Robeyns (2017).

[b]Stewart (1989).

Measuring Human Capital. https://doi.org/10.1016/B978-0-12-819057-9.00007-X
Copyright © 2021 Elsevier Inc. All rights reserved.

standardly wear, which in turn could be more expensive in high-income societies than in low-income ones."[g]

The HDI was seen as an important addition to the standard methods of measuring social progress through economic indicators, the most common being Gross Domestic Product (the GDP). However, as has been long acknowledged, this metric has major exclusions like the omission of nonmarket transactions including unpaid work. GDP is not cognizant of income and economic inequalities in society. Given that it measures gross flows, it does not account for the depletion of capital and ignores changes in assets such as a country's natural resources. This can undermine the sustainable management of these resources and distort priorities by signaling economic growth while natural resources are being depleted. In the words of the Stiglitz-Sen-Fitoussi Commission on the Measurement of Economic Performance and Social Progress, "what we measure affects what we do."[h] What we measure affects judgments about the current state of affairs and what policy responses are needed.

Ideas of human development draw substantially on the thinking and writings of Amartya Sen, who traces the origins of human development ideas back to Aristotle. Aristotle was seeing the difference between a good political arrangement and a bad one in terms of its successes and failures in enabling people to lead flourishing lives. "Wealth is evidently not the good we are seeking, for it is merely useful and for the sake of something else."[i]

When the HDI emerged in the first Human Development Report in 1990,[j] it was the culmination of an effort led by Mahbub Ul Haq, together with Amartya Sen and a group of scholars.[k] It was born out of dissatisfaction with GDP serving as the standard measure of development, with the idea of placing people and their well-being at the center of development. In the words of Ul Haq (1995), "[a]ny measure that values a gun several

hundred times more than a bottle of milk is bound to raise serious questions about its relevance for human progress." In many respects, the HDI has been remarkably successful in challenging the hegemony of income growth-centric thinking over time.[l]

This chapter is structured as follows. Section 4.2 provides a survey of basic ideas in human development and capabilities. Section 4.3 explores the measurement framework of human development. Section 4.4 reviews some aspects, challenges, and critiques of the choice of dimensions and indicators for the HDI. More details on the choice of indicators are presented in Section 4.5. Section 4.6 discusses the methods and approaches to combining indicators into the HDI, including the transformation, scaling, weighting, and aggregation. In Section 4.7, a summary of some important debates and critiques of the aggregation by the geometric mean is provided. Section 4.8 discusses ranking and classification by HDI, while Section 4.9 summarizes some data issues and perspectives. Section 4.10 concludes the chapter.

4.2 HUMAN DEVELOPMENT AND THE CAPABILITIES APPROACH

It is helpful to take a brief overview of some of the analytical distinctions that the human development and capabilities approach have articulated. In Amartya Sen's work on inequality, the question posed is: "inequality of what?" He made a fundamental analytical distinction between individual endowments, capabilities, functionings, achievements, entitlements, and vulnerabilities. Capabilities are those characteristics that provide the ability of individuals to exercise their freedoms and choices in terms of being and doing. At its very basic, these capabilities include the ability to read and write, lead a healthy life, and the ability to afford a decent standard of living: this is what is intended to be captured in the HDI. Endowments are those inherent and inherited attributes that form the basis for individual capabilities, and these are necessarily unequal between individuals, and range from innate talents to inherited wealth, whose distribution is beyond personal control. These include unique talents, skills and inherited traits that mark us all as individuals—and these gifts and talents determine the extent to which individuals are able to flourish given their capabilities. Functionings are the level of activation of capabilities that individuals are able to achieve, given their endowments, and these are influenced by context and a supportive, enabling environment. Achievements are those feats individuals are capable of achieving as a result of their endowments, capabilities, and functionings facilitated by an enabling environment. It is important to note that a

---

[g]Sen (2005), p. 154. Of course, clothing is used as an example of a broader point: the experience of not living in poverty includes a dimension of social inclusion, of dignity, for which the level of command over commodities is higher in countries with higher levels of income. People may have reasons to value higher incomes far beyond what is required to meet basic subsistence needs.

[h]Stiglitz et al. (2009), p. 7.

[i]Sen (1999).

[j]The Human Development Report is an independent report commissioned and published by the United Nations Development Programme. All editions are available at: http://hdr.undp.org/en/global-reports.

[k]According to Haq and Ponzio (2008), the group comprised of Sudhir Anand, Meghnad Desai, Keith Griffin, Gustav Ranis, Frances Stewart, and Paul Streeten.

[l]Gertner (2010).

consideration of merit and inequalities in endowments are essential when evaluating achievements. Entitlements are those protections offered to all members in society, irrespective of their individual characteristics and comprise of social protection, while vulnerability is the process through which those entitlements are eroded and individuals fall below a minimal socially acceptable threshold of existence. Given the tremendous human diversity, individuals have different levels of capabilities and endowments, which expose them to different vulnerabilities. If societies were to value people only instrumentally on the basis of their ability to use their human capital for productivity, then they would risk losing the most vulnerable and those with inherent limitations of endowments below a minimal threshold necessary for survival. There may be benefits for a community looking after its dependents and extending social protection, as it would reduce the burden of care on families and individuals.

The notion of human resources and human capital, therefore, needs to be mapped within the broader scope of the discussion of capabilities, endowments, and functionings—with policy issues relating to the enabling environment needed for full functioning and high achievements. Inequalities will inevitably emerge between individuals, given their particular attributes in terms of capabilities and endowments—but it is a matter of social choice as to which inequalities are acceptable and tolerable and which are not. This links back to the basic needs approach, which is particularly relevant to the issue of entitlements and vulnerabilities, and to the selection of what constitutes basic capabilities.

Human development is multidimensional in Sen's capability-functioning structure, where a functioning is what an individual chooses to do or to be. Examples of functionings are as follows: being educated, well nourished, healthy, having decent housing and standard of living, and enjoying safe and secure environment with available essential services. "However, it is not the achieved functionings that matter but the freedom that a person has in choosing from the set of feasible functionings, which is referred to as the person's capability."[m] In simple terms, human development refers to a process of enlarging people's choices— through improving their capabilities, expanding their opportunities and removing the social, cultural, or political barriers that may work against them. In a recent paper, Rodriguez (2020) provides a summary of the evolution of the capabilities approach and the human development paradigm, noticing that scholars differ in their views on the relation between

capabilities and human development—with an example of "Nussbaum (2011) who equates the terms, treating them as synonymous, and Robeyns (2017) who disputes this conflation, and argues that it is analytically problematic."

4.2.1 The Distinction Between Means and Ends

As Streeten (1994) pointed out, human beings are both ends in themselves and means of production, and development policy must recognize and respond to this distinction. First, and above all, human development is of intrinsic value, constitutive of wellbeing and an end itself, which needs no further justification. Second, it is also instrumental, as a means to higher productivity. A well-nourished, healthy, educated, skilled, alert labor force is the most important productive asset. Streeten identifies those who stress the means or productivity aspect, with a strong emphasis on income and production as the human-resource developers or who adopt the human capital approach. Those who stress the end aspect of wellbeing for all, are, what he terms, the humanitarians. He notes that while superficially there may appear to be a unity of interest between the human capital developers and the humanitarians, there are also fundamental differences which impact upon their policy outcomes. Although their motives are different, both may have the same cause at heart, and they could embrace each other (for example, when it comes to promoting education). Means are means toward ends, which presumably are the same ends in both camps. This harmony of interest is reinforced by the widespread notion that "all good things go together." Yet humanitarians are also concerned with dependents who are unproductive and unemployable: the old, infirm, disabled, and chronically sick. These people suffer from multiple disadvantages: they face greater difficulties in activating their capabilities, in earning income and in converting income into wellbeing. Moreover, the investments in the human capital of such dependents should not be measured in terms of their productivity output alone. A focus on human capabilities allows for a more multidimensional assessment of the impact of development on such vulnerable and at-risk groups. It encourages universal approaches which can lead to overall societal benefits rather than exclusionary, instrumentally targeted approaches that try to identify "deserving" or "productive" investments for spreading social welfare. In doing so, these are more equitable and comprehensive, and in keeping with broader human development.

The human development paradigm views the purpose of development to enable every person to live a

---

[m]Basu and Lopez-Calva (2011).

long, healthy, fully functioning life, equipped in terms of knowledge and agency to make choices from a range of accessible alternatives so to enhance person's wellbeing along the life course. "Human development puts people back at the center stage, after decades in which a maze of technical concepts had obscured this fundamental vision. [...] We should never lose sight of the ultimate purpose of the exercise, to treat men and women as ends, to improve the human condition, to enlarge people's choices" (Streeten, 1994).

4.2.2 Challenges for the Capabilities Approach

While there is much agreement as to things that are important to wellbeing, there is no common all-encompassing conceptualization of wellbeing, and indeed the use of the HDI itself has not been without its critics.[n] Even an individual's conception of his or her own wellbeing can be conflicted, and this conception needs to be examined and aggregated across individuals before we can arrive at an agreed concept of the wellbeing of society. As noted earlier, wellbeing primarily reflects a person's substantive freedom to lead a life they have reason to value. This language reflects a pluralistic approach to understanding wellbeing, drawn from Sen's capabilities approach. The language does not prescribe what it is that is valued, and it does not say how to aggregate across individuals.

There have been attempts to identify and comprehensively list all the important capabilities that matter for individual and collective wellbeing, starting with the list drawn up most significantly by Martha Nussbaum, who lists 10 "central human capabilities" that specify the political principles that every person should be entitled to as a matter of justice.[o] Yet, Sen disagrees with such a final listing, not least due to the importance he attaches to agency, the process of choice, and the freedom to reason with respect to the selection of relevant capabilities.[p] He argues that theory on its own is not capable of making such a final list of capabilities.[q] Instead, Sen argues that we must leave it to democratic processes and social choice procedures to determine the relevant capabilities at different times in different settings. In other words, when the capability approach is

used for policy work, it is the people who will be affected by the policies who should decide on what will count as valuable capabilities for the policy in question, and engages with theories of deliberative democracy and public deliberation and participation. It is in part for this reason that the human development approach is considered a fairly comprehensive and flexible formulation which allows for an open-ended and dynamic definition of human wellbeing, allowing one to track progress across different dimensions and over time.

4.3 MEASUREMENT FRAMEWORK OF HUMAN DEVELOPMENT

Sen (1985) makes an analogy between the "budget set," which in the commodity space represents a person's freedom to buy commodity bundle, and the "capabilities set," which in the functioning space represents a person's freedom to choose from possible ways of living. As one can measure the size of the budget set by personal income, similarly, the size of the capabilities set can be measured, in a crude way, by a composite measure—*a capabilities index*. The measurement of human development through an index of capabilities allows for keeping track of whether the capabilities set is expanding over time. The issue then becomes which capabilities should be included into the capabilities set?

While capabilities may not be measurable directly, its realizations in functionings are observable and measurable. The vast literature on socioeconomic indices suggests that there are many possible options in choosing indicators for a composite index—including for one of capabilities.[r] The choice of indicators can be guided by theory, axioms, or normative principles, but also by a set of quality criteria aimed at ensuring integrity, methodological soundness, and reliability of the resulting composite index.

The concept of human development is always broader than any particular set of capabilities and index derived from them. Moreover, the relevant capability set can change over time. So, any single index, no matter how smart its design, can hardly fully capture such complexity. However, a single index helps focusing attention and synthesizing the development in some basic dimensions. It may have a considerable political appeal, may easily draw public attention, may be good for advocacy, for initiating healthy competition among societies and for raising awareness. Nevertheless, such a focused single composite index cannot provide a comprehensive picture. A list (a table

---

[n]Castles (2014).

[o]These 10 capabilities are: Life; Bodily health; Bodily integrity; Senses, imagination and thought; Emotions; Practical reason; Affiliation; Other species; Play; and Control over one's environment. For more details, see Nussbaum (2006).

[p]Frediani (2010).

[q]Sen (2004).

---

[r]See for example OECD (2008).

or a dashboard) of many indicators related to the complex concept may allow a more comprehensive evaluation, but will likely be less effective in garnering public, media, and policy attention.

With this in mind, at the onset, the construction of the HDI followed six basic principles as guidelines (Ul Haq, 1995): to (i) measure the basic purpose of human development—to enlarge people's choices; (ii) to include a limited number of variables to keep it simple and manageable; (iii) to be composite rather than a plethora of separate indices; (iv) to cover both social and economic dimensions; (v) to be sufficiently flexible in both coverage and methodology to allow gradual refinements, once better alternatives became available; (vi) not be inhibited by lack of reliable and up-to-date data series.

The construction of the HDI has followed a general principle that the information contained in a composite index should be easy to communicate and should be of interest to a broad spectrum of potential users—from policy analysts and decision makers, to media and general public. This principle alone implies that the information must be restricted to a manageable number of indicators. However, the HDI has been criticized for its choice of dimensions and indicators, its computational methodology, its simplicity, and often for a lack of policy relevance. These criticisms also inspired the HDI evolution, triggered the changes, and brought improvements.[s]

In fact, the measurement of human development has evolved over time. A large literature is now concerned with conceptual and empirical aspects of human development: there is even an entire academic association, the Human Development and Capability Association (HDCA) with its associated Journal of Human Development and Capabilities, that is preoccupied with conceptual and empirical aspects of human development. The HDI is not only used by economists and social scientists, it is also utilized by a wide range of academic disciplines including the medical research community,[t] environmental science (Constatini and Monni, 2008; Ling Lai and Chen, 2020), demography (Hartgen and Vollmer, 2014), etc. The HDI has been replicated in numerous reports at national and regional levels in different countries and used as reference for the creation of various indicators of development.

The HDI was conceived to cover achievements in three basic dimensions—longevity, education, and living standard. These three dimensions have been kept throughout the three decades of the HDI existence. These dimensions indeed capture a set of basic capabilities: longevity—to lead a long and healthy life; educational attainment—to be knowledgeable, to communicate and participate in the life of community and in processes of the society; and income—to be able to afford a decent standard of living and physical quality of life. Longevity which enables a full lifetime free of avoidable afflictions and low morbidity is a constitutive element of human wellbeing. Education is often narrowly seen as providing human capital that can be transformed into earnings in the labor market. However, it is much more than that. It is one of the most important "social bases of self-respect" (Rawls, 1971). Education opens minds to understanding the world and interacting with others in a meaningful way. Skills give people the tools with which to shape their lives, to create new skills and to flourish. Skills promote social inclusion and encourage economic and social mobility, productivity, and well-being. The third dimension, income for access to resources needed for a decent standard of living, has a different status in the capability approach—it is means for other ends and as such it is instrumental in acquiring other capabilities, thus in enlarging the choices for lives people value. In this framework, economic growth makes important contributions to human development, but it is not the only determinant of human development. Also, the link between economic growth and human development is not automatic. Nutrition, health care, and education shape capabilities; and work, access to productive resources, and a conducive environment—enhance opportunities. Social, cultural, and political factors such

---

[s]For discussions on evolution and critiques of HDI and its policy relevance see Anand and Sen (1994, 1997, 2000a), Ul Haq (1995), Luchters and Menkhoff (1996), Hicks (1997), Noorbakhsh (1998a); Sen (2000), Panigrahi and Sivramkrishna (2002), Fakuda-Parr et al. (2009), Jahan (2009), Raworth and Stewart (2009), Ranis et al. (2006), Grimm et al. (2008), Alkire and Foster (2010), Kovacevic (2010), United Nations Development Program, 2010), Klugman et al. (2011a), Wolff et al. (2011), Hartgen and Klasen (2012), Ravallion (2012), Permanyer (2013), Shetty (2014), Mishra and Nathan (2018), Anand (2018), Fleurbaey (2018), Klasen (2018), Rodriguez (2020), among others.

[t]Qiu et al. (2018) pointed out that the relationship between the HDI and health has been studied in topics such as cancer (Bray et al., 2012), infant and maternal death (Lee et al., 1997), depressive episodes (Cifuentes et al., 2008), kidney cancer incidents (Patel et al., 2012), suicide (Shah, 2009), and prevalence of physical inactivity (Dumith et al., 2011).

as conflict or physical insecurity, discrimination, or lack of participation may all act to frustrate or enhance human potential.[u]

Klugman et al. (2011a) suggest that HDI can be characterized as an index of opportunity freedoms, based on Sen's (2002) distinction between two types of freedoms that are valued by the human development approach— the opportunity freedoms that give us greater opportunities to achieve what we value, and process freedoms that ensure that the process through which this happens is fair. While the HDI does not include process freedoms, the HDRs usually explore and discuss several process freedoms in the discussion of human development, such as empowerment, equity, and sustainability.

Although the HDI is a constantly evolving measure, it will never fully capture human development. Clearly, human development and the HDI should not be equated. Thus, the HDI is a summary index constructed to emphasize that people and their capabilities should be the ultimate criteria for assessing the progress of a country, not economic growth alone. Its purpose is to initiate relevant discussions, attract attention to the issues, and allow temporal and spatial comparison and benchmarking. For instance, Anand and Sen (1994) recognize that the Human Development Index "has been concerned only with the enhancement of very basic capabilities of people." They also acknowledge that for high income countries, differences are often due to small variations in life expectancy (this at a time when education was measured using literacy), and in order to capture the differences between "similar levels of achievements of basic capabilities, it becomes relevant to assess performance using more refined capabilities" (Anand and Sen, 1994). The broader point to emphasize is that the HDI is an index of basic capabilities, and that the agenda of human development metrics is open-ended and should evolve as the set of relevant capabilities also changes.

4.4 SIMPLICITY OF THE HDI AND RELATED CRITICISMS

Notwithstanding its success, the HDI has drawn criticisms from many sides, particularly on choice of dimensions and indicators and its computational methodology. Some argued that the HDI depicts an oversimplified view of human development based on only three capabilities and relying on only a few indicators and in that way it excludes other important dimensions such as equity, human rights, social security, political voice,

sustainability, and happiness, among others. Early critics include Lind (1992), Murray (1991), Srinivasan (1994), more recently, Shetty (2014), Biggeri and Mauro (2018), and others. Some criticism is concerned with the fact that the HDI presents averages and thus conceals wide disparities in the distribution of achievements across the population, leading to the suggestion of inequality adjustments to the HDI (Hicks, 1997; Foster et al., 2005; Seth, 2009).

Sen never prescribed a definitive list of capabilities, arguing that the selection and weighting of capabilities depend on personal value judgments and are context specific. However, he did suggest that the capabilities to "live long, escape avoidable morbidity, be well nourished, be able to read, write and communicate, take part in cultural and scientific pursuits and so forth could be considered as intrinsically valuable."[v] In a general context of multidimensional wellbeing, the choice of dimensions that matter has not been settled. Multidimensional theories of well-being are locked into a debate about value judgments. They seek to settle which dimensions should matter for measurement and policy, and, more importantly, on what grounds to decide what should matter. Moreover, there is a gulf between theory and practice, given that measurement and policy are rarely rooted in a coherent ethical framework (Burchi et al., 2014).

A possible alternative to the "narrow" HDI would have been to incorporate more dimensions into the HDI. Neumayer (2001, 2012) and Pineda (2012) proposed a sustainability dimension related to the environment, Graham (2010) discusses the implications of using happiness surveys, Cheibub et al. (2010) discusses the introduction of a dimension related to the political institutions. Burd-Sharps et al. (2010) provide a study for six developed countries: Australia, Canada, Japan, New Zealand, the United Kingdom, and the United States, in which new dimensions are added: inequality, happiness, civil rights, political freedom, violence, crime, environmental, governance, to name a few.

However, others argued that the current composition of the HDI is stable and that adding new dimensions may affect such stability. For example, Streeten (1994) voiced concerns against the addition of political freedom and human rights dimensions to the HDI on the grounds of subjectivity with which these dimensions are measured, less reliability and higher volatility, and the importance of each concept in its own, while putting

---

[u]Anand and Sen (2000b).

[v]A useful summary of historical debates about dimensions of human development and capabilities is given in Alkire (2002).

them together could be interpreted as leading to trade-offs. This further implies that discussions about human development should always be broader than based only on the HDI and the suite of measures that have been constructed so far.

It seems important to again quote Sen who wrote in the Foreword to the 2010 HDR "The human development approach is flexible enough to take note of the future prospects of human lives on the planet, including the prospects of those features of the world that we value, whether related to our own welfare or not (for example, we can be committed to the survival of threatened animal species on grounds that transcend our own well-being). It would be a great mistake to cram more and more considerations into one number like the HDI, but the human development approach is sophisticated enough to accommodate new concerns and considerations of future prospects (including forecasts of future levels of the HDI) without muddled attempts at injecting more and more into one aggregate measure."

In response to criticisms of this kind, rather than tinkering with the HDI to better capture broader aspects of human development such as gender disparity, equity and empowerment, inequality, and a broad poverty that goes beyond the income poverty, HDRs have presented additional complementary indices over time to reflect some of these aspects of human development. Complementary indices include the Gender Empowerment Measure and the Gender-Related Development Index[w] in 1995 replaced with the Gender Inequality Index[x] in 2010 and the Gender Development Index[y] in 2014, respectively. Also, the Human Poverty Index[z] was introduced in 1997 and replaced with the Multidimensional Poverty Index[aa] in 2010. In addition, the Inequality-adjusted HDI[ab] was introduced in 2010. The most recent addition is an experimental index, the Planetary pressures-adjusted Human Development Index which provides a guiding metric toward advancing human development while easing planetary pressures.[ac] It is worth noting that although these indices complement the HDI's explanatory power, they have not been as widely used as the HDI.

Table 4.1 presents human development composite indices, indicators, and dashboards along with the dimensions of human development that they integrate, categorized according to the level of aggregation/disaggregation of data they utilize.

A simple plot of a pair of human development composite indices can provide a strong additional insight into a complexity of human development and associations of different dimensions. For example, Fig. 4.1 presents a scatter plot of the relative gender gap in HDI versus HDI. The figure suggests a moderate negative association between the relative gender gap in HDI and the HDI—that is, the lower gender gap the higher HDI. The relative gender gap is another representation of the Gender Development Index (GDI): (1-GDI).

Some criticisms were directed to the fact that the HDI indicators are a mix of stocks and flows (Kelly, 1991; Ryten, 2000). Stock variables in the current, post-2010 HDI, are mean years of schooling and life expectancy and the flow variable is per capita GNI. The second education indicator—expected years of schooling—is based on the enrollment ratios, which are flow variables. In principle, economic stocks and flows variables have different units and cannot be meaningfully added or subtracted. However, in the case of the HDI, all indicators were rescaled to the interval [0,1]; thus, they are dimensionless, and their mixing can be done, provided they are interpreted as components in an index of capabilities. Perhaps, more important is the responsiveness of the HDI to changes in the respective domains. Due to a lag in the impact of policy changes in education on indicators of educational attainment and enrollment, the index has been criticized for measuring the outcomes of past efforts rather than the effects of present or recent policy changes.

4.5 CHOICE OF INDICATORS FOR THE HUMAN DEVELOPMENT INDEX

Table 4.2 contains indicators used in the post-2010 HDI along with the source, while Table 4.3 provides the choices of indicators in the HDI dimensions and evolution in calculation over the period 1990–2020.

The selection of indicators for the HDI has been guided by the criteria of statistical quality (OECD, 2008) mainly grouped around conceptual relevance, nonambiguity, reliability, consistency, and availability, including the coverage and timeliness. An often-asked question (e.g., Anand and Sen, 1994) is whether the selected indicators have a sufficient power of discrimination to differentiate (discriminate) both the developed and developing countries. Some of these

---

[w]UNDP (1995), p. 72.

[x]UNDP (2010), p. 7.

[y]UNDP (2014), p. 39.

[z]UNDP (1997), p. 27.

[aa]UNDP (2010), p. 7.

[ab]UNDP (2010), p. 26.

[ac]UNDP (2020), p. 13.

TABLE 4.1
Human development indices, indicators, and dashboards.

		Dimensions and determinants of human development					
		Health and longevity	Education	Standard of living	Environment	Empowerment	Other socio-economic
Average level		Human Development Index					
		Planetary pressures adjusted HDI					
Disaggregated by gender		Gender Development Index					
		Gender Inequality Index				Gender Inequality Index	
Micro level, distributions	Deprivation & Vulnerability	Multidimensional Poverty Index					
	Inequality	Inequality-adjusted HDI					
Dashboards: average level and disaggregated		Quality of human development; life-cycle gender gaps; women's empowerment; socioeconomic sustainability; economic enabling; work; human security; perceptions on community and well-being; environmental sustainability and environmental threats					

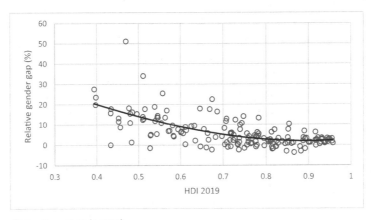

Note: Corr=-0.62 ($p<.001$)

Source: Based on Human Development Report Database. http://www.hdr.undp.org/en/data.

FIG. 4.1 HDI and the gap between the female and male HDI for 2019.

TABLE 4.2
Dimensions and indicators of the post-2010 HDI.

Dimension	Indicator	Source
Health	Life expectancy (at birth)	UN DESA—Population Division
Education	Expected years of schooling (at primary school entering age) Mean years of schooling (of population 25+)	UNESCO Institute for Statistics
Standard of living	Gross national income per capita (PPP$)	World Bank, UN Data, IMF

properties will be examined in more detail below. The statistical quality of data used in the construction of the HDI has often been a target of critique. While the data used in the construction of the HDI come from reputable international sources, there is always a room for improvement. The critiques have pointed out that the selected indicators do not truly capture intradimensional distribution and performance variations across countries in the relevant dimensions (Klugman et al., 2011a). For example, life expectancy as a measure of longevity does not tell us anything about the health profile of people while they are alive (Shetty, 2014). It does not reflect on some of the critical aspects determining health outcomes—quality of health care, availability, accessibility, and affordability.

TABLE 4.3
Evolution in calculation of the HDI 1990–2020.

Year	Ranked countries	Health and longevity	Education	Standard of living	Type of index/ aggregation
1990	130	Life expectancy (LE) in years, observed maximum and minimum set at 78.4 and 41.8	Adult literacy rate (ALR) for 25+: maximum=99%, minimum taken from data set at 12%	Logarithm of gross domestic product (GDP): maximum=3.68 ($4786 per capita in $PPP); minimum (taken from data set)=2.34 ($220)	Deprivation/ arithmetic mean
1991	160	LE: observed maximum and minimum, 78.6 and 42.0	ALR(%) and mean years of schooling (MYS) weighted 2/3 and 1/3. Minimum and maximum taken from data	Adjusted GDP pc obtained with the Atkinson formula with the minimum set at $4829 pc; maximum and minimum of discounted GDP taken from data set at $5070 and $350	As of 1990
1992–93	160 to 173	As of 1991	As of 1991	As of 1991	As of 1990
1994	173	LE: maximum and minimum set at 85 and 25	ALR(%), and MYS weighted 2/3 and 1/3, MYS: maximum and minimum set at 15 and 0	Maximum and minimum of discounted GDP was fixed at $5385 and $200, which was equivalent to fixing the real GDP to $40,000 and $200	Achievement/ arithmetic mean
1995–98	174	As of 1994	ALR(%) and combined enrolment ratio (primary, secondary, and tertiary, capped at 100, in %), weighted 2/3 and 1/3, respectively	Maximum for formula set at $5448 pc which is equivalent to $40,000, minimum is set at $100	As of 1994
1999	174	As of 1994	As of 1995	Logarithm of GDP pc: maximum=$40,000, minimum=$200	As of 1994
2000–09	174 to 182	As of 1994	As of 1995; ALR taken from age 15+combined enrolment ratio uncapped	As of 1999	As of 1994
2010	169	LE: observed maximum, 83.2, and fixed minimum, 20	Expected years of schooling (EYS) (observed maximum, 20.6, fixed minimum, 0) and mean years of schooling (MYS) for 25+ (observed maximum, 13.2, fixed min=0), weighted equally	Logarithm of gross national income per capita (GNI pc) in power purchasing parity dollars ($PPP): observed maximum $108,211, observed minimum $163	Achievement/ geometric mean
2011	187	LE: observed maximum, 83.4	EYS: fixed maximum 18; MYS, observed maximum 13.1	GNI pc: observed maximum $107,721, minimum fixed at $100	As of 2010
2013	187	LE: observed maximum, 83.6	MYS: observed maximum 13.3	GNI pc: observed maximum $87,478	As of 2010
2014–20	187 to 189	LE: Fixed maximum at 85	Fixed maximum for MYS at 15	GNI pc: fixed max at $75,000	As of 2010

4.5.1 Health Indicator

Life expectancy at birth, and its variants, has been the metric most commonly used by human development researchers and analysts. It is the only indicator that is retained in the HDI since 1990; the considered alternatives were either limited in country coverage or were of questionable reliability, although life expectancy does not capture all the aspects of the individual's current health that may affect functionings. It provides summary information about the longevity of the population but does not say how many years are lived in good health.

A number of health indicators have been used, but a measure that would integrate them into a summary measure of the health status of a population with ease of disaggregation by age, gender, and socioeconomic status is not regularly produced with the satisfactory quality. The ambitious Global Burden of Disease (GBD) project initiated in 1990, first led by the World Health Organization (WHO, 2008) and later by the Institute of Health Metrics and Evaluation of the University of Washington, is an important effort to expand information about health status beyond life expectancy at birth. One of the GBD main products, the Health-adjusted life expectancy (HALE), or healthy life expectancy, is an estimate of how many years a person might live in "good" health if the current patterns of mortality and morbidity stay throughout the person's life. In 2020, it was based on data on death and disability from more than 350 diseases and injuries in 195 countries, by age and sex. Data cover years since 1990 thus allowing temporal and spatial comparisons. Replacing life expectancy with the Healthy life expectancy would bring the "healthy" aspect to the "long and healthy life" dimension, something that has been envisioned when the idea of human development index was conceived (IHME, 2019). The 2020 HDR computes the HDI replacing life-expectancy at birth with HALEs, but the change makes little difference in terms of ranks of countries.

Many researchers have pointed out the quality problems of mortality data on which the life expectancy computation is based. The WHO highlights a weak national civil registration of deaths around the globe. "Worldwide, nearly half of deaths are registered with information on cause-of-death. However, incomplete death registration and incorrect or missing information on cause-of-death limit the use of these data in many countries" (WHO, 2021). Only 84 countries collect data of sufficient quality for monitoring trends in mortality by cause. Among them, just over half of upper-middle-income countries and over 80% of high-income countries collect medium- or high-quality

cause-of-death data. All other countries collect data of very low quality or do not register deaths at all. All low-income countries and two-thirds of lower-middle-income countries fall in this category.

4.5.2 Education Indicators

From the human development perspective both education at the early stages of a person's life prior to entry into the world of work, as well as continuing education and expansion of knowledge throughout a person's life are important, as human development concerns the expansion of capabilities. The quantity and quality of education received by the population is important. Basic education increases the efficiency and the participation of each individual in society.

Table 4.3 shows that the HDI has relied on two indicators for the dimension of education—adult literacy and gross enrollment ratio for school age children until 2010. The exceptions were 1990 when only literacy was used, and from 1991 to 1994, when in addition to literacy, mean years of schooling of adult population was used. From 2010, the second dimension of the HDI, education, is measured by expected years of schooling of children at school-entry age and mean years of schooling for adult population.

Literacy is considered a human capital stock variable, and in a sense, it represents the outcome of the education process. The adult literacy rate is based on a self-reported personal assessment and judgment that may be influenced by the social circumstances in which people describe themselves in a way that is different from what objectively their situation is. Lind (2004) argues that while "literacy is essential for development it is unimportant as a measure of development". It cannot be measured reliably. Even, if measured, "can it be compared between writing systems as different as Chinese and English?" (Harkness, 2007). Literacy becomes a nondifferentiating variable for most countries, e.g., in the HDR 2009, for 102 countries, it was ranging from 90% to 100%, and the average literacy rate was 83.9%.

The other indicator used in the HDI to proxy the knowledge dimension until 2010 was the combined gross enrollment ratio. Harkness (2007) criticized the use of enrollment data rather than school completion rates, which she considered as a more output-oriented indicator. Other researchers echoed Harkens and criticized the focus on enrollment rather than on completion, finding that the focus on enrollment was encouraging creation of large classes, and a little follow-up of real learning within countries. Completion of schooling is a significant problem in many developing countries. While enrollment has been increasing, many children drop out before finishing the fifth grade. Lack of data prevented the use of completion rates or even net enrollment rates, which exclude grade repetitions.

Mean years of schooling (MYS) of the adult population was a component indicator of the HDI in the period from 1991 to 1994. It was reintroduced in 2010 to replace the adult literacy indicator. MYS is estimated more frequently for more countries and discriminates better among countries. MYS poses many problems itself, mainly related to the significant variation in duration of each level of education across countries and across time that must be accounted for in order to achieve comparability. Barro and Lee (2000, 2013, 2015) take this variation into account by using information on the typical duration of each level of schooling within countries and an estimation methodology relying on cohort analysis applied to census data and modified by the information on school enrollment and school completion from the UNESCO Institute for statistics (UIS). UIS also started to formally estimate MYS for adult population in 2012 based on its tables on educational attainment of population. An issue of comparability between national school systems and programs still remains an important source of uncertainty. However, despite its limitations, MYS have provided a robust measure for the input of education into the formation of human capital (Chiswick, 1997) and as an indicator of "being knowledgeable" capability.

The gross enrollment rate was reframed and expressed in terms of years as the expected years of schooling (EYS). This indicator is produced by UIS under the name School Life Expectancy. As a component indicator of the HDI, it is interpreted, as part of the HDI, as expected years of schooling to avoid confusion with life expectancy. EYS is conceptually very similar to life expectancy. It is defined as the total number of years of schooling, which a child of a school-entry age can expect to receive in the future, assuming that the probability of his/her being enrolled in school at any particular age is equal to the current enrollment ratio for that age. This indicator, according to UNESCO, shows the overall level of development of an educational system in terms of the number of years of formal education that a child of primary school entry age can expect to achieve. In terms of statistical computation, it relies on data on school enrollment at all levels of education and on demographic data about population of official school-age. Higher EYS indicates that children can expect to spend more years in education. It must be noted that the expected number of years does not necessarily

coincide with the expected number of grades of education completed because of grade repetition. There is, however, a cautionary note attached to the utility of EYS for intercountry comparison for several reasons: (i) neither the length of the school-year nor the quality of education is necessarily the same in each country; (ii) as this indicator does not directly take into account the effects of repetition, it is not strictly comparable between countries with automatic promotion and those allowing grade repetitions; (iii) depending on the country, the enrollment data may not account for many types of continuing education and training. An idea suggested by the UNESCO is to complement this indicator with the repetition rates.[ad]

Overall, the two education indicators used since 2010 were motivated by their conceptual relevance. Mean years of schooling of adults is a better measure of knowledge attained than the literacy rate, which is based on a simple dichotomy of being able to read and write, or not. In addition, mean years of schooling covers all levels of education (excluding repetition) and has a higher power of discrimination across developed countries than adult literacy. Expected years of schooling complements the mean years of schooling and indicates the overall level of development of a country's educational system in terms of the average number of years of schooling that it offers to the eligible population, including those who never enter school. A relatively high EYS indicates a greater probability for children to spend more years in formal education and higher overall retention within the education system, a policy-relevant information that cannot be obtained from simple school enrollment data.

The content and quality of education matter in addition to enrollment and completion rates. Ideally, indicators of the knowledge dimension would go beyond estimating quantity to assessing quality. Several studies have shown that enrollment and completion indicators are not necessarily good or consistent predictors of knowledge and education outcomes.[ae] On the other hand, good measures of education quality do not exist for enough countries. Relevant cross-national assessments of science, mathematics and reading levels of young people, such as OECD's PISA, or TIMSS and PIRLS, are scarce in coverage and frequency. Their results are not necessarily comparable across countries (or group of countries) without additional harmonization.

[ad]UNESCO (2020).

[ae]For a review see Kovacevic (2010).

4.5.3 Indicator of Standard of Living

The third HDI component, standard of living, was measured by real Gross Domestic Product (GDP)[af] per capita in Purchasing Power Parity Dollars (PPP$)[ag] between 1990 and 2010. It was replaced with Gross National Income (GNI)[ah] per capita in constant PPP$.[ai] Many limitations of the GDP were pointed out over the years—starting with the limitations inherent in its own construction by excluding those goods and services not traded in markets, ignoring household productive activities such as taking care of own children, housekeeping, and food production for own consumption. Such activities are omnipresent and universally important, especially in developing countries. GDP includes all effects of economic activities, but ignore the costs of activities such as those that cause pollution.

The GNI per capita replaced the GDP per capita in the HDI in 2010. In a globalized world, differences can be large between the income of a country's residents (GNI) and its domestic production (GDP). Some of resident earnings are sent abroad, some residents receive international remittances and some countries receive sizeable aid flows. In other words, GNI expresses the income accrued to residents of a country, including some international flows, and excluding income generated in the country but repatriated abroad. Thus, GNI is a more accurate measure of a country's residents' ability to instrumentally use income to expand capabilities. For example, because of large remittances from abroad, GNI in the Philippines greatly exceeds GDP (for about 10% in 2019). In Ireland's case, GDP is actually larger than GNI because of repatriation of profits by companies resident in Ireland and repayments on the foreign elements of Ireland's national debt.

The 2009 Report by the Commission on the Measurement of Economic Performance and Social Progress[aj] mentions that "Income flows are an important gauge for the standard of living, but in the end it is consumption and consumption possibilities *over time* that matter." The Report then recommends using income or consumption rather than production; moreover, the Report suggests the use of wealth to take into account the temporal dimension. Income misses the various dimensions of wealth including financial and real wealth and natural wealth, which is central to evaluating sustainability. Foster (2013) entertained the idea of using one flow variable to indicate what is available for transformation into capabilities and to generate standard of living now, and one stock variable to indicate what is saved and transferred to the next generation.

The Commission also recommended that instead of using the averages of income, consumption, and wealth, it might be more insightful to use the medians as measures that pertain better to the "typical" individual or household than the mean (which may be distorted by extreme values at either end of the distribution). However, in practice, moving from means to medians may be difficult given that medians require microdata from household income surveys, whereas macroeconomic measures from the national accounts are based on a range of different macroeconomic sources and may not pertain to the same population. Many of the important properties of means, as well as the theories developed around the concepts such as welfare standards, may not translate directly to the median-based measures.

The standard of living dimension was settled for GNI per capita to account for income generated in the country plus some income received from abroad minus some sent abroad. Data on household income or consumption are neither readily available nor harmonized.

[af]Gross domestic product (GDP) per capita is the market value of all final goods and services made within the borders of a country (resident producers) plus any product taxes and minus any subsides not included in the value of the products in a year divided by midyear population. In other words, GDP is the monetary value of goods and services produced in a country irrespective of how much is retained in the country.

[ag]Purchasing power parities (PPPs) are the rates of currency conversion that try to equalize the purchasing power of different currencies, by eliminating the differences in price levels between countries.

[ah]Gross national Income (GNI) per capita is aggregate income of an economy generated by its production and its ownership of factors of production, less the incomes paid for the use of factors of production owned by the rest of the world divided by midyear population.

[ai]The use of GNI per capita in purchasing power parity dollars is important for international comparison, also expressing the GNI in real (or constant) terms is important to account for inflation and allow comparison over time.

4.6 FUNCTIONAL FORM OF THE HDI

Once a set of dimensions and indicators of human development was decided, the next step was to integrate them into an index. A construction of a composite index involves several steps after selecting the indicators—functional transformations, scaling (or normalization), weighting, and aggregation. These steps are not necessarily in a sequence, and often, they lead to adjustments

---

[aj]The Commission chaired by Stiglitz, Sen and Fitoussi. See Stiglitz et al. (2009).

of the previous steps, alterations, and corrections. Linked to these steps are the major decisions that must be made with respect to functional transformations, weighting for combining the components, which are often subject to debate.

4.6.1 Functional Transformation of Income

As pointed earlier in this chapter, income enters into the HDI not as a capability, but as a proxy for resources needed to have a decent standard of living, as well as to acquire other capabilities that are "critically dependent on one's economic circumstances" (Anand and Sen, 2000b). The issue regarding income then becomes how it is transformed into capabilities and not the extent to which it can substitute the health and education dimensions of the HDI. Such a transformation is supposed to capture the notion that "income transforms into capabilities at a decreasing rate," an idea that has been part of the human development thinking from the beginning. That is the notion that an increase of GNI per capita by $100 in a country where the average income is only $500 has a much greater impact on human development than the same $100 increase in a country where the average income is $5000 or $50,000. Fig. 4.2 illustrates the concave relationship between life expectancy, expected years of schooling, and mean years of schooling with gross national income per capita. The observed relationship suggests the plausibility of transforming by a nonlinear (concave) function before entering the HDI to reflect the decreasing marginal transformation into valuable capabilities. The type of nonlinearity was varied over years (Klugman et al., 2011a,b).

For example, the use of the logarithmic transformation of income implies that the effect of one additional dollar decreases with the level of income at which this happens. The logarithmic transformation was used in the first HDR in 1990. The logarithms were replaced in the 1991 HDR by a modified Atkinson formulation for the utility $W(y)$ derived from income y, $W(y) = \frac{y^{1-\varepsilon}}{1-\varepsilon}$. The elasticity of the marginal utility of income is ε. If $\varepsilon = 0$, there are no diminishing returns. As ε approaches 1, the equation becomes $W(y) = \ln(y)$.

The modified Atkinson formula (step-wise function) was used to transform the income component of the HDI for the years between 1991 and 1999, using different elasticity at different levels of income, the higher the income, the higher the diminishing return. This transformation was criticized for its inadequate diminishing of marginal returns, for not being continuously concave and because it was too severe on middle-income

countries.[ak] The Atkinson formula was replaced with the logarithmic transformation in 1999. The 1999 HDR lists three advantages of the logarithmic transformation over the Atkinson formula: the discounting is less severe, all levels of income are discounted uniformly, and middle-income countries receive recognition for increases in income that, under the Atkinson formula, would have been very heavily discounted.

Table 4.4 shows the basic statistics on GNI, ln(GNI) and income index, GNIx, obtained by the min-max scaling, calculated from the 2019 HDI data. The diminishing returns of the logarithmic transformation are computed as a simple ratio of the mean[al] of a quartile group to the overall mean. These ratios are compared across the quartile groups to assess the uniformity of discounting.

From Table 4.4, we see that the mean GNI for countries in the lower-middle quartile is about 43.5% of the overall mean. However, after the logarithmic transformation, it becomes 96.7% of the overall mean of logarithms, and finally after normalization, the mean GNI index settles at 93.7% of the overall mean GNI index. The lower-middle and low developed countries get a considerable boost from logarithmic transformation, which is then slightly reduced by the applied scaling (normalization) procedure. The directions of change in the first quartile group is opposite: The relative advantage of high HDI countries (2.56 times higher GNI on average) is considerably reduced by logarithmic transformation and capping at $75,000 (only 1.16 times higher ln(GNI) on average) and then the reduction is corrected by the applied scaling.

The real beneficiaries of the combination of logarithmic transformation and scaling are the countries in the low, lower-middle, and upper-middle development quartiles. The logarithmic transformation and the normalization move both ends of GNI distribution toward the overall mean. Fig. 4.3 presents the densities of the GNI, ln(GNI), and GNI index across 189 countries included in 2019 HDI (published in the 2020 HDR). It is evident that the logarithmic transformation corrects most of the skewness of the original distribution. The truncation effect, evident for the density of GNIx, is due to capping.

The choice of the logarithmic transformation of the per capita GNI is methodologically consistent with the idea that per capita income has diminishing

---

[ak]A good review of the treatment of income dimension and implications is given in Anand and Sen (2000b).

[al]The mean is calculated as an unweighted average across countries.

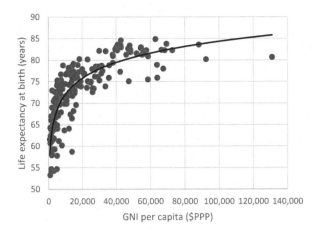

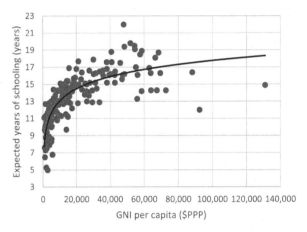

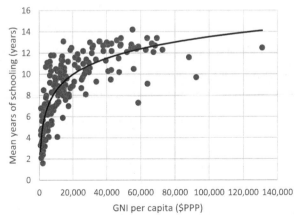

FIG. 4.2 Observed relationship between health and education indicators and income indicator in 2019. (Based on Human Development Report Database. http://www.hdr.undp.org/en/data.)

TABLE 4.4
Effects of logarithmic transformation of GNI.

		GNI	ln (GNI)	GNIx
All countries (189)	Overall mean	20,220	9.34	0.714
	% of overall mean	100	100	100
Highest HDI (47)	Mean	51,709	10.80	0.933
	% of overall mean	255.7	115.6	1.305
Upper-middle (47)	Mean	19,360	9.84	0.790
	% of overall mean	95.7	105.3	110.6
Lower-middle (47)	Mean	8795	9.04	0.669
	% of overall mean	43.5	96.7	93.7
Low (48)	Mean	2779	7.82	0.486
	% of overall mean	13.7	83.8	68.1

Based on Human Development Report Database. http://www.hdr.undp.org/en/data.

marginal returns, but it is not without problems. Some of the problems will be noted in the section on recent criticisms. There are other concave transformations of income with the same property, certainly each of them has the potential to generate a different ranking of countries.

A question that is often asked is why the principle of diminishing marginal returns is not applied to the other variables in the HDI? Why an additional year of life expectancy or education has the same effect on HDI no matter the level at which it occurs? There are arguments for and against transforming the health and education variables to account for diminishing marginal returns. It is true that health and education are not only of intrinsic value; they, like income, are instrumental to other dimensions of human development not included in the HDI (Sen, 1999). Thus, their conversion into other ends may likewise incur diminishing returns. However, the approach taken is to value each year of age or education equally, and therefore, the principle has been applied only to the income indicator. An explanation of this asymmetric approach is provided in Klugman et al. (2011a). "Because the functionings of being healthy and educated are *ends in themselves*, health and education capabilities grow with a change in health and education achievements in direct proportion to the absolute change in these achievements. Income, however, contributes to capabilities only instrumentally, that is, indirectly." Therefore, when variables are interpreted as estimates of capabilities, direct indicators should be distinguished from indirect indicators of capabilities and thus variables should receive differential treatment. In fact, the income dimension in the HDI could be interpreted as an index for other basic capabilities for which income matters—including the social standing that is socially expected in societies with different levels of income. The logarithmic transformation also implies that while income growth does increase the HDI, it does so less at higher levels of income, and thus does not imply that the HDI encourages unfettered growth or consumption.

4.6.2 Scaling (Normalization) of Indicators

Scaling of indicators is necessary for their comparability on the same scale. Each indicator is presented in its own units—income in dollars, life expectancy, expected years of schooling and mean years of schooling in years. Only after scaling they can be combined into a single scalar—a composite index. Scaling of indicators is indeed

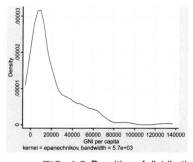
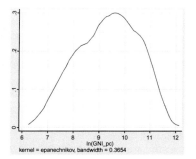
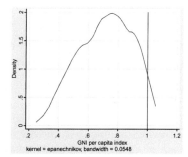

FIG. 4.3 Densities of distribution of the GDP per capita: original, log-transformed, and after rescaling (with capping at $75,000). (Based on Human Development Report Database. http://www.hdr.undp.org/en/data.)

another transformation of indicators and is usually applied as the last transformation before aggregation with other rescaled indicators into a composite index. The HDI has always been based on the linear transformation (min – max scaling) of its components:

$$I(x, m_x, M_x) = \frac{x - m_x}{M_x - m_x} = x \frac{1}{M_x - m_x} - \frac{m_x}{M_x - m_x}$$

where x, m_x, and M_x denote the indicator, and the minimum (lower) and maximum (upper) "goalposts" used for scaling, respectively. This scaling procedure allows indicators to be expressed in terms of their distance to the goalposts and hence tell us how far the country is from the minimum and how far it has to travel before it achieves the "ideal" or aspirational value.

As a linear transformation, the scaling of an original indicator has certain important properties: (i) normalization: $I(m, m, M) = 0$ and $I(M, m, M) = 1$; (ii) monotonicity: given m and M, an increase in x increases the index I; (iii) translation invariance: $I(x + c, m + c, M + c) = I(x, m, M)$; and (iv) homogeneity: for $c > 0$, $I(cx, cm, cM) = I(x, m, M)$.

By scaling life expectancy, education indicators and the natural log of income into indices, their range of variation is between 0 and 1, but the indices may range within different subintervals of $(0,1)$. The range of variation depends on the choice of the goalposts. The range implies the order of implicit weighting, the wider the range, the higher the implicit weighting and vice versa. The HDI scores and the corresponding rankings are sensitive to the choice of goalposts. Panigrahi and Sivramkrishna (2002) note that the sensitivity to the goalposts includes the possibility of an interchanging or reordering of country ranks. In other words, for given indicator values, with one set of goalposts we may have a situation where country 1 is ranked better than country 2; but with a different set, country 2 is ranked better than country 1.

Although the goalposts are determined according to some conceptual and computational principles, they remain arbitrary parameters. It further means that the HDI depends on the arbitrary choices of these parameters, particularly on the choice of the minima. Herrero et al. (2012) noticed that by deducting any positive value from the original indicators in the process of scaling, the position of lower performing countries worsens while the higher ranked countries are very little affected. In that way, the gap between high achieving and low achieving countries is artificially increased. The drawback of the use of minimum goalposts in the scaling is exacerbated in the case of aggregation by geometric mean because of its behavior when a rescaled

component approaches zero. Herrero et al. (2012) suggest scaling only with respect to the maximum goalposts to avoid the drawbacks of using the arbitrary minima.

From 1990 to 1993 (see Table 4.3) the HDI had the goalposts for all three components based on temporal-variable criteria—the observed minimum and maximum in the current year. Calculating the component indices using minimum and maximum values that change each year makes comparison between years difficult. From 1994 to 2009, all indicators of the HDI were rescaled with respect to fixed goalposts. From 2010 to 2013, the maxima were determined as the maximum achieved values over the period from 1980 to the present year, while the minima were kept as fixed values.[am] From 2014, the HDI has been again rescaled by fixed maxima and fixed minima goalposts.

Fixing the goalposts solves the problem of comparison over time. Although due to frequent data revisions by national and international statistical authorities, the HDRs recalculates the entire series of HDI based on the most recent series of the indicators available at the time of publishing every year. The differences in values of the HDI published in different editions of the Reports represent a combined effect of real changes in the HDI, changes in methodology, and data revisions. If the interest is to see the real changes in HDI, the users of HDI should use estimates based on the consistent series of data as published in the same year. These estimates are published in a separate table in Statistical Annex of the HDR, and consistent series of indicators are available in the online database http://hdr.undp.org/data.

The choice of goalposts is informed by a capability approach. Minimum goalposts are interpreted as minimum admissible values, a kind of subsistence level, below which capability is absent, and a society loses ability to develop and ultimately to exist. That is why the minimum goalposts are termed "natural zeros." Agreement on the natural zeroes is indispensable to the measurement exercise, once the natural zeroes have been decided upon, there should be little reason to change or update them.[an]

Maximum goalposts are regarded as an aspirational level or as an ideal level that societies are aspired to achieve. They may change over time in line of what is seen as possible for a country to achieve. Technically, the maximum goalpost keeps the range of index scores

---

[am]The exception was the minimum goalpost for the income component in 2010, which was set at $163 as observed in Zimbabwe in 2008.

[an]As discussed in Alkire and Foster (2010).

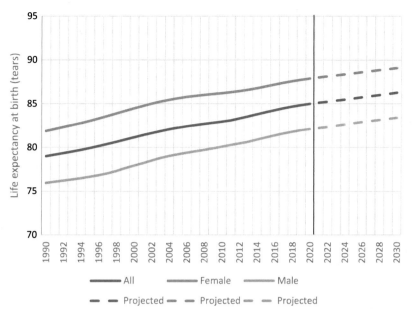

FIG. 4.4 Maximum life expectancy at birth, 1990–2030, estimates and projections. (Based on UNDESA, 2019. World Population Prospects, 2019 Update. UNDESA, New York, NY. https://population.un.org/wpp/.)

within a compact interval (0,1). The "aspirational" state of human development, as expressed by the current four maxima, is life expectancy at 85 years, expected years of schooling at 18 years, mean years of schooling at 15 years, and per capita GNI at $75,000 ($PPP).

In the dimension of health, the minimum value is set to the level that a society needs in order to survive over time. In 2010 it was set at 20 years based on historical evidence.[ao] If a society or a subgroup of society has a life expectancy below the typical age of reproduction, that society would die out. Lower values have occurred during some crises, epidemics, plagues, and wars. The statistical aspect of a selection of the goalpost values will be discussed later in this section. The two education indicators have natural minimum of zero, which is understood as a "natural zero," since societies can subsist without formal education and also there is a lot of learning outside school that is not reflected by the current educational indicators. For income, the minimum goalpost is set at $100 per capita, which is lower than the lowest value attained by any country in recent history

(Liberia in 1995).[ap] Should any country's per capita GNI fall close to or below $100, the minimum will be changed accordingly. The minimum value for income is set low, but it accounts for unmeasured subsistence and nonmarket production not captured in official statistics.

The upper goalpost of 85 years for life expectancy has been in use since 1990, except for 2010–13, when the maximum observed life expectancy (since 1980) was used. Fig. 4.4 presents the trend in maximum life expectancy since 1990 based on the data available from the UNDESA (2019). The maximum of life expectancy at birth exceeded 85 years in 2020. Keeping 85 years as the upper goalpost would mean that a binding capping of life expectancy is set. The binding cap can be interpreted as that years of life expectancy above 85 years are not contributing to human development, which is contrary to the basic idea of longevity in human development.

[ao]Maddison (2010), Riley (2005), Noorbakhsh (1998b), Wikipedia, Life expectancy, https://en.wikipedia.org/wiki/Life expectancy. Accessed on 15 May 2020.

[ap]Per capita GNI in constant $PPP is often revised due to revisions of population data, rebasing the series, new PPP conversion rates and a variety of updates in the system of national accounts. Liberia reached the historical minimum GNI per capita of $261 (constant 2011 $PPP) in 1995 according to data available in 2020.

The upper goalpost for expecting years of schooling (EYS) is set at 18 years which coincides to achieving a master's degree (or equivalent level)[aq] in most countries. Looking at the distribution of EYS used in the 2020 HDR, even 10 countries exceeded the upper goalpost of 18 years. Table 4.5 presents expected years of schooling along with the theoretical duration at each level of schooling for these 10 countries. The duration of the tertiary education level is left open-ended.

The inflated EYS come from the school gross enrollment rates (GER) exceeding 100% at the primary and the secondary level of schooling. It is possible that the GER is greater than 100% due to the inclusion of over-aged and underaged students. However, it should not be reflected in calculation of the expected years of schooling in a way that in some countries children may expect to achieve more than 7 years of primary education although the official duration of primary education is only 5 years. The progress and the advantage in EYS should not be based on the repetition of grades. Because of these concerns, the upper goalpost was set at 18 years. Setting the upper goalpost on EYS does not mean that there is an upper bound to what schooling can contribute to human development, but it allows more meaningful comparison across index scores.

The aspirational upper goalpost for mean years of schooling (MYS) was set at 15 years in 2013, which was a projected maximum for 2025. As Fig. 4.5 shows, MYS has increased steadily since 1990 but with periods of slower growth, which might be related to irregular updating of MYS, mainly based on decennial population censuses and surveys with different reference years for different countries. The annual values of MYS are obtained by linear interpolation at the country level.

Two educational indicators are first scaled by the corresponding upper goalposts and then aggregated by the arithmetic mean (with equal weights) into the education index. Between 2010 and 2013 the aggregation of educational indictors was done by the geometric mean, which was criticized as an unnecessary complexity of the new index and that the full substitutability between indicators should be allowed. Between 1991 and 2009, the education index was a weighted average of scaled adult literacy and gross enrollment ratio with respective weights of 2/3 and 1/3, representing roughly the relative sizes of subpopulations of adults (15 and older) and of school age.

The income variable (GDP per capita in $PPP) had the upper goalpost set at $40,000 between 1994 and 2009. At the time when the upper goalpost of income was introduced, it was not a binding cap. However, by 2009, even 13 countries had the GDP per capita (in $PPP) above the limit of $40,000. From 2010, the income variable has been gross national income (GNI) per capita. Between 2010 and 2013, the upper goalpost was set as the observed maximum across countries since 1980. Defined in that way, the upper goalpost was not binding but was likely to be an outlier of the income distribution across countries. From 2014, the upper goalpost was set at the fixed value of $75,000. The idea behind capping is to emphasize that increases in average income beyond $40,000 and later beyond $75,000 make no direct contribution to computation of the HDI. The critiques, however, identify the effect of capping the income as that the additional income beyond the cap would not yield increase in capabilities. Some critiques point out that an increase in average income increases the range of choices and capabilities at any income level and so enhance human development (Ranis, 2004). While this might be true, it is important to note that countries are not punished for exceeding the upper goalpost, rather any additional income over the upper goalpost does not directly boost the country's score or improve its ranking. However, any additional improvement in health or education due to this excess income is captured by indicators of health and education.

There are critics that find the upper goalpost of $75,000 being too high and advocate a lower capping. Hickel (2020) finds that the HDI pays no attention to ecology, and "retains an emphasis on high levels of income that—given strong correlations between income and ecological impact—violates sustainability principles." Hickel's analysis points out that the problem with the HDI is that all the top performers are exhibiting high and unsustainable levels of ecological impact while achieving very high incomes. Using data from the 2016 HDR, thus referring to 2015, Hickel finds that there are a number of countries with relatively low income that achieve very high levels of human development—Greece, Chile, and Portugal have higher life expectancy than the United States with less than half the income per capita. Costa Rica has a life expectancy that exceeds that of the United States with one-fourth of the income per capita. Similarly, he points out that there are a number of countries that score highly on the education index with relatively low levels of income—Kazakhstan's education levels rival Austria's, with half of the income per capita, Belarus exceeds

---

[aq]For international comparability purposes, the term 'Master's or equivalent level' is labeled as ISCED level 7. ISCED stands for the International Standard Classification of Education.

TABLE 4.5
Theoretical duration and expected years of schooling at each level of education.

	PRIMARY		SECONDARY		POSTSECONDARY NONTERTIARY		Tertiary	TOTAL EYS	
	Theoretical duration	Expected years	Theoretical duration	Expected years	Theoretical duration	Expected years	Expected years	Reported	Meaningful
Australia	7	7.02	6	7.64	1	0.76	5.08	22.00	19.1
Belgium	6	6.20	6	9.10	1	0.44	3.82	19.80	16.8
Denmark	7	7.04	6	7.64	–	–	4.11	18.90	17.1
Finland	6	6.02	6	8.80	1	0.36	4.29	19.40	17.3
Iceland	7	7.03	7	8.08	1	0.28	3.79	19.10	18.8
Ireland	8	8.07	5	7.71	2	0.40	3.58	18.70	18.6
Netherlands	6	6.30	6	8.02	1	–	4.24	18.50	17.2
New Zealand	6	6.06	7	7.98	1	0.65	4.19	18.80	18.2
Norway	7	7.01	6	6.96	1	0.10	4.06	18.10	18.1
Sweden	7	7.55	6	8.63	2	0.18	3.32	19.50	18.3

Based on UNESCO, 2020. UIS Glossary of Statistical Terms. http://uis.unesco.org/en/glossary.

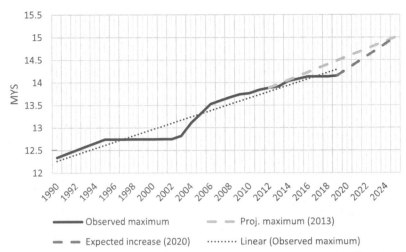

FIG. 4.5 Maximum mean years of schooling, 1990–2025, estimates and projections. (Based on Human Development Report Database. http://www.hdr.undp.org/en/data.)

Austria with one-third of the income per capita, while Georgia and Ukraine rival Austria with less than one-fifth of the income per capita. Based on his analysis, Hickel proposes a "sufficiency threshold" on per capita income at the level of $20,000. It should be noted that the logarithmic transformation implies that differences in income at higher levels of income are relatively small, and that the logarithmic transformation *plus* the cap can, together, make the way in which income is reflected in the HDI less of a concern than what transpires from this type of criticism.

Other group of critics finds the use of goalposts not only arbitrary but also unnecessary. Lind (2019) finds that limiting the HDI and its components by upper goalposts suggests that human development has an upper limit. Inspired by the construction of the Life Quality Index (Pandey et al., 2006), Lind suggests a new index of human development that combines the same three dimensions of the HDI but it is parameterized in such a way that all its parameters can be estimated from data without setting any upper limits: $H = (\text{LE}^c \cdot \text{GNI}^g)(s \cdot \text{EYS} + m \cdot \text{MYS})/R$, where R is the reference value that sets H equal to unity for the world in year 2000. The four parameters (c, g, s, and m) are derived from the observed relationships of the included indicators. For example, Lind observes that between 1990 and 2015, educational indicators grew by $\Delta\text{EYS} = 2.92$ years and $\Delta\text{MYS} = 2.41$ years. Under the assumption that this maximizes the overall utility, Lind then concludes that adding 1 year to EYS is valued equal to $2.41/2.92 = 0.825$ added years of MYS, and that the combined educational index is $\text{EDU} = 0.825 \cdot \text{EYS} + \text{MYS}$.

If the educational index of the current HDI with the upper goalposts of 18 and 15 for EYS and MYS, respectively, with the lower goalpost set at 0, is expressed in the Lind's proposed form it would be $\text{EDU} = 0.833 \cdot \text{EYS} + \text{MYS}$. Thus, it seems that there is no large difference in two approaches to parameterization of the educational index, although in the case of the HDI the parameters s and m are derived from order statistics (min and max) while Lind's proposal is based on estimated mean values.

Herrero et al. (2012) took aim on the lower goalposts in the HDI formula and pointed out the negative implications of using the nonzero lower goalposts when transforming the original values into relative gains. In addition to already mentioned arbitrariness in choosing the lower goalpost, they underlined that changing the minimum affects the net value of the variable $(x - \min(x))$ and so the ordering of the countries. However, most importantly, they pointed out that subtracting any positive value from the original variables worsens the standing of the countries with a lower performance. In particular, when aggregation across dimensions is by geometric mean, the use of min values in the normalization has an extra impact on the marginal rates of substitution because when one component is approaching zero values the associated marginal rates of substitution will increase substantially, but to a large extent artificially, because of the subtraction of the minimum. As a remedy, they suggest scaling of the original values X by a reference value X* chosen to allow the interpretation of the resulting score, X/X*. This

TABLE 4.6
Some basic statistics related to index scores of the 2019 HDI and its components.

	Mean[a]	Range (max-min)	Standard deviation
Health index	0.810	0.486	0.114
Education index[b]	0.659	0.694	0.173
Standard of living index	0.714	0.695	0.173
HDI	0.722	0.563	0.150

[a]Unweighted mean.
[b]Education index is the arithmetic mean of the EYS index and MYS index.Based on Human Development Report Database. http://www.hdr.undp.org/en/data.

normalization does not affect relative valuations of any two countries. Also, in the case of aggregation by geometric mean the ranking or the associated marginal rates of substitution are not affected. Such normalization implies that for the mapping to (0,1) interval using $X^* \geq \max(X)$ would be appropriate.

An important statistical criterion used in selecting the goalposts for the HDI indicators was to achieve a balance between the width of the range (max-min) and the spread of the index scores (standard deviation). Index scores that take too close values prevent countries from being meaningfully distinguished from one another. On the other hand, the index scores that are widely spread may prevent relatively similar countries from achieving similar scores. For example, once the lower goalpost (minimum) is fixed for income, the choice of the upper goalpost is decided to make index scores based on income better balanced and comparable with other index scores combined into the HDI. Table 4.6 presents the ranges and the standard deviations of the dimensional index scores and the HDI across 189 countries based on data for 2019.

Table 4.6 shows that the education index and the standard of living (GNI per capita) index are balanced in a very similar way, while the health (LE) index exhibits much lower range and a lower spread. This means that the health index has a lower power of differentiation between countries[ar] compared to other two indices and that it needs a "rebalancing" by selecting a new upper

goalpost. As it will be explained in the subsection on weighting, the lower variability of the health index also implies a lower implicit weight of this dimension.

Several critiques, including Anand and Sen (1994), raised a question about the ability of the chosen indicators to differentiate countries, especially at the top and at the bottom of the distribution. Hoyland et al. (2012) found that the difference in the HDI amongst developed countries is only the random noise and that information contained in the HDI cannot differentiate developed countries. Anand and Sen suggest that for countries at different level of human development different indicators can be used. The justification is based on observation that high developed countries differ very little in literacy rates, and that the difference in life expectancy at birth is becoming rapidly smaller over time. The proposed approach, combined with differential weighting of common indicators, would most likely solve the problem of a weak differentiation of countries at different levels of development but at the expense of loss of universality, strict comparability, and simplicity.

Both mentioned papers refer to the HDI in its pre-2010 form, thus with adult literacy, gross enrollment ratio and GDP per capita. The change in the HDI indicators in 2010 was supposed to increase the differentiation between countries, particularly by the education index. Fig. 4.6 presents the average distance between country scores in each index by the HDI category. The subsection on ranking and classification of countries has more on HDI categories.

The differentiation of countries by life expectancy index is weaker than by other dimensional indices. It is particularly weak in the very high HDI category. This is a signal to increase the upper goalpost for life expectancy and so increase the range. However, the differentiation between countries by all indices in the very high HDI and the high HDI categories is weaker compared to the differentiation in the medium and the low HDI category. As more countries are improving their HDI scores, they are moving up to higher HDI categories so that the absolute distance between countries within these categories is decreasing.

4.6.3 Weighting

Once the HDI indicators are normalized into dimensional index scores, some weighting is necessary in the process of aggregating them into a composite index. There is a general criticism of composite indices given the often arbitrary character of the procedures used to weigh their various components. Usually, there is a little understanding of normative implications of the choice of the weights, despite often well described and presented

---

[ar]The power of differentiation refers to the ability of a chosen indicator and the corresponding goalposts to differentiate countries, Kovacevic (2010).

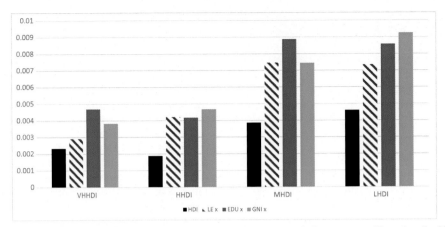

FIG. 4.6 Average distance between countries, by human development index category. (Based on the Human Development Report Database. http://www.hdr.undp.org/en/data.)

weighting procedures. The weights are perceived to be "importance weights." Also, a single set of weights is applied to the whole world, independently of the heterogeneity of people's preference toward income, health, education, etc. In principle, different weights could be used for different countries and for different years, recognizing differences in attitudes and preferences. Stiglitz et al. (2009), Ravallion (2010), Decancq and Lugo (2013), and Decancq et al. (2019) suggest allowing the weights to vary across countries, to take account of the preference of local people or policy-makers. However, such complexity would challenge practical and meaningful comparison across countries and across time.

The most common practice, though arbitrary as well, is to set equal weights for each component. Such a choice of weights is due to uncertainty about the correct weights arising from a lack of theoretical or other guidance.[as] Hence, one of major critiques about the HDI concerns the equal weights assigned to the three components. HDR 1991 justifies the equal weighting procedure by explaining that the three dimensions of the HDI are equally important and so the dimensional indices are equally important, and therefore, they are equally weighted. Streeten (1994) echoes the HDR's explanation of equal weighting and defends use of a simple average stating that it is a good tool for focusing on decreasing gaps between countries, and that there is a political appeal to a simple method. Kelly (1991) recognizes that it is difficult to justify any set of weights but that testing the sensitivity of the HDI and ranking to alternative weights would have been useful. Anand and Sen (1997), write: "Since any choice of weights should be

open to questioning and debating in public discussions, it is crucial that the judgments that are implicit in such weighting be made as clear and comprehensible as possible and thus be open to public scrutiny."

For HDI, weights of 1/3 for each of three dimensions and 1/2 for educational indices with the educational dimension are made explicit, and they reflect the "perceived" importance of each indicator involved. The approach taken by the HDI is normative, i.e., it depends on the value judgments about the trade-offs and are not based on the actual distribution of the achievements in the society under analysis. Several studies (UNDP, 1993; Noorbakhsh, 1998b; Kovacevic, 2010; Nguefack-Tsague, 2011) reported results of the principal component analysis (PCA) of the correlation matrix of the HDI components, showing that the data driven PCA-based weights are practically equal to 1/3, after normalization, and thus support the equal explicit weighting. The structure of the data and correlations between the indicators are the determinants of the implicit weights, i.e., "actual importance" of each indicator in the index (Paruolo, 2013; Becker et al., 2017). The structure of data includes the range of variation, the spread of variation, the chosen goalposts, and the correlations.

The implicit weights of the HDI components are estimated by applying methodology[at] developed by Paruolo (2013) and Becker et al. (2017) for the

---

[as]Seth and McGilverey (2018).

[at]The assessment is based on the coefficient of nonlinear association $\eta_i^2 = V_{x_i}(E_{x\sim i}(W|x_i))/V(W)$, where $E_{x\sim i}(W|x_i)$ is the mean of W when x_i is fixed, $x\sim i$ denotes all the components except x_i. $V(W)$ is the unconditional variance of the composite index W.

TABLE 4.7
Explicit (perceived) and implicit (actual) weights in HDI.

2019 HDI	Explicit weight	Implicit weight (η_i^2)	Standardized implicit weight	Difference	Relative difference (%)
Health	0.333	0.8409	0.3137	−0.0196	−5.9
Education	0.333	0.9213	0.3437	0.0104	3.1
Income	0.333	0.9186	0.3424	0.0091	2.7

Based on Human Development Report 2020 Database. http://hdr.undp.org/data.

assessment of the effect of each component x_i on the composite index $W(x)$. The estimated implicit weights are then compared to the explicit perceived importance weights and the deviation is estimated. The results of the assessment for the 2019 HDI are given in Table 4.7. Life expectancy is underweighted by slightly less than 6%, education is overweighted by 3.1%, and the income component is overweighted by 2.7%. This result coincides with the conclusion derived from the observed differences in range and spread of variation of three HDI components. From Table 4.7, it is clear that some rebalancing of life expectancy index should be considered.

4.6.4 Aggregation

Prior to 2010, the aggregation of the HDI component indices at the country level was done by the most widespread linear aggregation:

$$\text{HDI}(x, y, z) = \frac{1}{3}\left[I(x, m_x, M_x) + I(y, m_y, M_y) + I(z, m_z, M_z)\right]$$

From 2010, the aggregation is done by the geometric mean:

$$\text{HDI}(x, y, z) = \sqrt[3]{\left[I(x, m_x, M_x) \cdot I(y, m_y, M_y) \cdot I(z, m_z, M_z)\right]}$$

The change was justified in part to deal with the criticisms of perfect substitutability between dimensions implicit in the arithmetic mean. With the geometric mean, poor performance in any dimension is directly reflected in the HDI because there is no longer perfect substitutability across dimensions. This aggregation captures how well rounded a country's performance is across the three dimensions. There are some "positive side-effects" such as the independence of the ranking to the choice of the upper goalposts. Thus, changes in the upper goalposts would not imply changes in ranking. However, sensitivity to the choice of the lower goalposts remains. It should be emphasized that the HDI is introduced to represent an index of capabilities, not a

production or utility function meant to be maximized, even though it is possible to interpret degrees of substitutability in the context of generalized means, as discussed below.

Both the arithmetic mean and the geometric mean are special cases of the generalized mean defined as

$$W(x) = \begin{cases} \left\{\sum_{k}^{K} w_k (I(x_k))^\beta\right\}^{\frac{1}{\beta}}, \text{ for } \beta \neq 0 \\ \prod_{k}^{K} (I(x_k))^{w_k}, \text{ for } \beta = 0 \end{cases} \tag{4.1}$$

where $x = (x_1, \ldots, x_K)$ represents K indicators; for the sake of simplicity the component indices are expressed without an explicit writing of minimum and maximum used for scaling of x_k, i.e., $I(x_k) = I(x_k, m_k, M_k) = \frac{x_k - m_k}{M_k - m_k}$. The weights w_k sum to one. Parameter β is related to the elasticity of substitution between the component indices, $\sigma = \frac{1}{1-\beta}$ (Arrow et al., 1961).

When $\beta = 1$, the generalized mean becomes the arithmetic mean and the elasticity of substitution is infinite, thus making the dimensional indices to be perfect substitutes. Expression (4.1) suggests that the degree of substitutability is the same for all pairs of dimensions, which may not be sensible assumption to make. The marginal substitutability is discussed in more details in the next section.

When $\beta = 0$, the general mean takes the form of the geometric mean and the elasticity of substitution is equal to 1. An elasticity of 1 means that any two dimensional indices substitute each other in the same proportion, that is $p\%$ of one substitutes $p\%$ of the other.

The generalized mean satisfies a list of basic axioms: (i) continuity—$W(x)$ is continuous at all points, i.e., W does not change abruptly due to a change in any of its dimensions; (ii) normalization—if achievements in all dimensions are equal to μ, then $W = \mu$; (iii) linear homogeneity—if all achievements are doubled or tripled, W is doubled or tripled, respectively; (iv) symmetry in dimensions—permuting components does not change W, i.e., all dimensions are equally important; (v) monotonicity—if an achievement in one dimension increases, while others remain same, W increases; (vi) population replication invariance—if the same population is replicated more than once, the W remains the same; (vii) subgroup consistency—if the general mean of one subgroup rises and the other is unaltered, then overall general mean must rise.

There are other suggestions in the literature for composite indices with imperfect substitutability between components. Chakravarty (2003, 2011) suggested the arithmetic mean of discounted achievements in each dimension $\sum_{k}^{K} w_k (I(x_k))^r$, $0 < r < 1$. Mauro (2018) proposed a composite multidimensional synthesis indicator (MSI) in the context of monitoring well-being of a person/unit. Considering a country as a unit of interest, with the achievements $x = (x_1, \ldots, x_K)$ in K dimensions, their proposal takes the form:

$$1 - \left[\frac{1}{K} \sum_{k}^{K} (1 - I(x_k))^{1/g(x)} \right]^{g(x)}$$, where $g(x)$ is a generic

real-valued function of the scaled achievements x, with $g(x) \geq 1$. The function $g(x)$ allows a high degree of flexibility of the MSI. As a result, theoretical considerations regarding the structure of substitutability rates between achievements and the implied trade-offs can be considered with a higher flexibility. Krisnakumar (2018) revisited use of a composite index defined as $\min_{k=1, \ldots, K} \{I(x_k)\}$, which implies perfect complementarity. The approach has been discussed in the literature before by Segura and Moya (2009), who called it "the noncompensatory HDI." It is premised on the view that when basic dimensions such as health and education are concerned, allowing for substitutability does not make sense within the human development framework, and therefore, a min index is best suited as a measurement tool for temporal and spatial comparison of the country achievements.

Some authors add more axioms to gain better properties for the composite index. For example, Chakravarty (2003) requests that (viii) for any component indicator, the achievement difference is greater at lower attainment levels, given that the values of other attributes remain fixed. Herrero et al. (2012) introduce another set of axioms to characterize a family of social evaluation indices; (x) minimal lower boundedness, that requires the index to take on its minimal value whenever a variable attains its minimum level across all members of the society; (xi) ratio consistency—if two social state vectors have one component with the same value, then the ratio of the corresponding indices does not change if that common component changes to a different one. They note that the ratio consistency requirement is cardinal in nature and involves a separability feature in the evaluation index. Then, they prove that only geometric mean with equal weights satisfies the ratio consistency.

4.7 SUMMARY OF THE CRITIQUES AND A DEBATE ABOUT THE SWITCH TO THE GEOMETRIC MEAN

The switch to the geometric mean in 2010 generated intense debates and several critical papers—Klugman et al. (2011a,b), Ravallion (2010, 2011, 2012), Herrero et al. (2012), Zambrano (2014, 2017), Anand (2018), Seth and Villar (2017), Fleurbaey (2018), Rodriguez (2020), among others. While many scholars saw the new functional form as an improvement, others were critical.

We single out two main criticisms of the change to the geometric mean. The first, expressed among others by Sen (2013) and Anand (2018), is that the geometric mean is not very intuitive, simple, or transparent, thereby using it in the HDI as a method of aggregation is undercutting one of the key advantages of the HDI—simplicity. Anand was more specific highlighting issues related to disaggregation of the HDI to its component indicators and the sensitivity to the lower goalposts for scaling the component indicators. Further, the old HDI, based on the arithmetic mean, is additively separable in its component indicators so that the contribution of each component can be separately identified and quantified as a percentage of the overall index. By contrast, it is not possible to disaggregate or "decompose" the value of the HDI based on the geometric mean, although it is possible to disaggregate the logarithm of HDI and express the percentage contribution of the logarithm of each subcomponent to the logarithm of HDI. The HDI based on the geometric mean of the component indicators is extremely sensitive to the lower bound—when the value of an indicator approaches its lower bound, the HDI approaches zero and all corresponding marginal rates of substitutions degenerate beyond a reasonable interpretation. In the case of aggregation by the arithmetic mean, the lower bound is not critical.

The second argument concerns the different marginal rates of substitution between dimensions at different income levels in the case of the multiplicative form of the HDI (i.e., calculated by the geometric mean). Ravallion (2010, 2011, 2012) emphasizes the dramatic differences in valuation of an additional year in life expectancy between income-rich and income-poor countries. These extreme differences are partly related to the geometric mean, which is equivalent to a log transformation of each dimension, imposing an additional log transformation on the income component. In this way, the impact of higher incomes on HDI is heavily discounted. Ravallion also expressed a concern of the low absolute valuation of an additional year of life implicit in the HDI for poor countries. In 2010, Zimbabwe had the income level of $176, very close to the lower goalpost ($163) so that any marginal rate of substitution for Zimbabwe deemed degenerated. Ravallion finds these different trade-offs troubling and inferred that the value of life is far too low in poor countries and would lead to the policy conclusion to invest more in the health of rich countries where life is more valuable. Anand (2018) also emphasized how the partial derivative of the HDI with respect to life expectancy was no longer constant, but rather increasing with income and decreasing in life expectancy—he found problematic that the marginal contribution of life expectancy to the HDI increased with income because he interpreted this as implying attributing a higher dollar value to a longer life in richer countries. Fleurbaey (2018) suggested a different interpretation: to an impartial observer a year of life in a poorer country would be less desirable than in a richer country. Anand also took issue with the partial derivative to income, which is no longer inversely proportional to income, as with the arithmetic HDI, but in addition to income it inversely depends on an additional income term.

Klugman et al. (2011a,b), Zambrano (2017), Fleurbaey (2018), and Rodriguez (2020) argued that while it is the case that the differences in the trade-offs between poor and rich countries are very large, probably excessively so, they do not imply the conclusions that Ravallion draws. In a country that is very rich, additional income has hardly any human development impact, while in a poor country, it has a huge impact. So, instead of interpreting these figures as "values attached to human life," one should emphasize that they rather reflect differences in the importance of added income for human development (see also Klasen, 2018). Rodriguez (2020) wrote, "if a society is very near to its subsistence level of any variable, then it makes a lot of sense for it to strongly emphasize improvements in that dimension. Being near subsistence in the income dimension, means living on the edge of starvation, and if even a little additional income will help you avoid starving to death, it makes sense for you to give up a lot in terms of other valuable dimensions of your life to

ensure your survival." Also, the marginal substitution rate for life expectancy can be interpreted as an answer to a question—what percent of annual income per capita people would be inclined to trade for a year in life expectancy while keeping their current level of human development. In a country at the low level of the HDI, people would not be inclined to sacrifice a lot of income for keeping a low level of HDI, but in a country at a higher level of the HDI, people have "incentive" to trade-off more income and keep the higher HDI level.

The HDI is not a tool that is made for assessing policy consideration about an allocation of funds between countries, as Ravallion alluded, since a little or nothing is known about the costs of country-specific improvements and the world evaluation is completely missing. This point is particularly well emphasized by Fleurbaey (2018) who wrote "when the UNDP provides the list of country HDIs, it does not explicitly assess how much priority should be given to the less developed countries and this may confuse readers, suggesting that the list by itself plays the role of a social welfare function." If we were to construct a global social welfare function, there are strong reasons to expect that it places greater weight on marginal improvements in countries with lower standards of living, and therefore to advise for investing more resources in expanding capabilities in "Zimbabwe rather than Italy."

As a better choice of the functional form for the HDI, Ravallion suggested Chakravarty (2003) generalized HDI: $\sum_k^K w_k (I(x_k))^r, 0 < r < 1$, but also suggested a modification that concerns the income index, which, in the original Chakravarty's form, is based on the logarithmic transformation, $I(y) = \frac{[\ln(y) - \ln(m_y)]}{[\ln(M_y) - \ln(m_y)]}$. Instead, Ravallion suggests that income is not transformed so that $I(y) = \frac{y - m_y}{M_y - m_y}$. This change is important since it removes a source of the positive income effect on the weights implicit in the Chakravarty's HDI. Because of the exponent $0 < r < 1$, the diminishing marginal return to income is still in place.

Zambrano (2017) noticed an apparent paradox that the Chakravarty's HDI, one favored by Ravallion, produces more sensible trade-offs, but the HDI based on the geometric mean produces more sensible rankings. Zambrano finds that the strong concavity of the logarithmic transformation of income imbedded in the HDI was about 5 times more important than the multiplicative functional form of the index in explaining the tradeoffs between life expectancy and income across countries. The additive form of the modified Chakravarty's HDI has a higher degree of substitutability across dimensions and weakened diminishing returns of income component because of eliminating the log transformation, so that it is possible that a country ranks overall very high based on its high income only, with little or no regard to its attainments in other dimensions of the HDI. As a resolution, Zambrano suggested a "hybrid" HDI which keeps its multiplicative form but with the income component transformed by a concave power function y^r, $0 < r < 1$ rather than with the logarithmic function. The paper also provided a way to determine the power of the transformation based on a question on how much of income people are willing to trade for an additional year of life expectancy. However, this transformation could imply a stronger role for income in increasing the HDI than with the logarithmic transformation, taking the HDI farther away from the principle that income is instrumentally important as an enabler of basic capabilities other than health and education, and less and less so as income grows.

4.8 COUNTRY RANKING AND CLASSIFICATION BY HDI

The HDI is an ordinal measure designed with the general idea of ordering countries by their relative ranking according to the country's achievements in three basic capabilities. Using the HDI ranking the country can gauge its progress against the benchmark—rankings of other countries. A steady time series of rankings allows a country to study the dynamics of changes of its own ranking over time. However, ranking is a relative statistical operation, while it reflects the achievements of the country, it also depends on performance of other countries, particularly of those with similar HDI values. It also depends on the total number of ranked countries. For example, only 144 countries have HDI values and ranks in 1990, but even 189 in 2019. This makes the analysis of time series of ranking misleading because it is not the same being 50 among 144 countries and being 50 among 189. The change in ranking depends on the change in the HDI of the country but also on the magnitude of change for the "competing" countries. Then, it becomes important to mutually analyze both, the changes in HDI scores, which reflect achievements of the country only and rankings that show the relative position of the country vis a vis other countries. As it was underlined previously, the change in ranking should be assessed only from the consistent data and not by comparing ranks published in different editions of the reports. Beginning with the 2013 HDR, only three decimals of the HDI have been used for ranking of countries. Countries with the same rank are sorted

alphabetically within the rank. Another historical note, the HDI, was an index of deprivations from 1990 to 1993 (see Table 4.3) and countries were ranked accordingly, so in the 1990 HDR, Niger was ranked first and Japan was the last (146). From 1994, the HDI was an index of achievements and countries were ranked accordingly, the highest achieving country is the first, and the least achieving is the last.

In parallel, countries are divided into several categories of human development. Until 2009, there were three categories low, medium, and high defined with the fixed cut-off points of HDI at 0.5 and 0.8. In 2009, based on the value of HDI, countries were classified as low, medium, high, and very high human development countries. The ranges were 0–0.499 for low HDI, 0.500–0.799 for medium HDI, 0.800–0.899 for high HDI, and greater than 0.900 for very high HDI.

Between 2010 and 2013, countries were classified into four categories but defined in relative terms: very high human development category is the highest quartile of the HDI distribution, the next, the high human development category is the second highest quartile, and so on. Therefore, each category has the same number of countries. One benefit of a purely relative approach to classification is that there are no arbitrary numerical cutoffs whose meaning may vary with each new update of the goalposts or methodology in general.[au] However, without an absolute scale against which a country can judge its own progress independently of other possible influences, such relative classification may have less practical value for the country. A purely relative approach provides less or no incentives for determination of progress by the country. One quarter of all countries with HDI will always be in the low human development category. A country from the medium human development category must decline in its HDI and drop into the low category so that a country from the low can move up. A forward-looking government needs an absolute measure of progress so that the country can aim to changing the category, an objective whose achievements depends only on the country.

The Human Development Report 2014 reintroduced a system of fixed cut-off points for the four categories of human development achievements. The cut-off points (COP) are not completely arbitrary. They are obtained as the HDI values calculated using the 25th, 50th, and 75th percentile of the distributions of component indicators.

[au]Wolff et al. (2011).

TABLE 4.8	
Cut-off points for HDI categories.	
Very high human development	0.800 and above
High human development	0.700 to 0.799
Medium human development	0.550 to 0.699
Low human development	Below 0.550

HDR, 2020. Technical Notes. http://hdr.undp.org/en/content/hdr-technical-notes.

$$COP_q = HDI(LE_q, MYS_q, EYS_q, GNIpc_q), q = 1, 2, 3$$

The resulting HDI values are averaged over the 10-year interval (2004–13) and rounded to 0.55, 0.7, and 0.8. The ranges of the HDI are given in Table 4.8.

4.9 DATA ISSUES AND PERSPECTIVES

The HDI depends on data availability and data quality. Although data availability has improved over the years, it is still insufficient. Often, values for some indicators are nonexistent or not up to date for some countries. Such data gaps severely limit a possibility of enhancing the global human development composite measures by means of adding new indicators or improving the coverage.

Collecting data to measure human development is far from being straightforward. The main sources of data for development have been known to overlook or underrepresent certain population groups. The most marginalized groups may be invisible to standard survey techniques, including those who are refugees, migrants, homeless, indigenous, disabled, or old. It is still true that many indicators do not disaggregate by age or gender. For example, many countries do not publish male and female average incomes separately. These data gaps prevent efficient monitoring of some essential human development issues such as gender equity in the workplace.

When data are based on different methodologies, originate from different data sources with different timelines and possibly different indicator definitions across countries, the comparability of human development measures is extremely limited. Statistics published by national statistical offices often cannot be directly compared between two countries, since they might use different methodologies to collect and process the data and different data sources, timelines, or indicator definitions. International statistical agencies produce regional and global statistics, aggregating national data but also calculating estimates when national data are missing. Discrepancies between statistics available from national statistical offices and international statistical agencies have been a major concern in monitoring human development. Governments may argue that data that international agencies use to monitor development advances in their country are not the most recent or do not correspond to their own records. To comply with transparency, ensure trust in official statistics and base policies on accurate information, the origins of these discrepancies must be understood. Fig. 4.7 presents a summary of quality of data for four indicators used to compute the 2019 HDI for 189 countries.

Apart from the above data and methodological challenges in measuring human development by the HDI, there are also various practical difficulties, which pose critical challenges for a wider human development assessment mainly due to lack of data and underdeveloped methodologies[av]:

- The measurement of material wellbeing involves significant difficulties with measuring quality (e.g., or education or health) and nonmarket (e.g., unpaid housework and care) services.
- The measurement of opportunities and capabilities involves attempting to measure what people could do (capabilities), as opposed to what they actually do (functionings).
- The measurement of self-reported subjective wellbeing is complicated by the various types of wellbeing that could be reported (e.g., mood happiness, life satisfaction or feelings of agency and autonomy).[aw]
- The estimation of future wellbeing involves taking a position on (at least) future preferences, discoveries, technological developments, population growth, intergenerational and environmental constraints, as well as planetary boundaries, which are currently not incorporated.
- The centrality of human beings in this anthropocentric development narrative overlooks the interdependence of species as well as issues of environmental and planetary pressures—as explored in the 2020 HDR, issues that the Covid-19 pandemic and climate change illustrate as unprecedented risks for the human civilization in a way not confronted before (there have been other pandemics, but there has

[av]Gruen and Spender (2014).

[aw]Agency in this context refers to the capacity to act with purpose to one's advantage. This capacity is considered to be more important for subjective wellbeing as society becomes richer and basic material needs are met.

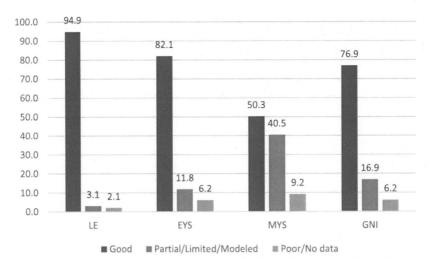

FIG. 4.7 Quality of HDI component indicators data. (Based on Human Development Report Database. http://www.hdr.undp.org/en/data.)

been an increase in the frequency of zoonotic diseases, which is tied to increased planetary pressures).

- The dual issue of intergenerational and intragenerational equity—whether the patterns of consumption in society are fair and efforts to improve human development are sustainable over time, or they are depleting natural resources and stealing opportunities from future generations.

The HDI and the complementary composite indices comprise of indicators that correspond to 12 different Sustainable Development Goals (SDG), and remain relevant for the assessment of the human development aspects of the 2030 Agenda[ax]; e.g., how much people expanded their capabilities while achieving SDGs.

4.10 CONCLUSION

This chapter has outlined some important aspects of human development paradigm and its measurements, with a focus on contributions of the HDI to thinking about development. It also surveyed some major challenges and criticisms and provided notes on how these criticisms were addressed and hints about a possible future evolution.

[ax]The Sustainable Development Goals are a collection of 17 interlinked global goals designed to be a "blueprint to achieve a better and more sustainable future for all". The SDGs were set in 2015 by the United Nations General Assembly and are intended to be achieved by the year 2030, hence 2030 Agenda.

The simplicity of its methodology—the shift to the geometric mean notwithstanding, with Klasen (2018) noting that, in reality, differences in rankings are relatively minor compared with the use of the arithmetic mean—the reliance on publicly available national data, the transparency of procedures, and ease of interpretation of the results have been the main factors in the success of the HDI over the past three decades. HDI and related human development measures are evolving based on many inputs from a wider community of researchers and users. It is pointed out that occasionally some of critiques are based on misunderstanding and misinterpretation of the HDI. Although the simplicity of the HDI brought its prominence, the HDI has never been as simple as one might think, particularly in the domain of interpretation and communication.

The HDI may not have achieved everything, but it has achieved a lot. With all its limitations, the HDI, as a simple, robust, and transparent measure of broader human well-being, is credited, among other achievements, with the following:

- It helped establishing human development framework within which a rich pluralism of ideas, thoughts, methods, and approaches about social, economic, and environmental development coexist.
- It has changed the way development is perceived and analyzed, and development outcomes are measured. Income is no longer seen as the sum of human life.
- It has served as a powerful instrument of public and policy advocacy. It has contributed a lot to public

communication, with a strong advocacy role. It has also affected policy-making and targeting.

- It has led to exercises for generating more systematic and reliable data. The national and regional Human Development Reports—with more than 800 so far—have been major vehicles. Some of them have also pursued innovative approaches to constructing the HDI reflecting better their conditions and preferences.
- It has motivated healthy competition among countries, particularly neighboring countries, to surpass neighbors or competitors in ranking.
- It has provided ammunition to civil society for to putting pressure on governments to undertake in advocacy for human development-friendly strategies, to instigate debates among political parties to hold each other accountable on their human development progress records.
- It has sparked serious academic research and empirical studies that have suggested refinements. The academic interest in the HDI at least partly contributed to the birth of academic journals like the *Journal of Human Development and Capabilities*.

In many Human Development Reports, it was underlined that the HDI is not and was never intended to be an overarching definitive measure of development. As Klugman et al. (2011a) asserted "by design, the HDI is a partial measure that uses imperfect indicators and that attempts to provide a broad vision of the advance of countries in furthering capabilities. The HDI should be understood as the starting point of a conversation about what we mean by development, rather than as its endpoint."

When HDI is disaggregated, it can spotlight inequalities and disparities on various planes and guide all kinds of policies including resource reallocation. This has been done in many countries. Recently, Permanyer and Smits (2020) have presented geographical subnational human development indices for 1600 subnational regions in 160 countries covering 99% of global population. Such disaggregated HDI provides a picture of within the country social and economic inequalities. It can help discovering the clusters of subnational regions at a similar level of HDI and help targeting the changes by the subnational or national governments.

The HDI with all its limitations plays a role in policy-relevant analyses. For example, the UNDP Human Development Reports consistently show that countries with comparable resource endowments and levels of economic development often diverge in terms of human development achievements due to policy

differences. Often such analysis demonstrates the importance of policy intervention, and thereby the centrality of metrics to track and plan such interventions.

The human development approach remains indispensable in current times. It can be easily considered as instrumental to achieving sustainable development and the SDGs. HDI and the family of human development composite measures and indicators complement SDG indicators by offering summaries and analyses of development achievements across SDGs.

As evident in the first two decades of the 21st century, the challenges facing the world are far more complex than a simple divide between developed and developing countries. It is therefore important to have metrics that will be able to track and measure dynamic developments which have long-term and intergenerational impact. Efforts are not spared to adapt the HDI to these challenges, continuously resulting in novel tools—Inequality-adjusted HDI, Gender Development Index and Gender Inequality Index, Multidimensional Poverty Index, Planetary pressures adjusted HDI, as well as in informative dashboards of indicators that are able to track these multidimensional and often methodologically incomparable aspects of wellbeing even if these are not developed into a single metric.

REFERENCES

Alkire, S., 2002. Dimensions of human development. World Dev. 30 (2), 181–205. https://doi.org/10.1016/S0305-750X(01)00109-7.

Alkire, S., Foster, J., 2010. Designing the inequality-adjusted Human Development Index. Human Development Research Paper Series, 2010-28. http://www.hdr.undp.org/sites/default/files/hdrp_2010_28.pdf.

Anand, S., 2018. Recasting human development measures. UNDP-HDRO Occasional Paper http://www.hdr.undp.org/en/content/recasting-human-development-measures.

Anand, S., Sen, A.K., 1994. Human Development Index: methodology and measurement. HDR Occasional Papers.

Anand, S., Sen, A.K., 1997. Concepts of human development and poverty: a multidimensional perspective. Human Development Papers, Human Development Report Office (UNDP).

Anand, S., Sen, A.K., 2000a. Human development and economic sustainability. World Dev. 28 (12), 2029–2049.

Anand, S., Sen, A.K., 2000b. The income component of the Human Development Index. J. Hum. Dev. 1 (1), 83–106.

Arrow, K.J., et al., 1961. Capital-labor substitution and economic efficiency. Rev. Econ. Stat. 43 (3), 225–250.

Barro, R.J., Lee, J.-W., 2000. International data on educational attainment: updates and implications. Working Paper 42, Center for International Development, Harvard University.

Barro, R.J., Lee, J.-W., 2013. A new data set of educational attainment in the world, 1950-2010. J. Dev. Econ. 104, 184–198.

Barro, R.J., Lee, J.-W., 2015. Education Matters: Global Schooling Gains From the 19th to the 21st Century. Oxford University Press, Oxford, UK.

Basu, K., Lopez-Calva, L.F., 2011. Functionings and capabilities. In: Arrow, K.J., et al. (Eds.), Handbook of Social Choice and Welfare. vol. II. North-Holland, Amsterdam, The Netherlands, pp. 153–187 (Chapter 16).

Becker, W., et al., 2017. Weights and importance in composite indicators: closing the gap. Ecol. Indic. 80, 12–22. https://doi.org/10.1016/j.ecolind.2017.03.056.

Biggeri, M., Mauro, V., 2018. Towards a more 'sustainable' Human Development Index: integrating the environment and freedom. Ecol. Indic. 91, 220–231. https://doi.org/10.1016/j.ecolind.2018.03.045.

Bray, F., et al., 2012. Global cancer transitions according to the Human Development Index (2008–2030): a population-based study. Lancet Oncol. 13 (8), 790–801. https://doi.org/10.1016/S1470-2045(12)70211-5.

Burchi, F., et al., 2014. Which dimensions should matter for capabilities? A constitutional approach. Ethics Soc. Welf. 8 (3), 233–247. https://doi.org/10.1080/17496535.2014.932415.

Burd-Sharps, S., et al., 2010. Twenty years of human development in six affluent countries: Australia, Canada, Japan, New Zealand, the United Kingdom, and the United States. Human Development Research Paper 2010-27 http://www.hdr.undp.org/en/content/twenty-years-human-development-six-affluent-countries.

Castles, I., 2014. Measuring wealth and welfare: why HDI and GPI fail. In: Podger, A., Trewin, D. (Eds.), Measuring and Promoting Wellbeing: How Important Is Economic Growth? ANU Press, Acton, ACT, Australia, pp. 253–270. www.jstor.org/stable/j.ctt6wp80q.15.

Chakravarty, S.R., 2003. A generalized Human Development Index. Rev. Dev. Econ. 7, 99–114. https://doi.org/10.1111/1467-9361.00178.

Chakravarty, S.R., 2011. A reconsideration of the tradeoffs in the new Human Development Index. J. Econ. Inequal. 9, 471–474. https://doi.org/10.1007/s10888-011-9190-3.

Cheibub, J., et al., 2010. Democracy and dictatorship revisited. Public Choice 143 (1/2), 67–101. http://www.jstor.org/stable/40661005.

Chiswick, B.R., 1997. Interpreting the coefficient of schooling in the human capital earnings function. Policy Research Working Paper Series 1790, The World Bank. https://ideas.repec.org/p/wbk/wbrwps/1790.html.

Cifuentes, M., et al., 2008. The association of major depressive episodes with income inequality and the Human Development Index. Soc. Sci. Med. 67 (4), 529–539. https://doi.org/10.1016/j.socscimed.2008.04.003.

Constatini, V., Monni, S., 2008. Environment, human development and economic growth. Ecol. Econ. 64 (4), 867–880. https://doi.org/10.1016/j.ecolecon.2007.05.011.

Decancq, K., Lugo, M.A., 2013. Weights in multidimensional indices of well-being: an overview. Econ. Rev. 32 (1), 7–34. https://doi.org/10.1080/07474938.2012.690641.

Decancq, K., et al., 2019. Multidimensional poverty measurement with individual preferences. J. Econ. Inequal. 17, 29–49. https://doi.org/10.1007/s10888-019-09407-9.

Dumith, S.C., et al., 2011. Worldwide prevalence of physical inactivity and its association with Human Development Index in 76 countries. Prev. Med. 53 (1), 24–28. https://doi.org/10.1016/j.ypmed.2011.02.017.

Fakuda-Parr, S., et al., 2009. Using the HDI for policy analysis. In: Fukuda-Parr, S., Kumar, A.K.S. (Eds.), Handbook of Human Development: Concepts, Measures and Policies. Oxford University Press, New Delhi, India, pp. 177–187 (Chapter 2.5).

Fleurbaey, M., 2018. On human development indicators. UNDP-HDRO Occasional Paper http://www.hdr.undp.org/en/content/human-development-indicators.

Foster, J.E., 2013. Reflections on the Human Development Index. In: Presented at the UNDP's Second Conference on Measuring Human Progress. March 4-5. http://www.hdr.undp.org/en/second-conference-measuring-human-progress.

Foster, J.E., et al., 2005. Measuring the distribution of human development: methodology and an application to Mexico. J. Hum. Dev. 6 (1), 5–29.

Frediani, A., 2010. Sen's capability approach as a framework to the practice of development. Dev. Pract. 20 (2), 173–187. www.jstor.org/stable/27806685.

Gertner, J., 2010. The rise and the fall of the G.D.P. N. Y. Times. May 13 https://www.nytimes.com/2010/05/16/magazine/16GDP-t.html.

Graham, C., 2010. Challenges of incorporating empowerment into the HDI: some lessons from happiness economics and quality of life research. Human Development Research Paper 2010/13 http://www.hdr.undp.org/sites/default/files/hdrp_2010_13.pdf.

Grimm, M., et al., 2008. A Human Development Index by income groups. World Dev. 36, 2527–2546. https://doi.org/10.1016/j.worlddev.2007.12.001.

Gruen, D., Spender, D., 2014. The need for wellbeing measurement in context. In: Podger, A., Trewin, D. (Eds.), Measuring and Promoting Wellbeing: How Important Is Economic Growth? ANU Press, Acton, ACT, Australia, pp. 209–222. Retrieved July 30, 2020, from www.jstor.org/stable/j.ctt6wp80q.12.

Haq, K., Ponzio, R. (Eds.), 2008. Pioneering the Human Development Revolution: An Intellectual Biography of Mahbub ul Haq. Oxford University Press, Oxford, UK.

Harkness, S., 2007. Social and political indicators of human well-being. In: McGillivray, M. (Ed.), Human Well-Being. Studies in Development Economics and Policy. Palgrave Macmillan, London, UK, pp. 88–112, https://doi.org/10.1057/9780230625600_4.

Hartgen, K., Klasen, S., 2012. A household based Human Development Index. World Dev. 40 (5), 878–899. https://doi.org/10.1016/j.worlddev.2011.09.011.

Hartgen, K., Vollmer, S., 2014. A reversal in the relationship of human development with fertility? Demography 51 (1), 173–184. https://doi.org/10.1007/s13524-013-0252-y.

Herrero, C., et al., 2012. A newer Human Development Index. J. Hum. Dev. Capab. 13 (2), 247–268. https://doi.org/10.1080/19452829.2011.645027.

Hickel, J., 2020. The sustainable development index: measuring the ecological efficiency of human development in the anthropocene. Ecol. Econ. 167, 106331. https://doi.org/10.1016/j.ecolecon.2019.05.011.

Hicks, D.A., 1997. The inequality-adjusted Human Development Index: a constructive proposal. World Dev. 25 (8), 1283–1298. https://doi.org/10.1016/S0305-750X(97)00034-X.

Hoyland, B., et al., 2012. The tyranny of international index rankings. J. Dev. Econ. 97 (1), 1–14. https://doi.org/10.1016/j.jdeveco.2011.01.007.

Institute of Health Metrics and Evaluation, 2019. Global Burden of Disease. http://www.healthdata.org/gbd/2019.

Jahan, S., 2009. Evolution of the Human Development Index. In: Fukuda-Parr, S., Kumar, S.A.K. (Eds.), Handbook of Human Development: Concepts, Measures and Policies. Oxford University Press, New Delhi, India, pp. 152–163 (Chapter 2.3).

Kelly, A., 1991. The Human Development Index: "Handle with care". Popul. Dev. Rev. 17 (2), 315–324. https://doi.org/10.2307/1973733.

Klasen, S., 2018. Human development indices and indicators: a critical evaluation. Human Development Report Background Paper http://www.hdr.undp.org/en/content/human-development-indices-and-indicators-critical-evaluation.

Klugman, J., et al., 2011a. The HDI 2010: new controversies, old critiques. Human Development Research Paper 2011-1 http://www.hdr.undp.org/en/content/hdi-2010-new-controversies-old-critiques.

Klugman, J., et al., 2011b. Response to Martin Ravallion. J. Econ. Inequal. 9, 249–288. https://doi.org/10.1007/s10888-011-9178-z.

Kovacevic, M., 2010. Review of HDI critiques and potential improvements. Human Development Research Paper 2010-33, UNDP-HDRO. http://www.hdr.undp.org/sites/default/files/hdrp_2010_33.pdf.

Krisnakumar, J., 2018. Trade-offs in a multidimensional Human Development Index. Soc. Indic. Res. 138 (3), 991–1022. https://doi.org/10.1007/s11205-017-1679-0.

Lee, K., et al., 1997. Human development index as a predictor of infant and maternal mortality rates. J. Pediatr. 131 (3), 430–433. https://doi.org/10.1136/jech.57.7.493.

Lind, N.C., 1992. Some thoughts on the Human Development Index. Soc. Indic. Res. 27, 89–101. https://doi.org/10.1007/BF00300511.

Lind, N.C., 2004. Values reflected in the Human Development Index. Soc. Indic. Res. 66 (3), 283–293. https://doi.org/10.1023/B:SOCI.0000003587.32655.b7.

Lind, N.C., 2019. A development of the Human Development Index. Soc. Indic. Res. 146, 409–423. https://doi.org/10.1007/s11205-019-02133-9.

Ling Lai, S., Chen, D.-N., 2020. A research on the relationship between environmental sustainability management and human development. Sustainability 12, 9001. https://doi.org/10.3390/su12219001.

Luchters, G., Menkhoff, L., 1996. Human development as statistical artifact. World Dev. 24 (8), 1385–1392. https://doi.org/10.1016/0305-750X(96)00038-1.

Maddison, A., 2010. Historical Statistics of World Economy: 1-2008 AD. Organization for Economic Cooperation and Development, Paris. http://www.ggdc.net/maddison/oriindex.htm.

Mauro, V., 2018. Measuring and monitoring poverty and well-being: a new approach for the synthesis of multidimensionality. Soc. Indic. Res. 135, 75–89. https://doi.org/10.1007/s11205-016-1484-1.

Mishra, S., Nathan, H.S.K., 2018. A manush or humans characterisation of the Human Development Index. J. Hum. Dev. Capab. 19 (3), 398–415. https://doi.org/10.1080/19452829.2017.1422703.

Murray, J.L., 1991. Development data constraints and the Human Development Index. In: Westerndorff, D.G., Ghai, D. (Eds.), Monitoring Social Progress in the 1990s. UNIRSD, Geneva, Switzerland, pp. 40–64.

Neumayer, E., 2001. The Human Development Index and sustainability: a constructive proposal. Ecol. Econ. 39 (1), 101–114. https://doi.org/10.1016/S0921-8009(01)00201-4.

Neumayer, E., 2012. The Human Development Index and sustainability—a constructive proposal. Ecol. Econ. 39 (1), 101–114. https://doi.org/10.1016/S0921-8009(01)00201-4.

Nguefack-Tsague, G., 2011. On weighting the components of the Human Development Index: a statistical justification. J. Hum. Dev. Capab. 12 (2), 183–202. https://doi.org/10.1080/19452829.2011.571077.

Noorbakhsh, F., 1998a. A modified Human Development Index. World Dev. 26 (3), 517–528. https://doi.org/10.1016/S0305-750X(97)10063-8.

Noorbakhsh, F., 1998b. The Human Development Index: some technical issues and alternative indices. J. Int. Dev. 10, 589–605. https://doi.org/10.1002/(SICI)1099-1328(199807/08)10:5<589::AID-JID484>3.0.CO;2-S.

Nussbaum, M., 2006. Frontiers of Justice: Disability, Nationality, Species Membership (The Tanner Lectures on Human Values). Harvard University Press, Cambridge, MA.

Nussbaum, M., 2011. Creating Capabilities: Human Development Approach. Harvard University Press, Cambridge, MA.

OECD, 2008. Handbook on Constructing Composite Indicators: Methodology and User Guide. OECD and EU Joint Research Centre, Paris, France. https://www.oecd.org/sdd/42495745.pdf.

Pandey, M.D., et al., 2006. The derivation and calibration of the life-quality index (LQI) from economic principles. Struct. Saf. 28, 341–360. https://doi.org/10.1016/j.strusafe.2005.10.001.

Panigrahi, R., Sivramkrishna, S., 2002. An adjusted Human Development Index: Robust country ranking with respect to choice of fixed maximum and minimum indicator values. J. Hum. Dev. 3 (2), 201–311. https://doi.org/10.1080/14649880220147365.

Paruolo, P., 2013. Ratings and rankings: voodoo or science? J. R. Stat. Soc. A. Stat. Soc. 176, 609–634. https://doi.org/10.1111/j.1467-985X.2012.01059.x.

Patel, A.R., et al., 2012. The association of the human development index with global kidney cancer incidence and mortality. J. Urol. 187 (6), 1978–1983. https://doi.org/10.1111/bju.13875.

Permanyer, I., 2013. Using census data to explore the spatial distribution of human development. World Dev. 46, 1–13. https://doi.org/10.1016/j.worlddev.2012.11.015.

Permanyer, I., Smits, J., 2020. Inequality in human development across the globe. Popul. Dev. Rev. 46 (3), 583–601. https://doi.org/10.1111/padr.12343.

Pineda, J., 2012. Sustainability and human development: a proposal for a sustainability adjusted HDI (SHDI). Munich Personal RePEc Article Paper Series, No. 39656 https://mpra.ub.uni-muenchen.de/39656/.

Qiu, Q., et al., 2018. Using spatial factor analysis to measure human development. J. Dev. Econ. 132, 130–149. https://doi.org/10.1016/j.jdeveco.2017.12.007.

Ranis, G., 2004. Human development and economic growth. Yale University Economic Growth Center discussion paper no. 887, Yale University EGC, New Haven, CN. https://papers.ssrn.com/sol3/papers.cfm?abstract_id=551662.

Ranis, G., et al., 2006. Human development: beyond the Human Development Index. J. Hum. Dev. 3, 323–358. https://doi.org/10.1080/14649880600815917.

Ravallion, M., 2010. Mashup indices of development. In: Policy Research Working Paper Series 5432. The World Bank. https://ideas.repec.org/p/wbk/wbrwps/5432.html.

Ravallion, M., 2011. The Human Development Index: a response to Klugman, Rodriguez and Choi. J. Econ. Inequal. 9, 475–478. https://doi.org/10.1007/s10888-011-9193-0.

Ravallion, M., 2012. Troubling tradeoffs in the Human Development Index. J. Dev. Econ. 99 (2), 201–209. https://doi.org/10.1016/j.jdeveco.2012.01.003.

Rawls, J., 1971. A Theory of Justice. Harvard University Press, Cambridge, MA.

Raworth, K., Stewart, D., 2009. Critiques of the Human Development Index: a review. In: Fukuda-Parr, S., Kumar, A.K.S. (Eds.), Handbook of Human Development: Concepts, Measures and Policies. Oxford University Press, New Delhi, India, pp. 164–176 (Chapter 2.4).

Riley, J.C., 2005. Poverty and Life Expectancy. Cambridge University Press, Cambridge, UK.

Robeyns, I., 2017. Critiques and debates. In: Robeyns, I. (Ed.), Wellbeing, Freedom and Social Justice: The Capability Approach Re-Examined. Open Book Publishers, Cambridge, UK, pp. 169–210 (Chapter 4) http://books.openedition.org/obp/486.

Rodriguez, F., 2020. Human development and capabilities: conceptual and measurement advances. HDRO Series of Background Papers, UNDP-HDRO.

Ryten, J., 2000. The Human Development Index and beyond: which are the prerequisites for a consistent design of development indicators—should there be a Human Development Index? In: International Association of Official Statistics Conference "Statistics, Development and Human Rights" Montreux, Switzerland, May 4-8.

Segura, L.S., Moya, E.G., 2009. Human Development Index: a non-compensatory assessment. Cuad. Econ. 28 (50), 223–235. https://revistas.unal.edu.co/index.php/ceconomia/article/view/10791/11252.

Sen, A., 1985. Commodities and Capabilities. North-Holland, Amsterdam, Netherlands.

Sen, A., 1999. Development as Freedom. Oxford University Press, Oxford, UK.

Sen, A., 2000. Freedom, Rationality, and Social Choice: The Arrow Lectures and Other Essays. Oxford University Press, Oxford, UK.

Sen, A., 2002. Rationality and Freedom. Harvard University Press, Cambridge, MA.

Sen, A., 2004. Dialogue capabilities, lists, and public reason: continuing the conversation. Fem. Econ. 10 (3), 77–80.

Sen, A., 2005. Human rights and capabilities. J. Hum. Dev. 6 (2), 151–166. https://doi.org/10.1080/14649880500120491.

Sen, A., 2013. Panel on measuring human progress. In: Discussion With J. Stiglitz, J-P. Fitoussi and J.A. Ocampo. UNDP's Second Conference on Measuring Human Progress. March 4-5, New York, NY. http://www.hdr.undp.org/en/second-conference-measuring-human-progress.

Seth, S., 2009. Inequality, interactions, and human development. J. Hum. Dev. Capab. 10, 375–396. https://doi.org/10.1080/19452820903048878.

Seth, S., McGilverey, M., 2018. Composite indices, alternative weights, and comparison robustness. Soc. Choice Welf. 51, 657–679. https://doi.org/10.1007/s00355-018-1132-6.

Seth, S., Villar, A., 2017. Measuring human development and human deprivations. Oxford Poverty and Human Development Initiative (OPHI), Working Paper 111 https://ophi.org.uk/human-development-inequality-and-poverty-empirical-findings/.

Shah, A., 2009. The relationship between elderly suicide rates and the human development index: a cross-national study of secondary data from the World Health Organization and the United Nations. Int. Psychogeriatr. 21 (01), 69–77. https://doi.org/10.1017/S1041610208007527.

Shetty, N.S., 2014. Human development: not a bird's eye view but a worm's eye view required. Nitte Manag. Rev. 8 (1), 14–23. http://informaticsjournals.com/index.php/nmr/article/view/18381/15341.

Srinivasan, T.N., 1994. Human development: a new paradigm or reinvention of the wheel? Am. Econ. Rev. 84 (2), 238–243. https://www.jstor.org/stable/2117836.

Stewart, F., 1989. Basic needs strategies, human rights, and the right to development. Hum. Rights Q. 11 (3), 347–374. https://doi.org/10.2307/762098.

Stewart, F., et al., 2018. Advancing Human Development: Theory and Practice. Published to Oxford Scholarship

Online: March, https://doi.org/10.1093/oso/9780198794455.001.0001.

Stiglitz, J.E., et al., 2009. 2009 Report by the Commission on the Measurement of Economic Performance and Social Progress, Paris, France. http://www.stiglitz-sen-fitoussi.fr/en/index.htm.

Streeten, P., 1994. Human development: means and ends. Am. Econ. Rev. 84 (2), 232–237. https://www.jstor.org/stable/2117835.

Ul Haq, M., 1995. Reflections on Human Development. Oxford University Press, New Delhi, India.

UNDESA, 2019. World Population Prospects, 2019 Update. UNDESA, New York, NY. https://population.un.org/wpp/.

UNDP, 1990. Human Development Report 1990. UNDP, New York, NY. http://www.hdr.undp.org/en/reports/global/hdr1990.

UNDP, 1993. Human Development Report 1993. UNDP, New York, NY. http://www.hdr.undp.org/en/reports/global/hdr1993.

UNDP, 1995. Human Development Report 1995. UNDP, New York, NY. http://www.hdr.undp.org/en/content/human-development-report-1995.

UNDP, 1997. Human Development Report 1997. UNDP, New York, NY. http://www.hdr.undp.org/en/content/human-development-report-1997.

UNDP, 2010. Human Development Report 2010. UNDP, New York, NY. http://www.hdr.undp.org/en/content/human-development-report-2010.

UNDP, 2014. Human Development Report 2014. UNDP, New York, NY. http://www.hdr.undp.org/en/content/human-development-report-2014.

UNDP, 2020. Human Development Report 2020. UNDP, New York, NY. http://www.hdr.undp.org/en/content/human-development-report-2020.

UNESCO, 2020. UIS Glossary of Statistical Terms. http://uis.unesco.org/en/glossary.

WHO, 2008. The World Health Report 2004—Changing History. WHO, Geneva, Switzerland. https://www.who.int/healthinfo/global_burden_disease/GBD_report_2004update_full.pdf.

WHO, 2021. Civil registration of deaths. In: Global Health Observatory (GHO). WHO, Geneva, Switzerland. https://www.who.int/gho/mortality_burden_disease/registered_deaths/text/en/.

Wolff, H., et al., 2011. Classification, detection and consequences of data error: evidence from the Human Development Index. Econ. J. 121 (553), 843–870. https://doi.org/10.1111/j.1468-0297.2010.02408.x.

Zambrano, E., 2014. An axiomatization of the Human Development Index. Soc. Choice Welf. 42, 853–872. https://doi.org/10.1007/s00355-013-0756-9.

Zambrano, E., 2017. The 'troubling tradeoffs' paradox and a resolution. Rev. Income Wealth 63 (3), 520–541. https://doi.org/10.1111/roiw.12235.

FURTHER READING

Ul Haq, M., 2009. The birth of the human development. In: Fukuda-Parr, S., Kumar, S.A.K. (Eds.), Handbook of Human Development: Concepts, Measures and Policies. Oxford University Press, New Delhi, India, pp. 127–137 (Chapter 2.1).

CHAPTER 5

Summary of Lim, S. S., et al., "Measuring human capital: A systematic analysis of 195 countries and territories, 1990–2016"*

BARBARA M. FRAUMENI[a,b,c,d,e,*] • GANG LIU[f]
[a]Central University of Finance and Economics, Beijing, China, [b]University of Southern Maine, Portland, ME, United States, [c]National Bureau of Economic Research, Cambridge, MA, United States, [d]IZA Institute for Labor Economics, Bonn, Germany, [e]Hunan University, Changsha, China, [f]Statistics Norway, Oslo, Norway
*Corresponding author: Barbara_Fraumeni@hotmail.com

Both the World Bank and the Institute for Health Metrics and Evaluation (IHME) acknowledged the importance of global human capital by publishing their first estimate of a human capital index for a large number of countries in 2018. Human capital contributes to economic productivity in concert with physical capital. Education, training, skills, and health comprise the characteristics of human capital, along with intangible attributes that are difficult to identify. To better understand human capital's contribution to economic growth, IHME recognized the importance of creating an internationally comparable human capital measure.

IHME is well known for its Global Burden of Disease (GBD) database, which comprehensively documents causes of death, diseases, and injuries, and risk factors in more than 200 countries and territories. However, a globally comparable measure of human capital is a far larger and more difficult undertaking as it entails tracking other aspects of human capital, such as education. To be able to better isolate and track progress toward improved human capital, an index, whose components could be amenable to policy interventions, was computed by IHME. Both IHME and the World Bank found that too little investment in human capital had been occurring relative to investment in physical capital.

IHME defined its forward-looking human capital index as the expected years lived from age 20 to 64 years, adjusted for educational attainment, learning, health, and survival. Four components were included annually for 195 countries from 1995 to 2016. Table I.1 of the Introduction to this book summarizes the major components of the IHME human capital index, as well as those of the World Bank and the United Nations Development Programme. This chapter of the book provides more details on the IHME index and summarizes its important results.

5.1 METHODS

IHME first systematically determined what data were available. Education and functional estimates by sex and by 5-year age groups were constructed for educational attainment (from age 5 to 64) and learning as measured by performance on standardized tests of reading, mathematics, and science (from age 5 to 19) and seven health conditions (from age 5 to 64). Among more than 300 diseases and injuries currently covered by GBD 2016, a small number of components or aggregates were picked up, which were thought to contribute most to economic productivity. The chosen seven included wasting, stunting, anemia, cognitive impairment, severe vision loss or blindness, hearing loss, and three infectious disease aggregates. In addition, mortality rates from GBD 2016 by location, age, sex, and year entered into the index.

*See Lim et al. (2018).

Measuring Human Capital. https://doi.org/10.1016/B978-0-12-819057-9.00004-4

A variety of sophisticated statistical and econometric techniques were used to create complete time series.[a]

5.1.1 Educational Attainment

Estimates based on more than 2500 censuses and household surveys were made following an approach pioneered by Gakidou et al. (2010) to determine educational attainment, which was also referred to as the quantity of education. The lowest level of education completed is 1 year of preschool, followed by first grade, through at least 1 year postgraduate, for a total of 18 years at a maximum. In some cases, educational attainment was available by a 10-year age group instead of a 5-year age group and by multigrade education completed bins. In the bin cases, the data were distributed using information from almost 1800 single years of education data sources. In each bin case, the final educational attainment figures by single years of education were determined from the 12 single grade datasets considered to be most similar by geography and year.

The next step in the imputation depended on the relative constancy of educational attainment after age 25. Data for 5-year age cohorts were projected backward and forward from age cohort 25–34 for 5-year intervals, for example, for 1990, 1995, 2000, and so on. All original data and the imputed cohort data were the basis for estimating complete single grade attained with age-period models for 1950–2016 by age, sex, and location. The mean level of educational attainment was calculated separately by year, sex, age, and GBD location. The maximum mean attainment was set at 3 for ages 5–9, 8 for ages 10–14, 13 for ages 15–19 years, and 18 for all older age groups. Natural spline for age and a Gaussian process regression were additional techniques used to complete the data set estimation, with associated uncertainty intervals.

5.1.2 Learning

Learning, also referred to as the quality of education, was determined from international and national assessments of reading, mathematics, and science. Almost 1900 tests across almost 300 unique locations were the basis for the database construction. The four major programs providing substantial test results include the Programme for International Student Assessment (PISA) of the Organisation for Economic Co-operation and Development (OECD), the Progress in International Reading Literacy Study (PIRLS) of the International Association for the Evaluation of Educational Achievement (IEA), the Trends in International Mathematics and Science Study (TIMSS), and several other tests covering literacy and science from IEA. Regional testing programs supplemented information from these four, and so did representative studies measuring intelligence quotient in school-aged children. Trends through time observed along demographic information implied by grade levels and information by subject (reading, mathematics, and science) were kept separate for analysis purposes. Test results from the diverse sources were normalized to the TIMSS mathematics and science tests and PIRLS readings tests.

Gaussian process regression was the basis for estimating test scores for all countries, years and 5-year age groups, which were rescaled to a 0–1 score, with 1 set to one standard deviation above the mean score (600) on the original TIMSS exam.

5.1.3 Functional Health Status

Policy trials and observational studies determined the seven diseases or impairments notably adversely impacting on learning and productivity. Wasting and stunting for those aged 5 or below was determined by being at least two standard deviations below the mean values of these components. Anemia, cognitive, and vision standards each relied on three categories: mild, moderate, or severe for anemia; moderate, severe, or profound developmental delay for cognitive; and moderate impairment, severe impairment, or blindness for vision. The three infectious disease GBD 2016 aggregates included HIV/AIDS, tuberculosis, malaria, neglected tropical diseases, diarrhea, and several other common infectious diseases. These seven functional health status measures were then combined into a single measure using principal components analysis (PCA).

5.1.4 Survival

As was noted previously, GBD 2016 was the source for mortality rates. A wide variety of sources were used to construct the GBD estimates.

5.1.5 Uncertainty Analysis

Overall uncertainty in the final dataset at the level of each of the four components (educational attainment, learning, functional health status, and survival) was estimated with 1000 estimates of expected human capital using 1000 draws from their respective posterior distribution.

---

[a]It is recommended that a reader interested in the statistical and econometric techniques refer to the article itself as the details of these techniques are not reported in this summary.

5.1.6 Association Between Expected Human Capital and Gross Domestic Product (GDP)

The association was examined between expected human capital estimated in the study and GDP per capita by country, which was taken from a study by Dieleman et al. (2018). The cross-sectional association pattern, with GDP per capita in both logarithms and levels, was examined in 1990 and 2016. In addition, the median and Interquartile Range (IQR) of GDP per capita were computed and examined for the end-point years in expected human capital by quartiles, as were the median and IQR for the annualized rate of change in GDP per capita between 1990 and 2016 based on quartiles from the absolute change in expected human capital.

5.1.7 Overall Index of Expected Human Capital

Expected human capital, with the four dimensions (educational attainment, learning, functional health status, and survival) as the variables, was calculated, as previously indicated, as:

$$IHME\,HCI = \left(\frac{\sum_{x=20}^{64} nL_{xt}FH_{xt}}{l_0}\right) * \left(\frac{\sum_{x=5}^{24} Edu_{xt}Learn_{xt}}{18}\right),$$

(5.1)

where

nL_{xt} = expected years lived in age group x for year t;

FH_{xt} = functional health status in age group x in year t, transformed to a 0 to 1 scale;

l_0 = starting birth cohort;

Edu_{xt} = years of education attained during age group x for year t;

$Learn_{xt}$ = average standardized test score in age group x for year t, transformed to a 0 to 1 scale.

The following components by age, all sex and age-specific, were entered into the final measure:

Educational attainment: from age 5 to 24.

Functional health status: from age 20 to 64 by 5-year age groups, with wasting and stunting for those aged 5 or under.

Learning: from age 5 to 24.

Survival: from birth to age 64.

5.2 RESULTS

Results are presented in a variety of color-coded formats for easier viewing: with individual scores, bar graphs, and plots. Breakouts of four components of expected human capital for 20 of the most populous countries by 2016 total population are shown in bar graph form

for 1990 and 2016: expected years lived (age 20–64), the educational attainment adjustment, educational attainment and learning adjustment, and educational attainment, learning, and functional health adjustment. Also, for 1990 and 2016, but for all 195 countries, the expected human capital and its components—expected years lived (from age 20, for an additional 0–45 years), functional health status (0–100), educational attainment (0–18 years), and learning (0–100)—were listed in a figure. The nine color codes range from dark green for the best performance, fading to yellow for average performance, to dark red for the worst performance. Two world maps with the same color-coding summarize the expected human capital results by country in 1990 and 2016. There are three versions of plots, one version for the change between 1990 and 2016, the second version for the 2016 difference between men and women, and the third for expected human capital versus GDP per capita or log GDP per capita in 1990 and 2016.[b] In all three versions, the dots in the plots were color coded for high income countries and those in six regions, which were the seven GBD super-regions.[c] In the first two versions, a plot was included by expected human capital and by each of its four components. In the last version, the plots were only for expected human capital in 1990 and 2016. A final series of bar graphs looks at quartiles of expected human capital in 1990 and 2016 and the quartiles of the change in human capital between 1990 and 2016. A significant amount of information was presented in this article.

Looking at the results for the 20 most populous countries and for all 195 countries covered in 2016, Japan had the highest overall index of expected human capital at 24, with expected years lived at almost 44 years, a functional health score of 85, an expected educational attainment of 12, and a learning score of 94.[d] A number of other countries in the world had expected years lived of 44 out of a maximum of 45 in 2016. Many countries in the top 100 (of 195 ranked

---

[b]Gross Domestic Product was measured using purchasing power parities (PPPs).

[c]The six regions were as follows: (1) Central Europe, (2) Latin America and Caribbean, (3) North Africa and Middle East, (4) South Asia, (5) Southeast Asia, east Asia, and Oceania, and (6) Sub-Saharan Africa.

[d]In the results and discussions of the IHME article, the levels are, when possible, rounded to be consistent with the numbers presented in the figures. Numbers for the overall index of expected human capital and its 4 components for the 20 most populous countries and all countries are listed in figures 1 and 2, respectively, in the article.

countries) achieved the same level of educational attainment; even some countries in the next 50 were at this level. Finland had the highest level of educational attainment of any of the covered countries at 15 out of a maximum of 18. Out of 100, only Singapore at 98 and South Korea at 96 of all countries covered had higher learning scores than Japan. Many counties in the top 50 of the covered countries had a functional health score of 85 or above out of 100, but only Greenland had a similar level of functional health among the remaining 135.

In 2016, out of all 195 countries, Finland ranked number 1 at 28 for the overall index of expected human capital with only 5 countries at a level of 26 or 27, with Japan ranked 13th. Finland scored 45 for expected years lived, 89 for functional health status, 15 for educational attainment, and 91 for learning. The only component for which Finland did not score at the highest level among all countries is for functional health status as the Netherlands and Norway were at 90. By 2016, all of the top 15 countries had an expected human capital rating of at least 25; in 1990, this rating was at least 21.

Among the 20 most populous countries, Ethiopia fared the worst in 1990, and in 2016, although, the expected human capital rose from one to five between those years. Of the 20 most populous countries, the Democratic Republic of the Congo and Nigeria also had an expected human capital ranking of 5 in 2016. Ethiopia scored 38 for expected years lived, 49 for functional health status, 7 for educational attainment, and 62 for learning. In 1990, among the 20 most populous countries, the next lowest score to Ethiopia's was 3, with the Democratic Republic of the Congo and Nigeria receiving that score.

Out of the 195 countries in 2016, Niger had the lowest expected human capital at 2, followed closely by Chad and South Sudan, both at 2. Niger scored 35 for expected years lived, 38 for functional health status, 4 for educational attainment, and 52 for learning. All other countries had higher expected human capital. All three countries ranked among the bottom five in 1990, although the expected human capital number of each increased by one or two between 1990 and 2016. In 1990, the lowest score, a zero for expected human capital, was received by Mali and South Sudan.

There has been a significant amount of consistency as well as a significant amount of movement among the most highly rated countries. Of the six Nordic countries (Denmark, Finland, Iceland, Greenland, Norway, and Sweden), only Greenland at 64 in 1990 and 69 in 2016 ranked below the top 15 in 1990 and 2016. In fact, Finland, Iceland, and Norway were ranked one, two,

and three, respectively, in both years. The two countries dropping out of the top 15 with substantial downward movement are Greece and the United States, which dropped 14 and 21 points, respectively, in the rankings between 1990 and 2016. In both cases, with one exception, the change in ranking was not due to the countries performing less well on the components, rather that other countries improved their performance to a greater extent.[e] For example, Finland's overall score for expected human capital increased from 25 to 28 between 1990 and 2016, with the components for expected years lived, functional health status, educational attainment, and learning increasing from 42 to 44, 86 to 89, 14 to 15, and 89 to 91, respectively. The statistics for the 15th ranked country in 1990 (Andorra) were 21, 43, 88, 12, and 85, respectively; the statistics for the 15th ranked country in 2016 (Sweden) were 24, 44, 89, 13, and 87, respectively. The good news is that even in countries with a relatively high level of expected human capital, improvements were being made.

Table 5.1 documents that between 1990 and 2016, there was clear progress in raising the level of expected human capital and educational attainment for both the 20 most populous countries and for all 195 countries covered in the study.[f] There was a substantial drop in the number of countries having a level of expected human capital of 7 or less, a substantial increase in the number of countries having a level of expected human capital of 19 or greater, and a substantial decrease in the number of countries with educational attainment less than 9. Seven of the 20 most populous countries had an increase of at least 6 in expected human capital: Brazil, China, Egypt, Iran, Thailand, Turkey, and Vietnam. A typical driver of an increase in expected human capital was the increase in the educational attainment component of a country. Turkey's increase in expected human capital, which was the largest of all 195 countries at 12, was broad based among the 4 components, with educational attainment at 75% contributing the most; however, the other components all increased between 8% and 15%. For all 7 of the 20 most populous countries with the largest absolute increase, the percentage increase in educational

---

[e]The one exception is that the United States educational attainment component went down from 13 to 12 between 1990 and 2016.

[f]The break points of 7 and 19 were picked for the level of expected human capital as in 2016 for the most populous countries the next highest level of expected human capital from 7 was 3 points higher and the next lowest level from 19 was 3 points lower.

TABLE 5.1
Level of expected human capital and educational attainment, 1990 versus 2016.

	7 or less	19 or greater	Educational attainment below 9
1990—20 most populous countries	10	3	8
2016—20 most populous countries	6	6	2
1990—all 195 countries	80	39	63
2016—all 195 countries	54	50	22

TABLE 5.2
Increases in expected human capital between 1990 and 2016 of at least six.

Increase from 1990 to 2016	Country by 1990 level in parentheses	% Change
6	Myanmar (3), Egypt (6)[a], Sri Lanka (7), Algeria (8), Iran (9)[a], United Arab Emirates (10), Poland (17), South Korea (20)	200, 100, 86, 75, 67, 60, 35, 30
7	Saint Lucia (7), Vietnam (7)[a], Malaysia (8), Tunisia (8), Brazil (9)[a], Singapore (17)	100, 100, 88, 88, 78, 41
8	Maldives (4), Oman (6), Libya (8), Thailand (8)[a], Kuwait (9)	200, 133, 100, 100, 89
9	China (12)[a]	75
10	Saudi Arabia (7)	143
12	Turkey (8)[a]	150

[a]One of the 20 most populous countries in 2016.

attainment contributed the most. However, it is possible that it was more difficult to make substantial changes over a relatively short period of time in the three other components. Between 1990 and 2016, among the 20 most populous countries, the United States had the smallest increase of expected human capital of 1; the Democratic Republic of Congo and Nigeria at 2 had the next smallest absolute increase. However, as both the Democratic Republic of Congo and Nigeria started with a base of 3, their increase was much more noteworthy than the increase of the United States from an expected human capital level of 22 to 23. With 2 exceptions (Swaziland and Zimbabwe) of the 195 countries, the expected human capital rose between 1990 and 2016. The only 5 countries of the 195 for which the expected human capital rose only by 1 were Chad, Lesotho, South Africa, Tajikistan, and as previously mentioned the United States. Many countries that were not among the 20 most populous had an increase in expected human capital of 2.

In measuring progress, it matters not only by how much expected human capital rose, but also by the 1990 starting point for the increase. Table 5.2 lists the starting point by the increase in expected human capital and the percentage change in expected human capital. The expected human capital of 8 countries rose by 6, 6 countries rose by 7, 5 countries rose by 8, and 1 country each rose by 9, 10, or 12, respectively. As expected, for each of the countries listed in Table 5.2, the increase in educational attainment is clearly the largest increase of all of the four components. Most impressive is the performance of Myanmar, Maldives, Oman, Saudi Arabia, and Turkey whose expected human capital rose by

more than 100%. There are arguments for saying that it is more difficult for a country to raise its expected human capital starting from a very low level (e.g., the case of Maldives and Myanmar), but alternatively, it could be argued that it is more difficult to raise expected human capital starting from a relatively high level (e.g., the case of Poland, Singapore, and South Korea).

Although the status of the top-ranked countries is of interest, of greater interest is the relative status of lower ranked countries and whether those closer to the bottom of the ranking have been making substantial progress.

By region of the world, the levels of expected human capital varied widely, but by level ranges, no region exhibited a consistent level or trend for all the countries in that region.[g] Many countries in sub-Saharan Africa and much of south Asia had expected levels of human

[g]In Fig. 3 of the article, the ranges of expected human capital that were identified by color included (1) <2.83, (2) 2.83 to <4.71, (3) 4.71 to <6.94, (4) 6.94 to <8.58, (5) 8.58 to <10.88, (6) 10.88 to <13.65, (7) 13.65 to <16.09, (8) 16.09 to <18.72, (9) 18.72 to <22.14, and (10) ≥22.14. In these categories, categories (1) through (4) were coded from red to orange (poorest performances), (5) yellow, or neutral, as not being a bad or good performance; categories (6) through (10) were coded from light green (somewhat good performance) to dark green (best performance).

capital less than five. No covered countries in Africa were at the somewhat good or better level in 1990; by 2016, there were five. The level of expected human capital in all covered countries in South America was below 16 in 1990, yet by 2016 all but 2: Guyana and Suriname had achieved expected human capital levels of at least 11. The level of expected human capital in all covered countries in Africa was in the not so good categories; however, by 2016, Algeria, Egypt, Gabon, and Libya had made it into one of the two lower at least somewhat good categories. Within Western Europe, all covered countries were in one of the fairly good categories or better in 1990 and 2016. Most of covered Eastern European countries, including the ex-USSR countries, were in one of the better categories in 1990, all were by 2016. Notable improvements in expected human capital occurred in covered south Asia, Caribbean, and Middle East countries, but a number of them were still in one of the three worst categories in 2016, for example, Afghanistan, Bangladesh, India, Nepal, Pakistan, Papua New Guinea, and Yemen. The expected human capital level of all countries in southeast and east Asia increased to a higher expected human capital category between 1990 and 2016, except that some did not advance to a green-coded level. Differential progress within regions was common in the world.

The results again point out to the importance of educational attainment when looking at differences between men and women. The revealed pattern of educational attainment translates into a clear separation at a threshold of 10 years of expected human capital. In general, above this threshold, expected human capital tends to be higher for women than for men, whereas below this threshold, expected human capital tends to be lower for women than for men, although expected years lived were greater for women than men, and functional health status was greater for women than for men except in high income countries. In addition, learning was lower for women than for men when learning was at the lower or middle level of learning, but this was not so for higher income countries or when learning levels were higher. Educational attainment of women versus men was the best indicator of expected human capital of women compared to men.

Higher levels of expected human capital occurred in countries with higher levels of GDP per capita in both 1990 and 2016; in addition, higher levels of growth in expected human capital occurred in countries with higher levels of growth in GDP per capita between 1990 and 2016. Plots of expected human capital versus GDP per capita and log of GDP per capita, and IQR analysis for levels in 1990 and 2016 and change between years conformed this. Although the analysis conducted did not attempt to determine if there was any causal relationship, the article noted that these results are suggestive because of this association.

5.3 DISCUSSION

As was noted in the beginning of this summary of the IHME article, this project was initiated as it recognized, as has the World Bank, the importance of human capital. It produced human capital results with details on underlying components for more countries than other efforts.[h]

The article notes that annual measurement of human capital could be used to make loan decisions; incentives could be created for governments to institute programs and policies to increase human capital, particularly in those with low human capital who may have the greatest need for such loans. The discussion in the article states that there are a number of strategies that could be implemented. Reducing or eliminating school fees have been used to increase school enrollments and completions in many countries. School infrastructure, even bathrooms particularly for girls, teacher training and support, grouping students by ability, could also help with improving educational attainment. There are many effective interventions to reduce incidence of infectious diseases and to improve vision and hearing, which can help survival and improve functional health status. Several countries, including Brazil, Poland, Singapore, Thailand, and Turkey, already have education, learning, and health programs, which have increased their country's human capital. Use of evidence-based effective interventions, supported by funding to implement them, can clearly raise expected human capital if national governments set them as priorities. In our global economy that more heavily relies on digital technology than in the past, the article notes that it is even more important that increasing numbers of workers be highly skilled and healthy.

The authors also note several advantages of this study over others, such as that by Barro and Lee.[i] First, the estimates depend on censuses and household surveys rather than enrollment data, which can be inaccurate. Second, the IHME project used more unique sources than others, for example, 2522 compared to 621 of Barro and Lee. Third, binned levels of education were separated into

---

[h]The World Economic Forum released a human capital measure with underlying components for 130 countries in 2017.
[i]Barro and Lee (1993).

education by single grades. Fourth, annual estimates for 5-year age groups were created. A limitation in the data is that only mean estimates of education completed without information on distributions were included in the expected human capital measure.

The authors note some other limitations of their estimates. The quality of the learning estimates was adversely impacted by 56 countries not participating in international student assessments tests. In addition, there was a lack of quality metrics for tertiary education and on-the-job training. The health measures relied on PCA, which may not fully capture the differential impact of health status on economic productivity. Other health status elements, such as mental health and substance abuse, which were not included in the IHME study because of lack of data, may have important implications for economic productivity. It would be desirable to obtain better measures of stunting and wasting. A geospatial analysis would be preferred to the IHME national level analysis for many reasons. All of these limitations suggest opportunities for future research by IHME and others, as well as to attempt to determine the causal relationship between per capita GDP and human capital.

The article concludes that the IHME expected human capital estimates can serve as a metric to help countries focus on investing in their human capital to a greater extent as the World Bank recommends.

REFERENCES

Barro, R.J., Lee, J.-W., 1993. International comparisons of educational attainment. J. Monet. Econ. 32 (3), 363–394.

Dieleman, J.L., et al., 2018. Trends in future health financing and coverage: future health spending and universal health coverage in 188 countries, 2016-40. Lancet 391, 1783–1798.

Gakidou, E., et al., 2010. Increased educational attainment and its effect on child mortality in 175 countries between 1970 and 2009: a systematic analysis. Lancet 376, 959–974.

Lim, S.S., et al., 2018. Measuring human capital: a systematic analysis of 195 countries and territories, 1990–2016. Lancet 392, 1217–1234.

CHAPTER 6

Summary of World Economic Forum, "The Global Human Capital Report 2017—Preparing people for the future of work" ☆

BARBARA M. FRAUMENI[a,b,c,d,e,*] • GANG LIU[f]
[a]Central University of Finance and Economics, Beijing, China, [b]University of Southern Maine, Portland, ME, United States, [c]National Bureau of Economic Research, Cambridge, MA, United States, [d]IZA Institute for Labor Economics, Bonn, Germany, [e]Hunan University, Changsha, China, [f]Statistics Norway, Oslo, Norway
[*]Corresponding author: barbara_fraumeni@hotmail.com

As the title of the report suggests, the World Economic Forum's (WEF's) human capital index focused on building the workforces of tomorrow. Its 2017 report presented indices for 130 countries, which it hopes leaders will use as a tool to help human beings realize their potential in preparing for the political, societal, economic, and moral challenges of the Fourth Industrial Revolution.[a] WEF defines the Fourth Industrial Revolution as occurring with the adoption of cyber-physical systems, which require that workforces' skills be developed, realized, and enhanced throughout their whole lifetime.[b] WEF's actions, including the construction of the human capital index, are based on the principle that the future should be inclusive and human-centric. WEF believes that a deeper investment in human capital and a revolution in education systems are needed to accomplish the goal of maximizing human capital in each of the critical four human capital dimensions it quantified in the report.

WEF is an internationally known public-private cooperation organization, perhaps best known for its annual gathering in Davos, Switzerland. Recently, it released its second manifesto, which calls for stakeholder capitalism. This 2020 manifesto states "companies should pay their fair share of taxes, show zero tolerance for corruption, uphold human rights throughout their global supply chains, and advocate for a competitive level playing field—particularly in the 'platform economy.'"[c] In doing so, the manifesto asserts, and companies will serve all stakeholders: employees, customers, suppliers, local communities and society at large. The principles in the earlier 1973 manifesto are consistent with the principles in the 2020 manifesto.[d]

By "human capital" WEF means the knowledge and skills people possess that enable them to create value in the global economic system. The WEF human capital index was constructed from four equally weighted thematic components (subindexes): capacity, deployment, development, and know-how. Each component (subindex) comprises several subcomponents (indicators). Except in the case of unemployment (an indicator), the following equation was implemented to construct subcomponent (indicator):

$$\text{Country indicator} = \frac{\text{Country indicator value} - \text{logical minimum value}}{\text{Logical maximum value} - \text{logical minimum value}}$$

(6.1)

☆See World Economic Forum, 2017. The Global Human Capital Report 2017—Preparing People for the Future of Work. https://www.weforum.org/.

[a]The indicators and construction of the human capital index in the 2017 report were substantially revised from that in previous reports, such as the World Economic Forum's (WEF's) (2015) report The Human Capital Report 2015.

[b]World Economic Forum (n.d.-a), "What is the Fourth Industrial Revolution?"

[c]World Economic Forum (n.d.-b), "Why we need the Davos manifesto for better kind of capitalism."

[d]World Economic Forum (n.d.-b), "Why we need the Davos manifesto for better kind of capitalism."

Measuring Human Capital. https://doi.org/10.1016/B978-0-12-819057-9.00008-1

The subcomponents (indicators) detailed results for relevant age groups: 0–14 years, 15–24 years, 25–54 years, 55–64 years, and 65 years and over. The subcomponents with age groups were weighted by population share of each age group. The most recent data were used in calculating the index; however, data older than 10 years were considered to be too out-of-date to use. Countries omitted from the study included those for which their recent information were thought to be of poor quality, and those for which a WEF Executive Opinion Survey (EOS) had not been conducted within the past 2 years, as well as those for which civil or military unrest made obtaining quality data difficult. The report includes a single page for each of the 130 countries covered with a score card for the four components (subindexes) by relevant age groups, its rank, overall human capital score, and a large number of useful key indicators from a variety of sources.[e] This summary begins with a description of each of the four components (subindexes).

6.1 CAPACITY

The construction of the capacity component began with educational attainment by age groups and continued with analysis of fields of study by age groups based on LinkedIn membership information. Literacy and numeracy were calculated at least for ages 15–24; primary and secondary educational attainment for ages 15–24, 25–54, 55–64, and 65+ age groups; and tertiary educational attainment and field of study for ages 25–54, 55–64, and 65+. Data were excluded from construction of this component when indicators were available for less than two of the capacity subcomponents for the relevant age group. Of the 19 most populous countries in the world covered by WEF, the

percentage of the population with tertiary education in the 25–54 age group was highest for Japan (51%) and lowest for Ethiopia (3%), with the next lowest tertiary percentage for a most populous country being above 6%.[f,g] Of all 130 covered countries, Japan has, by far, the highest tertiary rate for the 25–54 age group, followed by the United States (32%) and the Russian Federation (30%); Yemen had the lowest tertiary rate (2%) followed by Ethiopia (3%) and Mali (3%). Literacy and numeracy, and primary and secondary education attainment were 100% for Finland, the top-rated human capital country of the 130. Literacy and numeracy and primary education attainment were 100% for each of the top 10-rated human capital countries of the 130. There was a large range in the literacy and numeracy scores among the bottom 10 of the 130 countries, from 55 or below for Chad, Guinea, and Mali, to 85 or above for Lesotho, Swaziland, and Yemen. Other factors than literacy and numeracy clearly had an adverse capacity impact on those at the bottom of the ranking, whereas at the top of the ranking literacy and numeracy and at least education attainment below the tertiary level were quite consistently high.

Some skills are developed through education and others by on-the-job learning. The report noted that as a greater diversity of lifetime skills becomes more important, the movement toward greater specialization in tertiary degrees may be misguided, although a deeper lifetime specialization could be important. The LinkedIn membership data indicated that some of the top 100 undergraduate degrees, such as business administration and management, have retained their share of all degrees across generations. The share of others such as computer science has been growing, while that of some others such as economics has been decreasing. The share of some others such as psychology, higher among those aged 55 and over, has become more important among those aged 25–34.[h] In general, there was quite a bit of diversity across generations in tertiary degree fields of study.

---

[e]The key indicators, not specifically included in the human capital index, are total population, gross domestic product (GDP) per capita (US$, purchasing price parity—PPP), mean years of education, median age of population, healthy life expectancy, working age population, labor force participation rate, unemployment rate, youth not in employment, education or training rate, output per worker (US$, PPP), mean monthly earnings (US$, PPP), mean monthly earnings for high-skilled workers (US$, PPP), mean monthly earnings for medium-skilled workers (US$, PPP), mean monthly earnings for low-skilled workers (US$, PPP), public spending on education (% of GDP), public spending on social security, working age (% of GDP), public spending on social security, retired (% of GDP), and pension scheme coverage share (% of working age population).

---

[f]In this summary, the list of the 20 most populous countries in 2016 comes from Lim et al. (2018). Of these 20, all but the Democratic Republic of Congo were covered by the WEF report.

[g]In this summary, all numbers are rounded.

[h]The top four undergraduate fields of study on average across ages 15–55+ among the 50 identified were business administration, computer science, economics, and psychology. The share for business administration was 6%; the share for the others was 4%.

Through LinkedIn membership, the field of study used in 10 industries and in 52 countries was documented.[i] The extent to which industries employed individuals across fields of study differs.[j] In most of the countries, the share for either business administration and law or information and communication technologies aggregate fields of study was the largest. The share of arts and humanities was unusually high at 10% or above for the high-income countries of Denmark, France, Ireland, and the United Kingdom. As one might expect, the share of engineering, manufacturing, and construction was high among countries with an abundance of oil.

The report ends the capacity section by concluding that the availability of information on online platforms, such as LinkedIn, presents the opportunity for aligning education and training to the demonstrated fields of study utilized by individual industries.

6.2 DEPLOYMENT

Four subcomponents made up the deployment score: (1) labor force participation rate, (2) employment gender gap, (3) unemployment rate, and (4) underemployment rate. Data were excluded from construction of this component when indicators were available for less than two of the deployment subcomponents for the relevant age group. The labor force participation rate was defined as the percentage of the population in the age category who were working or looking for work. The employment gender gap was defined as the ratio of the female labor force participation rate to the male labor force participation rate. The unemployment rate was defined as the percentage of those looking for work of those in the labor force. The indicator for the unemployment rate was constructed in a manner different from other human capital index indicators as its value was heavily skewed toward one end of the distribution[k]:

$$\text{Unemployment country indicator} =$$
$$\frac{[\log(\text{country indicator value} + 1)/2]*100 - \text{logical minimum value}}{\text{logical minimum value} - \text{logical maximum value}}$$

$$(6.2)$$

The underemployment rate was defined as the percentage of those who were employed but would like to work more hours in their current job, a new job, or by holding more than one job. The underemployment rate was not available for all countries and the unemployment rate may be available for only younger workers: those aged 15–24. Age categories for all four categories, when the data were available, were for those aged 15–24, 25–54, 55–64, and 65 or above. By age, the youngest and the oldest have the lowest deployment score. By gender, women typically have a lower labor force participation rate than men.[l] The report notes that rigid gender roles, insufficient and low fit opportunities, the increase in the number of youths in emerging countries, and the changing nature of work were often a problem causing low deployment. The report also raised a concern that along with new opportunities, there might also be issues regarding income inequality and differences in employment opportunities within and between countries.

The countries that one would expect to be the highest rated in any of the human capital components were not the ones that were rated highest in the deployment component, yet the country rated the lowest in the deployment component received very low scores on all components. Burundi and Rwanda, both with a

---

[i]The 10 industries include (1) basic and infrastructure, (2) consumer, (3) energy, (4) financial services, and investment, (5) healthcare, (6) information technology and telecoms, (7) media, entertainment and information, and (8) mobility, (9) professional services, and (10) public-sector and nonprofits.

[j]The analysis by industry and field of study was done for 10 aggregated fields of study; the analysis by country and field of study was done for nine aggregated fields of study. The 10 aggregated fields of study included (1) agriculture, forestry, fisheries, and veterinary, (2) arts and humanities, (3) business administration and law, (4) education, (5) engineering, manufacturing, and construction, (6) health and welfare, (7) information and communication technologies, (8) natural sciences, mathematics, and statistics, (9) services, and (10) social sciences, journalism, and information. The agriculture, forestry, fisheries, and veterinary aggregated field of study was not included in the study by country.

[k]The formula used for other subcomponent country indicators is listed in the section above.

[l]*The Global Human Capital Report 2017* used two measures of the gender gap, one in deployment and the other in development. Other reports by WEF include a number of additional means to quantify the gender gap. For example, see the WEF, *Global Gender Gap Report 2020*, p. 44. This report, which is summarized briefly in a later section in this summary, includes a number of ways to quantify the gender gap. The economic participation and opportunity subindex in this gender gap report contains three concepts: the participation gap, the remuneration gap and the advancement gap. These are most similar to the deployment gender measure in *The Global Human Capital Report 2017*. The *Global Gender Gap Report 2020* also has subindexes on educational attainment, health and survival, and political empowerment (p. 46). The development component in *The Global Human Capital Report 2017* includes a secondary enrollment gender gap subcomponent.

deployment score of 90, received the highest ranking among the 130 countries; Uganda with a deployment score of 84 received the next highest ranking. The labor force participation rate of both of the leaders for the core working age categories, 25–54 and 55–64, was at least 85; the employment gender gap for these ages was at least 97. The factor reducing their deployment score was that the unemployment rate, only available for the young, aged 15–24, was in the 68% to 70% range. In contrast for the country, Yemen, receiving the lowest deployment rating, a score of 34, the labor force participation rate for those aged 25–54 was 62%, dropping to 43% for those aged 55–64. For the country receiving the next lowest deployment rating at 35, Jordan, the statistics were 54% and 20%, respectively. The employment gender gap was particularly large for Yemen, as for those aged 25–54, female labor force participation was 13% of that of males; for Jordan it was 29%. Unemployment information was available for both Yemen and Jordan for all five age groups. For those aged 25–54, Yemen's unemployment rate was 46% and Jordan's unemployment rate was 39%. As was true with the countries having the highest deployment score, there was a notable gap in the ranking, in this case between the two lowest deployment ranked countries and that ranked as the next lowest: Iran, one of the 19 most populous countries in the world, was at 41.

A figure classified countries according to their capacity and deployment components into four quadrants: low capacity and deployment, high capacity and deployment, low capacity with high deployment, and high capacity with low deployment. The low versus high categories were separated by the mean values for these components, which were about 65 for both capacity and deployment. All of the 10 top-ranked human capital index countries fell in the high capacity and deployment category, along with a number of others such as China, the Russian Federation, Singapore, and the United Kingdom. Eight of the 10 lowest-ranked human capital index countries fell in the low capacity and deployment category, along with a number of others, notably four of the 19 most populous countries: Bangladesh, Ethiopia, India, and Pakistan. Guinea ranked at 121st and Chad at 122nd for the overall human capital index; both did well on deployment, but poorly on capacity. It was noted in the report that Sub-Saharan African countries frequently fell in the low capacity with high deployment category. A number of the most populous countries were marginally in one or both of the low capacity or deployment categories; these included Brazil, Indonesia, Mexico, the Philippines, and Vietnam. Four other most populous countries were in the low

deployment category, but basically on the border between the low and high capacity areas: Egypt, Iran, Thailand, and Turkey. Most countries did not fall in the high capacity and deployment category.

The report stressed the importance of policies and programs to raise the components with low score. Targets mentioned include gender related issues, re- and up-skilling, structural impediments that limit the availability and utilization of high-skilled workers, and work opportunities.

6.3 DEVELOPMENT

The development component of the human capital index included a number of enrollment subcomponents, two quality subcomponents, and two other measures. The enrollment subcomponents were primary, secondary, vocational, and tertiary education enrollment rates. In addition, there was a secondary enrollment gender gap subcomponent. The two quality subcomponents were for quality of primary schools and quality of education system. Of the nine subcomponents, the two remaining were skill diversity of graduates and extent of staff training. Data were excluded from construction of this component when indicators were available for less than three of the development subcomponents for the relevant age group. Three of the nine subcomponents, quality of primary schools, quality of education system, and extent of staff training, depended upon the WEF's EOS, which is a survey of business leaders around the world. The respondents were asked to rank these measures from 1 (lowest) to 7 (highest). The 0–14 age group was specified as the universe for the quality of primary schools' subcomponent, and the 15–24 age group was specified as the universe for the quality of education system subcomponent. The extent of staff training subcomponent did not list a specific age group, but clearly it was a question about workers. The skill diversity of graduates score was calculated using the Herfindahl-Hirschman index, which is a measure of concentration.[m] Further information on the skill diversity of individuals was collected from LinkedIn member records.

The needs of countries can differ according to the age composition of their country, for example, the

---

[m]The percentage of students in tertiary education enrolled in 1 of 10 programs plus unspecified were inputs to the Herfindahl-Hirschman index. The percentages came from the Institute of Statistics of the United Nations Educational, Scientific, and Cultural Organization. These 11 programs except for the unspecified were used in previous analysis.

preponderance of younger cohorts in Sub-Saharan Africa and the aging of many developed countries such as Japan and the United States and in Western European countries. Most of the development subcomponents speak to the issue of economies with younger populations rather than to those with older populations. The report maintains that lifelong learning initiatives should be implemented in countries with older populations.

The report notes that all learning systems would benefit from a forward-looking perspective, particularly given the nature of the Fourth Industrial Revolution. Building economic systems is of critical importance, with a focus on broad-based literacy, including linguistic and Science, Technology, Engineering, and Mathematics (STEM) literacies, as a basis for digital literacy. In a way consistent with the 2020 WEF manifesto, efforts to improve education should involve all stakeholders. Higher quality teaching, technical and vocational education and training, and lifelong learning are all important in this effort, supported by both private and public entities and by funding to ensure success and access to education and training across an individual's life.

Not all of the countries rated in the top 10 for the overall human capital index were also rated in the top 10 for development, however all scored at least in the high 70s. The top 10 for development all scored 80 or above, which was at least double of the scores being rated the lowest (Chad, Mauritania, and Yemen), with Finland at 89 scoring the highest. The primary and secondary education subcomponents were all done for ages 0–14; all other subcomponents, except that for staff training, were done for ages 15–24. It is no surprise that Finland received the highest development rating overall, but it scored relatively poorly on the secondary education enrollment rate and skill diversity of graduate subcomponents of development at 25th and 23rd, respectively. Algeria scored very high marks in secondary education enrollment rate and secondary enrollment gender gap at 99% and 100%, respectively. Canada received the highest rating for skill diversity of graduates but ranked poorly in the vocational education component at 97th and in the tertiary education enrollment rate at 43rd. Although Chad's, Mauritania's and Yemen's primary education enrollment rates were all at 79% or above, their rankings for this and all other subcomponents, except in the case of skill diversity of graduates, were all below 100.[n] Although Japan ranked 1st for the tertiary education attainment capacity subcomponent for those aged 25–54, it ranked only 37th for the

tertiary education enrollment rate development subcomponent. This indicates that its lead in the tertiary education attainment capacity subcomponent likely will be lost in the future. Greece led in tertiary education enrollment; Norway led in quality of primary schools, and Switzerland led in quality of education and extent of staff training.

A figure relating capacity and development, similar to the figure which classified countries according to their capacity and deployment components, was constructed with about the same mean value delineations of quadrants. There were only a few countries in the low capacity, high development quadrant. Aside from the countries typically rated highly in subcomponents, such as Finland, Norway, and Switzerland, Argentina, China, the Czech Republic and Kazakhstan were also in the high capacity, high development quadrant. There were few surprises in the low capacity, low development quadrant, although note that both India and Kenya were near one or the other of the borders of this quadrant. Egypt was near the high capacity border of the high capacity, low development quadrant; Mexico and Paraguay were highlighted as being clearly within the high capacity, low development quadrant.

Fifty-two cross-functional skills of LinkedIn members were identified by ages 18–24, 25–34, 35–44, 45–54 and 55+ and by nine degree specializations. The cross-functional skills covered a wide variety of skills. The nine degree specializations were the same as used earlier in the report. For those aged 18–24, four of the top nine cross-functional skills listed by at least 20% of the members involved a Microsoft product (Excel, Office, PowerPoint, and Word). Also included in the top nine for this age group were customer service, leadership, management, public speaking, research, and social media. For those aged 25–34, leadership, project management, and public speaking no longer were mentioned by at least 20% of the members. The number of skills being mentioned by 20% or more of the members shortened significantly for those above 34. For those aged 35–45, only management and Microsoft office made the 20% mark; for those above 44 only management and leadership made the 20% mark. The natural sciences, mathematics, and statistics degree concentration had the most concentrated set of cross-sectional skills as only two cross-sectional skills were listed by 20% more of the members with this degree specialization: Microsoft office and management. Other degree specializations mentioned at least three cross sectional skills at least 20% of the time.

The report also focused on about 200 specialized information, communications and technology (ICT)

---

[n]There was no information on skill diversity of graduates for Yemen.

skills of LinkedIn members for 10 degree specialties used previously in analysis. In terms of these ICT skills, there were two groups of degree specializations for which there seemed to be a commonality. The first was the group of engineering-track, natural sciences, and mathematics-track and ICT-track specializations; the second was the group of arts and humanities-track specializations; business, administration and law specializations; and social science, journalism, and information specializations. The report concluded that these commonalities suggest that individuals could move between the tracks within these groups with partial reskilling.

The distribution of specialist ICT skills by age and country highlighted the preponderance of those under 35 with these skills in certain countries: Brazil, Jamaica, Lithuania, Mauritius, and Trinidad and Tobago. In each of these countries the percentage of individuals under 35 with ICT skills was at least 75% or so. This was in contrast to the five countries at the lower end of the distribution with the percentage of individuals under 35 with ICT skills at around 55% or lower: Australia, Belgium, Luxembourg, the Netherlands, and Sweden. The ICT skills share for individuals under 35 for about half of the 52 countries for which statistics were tabulated was below 60%.

6.4 KNOW-HOW

In a global economy, skills are particularly important. The know-how component of the human capital index included three skills measures: medium-skilled and high-skilled employment share and availability of skilled employees. The International Labour Organization's Statistics Division, ILOSTAT, was the source for the employment shares. WEF's EOS was the basis for the availability of skilled employee measures. The fourth subcomponent of know-how was economic complexity. Hausmann et al.'s (n.d.) atlas was the basis for this measure. None of the subcomponents were available for a specific age group, but all were measures about workers; however, data were excluded from construction of this component when indicators were not available for at least one subcomponent.

In the overall know-how index, those who scored the highest and lowest were both fairly tightly bunched with a difference of six from the country ranked tenth (United Kingdom) to that ranked first (Switzerland) and from the country ranked last at 130th (Ethiopia) to that ranked 121st (Cambodia); those in the top 10 scored from 70 to 76 and those in the bottom 10 scored from 35 to 41. For the top 10 countries, there was a lot of diversity in the subcomponent rankings. In addition, of the

countries who ranked first in one of the four know-how subcomponents, only Norway scored in at least the top 25% of all ranked countries in all of the know-how subcomponent results. Luxembourg ranked first in high-skilled employment share, Kuwait ranked first in medium-skilled employment share, Japan ranked first in economic complexity, and Norway ranked first in availability of skilled employees.

The relationship between capacity and know-how was examined in a figure similar to previous figures relating capacity to one of the other components; in addition, the relationship between deployment and know-how was featured in a figure. As the mean for know-how was about 55, the position of the quadrants differed from the previous figures relating capacity to deployment or capacity to development. A very few countries were in the low capacity and low know-how or low deployment and low know-how quadrants. The report suggests that countries with high capacity and low know-how, such as Peru, Mongolia, and South Africa, have an opportunity to raise their know-how through a variety of mechanisms, including by participating in a global supply chain. In addition, the suggestion was that countries in the low deployment and low know-how quadrant, such as France, Germany, Italy, and the United Arab Emirates, could raise their low know-how scores by up-skilling and utilizing in skill intensive industries their large pool of workers with medium-level skills. About one-third of all countries were in the low deployment and low know-how quadrant. With one exception for a country with borderline high know-how, all countries in the high deployment and high know-how quadrant had a deployment score of less than 80.

6.5 OVERALL HUMAN CAPITAL INDEX

The human capital index was presented in detail by country, and by regions, income groups, and by two political entities: the G20 and the European Union. As WEF hopes that countries will prepare for the Fourth Industrial Revolution, the initial emphasis was on gaps in human capital development. The smallest gap by region was that for North America at 26%; the largest gap by region was for Sub-Saharan Africa at 47%.[o,p]

---

[o]Eight regions were considered: (1) East Asia and the Pacific, (2) Eastern Europe and Central Asia, (3) Latin America and the Caribbean, (4) Middle East and North Africa, (5) North America, (6) South Asia, (7) Sub-Saharan Africa, and (8) Western Europe.

[p]The North America region included only two countries: Canada and the United States.

The global average gap was 38%. As the report states, of the 130 covered countries, there were 25 countries whose gap was 30% or less, 50 countries whose gap was between 31% and 40%, 41 countries whose gap was between 41% and 50%, and 14 countries whose gap was at 51% or more. The 10 countries that had the smallest gap (in order from ranked number 1 to number 10) were Norway, Finland, Switzerland, the United States, Denmark, Germany, New Zealand, Sweden, Slovenia, and Austria. The 10 countries who had the largest gap (in reverse order from ranked number 130th to number 121th) were Yemen, Mauritania, Senegal, Ethiopia, Mali, Pakistan, Lesotho, Swaziland, Chad, and Guinea. Among the top rankings were Nordic countries and smaller European countries, along with two countries that were among the 19 most populous countries in the world (Germany and the United States), plus New Zealand. Seven of the countries with the largest gap were Sub-Saharan countries, 2 were from the Middle East and North Africa region, 1 was from South Asia, and 2 were among the 19 most populous counties in the world (Nigeria and Pakistan). Regional differences in human capital gaps certainly existed.

There was a greater dispersion in human capital scores among the G20 countries than among the 28 members of the European Union.[q] The highest human capital score among the G20 countries was 75 (United States, ranked 4th) and the lowest was 55 (India ranked 103rd). The highest human capital score among the European Union countries was 77 (Finland, ranked 2nd) and the lowest was 65 (Greece, ranked 48th). As the report notes, the G20 has recognized the importance of developing global human capital, through both government and private action. The report also notes that the European Union recognized the importance of digital skills by launching a new initiative in 2016.

The widest dispersion in human capital scores by region was for the Middle East and North Africa region, the least dispersion was for the North America region, followed by the Latin America and the Caribbean region. The highest score among the Middle East and North Africa countries was 72 (Israel, ranked 18th) and the lowest 35 (Yemen, ranked last at130th). There were only two North American region countries: Canada at 73, ranked 14th, and the United States at 75, ranked 4th. The highest human capital score among the Latin America and the Caribbean countries was 64 (Argentina, ranked 52nd) and the lowest at 56 (Honduras, ranked 101st).

---

[q]The United Kingdom left the European Union after the writing of the WEF report.

6.5.1 East Asia and the Pacific

There were 16 countries ranked in the East Asia and the Pacific region. This region includes 6 of the 19 most populous countries in the world: China, Indonesia, Japan, Philippines, Thailand, and Vietnam. The difference between the countries with the highest human capital scores and the lowest was among the largest of all regions; however, there was a sign of a better future coming. Although only 20% of the region's population aged 0–14 was enrolled in secondary school, the educational attainment rates in the capacity component for the younger generation were greater than those of the older generation. The countries with the highest human capital ratings in the region, Japan, South Korea, and Singapore, were in contrast to those with the lowest: Cambodia, Lao PDR, and Myanmar. In spite of ranking last for the region, the latter three countries did well in the deployment component. China, the most populous country in the world (followed by India), did very well in the deployment component and achieved a very high secondary enrollment rate, which was an indicator in the development component. Thailand did well in the development component; Malaysia did poorly mainly because of its employment gender gap. Countries with younger populations such as Indonesia and Vietnam did well on the enrollment subcomponents of the development component, in contrast to countries with older populations such as the Republic of Korea and Japan, who did well on the attainment subcomponents of the capacity component. Although Australia and New Zealand did very well in the ratings, their human capital score would be improved if unemployment and underemployment were less.

6.5.2 Eastern Europe and Central Asia

There were 21 countries ranked in the Eastern Europe and Central Asia region. One of these countries, the Russian Federation was among the 19 most populous countries in the world. Six countries in this region ranked in the top 25, all with human capital scores above 70: Czech Republic, Estonia, Lithuania, Russian Federation, Slovenia, and Ukraine. Macedonia, FYR, and three countries in Eastern Europe: Albania, Moldova, and Romania were at the bottom of the rankings for the whole region. The Kyrgyz Republic, Russian Federation, and Tajikistan all performed well on the educational attainment indicators of the capacity component, but were lagging in either the deployment or know-how components.

6.5.3 Latin America and the Caribbean

There were 22 countries ranked in the Latin America and the Caribbean region. Two of these countries, Brazil and

Mexico, which ranked at about the middle of the index at 77th and 69th respectively, were among the 19 most populous countries in the world. Venezuela and some Central America countries, such as Honduras, did poorly in the overall ranking and in the capacity component because of low education attainment rates at levels above primary education. Peru, which also ranked at about the middle of the distribution at 66th, nonetheless received the highest deployment score in the region because of high levels of labor force participation. Although many of the individuals in several countries in the Latin America and the Caribbean region had not obtained basic education, there was little evidence of an education gender gap. Many countries had a high youth unemployment, but relatively low unemployment in the 25–54 prime working age group and a high-skilled employment share in the 20% range. Hopefully this portends for a greater utilization of human capital when the youths age. Because many individuals continue to work at aged 65 and above which was beyond their country's expected health life-span for individuals, it may be that the country's social net was not adequate.

6.5.4 Middle East and North Africa

There were 15 countries ranked in the Middle East and North Africa region. Three of these countries: Egypt, Iran, and Turkey were among the 19 most populous countries in the world. Each of these populous countries did poorer on the deployment and know-how components than on the capacity and development components, and scored between 55 and 60 on the overall human capital measure. Each of them ranked the worst in deployment, with employment gender gap rankings below 100. Three gulf states in the region, Bahrain, Qatar, and the United Arab Emirates, did the best of all of the Arab states; however, as they were among the six high-income countries in the region, it was maintained in the report that they could possibly use their wealth to further the level of their human capital. Notably, relative to the rest of the region, they scored poorly on vocational and tertiary education enrollment and on skill diversity of graduates. Both Kuwait and Saudi Arabia, also high-income countries, have high youth unemployment and a high employment gender gap, and ranked in the bottom 40% of the 130 countries. Wealth alone does not mean that human capital will be high. None of the North Africa countries, Algeria, Mauritania, Morocco, Tunisia, or Yemen, ranked above 100th. As previously noted, this region had the highest dispersion of human capital scores among the eight regions, with Israel, a high-income country, ranking 18th and Yemen, a lower-middle income country, ranking 130th.

6.5.5 North America

Both countries in this region, Canada and the United States, were among the 20 highest human capital ranked countries. The United States was among the most populous 19 countries in the world. The biggest component ranking difference between the two countries was for development, with Canada ranked 22nd and the United States ranked 4th, although Canada did much better than the United States in the primary and secondary enrollment rates, the quality of primary school indicators, and the skill diversity of graduates subcomponents. The United States did better in the tertiary education enrollment rate and in the extent of staff training subcomponents. Both did the poorest in the deployment category, with both ranking below 50th in the labor force participation rate subcomponent.[r]

6.5.6 South Asia

There were five countries ranked in this region, with three of them: Bangladesh, India, and Pakistan, among the 19 most populous countries. Only Sri Lanka of all countries in the region, had utilized 60% or more of its human capital. Its ranking was lower than it would be otherwise as more than 20% of those aged 15–24 were unemployed. India had made significant progress in improving its human capital; however, 11% of its youth still were not literate or did not have the ability to understand and work with numbers. In addition, it ranked among the worst of all 130 countries in the employment gender gap subcategory and did poorly in the labor force participation rate category except for those 65 years of age or older. Since the healthy life expectancy in India was 60 years, a labor force participation rate of those 65 and above at 26% was a bit surprising. The results for both Bangladesh and Pakistan indicated the inadequacy of their education system particularly below the tertiary level. Both countries finished among the lowest third for all age groups for literacy and numeracy, primary and secondary attainment and enrollment rates, and quality of primary schools. Both countries also experienced significant employment gender gaps. This region's human capital gap at 46% was only 1 percentage point lower than that of the region with the greatest gap: Sub-Saharan Africa.

6.5.7 Sub-Saharan Africa

There were 29 countries ranked in this region, with two of them, Ethiopia and Nigeria, among the 19 most

---

[r]There was no United States' information for underemployment rate or vocational education enrollment rate, in the deployment and development components, respectively.

populous countries. Both of these countries ranked near the bottom of the human capital rankings, with Nigeria being the only country of the two scoring better than 98th on any component. Ethiopia ranked close to 100th on deployment and development in spite of a respectable youth labor force participation rate, but with across all age groups, high unemployment rates (41%–52%) and underemployment rates (20%–47%). There were two bright spots in the development component: secondary enrollment gender gap and vocational education enrollment rate. Ethiopia ranked last of the 130 countries ranked in know-how and near last in capacity. Nigeria ranked near to last in development and know-how, with only about two-thirds of those aged 0–14 enrolled in primary schools, which were ranked to be of poor quality. Clearly, in the future there was much room for these populous countries to improve their human capital to significantly raise their own human capital and the average human capital of the region.

Although just over half of the countries in the region were in the lower income group and the remaining were spread fairly evenly among the two middle income categories, the relative performance of all of the countries in the region among the four components and across age groups was fairly similar. Five of the top 10 rated countries in the deployment category were from this region, mainly due to high labor force participation. However, the capacity and know-how ratings were typically below average, which suggests that their human capital would benefit from development efforts.

The two top-ranked countries in the region, Ghana and Rwanda, as well as Kenya, could all do better if their secondary enrollment rates were improved. Neither Ghana nor Rwanda had employment and secondary education gender gaps, which helped. All three countries benefit from having a high medium-skill employment share in the know-how component, and relatively high quality of education system and extent of staff training in the development category.

South African countries, Botswana, Namibia, South Africa, and Zambia, did better than the rest of the region on the development component, although they performed below the region average on the deployment component. South Africa has the highest workforce share of high-skilled employees of all in the region and did well in staff training in spite of not doing well in the quality of education system subcomponent.

6.5.8 Western Europe

There were 20 countries ranked in this region, with only 1 of them: Germany, among the 19 most populous countries in the world. Six countries in the region ranked in the human capital top 10: Denmark, Finland, Germany, Norway, Sweden and Switzerland, with four other countries not far behind: Belgium, France, the Netherlands, and the United Kingdom. Only three countries ranked in the 40s range: Greece, Portugal, and Spain, which places them in the bottom of the regional list.

In spite of these high human capital rankings, most of the region's countries performed below average in youth deployment. The reason for this lower than average deployment ranking was a generally low labor force participation rate, and a generally high unemployment and underemployment rate for this age category. Greece was plagued with a 48% unemployment rate among its young. Seventeen of the top 30 ranked countries in the know-how component were in this region.

Two countries that were midranked were among those in the region, France and the United Kingdom, were being held back by their rankings on deployment and capacity, respectively. Italy was held back by a variety of factors, including a low labor force participation rate, high youth unemployment, the extent of its staff training, and somewhat larger gender gaps than others in the region.

6.6 INCOME (GROSS NATIONAL INCOME PER CAPITA)

There were 46 high-income countries, with three, Germany, Japan, and the United States, among the 19 most populous countries.[5] All but 3 of the high-income countries scored 60 or above in human capital, with 23 scoring 70 or above. The 3 who scored below 60 were Barbados, Kuwait, and Saudi Arabia.

The situation was quite different for the 31 countries in the upper-middle income category as only 1 country: the Russian Federation, scored above 70 in human capital. The Russian Federation was among the 19 most populous countries. The rest of the countries in this category were fairly evenly split between earning scores of

---

[5] The World Bank income categories as of July 2017 were used in the report. These were based on Gross National Income (GNI) per capita in current US dollars. Low income countries were those for which this GNI per capita was $1005 or less; lower-middle income countries were those for which this GNI per capita was $1006 to $3955; upper-middle income countries were those for which this GNI per capita was $3956 to $12,235; and high income countries were those for which this GNI per capita was $12,236 or more. These figures were calculated by the World Bank by using the Atlas method, which smooths exchange rate fluctuations by using a three-year moving average, price-adjusted conversion factor.

60 to less than 70 and 50 to less than 60, with 17 in the first and 14 in the second range.

The vast majority of the 19 most populous countries were in a middle-income category, with 7 in the upper-middle income category and 8 in the lower-middle income category.

There were 35 lower-middle income countries, with just 1 country: Ukraine, scoring above 70 in human capital. Twelve scored in the 60 to less than 70 range, 16 in the 50 to less than 60 range, and 6 scored below 50.

An equal number of countries in the lower-middle income category and the lower income category were in the bottom 10 for their human capital scores.

There were 17 lower income countries, with only 1, Rwanda, scoring above 60 in human capital and only 1 country: Ethiopia, among the 19 most populous countries. The rest of the countries were evenly split between the next two ranges with eight earning scores of 50 to less than 60 and eight earning scores just below 50.

6.7 BRIEF SUMMARY OF HUMAN CAPITAL COMPONENTS IN OTHER RECENT WEF REPORTS

There are two recent WEF reports that contain substantial indicators of human capital: *The Global Competitiveness Report 2019* and the *Global Gender Gap Report 2020*. The former report covered 141 countries and the latter 153 countries.[t] As the results for human capital related components of these two WEF reports frequently varied from those in *The Global Human Capital Report 2017*, one's perspective on a country's human capital could easily depend on which report is referenced.

6.7.1 The Global Competitiveness Report 2019[u]

The 12 pillars of the overall 2019 4.0 competitiveness index were as follows: institutions, infrastructure, ICT adoption, macroeconomic stability, health, skills, product market, labor market, financial system, market size, business dynamism, and innovation capability (World Economic Forum, 2017, 2019, 2020). These 12 pillars were further identified as part of four broader categories: enabling environment, human capital, markets, and innovation ecosystem. In addition to the pillars, five selected contextual indicators and four social and environmental performance indicators, which did not enter into the competitiveness calculation, were listed by country. The broader human capital aggregate, which contained the health and skills pillars (5th and 6th, respectively), is certainly the one most relevant for WEF's *The Global Human Capital Report 2017* human capital index. Each pillar, and each subcomponent of a pillar, and each indicator within a subcomponent were equally weighted in the competitiveness index. Accordingly, the broader human capital aggregate accounted for 16.7% of the competitiveness index score. As there was only one subcomponent of health, it accounted for the full 8.3% of that pillar's score.[v,w] Table 6.1 shows the contributions of the nine individual indicators which comprise the 6th pillar.[x] Mean years of schooling was included instead of the disaggregated education attainment level and age breakouts in *The Global Human Capital Report 2017*. Table 6.1 shows the extent to which the reliance on WEF's EOS increased between the human capital and competitiveness report. In the human capital report, two subcomponents also available in the competitiveness report used the WEF EOS: Extent of staff training and availability of skilled employees. The graduate skill

---

[t]There were four countries in *The Global Human Capital Report 2017*, but not in *The Global Competitiveness Report 2019*: Guyana, Liberia, Myanmar, and Sierra Leone. There were 15 countries in *The Global Competitiveness Report 2019*, but not in *The Global Human Capital Report 2017*: Angola, Azerbaijan, Bosnia and Herzegovina, Burkina Faso, Cape Verde, the Democratic Republic of the Congo, Georgia, Haiti, Hong Kong, Lebanon, Montenegro, Oman, Seychelles, Taiwan, and Zimbabwe. There were two countries in *The Global Human Capital Report 2017*, but not in the *Global Gender Gap Report 2020*: Gabon and Guyana. There were 25 countries in the *Global Gender Gap Report 2020*, but not in *The Global Human Capital Report 2017*: Angola, Azerbaijan, Bahamas, Belarus, Belize, Bhutan, Bosnia and Herzegovina, Burkina Faso, Cape Verde, the Democratic Republic of Congo, Cuba, Fiji, Georgia, Iraq, Lebanon, Maldives, Montenegro, Oman, Papua New Guinea, Suriname, Syria, Timor-Leste, Togo, Vanuatu, and Zimbabwe. Swaziland became Eswatini in 2018; Macedonia became North Macedonia in 2019.

[u]A competitiveness report by the WEF was released late in 2020: Schwab and Zahidi (2020) *How Countries are Performing on the Road to Recovery*. This report did not provide country rankings, accordingly it is not discussed in detail in this summary of WEF human capital measures. In the human capital section of this 2020 report (pp. 21–26), there were three sections: "What are the human capital-related priorities emerging from the past decade," "What are the priorities for human capital development in the short-term revival of economies," and "What are the priorities for empowering human capital to drive the long-term transformation of economies?."

[v]This information was obtained from the Institute for Health Metrics and Evaluation's Gross Burden of Disease 2017.

[w]The sole indicator for the health pillar was healthy life expectancy.

[x]This table was derived from the listing on p. 612 of *The Global Competitiveness Report 2019*.

TABLE 6.1
6th pillar: skills.

	% of skills component score	Sum of right-most %s	Source
Current workforce	50		
Education of current workforce	25		
Mean years of schooling	25		UNESCO[a]
Skills of current workforce	25		
Extent of staff training	5		WEF EOS
Quality of vocational training	5		WEF EOS
Skillset of graduates	5		WEF EOS
Digital skills of active population	5		WEF EOS
Ease of finding skilled employees	5		WEF EOS
Future workforce	50		
Education of future workforce	25		
School life expectancy	25		UNESCO
Skills of future workforce	25		
Critical thinking in teaching	12.5		WEF EOS
Pupil-to-teacher ratio in primary education	12.5		World Bank
		100	

[a]UNESCO is the abbreviation for the United Nations Educational, Scientific, and Cultural Organization.

indicator from *The Global Human Capital Report 2017* (skill diversity of graduates) differed in concept and source from what appeared in *The Global Competitiveness Report 2019* (skillset of graduates). Availability of skilled employees in the human capital report was retitled to ease of finding skilled employees in the competitiveness report. The other seven 6th pillar indicators were all different from indicators in the human capital report. There was no health component in the human capital report; accordingly, the 5th health pillar was a new subcomponent of human capital compared to that in the human capital report.

How human capital was measured in the two reports did impact on the rankings of countries included in both reports. All countries ranked in the top 10 in *The Global Human Capital Report 2017* were also covered in *The Global Competitiveness Report 2019*. The average health pillar 5 ranking of the top 10 from the human capital report was 26th, with Switzerland having the highest ranking at 5th and the United States substantially lowering the average at 55th. All but 2 of the top 10 in the human capital report were also in the

top 10 in the skill pillar 6 of the competitiveness report, and several received top scores for this pillar. Switzerland ranked first overall in pillar 6, ranking first in three of the nine pillar indicators. Finland ranked first in two of the nine skills pillar indicators; Germany and the United States each ranked first in one of the nine skills pillar indicators. There were multiple countries that tied with perfect scores in 2 of the pillar indicators, with half of the top 10 countries having perfect scores in one of the skill pillar indicators with ties and with 2 of top 10 having perfect scores in the other indicator with ties. In the one indicator that was the same in both reports (availability of versus ease of finding skilled employees), the United States scored 5th in the human capital report and 1st in the competitiveness report. Finland scored first overall in the human capital report and Switzerland scored first in the competitiveness report skills pillar 6.

A number of countries not included in *The Global Human Capital Report 2017* ranked in the bottom 10 in *The Global Competitiveness Report 2019*. For a fair comparison, only those countries covered in both are

TABLE 6.2
Component and indicator % weights.

	Weights	Sum of right-most %s
Economic participation and opportunity	25	
Labor force participation rate	19.9	
Wage equality for similar work	31.0	
Estimated earned income	22.1	
Legislators, senior officials, and managers[a]	14.9	
Professional and technical workers	12.1	
		100
Educational attainment	25	
Literacy rate	19.1	
Enrollment in primary education	45.9	
Enrollment in secondary education	23.0	
Enrollment in tertiary education	12.1	
		100
Health and survival	25	
Sex ratio at birth[a]	69.3	
Healthy life expectancy	30.7	
		100

[a]These two categories are significantly different from those included as part of human capital in other WEF reports.

included as being 1 of the 10 lowest ranked countries. In health pillar 5 ranking, only three countries ranked at the bottom in the human capital report were also in the bottom 10 in the competitiveness report. Lesotho, which was not in the bottom 10 in the human capital report, ranked the lowest, 141st, in the only pillar 5 indicator: healthy life expectancy. In the skills pillar 6 ranking, all but 2 of the 10 ranked at the bottom in the human capital report were also in the bottom 10 in the competitiveness report. The only country ranked in the human capital report bottom 10 to be ranked last in the health indicator or any one of the nine skills indicators was Mauritania, which ranked last in one of the skills indicators. Yemen was ranked last overall in the human capital report at 130th and next to last in the competitiveness report at 140th; Chad ranked 122nd in the human capital report and last in the competitiveness report skills pillar 6 at 141st.

6.7.2 Global Gender Gap Report 2020

Because this is a report on the gender gap, its included human capital-related indicators were the ratio of females to males. There were four major components

in this report: economic participation and opportunity, educational attainment, health and survival, and political empowerment, with five, four, two, and three indicators in each. Each of the four components was equally weighted in the overall index. In addition to the gender gap indicators, 53 contextual data indicators, which did not enter into the gender gap calculation, were listed by country. To be included in the report with a composite score, a country must have had data on at least 12 of the 14 indicators. Nine of the 14 indicators, including all but 2 of the 11 listed in Table 6.2, were similar to human capital indicators in other WEF reports, but with a focus on women. Each of the four components was equally weighted in the overall index, but the contribution of individual indicators to a component depended upon a normalization through equalized standard deviations. Table 6.2 lists the indicator weights within each component for all but the political empowerment component, which did not contain any of the similar indicators. The indicators were listed for females and males, and for the ratio of the female to male indicator, with a country's rank depending on the ratio.

Almost all countries ranked in the top 10 in *The Global Human Capital Report 2017* did very well in the educational attainment component of the *Global Gender Gap Report 2020*, but few did well in the other two human capital-related components. Note that all countries ranked in the top 10 in the human capital report were also covered in the gender gap report. Four of the top 10 were in a tie for first with 21 other countries, with all but one of the top ten scoring at least 0.992, for a 77th ranking, with 1.000 being a perfect score. Germany ranked last of the top 10 countries at 103rd. None of the top 10 in the human capital report were ranked in the top 10 in the gender gap report, although two were close (Norway at 11th and Slovenia at 12th) and all but 1 of the top 10 ranked 50th or above. The lowest average ranking for the top 10 was in the health and survival component, although Slovenia, one of the top 10, tied for first with 38 other countries. The average ranking for the other 9 top 10 countries was 92nd. This low average ranking was due to low healthy life expectancy indicator scores as all but 1 of the top 10 were tied with a number of other countries for a first ranking in the sex ratio at birth indicator subcomponent.

Three of the countries ranked among the bottom 10 in *The Global Human Capital Report 2017* were ranked among the bottom 10 in the overall gender gap ranking in the *Global Gender Gap Report 2020*, but the bottom 10 in the human capital report fared better when considering only those gender gap components more directly related to human capital.[y] For example, Guinea ranked 10th in the gender gap report economic participation and opportunity component, although it ranked 11th from the bottom in the health and survival component. In addition, three countries ranked in the bottom 10 in the human capital report were among the 39 countries tied for first in the health and survival component; 1 country ranked in the bottom 10 in the human capital report was among the 24 countries tied for first in the educational attainment component. Up to four bottom ranked countries were tied for first place in the literacy rate, enrollment in primary education, or enrollment in secondary education indicators of the educational attainment component. Iraq, which was not covered in the human capital report, ranked last in the gender gap report economic participation and opportunity component; Chad, 1 of the 10 lowest ranked countries in the human capital report, ranked last in the educational attainment component; and China, not 1 of the 10 lowest ranked countries in the human capital report,

ranked last in the gender gap report health and survival component. The results for countries ranked among the bottom 10 in the human capital report varied significantly in their rankings in the gender gap report.

6.8 CONCLUSION OF THE WEF 2017 HUMAN CAPITAL REPORT

The World Economic Forum provides an abundance of information on human capital. In its conclusion, it made a number of recommendations. It called for greater connection between education and the skills needed for labor markets. It asserts that behavioral and noncognitive skills were becoming increasingly important as were lifelong-learning, innovation, and training. In addition, in many countries, youths may not have access to the education they need; in other countries, substantial increases in funding have yielded little return and not been directed sufficiently toward early child education and teacher training to produce high quality teachers. Technology can change the relationship between human capital and physical capital. The experts were unsure if the use of human capital will decrease or increase as a result. It noted that generational shifts were occurring in many countries, with the older workforce retiring and the younger workforce having different objectives and worldviews. These uncertainties raise questions about the long-term future. The WEF report states that all of those involved in or impacting on human capital: government officials, business leaders, education providers, and individuals, must be aware of the potential future changes to be able to respond to them. A set of knowledge tools has been provided by WEF's System Initiative on Shaping the Future of Education, Gender and Work. The report concludes that WEF's global human capital index will impact on private-public collaborations, discussions about global multistakeholder's collaborations, shared visions impacting education, employment, and investment given the Fourth Industrial Revolution.

REFERENCES

Hausmann, R., Hidalgo, C., et al., n.d.. The Atlas of Economic Complexity. https://atlas.cid.harvard.edu/.

Lim, S.S., et al., 2018. Measuring human capital: a systematic analysis of 195 countries and territories, 1990–2016. Lancet 392 (October 6), 1217–1234.

Schwab, K., Zahidi, S., 2020. How Countries Are Performing on the Road to Recovery (Special edition 2020, December 16) http://www3.weforum.org/docs/WEF_TheGlobalCompetitivenessReport2020.pdf.

World Economic Forum, 2015. The Human Capital Report 2015, Employment, Skills, and Human Capital Global

---

[y]For a fair comparison, again only those countries covered in both are included as being 1 of the 10 lowest ranked countries.

Challenge Insight Report. http://www3.weforum.org/docs/WEF_Human_Capital_Report_2015.pdf.

World Economic Forum, 2017. The Global Human Capital Report 2017—Preparing People for the Future of Work. https://www.weforum.org/.

World Economic Forum, 2019. The Global Human Competitiveness Report 2019. http://www3.weforum.org/docs/WEF_TheGlobalCompetitivenessReport2019.pdf.

World Economic Forum, 2020. Global Gender Gap Report 2020. https://www.weforum.org/.

World Economic Forum. What Is the Fourth Industrial Revolution?. https://www.weforum.org/agenda/2016/01/what-is-the-fourth-industrial-revolution/, n.d.-a, 26 December 2020.

World Economic Forum. Why We Need the Davos Manifesto for Better Kind of Capitalism. https://www.weforum.org/agenda/2019/12/why-we-need-the-davos-manifesto-for-better-kind-of-capitalism/, n.d.-b, 26 December 2020.

CHAPTER 7

Human Capital of Mainland China, Hong Kong and Taiwan, 1997–2018

XIANFANG XIONG[a] • XING CHEN[b] • YUZHE NING[c] • HAIZHENG LI[c,d,*] • BELTON M. FLEISHER[e,f]

[a]Center for Economics, Finance and Management Studies, Hunan University, Changsha, China, [b]Economic Research Institute of State Grid Henan Electric Power Company, Zhengzhou, China, [c]China Center for Human Capital and Labor Market Research, Central University of Finance and Economics, Beijing, China, [d]School of Economics, Georgia Institute of Technology, Atlanta, GA, United States, [e]Department of Economics, Ohio State University, Columbus, OH, United States, [f]IZA Institute of Labor Economics, Bonn, Germany
*Corresponding author: haizheng.li@econ.gatech.edu

7.1 INTRODUCTION

We contribute to the literature by providing a comprehensive description and discussion of human capital development in Beijing, Shanghai, Hong Kong, and Taiwan, starting from the date of Hong Kong's return to China in 1997. To compare these regions, we construct alternative human capital measures under various frameworks and mechanism implications. Our focus on how human capital development has contributed to the narrowing economic gap between Mainland China, Hong Kong, and Taiwan is based on the accepted belief that human capital is a key factor in economic development (Fleisher et al., 2010). The analysis sheds new light on the role of human capital in China's development and on economic growth, in general, and our results should be useful for various policy analyses and related research.

We analyze human capital trends and dynamics based on traditional education-based human capital indexes, and we develop a new comprehensive human capital measure for China based on the Jorgenson-Fraumeni (J-F) lifetime income framework. The J-F measure has been widely adopted in human capital research, including the World Bank estimation of country level human capital (Lange et al., 2018) and in published papers (Fraumeni et al., 2019). Limitations of traditional education-based measures of human capital include neglecting adjustments for education quality, on-job learning, health, and other influences. The J-F

avoids these limitations and, moreover, provides a monetary value of the human capital stock, which facilitates comparisons across locations and over time.

The drastic geographical economic disparities within Mainland China leads us to compare two of Mainland China's most advanced cities, Beijing and Shanghai, with Hong Kong and Taiwan. Given the significant changes for Hong Kong after returning to China in 1997, our comparisons mainly cover the years 1997–2018, the latest year with available data.

In 2018 per capita GDP was 6.6 thousand 1997 US dollars (USD) in Mainland China, 21.0 thousand in Taiwan, and 37.4 thousand Hong Kong. The comparable figures for Beijing and Shanghai, within the Mainland China, were 14.1 thousand 1997 USD in Beijing and 13.4 thousand in Shanghai. Fig. 7.1 shows the trend of GDP per capita in all regions. As can be seen, Beijing and Shanghai are much closer to Hong Kong and Taiwan in terms of their development stage throughout the 1997–2018 time period.

In contrast to their levels, the growth relative annual growth rates of GDP per capita, 10.8% and 10.7% for Beijing and Shanghai, respectively, vastly exceed those for Hong Kong and Taiwan, which are, respectively, only 2.6% and 2.9%. Fig. 7.1 illustrates the three regions' potential convergence of per capita GDP. In view of their economic growth gaps, we compare underlying forces including relative performance measures of

Measuring Human Capital. https://doi.org/10.1016/B978-0-12-819057-9.00005-6

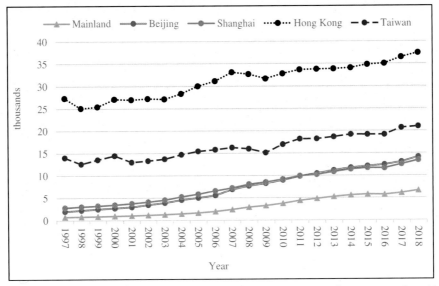

FIG. 7.1 GDP per capita. Data is from http://humancapital.cufe.edu.cn, https://www.censtatd.gov.hk and https://statdb.dgbas.gov.tw; GDP data are first converted to real 1997-based GDP, then converted to USD with the 1997 exchange rate.

labor-market performance and trends in human capital accumulation.

While our main focus is to investigate the regional gaps in alternative measures of human capital and their trends, we also assess the interactions of human capital trends with those of population aging and their impact on population dividends. We seek to measure the extent to which human capital growth potentially retards the effect of population aging on the shrinking of population dividends.

The remainder of this chapter is organized as follows. The next section reviews the literature on human capital measurements. Section 7.3 discusses labor force composition and age structure in Mainland China including the major markets in Beijing and Shanghai, Hong Kong, and Taiwan. Section 7.4 presents an overview of the education systems in Mainland China, Hong Kong, and Taiwan. Section 7.5 discusses education-based human capital measures. Section 7.6 presents J-F calculation measures of human capital. Section 7.7 further assesses the J-F human capital measure, comparing it with the behavior of GDP and physical capital. Section 7.8 discusses human capital development and its effect on population aging and population dividends. Section 7.9 concludes the chapter.

7.2 HUMAN CAPITAL MEASUREMENTS

We briefly review the broad literature of human capital measurement and its impact on economic growth and development, focusing on China's development and the growth trends of Mainland China, Hong Kong, and Taiwan.

The measurement of human capital has evolved along three main approaches: (i) education-based, (ii) cost-based, and (iii) income-based. The education-based approach measures human capital with various schooling indicators, such as average schooling years (Barro and Lee, 1993; Cohen and Soto, 2001) and schooling enrollment ratios (Barro and Lee, 2013). Typically, education-based measures do not reflect schooling quality. By definition, they do not measure human capital elements such as health and learning-by-doing via work experience. Recently, the work of Hanushek and Ludger (2012) measures human capital based on cognitive skills instead of formal schooling.

The cost-based approach incorporates measures of aggregate expenditures on tangible and intangible components of human capital, examples include Kendrick (1976) and Eisner (1985). Tangible components of human capital capture expenditure on quantities, while intangible components reflect expenditures on human capital quality. The cost-based approach is limited in use because of data limitations; for example, relevant prices are often difficult to identify, nor do they directly measure value.

A third measure of human capital is the income-based approach, based on the discounted values of future labor income flows. The income-based approach is regarded by many as the most reliable and is proposed by (Jorgenson and Fraumeni 1989, 1992a,b). The Jorgenson-Fraumeni (J-F) lifetime income-based human capital measurement has been widely applied, for example, in Mulligan and Sala-i-Martin (1997), Mira and Liu (2010), and in the work of the OECD (2010), World Bank (Lange et al., 2018), and UNEP and Urban Institute of Kyushu University (Managi and Kumar, 2018).

The income-based approach, based on the value of output produced by human capital, avoids many of the difficulties associated with identifying the costs of inputs and the limitations imposed by the narrowness of the education-based approach. Output price has the further advantage of reflecting differences in the value of human capital across areas and regions that are not captured by regional variation of inputs.

An important part of our approach is to develop procedures to calculate the J-F income-based measure of human capital (Jorgenson and Fraumeni, 1989, 1992a,b). Among scholars studying the relationship between human capital and China's economic growth, the team of Li et al. (2010, 2013b) adapted the J-F lifetime income methodology and used available data for the Chinese economy to construct various human capital measures, including the J-F human capital measure. Their methodology modifies the J-F framework by incorporating the well-known Mincer model of the income, education, and work experience relationship to impute estimates of earnings that are not generally available at the required level of detail. At the national level, the authors find that total and per capita human capital in China have grown steadily, but at a slower rate than GDP and physical capital; moreover, per capita human capital in China remains well below that in more developed economies (Li et al., 2013a,b; Managi and Kumar, 2018).

In extensions of the work described above, Li et al. (2013a,b, 2014) provides calculations of China's total human capital of the population and the labor force, as well as per capita measures of both across provinces. The results are adjusted for cross-provincial differences in the cost of living and are disaggregated into gender and rural-urban subgroups. Various components of these measures are incorporated in a production-function framework to account for China's economic growth attributable to physical capital, human capital, and multifactor productivity.

Liu et al. (2018) and Fraumeni et al. (2019) use a Divisia decomposition method along with dynamic panel models to capture components and structure of the development of human capital in China. They apply these measures to identify various contributions to the quantity and quality growth of human capital and to its regional disparity. They show that the regional human capital gaps in China are growing, in general, and that J-F measurement can better reflect the gaps among regions than traditional measures of human capital do.

7.3 LABOR FORCE COMPOSITION AND AGE STRUCTURE

Measures of human capital are generally specified over specific population groups. The major groups we specify include (i) total population of a country or region; (ii) active population, i.e., those below retirement age, including labor force, those in legal labor force age but in school, and those younger than legal working age; (iii) total labor force, including those above legal work age and below the retirement age but not in school, representing human capital currently used in market production; and (iv) reserve population, including young people below the legal working age and those within the legal labor force age but in school. Clearly, the active population includes both those in the labor force and in the reserve population.

We analyze trends in the labor force size and age structure defined by legal minimum working age and retirement age for Mainland China, Hong Kong, and Taiwan.

7.3.1 Labor Force Definition and Size

The total population of China is about 1.4 billion, including over 700 million males and just fewer than 700 million females in 2018.[a] The total population of Hong Kong, a special region of China, equaled 7.5 million, 3.42 million males and 4.08 million females in 2019.[b] Taiwan's population in 2018 consisted of 23.59 million people, including 11.71 million males and 11.88 million females.[c] In contrast to Mainland China, both Hong Kong and Taiwan have slightly higher proportions of females than males.

Table 7.1 summarizes the legal working ages and retirement ages in Mainland China, Hong Kong, and Taiwan, which serve as labor-force definitions throughout this study. In some cases, there is no mandatory retirement age, and the legal retirement age simply

---

[a]Ministry of Education of PRC website: http://data.stats.gov.cn/easyquery.htm?cn=C01.

[b]Statistics Department of the Hong Kong Government: https://www.censtatd.gov.hk/hkstat/sub/so20_tc.jsp.

[c]Taiwan Department of Household Registration website: https://win.dgbas.gov.tw/dgbas03/ca/yearbook/index2.htm.

TABLE 7.1
Labor force age and retirement age (years).

	Mainland	Hong Kong	Taiwan
Minimum labor force age	16	15	15
Retirement age for males	60	65	60
Retirement age for females	55	60	60

defines the point at which a worker has the right to receive pension benefits. Note that legal working and retirement ages may differ from actual working and retirement ages.

China's laws set 16 years as the youngest age that workers can enter the labor force. The legal retirement age since 1995 is 60 years old for males, 50 years old for female workers, but 55 years old for female public servants.[d] The mandatory, legal retirement ages in China are very young compared with many countries; thus, the working years of China's labor force are relatively less than those of its international counterparts'.[e]

Hong Kong's legal minimum age to enter the labor force is 15 years, but there is no general mandatory retirement age.[f] Many employers set a retirement age in the range of age 60–65. The civil servant system requires mandatory retirement for all employees, and the retirement age is generally 65 years old for those employed after 2015.[g] Hong Kong's first retirement security system was established in 1992. The Mandatory Provident Fund Schemes ordinance was passed in 1995 and it insured employees' pensions and set 65 years as the age at which employees can begin to receive pensions.[h] In light of the varying retirement ages in Hong Kong, we set the age range of its labor force as 15–60 years old for females and 15–65 years old for males.

The minimum legal working age in Taiwan is 15 years. Employees and civil servants in Taiwan have different voluntary retirement ages at which to begin receiving their pensions. In general, the qualified ages for retirement are determined jointly by an individual's age and years of work, and retirement is mandatory at age 65.[i] Based on the general retirement age and to be more comparable with the Mainland, we set the Taiwan's retirement age at 60 years to calculate the labor force.

As shown in Table 7.2, the labor force in Mainland China rose from 753 to 884 million from 1997 to 2018, and it declined after 2012. China's population structure is undergoing a major transition, largely due to aging exacerbated by the one child policy that was introduced in 1979. The population declined by 2.8% between 2012 and 2018. In 2018, 27% of the employed were in primary industries, 28% in secondary industries, and 44.9% in the tertiary sector.[j]

Between 1997 and 2018, the labor forces of Beijing, Shanghai, Hong Kong, and Taiwan grew approximately 68%, 53%, 17%, and 4%, respectively. The rapid growth of Beijing and Shanghai labor forces is due to large-scale immigration from other parts of the country. Hong Kong's relatively rapid labor force growth is also probably due to immigration—principally from the Mainland. Taiwan's labor force, in contrast, has changed little over this period.

In 1997, the labor forces of Beijing and Shanghai were much smaller than in Taiwan's, but given their much faster growth, they have reached rough parity with Taiwan's, ranging between 15 and 16 million individuals since 2012. Hong Kong's labor force is about one-third in the size of Beijing or Shanghai.

7.3.2 Labor Force Aging

According to the China National Committee on Aging, China entered the group of aging societies in 1999.[k] The respective labor forces' average ages are shown in

---

[d]The National People's Congress of the People's Republic of China website:http://www.npc.gov.cn/wxzl/wxzl/2000-12/07/content_9552.htm.

[e]China's mandatory, legal retirement age policy forces some labor force who don't want to retire leave the labor market.

[f]https://www.news.gov.hk/chi/2018/09/20180916/20180916_142224_858.html.

[g]https://www.csb.gov.hk/tc_chi/admin/retirement/183.html.

[h]Hong Kong Labor Department website: https://www.swd.gov.hk/tc/index/site_pubsvc/page_socsecu/sub_ssallowance/.

[i]Taiwan Legislative Yuan website: https://www.mol.gov.tw/topic/3078/3302/25656/.

[j]According to the Industrial Classification of National Economy of China, primary industry is defined as agriculture, forestry, animal husbandry and fishery; secondary industry is defined as mining, manufacturing, power, heat, gas and water production and supply industry, and construction industry; tertiary industry is defined as service industry, including all other industries except the primary industry and the secondary industry.

[k]China National Committee on Aging of PRC: http://www.cncaprc.gov.cn/llxw/572.jhtml.

TABLE 7.2
Size of the labor force (millions).

Year	Mainland	Beijing	Shanghai	Hong Kong	Taiwan
1997	753	9.0	9.9	4.5	14.9
2002	809	10.7	12.1	4.8	15.3
2007	866	13.1	14.5	5.0	15.9
2012	909	15.5	16.4	5.2	16.1
2018	884	15.1	15.1	5.3	15.5

TABLE 7.3
Average age of labor force (years).

Year	Mainland	Beijing	Shanghai	Hong Kong	Taiwan
1997	33.9	34.7	36.3	36.2	35.0
2002	35.4	35.6	37.2	37.5	36.7
2007	36.1	35.5	36.5	38.8	37.8
2012	36.8	36.0	36.8	39.2	38.2
2018	38.4	37.7	38.4	39.0	39.5

Table 7.3. For Mainland China as a whole, the labor force aged more rapidly than either Hong Kong or Taiwan, from an average age of 33.9 years in 1997 to 38.4 years in 2018, an increase of 4.5 years.

The labor forces of Hong Kong and Taiwan are on average older than that of the Mainland, in part because their older retirement ages more than offset their lower labor-force entry ages. Despite this complication, we can compare their relative trends of labor force aging, and it is quite clear that Taiwan's labor force is aging faster than those of Beijing, Shanghai, and Hong Kong. The average age of the Taiwan labor force rose about 4.5 years from 1997 to 2018, during which time, the average age in Hong Kong, Beijing, and Shanghai rose by 2.8, 3, and 2.1 years, respectively (Table 7.3). Although Beijing appears to be aging faster than Hong Kong, in 2018, Beijing still had the youngest labor force, probably due to a larger inflow of young workers.

7.4 OVERVIEW OF THE EDUCATION SYSTEMS

Human capital theory emphasizes human capital accumulation arising mainly from formal schooling and on-the-job training (OJT) (Mincer, 1974). Thus, education is a critical component in any human capital measurement. As discussed above, traditional measures directly utilize education as a proxy for human capital. Other more comprehensive measures also incorporate education implicitly as a critical component. Given the importance of education in human capital, we briefly review the education systems in Mainland China, Hong Kong, and Taiwan.

7.4.1 Education Systems in Mainland China

In 1986, China adopted its compulsory education law, initiating rapid development of China's education since then. China requires 9-years' minimum education, through primary school and middle school. Students who graduate from middle school can choose vocational education or general high-school education.[1]

Those who choose vocational education can obtain their secondary vocational education degree after 3 years and can then choose to pursue an advanced vocational education degree, which generally requires three additional years.

Students who graduate from general high school after 3 years of study can pursue tertiary-level schooling. Higher education options include junior college and bachelor programs, master's, and doctoral programs at the university level.

Admission to colleges and universities requires that high-school graduates pass the 2-day national college entrance examinations (*gaokao*). Obtaining a bachelor's degree normally requires 4 years. With a bachelor's

---

[1] Ministry of Education of PRC: http://www.moe.edu.cn/publicfiles/business/htmlfiles/moe/s623456/201201/1464528.html.

degree, students can apply for a master's program. Students with a master's degree can apply for a doctoral program. Admission to a master's or a doctoral program normally requires passing entrance examinations, but admission via recommendations with a waiver of examination is possible in some universities.

Since the resumption of higher education after the Cultural Revolution in Mainland China, enrollment in colleges and universities has greatly increased. In 1999, the Chinese government implemented a dramatic expansion of higher education.[m] The initiation of the plan for expanding the enrollment for higher education aimed to boost domestic demand, stimulating consumption, and easing employment pressure.[n] In 1999, the number of students rose by at an unprecedented 47%, to 1,596,800, followed by 38% expansion in 2000, 22% in 2001 and 19% in 2002.[o]

As an example of encouraging enrollment in higher education, in the year 2000, Beijing, Shanghai, and Anhui Province initiated their spring admission policies. In 2001, the ministry of education issued a new policy to allow people over 25 to take the university entrance exam, removing the age limit for regular college admission.[p] While the expansion of higher education has increased overall education in China, there has been some concern regarding education quality and job opportunities for college students.

Professional education has taken off since 1978, and various policies have promoted secondary vocational education. The law on vocational education was passed in 1996, and it established professional education is an important part of national education. The expansion of higher education in the late 1990s induced more middle school graduates to choose general high schools instead of vocational high schools, in order to gain access to enrollment in regular colleges, at the same time possibly slowing growth of secondary vocational education.

To attract more students to enroll in professional education, in 2009, the government initiated a tuition-free policy for rural students from poor families who enrolled in professional education and for students majoring in agriculture. In 2019, the government for the first time proposed to expand enrollment in professional schools to 1 million students.

7.4.2 Education Systems in Hong Kong

Hong Kong initiated compulsory primary education in 1971, and in 1978, free and compulsory 9-year compulsory education was fully implemented.[q] Since then, the education System in Hong Kong has included the 9-year compulsory education (primary school and middle school), secondary education (high school and preparatory education), and higher education (college, university, or above).[r]

Government-funded or subsidized schools provide 6-year primary and 3-year middle school courses for school-age children. Those who choose secondary education can obtain their diploma after 2 years and can then choose to pursue a college-preparatory high school education, which generally requires two additional years to complete.

After 2009, the education system advanced to 12-year free education, including primary school, middle school, and high school. After middle school, students can choose vocational schools as an alternative to college preparatory education.[s]

College and university curriculums generally require 3 or 4 years following college-preparatory high school. Students can choose vocational education after middle school or 2-year high school (Ying, 2007).

7.4.3 Education Systems in Taiwan

Taiwan established its education law in 1979, stipulating that children aged 6 to 15 must enroll in 9 years' compulsory education, including primary school and middle school.[t] The 9-year compulsory education is funded by the Taiwan government. In 2014, compulsory schooling in Taiwan was extended to 12 years, adding high school education.[u] The current schooling system in Taiwan includes 12-year compulsory schooling and a higher education system.[v]

[m]Ministry of Education of PRC: http://www.moe.gov.cn/s78/A03/moe_560/moe_571/moe_563/201002/t20100226_7790.html.

[n]Ministry of Education of PRC: http://www.moe.gov.cn/jyb_xwfb/xw_zt/moe_357/jyzt_2019n/2019_zt19/zhengce/201909/t20190906_397979.html.

[o]Ministry of Education of PRC: http://www.moe.gov.cn/s78/A03/moe_560/moe_568/moe_581/201002/t20100226_10560.html.

[p]Ministry of Education of PRC: http://www.moe.gov.cn/s78/A03/moe_560/moe_567/moe_585/201002/t20100226_7965.html.

[q]See website for the information: https://baike.baidu.com/item/%E9%A6%99%E6%B8%AF%E6%95%99%E8%82%B2%E5%88%B6%E5%BA%A6/15763327?fr=aladdin.

[r]Hong Kong Education Bureau website:https://www.gov.hk/sc/residents/education/preprimary/index.htm.

[s]https://www.gov.hk/sc/residents/education/.

[t]https://www.moe.gov.tw/policy/.

[u]http://history.moe.gov.tw/policy_list.asp.

[v]Taiwan History of Ministry of Education website: http://history.moe.gov.tw/policy_list.asp.

The education system in Taiwan also includes technical vocational education. After middle school, students can choose either 3-year vocational education, equivalent to high school education or 5-year vocational education, equivalent to junior college.[w]

Higher education in Taiwan is divided into colleges, independent colleges, and universities. There are two channels of tertiary education: 3-year college and general 4-year university.[x] The length of schooling in junior college varies according to entrance qualifications. Colleges and universities in Taiwan mostly recruit high school graduates or students who have passed the entrance examination after high school graduation. Taiwan's private educational institutions are important parts of the education system.

Universities or departments of independent colleges may set up research institutes to recruit postgraduate or doctoral students. A master's degree requires 2 to 3 years, and a doctoral degree requires 3 to 4 years in Taiwan. For comparison, in Hong Kong, a master's degree requires 1 to 3 years and a doctoral degree requires 4 years. In the Mainland China, a master's degree requires 2 to 3 years and a doctoral degree 4 to 7 years.

7.5 EDUCATION-BASED HUMAN CAPITAL MEASURES

The education-based measure on human capital has been at the core of traditional human capital measurement. Education-based measures are generally based years of education, literacy rates, enrollment rates, and/or proportions of labor force or population with various level of education attainments.

Fig. 7.2 shows the trends of average schooling years of the labor force of Mainland China, which rose from 8.0 years in 1997 to 10.4 years in 2018. During the same period, the average schooling in the rural area rose from 7.2 to 9.0 years, while in the urban areas it increased from 9.6 to 11.3 years. In 2018, the national average year of education was above 9 years, approximately 2 years of high school. The urban areas lead rural areas by an average of 2.3 school years.

In addition to years of schooling, we consider the proportions of the labor force that have achieved various levels of education. These measures represent different various benchmarks of labor force education that is less clearly revealed by average years of schooling. For example, the proportion of workers in the labor force who have graduated from college or higher reflects the proportion of workers who are qualified for jobs at the highest skill levels, which is less accurately inferred from data on average years of schooling.

For Mainland China, as shown in Fig. 7.3, the percentage of labor force with high school education or above increased from 17.3% in 1997 to 39.8% in 2018, more than doubling in 21 years. For higher education, the enrollment of undergraduate college students in Mainland China rose from about 1 million in 1997 to about 7.49 million in 2017.[y] Fig. 7.3 also shows that the proportions of the labor force with education level of college or above in Mainland China rose from 3.8% in 1997 to 19.2% in 2018, a more than fourfold increase, seen to be even more dramatic considering that the large expansion of higher education began in 1999. The proportion of the labor force with university education rose from 1.1% in 1997 to 9.2% in 2018.

Education attainments of the labor force in Hong Kong and Taiwan are higher than in Mainland China. The labor force proportion of individuals with schooling at the level high school or above in Taiwan rose from 50.0% in 1997 to 88.2% in 2018, while in Hong Kong it rose from 55.5% in 1997 to 76.1% in 2018 (Table 7.5). The labor force proportion of those with college education or above in Taiwan rose from 17.2% in 1997 to 56.0% in 2018, while Hong Kong experienced slower growth, rising from 17.6% in 1997 to 43.3% in 2018 (Table 7.6). Although the definitions of labor force are different, the proportions of workers with higher education in both Hong Kong and Taiwan exceed the Mainland's proportion.

Because Hong Kong and Taiwan are much further advanced in education than Mainland China as a whole, we compare them with the Mainland's most developed cities, Beijing and Shanghai. Beijing and Shanghai have benefited from reform under more modern conditions and the inflow of highly educated migrants.

Average years of schooling of the labor forces among the four regions are compared in Table 7.4. In 2018, the labor force average years of schooling of Taiwan was 13.7 years, exceeding that in Hong Kong (12.4 years). Although both regions exceed that in Mainland China by more than 2 years, their average schooling is quite close to Beijing's (13.0 years) and Shanghai's (12.0 years). In fact, Beijing's average years of schooling of the labor force has exceeded that in Hong Kong since 1997.

---

[w]http://history.moe.gov.tw/policy.asp?id=4.

[x]Taiwan Ministry of Education website: https://www.moe.gov.tw/policy/overview/s9789/636245.html.

[y]China Educational Statistic Yearbook 1998 to 2018, various years.

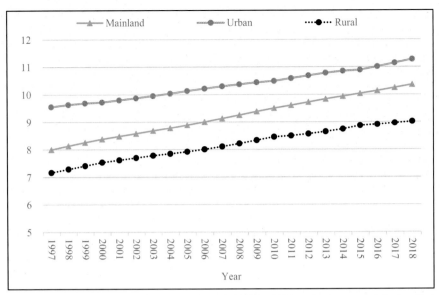

FIG. 7.2 Average years of schooling of the labor force in Mainland China. Average years of school is from the 2020 human capital project.

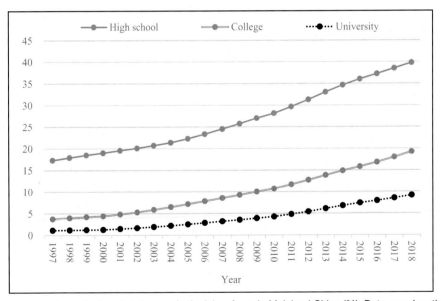

FIG. 7.3 Proportions of education degrees in the labor force in Mainland China (%). Data on education degrees is from the 2020 human capital project.

Table 7.5 compares the proportion of the four regions' labor forces with education at levels of high school or above between 1997 and 2018. The proportion in Taiwan is higher than that in Hong Kong, and both are much higher than that in Mainland China, but they exhibit smaller gaps with Beijing and Shanghai. Beijing's share of its labor force with high school education or above is actually in line with Hong Kong's.

TABLE 7.4
Average years of education of labor force.

Year	Mainland	Beijing	Shanghai	Hong Kong	Taiwan
1997	8.0	10.5	9.9	10.4	10.4
2002	8.6	11.0	10.2	10.7	11.4
2007	9.1	11.6	10.7	11.0	12.4
2012	9.7	12.2	11.3	11.8	13.0
2018	10.4	13.0	12.0	12.4	13.7

TABLE 7.5
Proportions of high school or above in the labor force (%).

Year	Mainland	Beijing	Shanghai	Hong Kong	Taiwan
1997	17.3	45.5	38.5	55.5	50.0
2002	20.1	50.4	40.9	58.9	63.0
2007	24.5	56.7	46.7	62.2	75.7
2012	31.3	64.8	52.8	70.2	82.2
2018	39.8	72.3	59.3	76.1	88.2

TABLE 7.6
Proportions of college or above in the labor force (%).

Year	Mainland	Beijing	Shanghai	Hong Kong	Taiwan
1997	3.8	17.7	11.0	17.6	17.2
2002	5.3	22.0	13.9	19.8	27.3
2007	8.6	30.4	20.8	26.0	38.2
2012	12.3	39.4	28.7	34.4	44.8
2018	19.2	52.8	39.5	43.3	56.0

Table 7.6 compares the proportion of workers with education at college or above in the labor forces. The proportion in Taiwan is higher than in Hong Kong, and both are much higher than in Mainland China. However, in 2018, the share of Beijing's labor force with schooling level at college or above is higher than Hong Kong's and in line with that in Taiwan. While Shanghai's labor force's share of workers with college or above schooling is lower than Beijing's share, it is still in line with that in Hong Kong.

In sum, since 1997, the labor force's education in Mainland China has increased rapidly, quickly reducing the gap with Hong Kong and Taiwan. The enforcement of 9-year compulsory education, the increased availability of higher education from mainly to the elite to a more representative share of the population, and the shifting of higher education to a tuition-based system have all contributed to the rapid advancement of education in the Mainland.

Although education achievement in Mainland China as a whole remains largely behind that in Hong Kong and Taiwan, in recent years, its most developed cities such as Beijing and Shanghai have achieved labor force schooling levels and proportions of highly educated workers that are comparable to or that even surpass those in Hong Kong and Taiwan.

7.6 JORGENSON-FRAUMENI MEASURE OF HUMAN CAPITAL

In the preceding section, we analyze human capital of the labor force based on various measures of education attainments. However, because education quality differs across regions, comparison of education level alone is unlikely to provide a complete picture of human capital variation.

In this section, we estimate human capital based on the Jorgensen-Fraumeni framework. The J-F approach utilizes an individual's lifetime labor earning to estimate the value of human capital, thus reflecting education quality without needing a direct measurement. Other advantages of the J-F method are as follows: (i) it quantifies human capital in monetary value; (ii) it measures the human capital of those in the labor force and those who have not yet entered the labor market.

7.6.1 Estimating Individual Labor Earnings

Application of the J-F approach requires measures of earnings at different ages and education attainments. Because such data are not universally available at the individual level for China, we use survey data to estimate earnings that are assigned to individuals.

We estimate the earnings by means of the standard Mincer equation:

$$\ln(yinc) = \alpha + \beta Sch + \gamma Exp + \delta Exp^2 + u \qquad (7.1)$$

where $\ln(yinc)$ represents the logarithm of annual income, Sch represents years of schooling, Exp is years of work experience, and β represents the returns to education. The return to education is determined in the labor market for workers at a specific education level and is assumed reflect education quality as it affects worker productivity.

There are many technical issues related to estimating Mincer equations, not the list of which is the well-known omitted ability problem (Heckman et al., 2006). For simplicity, we ignore these issues and simply estimate Eq. (7.1) by means of ordinary least squares (OLS).

We estimate the Mincer equations for the Mainland, Beijing, and Shanghai for every year from 1997 to 2018, requiring a large amount of survey data. For Mainland China, we use five Chinese household databases for the various years they are available, including UHS (Urban Household Survey), CHIP (Chinese Household Income Project Survey), CHNS (China Health and Nutrition Survey), CHFS (China Household Finance Survey), and CFPS (China Family Panel Studies). Those data cover different years with information on

individual labor market earnings and other characteristics. For years where we have multiple data sets, we average the estimates weighted by the sample sizes. For some years, there is no survey data available, and we impute estimated parameters (see Li et al., 2014 for details).

One particular challenge to the estimation is small sample sizes for Beijing and Shanghai. To resolve this problem, we combine the city level data with the individual data to augment the Mincer model to obtain city specific returns to education. In particular, the provincial-level Mincer model is specified as (see Fraumeni et al., 2019 for details)

$$\ln yinc_{ij} = \beta_1 \ln avwage_j + \beta_2 sch_{ij} + \beta_3 sch_{ij} \cdot PGDP_j \\ + \beta_4 sch_{ij} \cdot \Pr_j + X_{ij}\delta + u_{ij} \qquad (7.2)$$

for individual i in province j where X_{ij} includes the intercept and other control variables, and u_{ij} is the error term. For province level variables, $avwage$ is the average wage of the province j, $PGDP$ is province GDP per capita, and Pr is the proportion of the labor force employed in primary industry. Those variables are included to capture specific labor market conditions that affect returns to education and the intercepts (e.g., the starting wages differentials).[z]

For Hong Kong, the data on population are from the Hong Kong Statistics Department and those on students are from the Education Department. To estimate the Mincer model, we used the Hong Kong Census and Interim Population Survey, which is collected by the Hong Kong Census and Statistics Department. The data include the 1% sample of the 1981 census, the 1% sample data of the 1986 midterm population survey, the 5% sample data set of the 1991, 2001, and 2011 censuses, and the 5% sample data set of the 1996 and 2006 midterm population surveys.[aa]

For Taiwan, the data on population are from various statistical yearbooks, and the data on students are from various Ministry of Education statistics. To estimate Taiwan's Mincer model, we use the database of Household Income and Expenditure Surveys in Taiwan from 1985 to 2006.[ab] The surveys are organized by Directorate-

---

[z]We estimate Eq. (7.2) separately using samples for each of the rural/urban and male/female combinations using survey data.

[aa]A caveat note: due to data availability, the latest year of data for estimating Hong Kong's Mincer model is 2011. The related parameters are imputed for the years after.

[ab]Similar to the caveat note for Hong Kong, the latest year of survey data used for Taiwan is 2006 and the parameters for the years after that are imputed.

General of Budget, Accounting and Statistics of the Taiwan Government.[ac]

7.6.2 Estimating Lifetime Income

With the individual level earnings estimated as described in the above section, we can calculate an individual's lifetime income within the J-F framework. In the J-F income-based approach, aggregate human capital is calculated based on the sum of the present value of expected lifetime income for individuals with the same human capital characteristics, including gender, age, education, and location. The formula is expressed as

$$H_t = \sum_g \sum_a \sum_e \sum_r inc_{g,a,e,r,t} * n_{g,a,e,r,t} \qquad (7.3)$$

where t, g, a, e, and r refer to year, gender, age, years of education, and region, respectively; inc indicates average expected lifetime labor income; and n represents the corresponding populations with the particular combination of four-dimensional characteristics.

Estimation of lifetime income is calculated backward recursively through five lifetime stages: preschool, school only, work-school, work only and retirement, based on income of a matching individual 1-year older. For example, when an individual is at the work-school stage, the expected lifetime income is estimated as

$$
\begin{aligned}
inc_{s,a,e,r,t} = {} & yinc_{s,a,e,r,t} * epr_{s,a,e,r,t} \\
& + svr_{s,a+1,r,t+1} [enr_{s,a+1,e+1,r,t+1} * inc_{s,a+1,e+1,r,t} \\
& + (1 - enr_{s,a+1,e+1,r,t+1}) * inc_{s,a+1,e,r,t}] * \frac{1+G}{1+R} \qquad (7.4)
\end{aligned}
$$

where $yinc$ is an individual's annual earnings as estimated above based on the Mincer model, epr the employment rate, svr the survival rate, enr the school enrollment rate, G the exogenous real income growth rate, and R the discount rate. In other words, an individual's lifetime income at age a is equal to the lifetime income of an individual at age $a+1$ plus annual income adjusted with the survival rate, probability of work, the exogenous real income growth rate, and the discount rate. Other stages are calculated accordingly (see Fraumeni et al., 2019; Li et al., 2013a,b; Li et al., 2014 for details).

The data on population are from various censuses, and those on school admission, employment rates, survival rates, etc. are from various multiple-year statistical yearbooks from Mainland China, Hong Kong Bureau of Statistics, and the Taiwan Bureau of Statistics. The

exogenous real income growth rate is calculated separately for rural and urban area based on the net income per person and the CPI index in each area. A general discount rate, 4.58% per year, from OECD is used in the calculation of income-based human capital. This discount rate has been used in OECD member states.

Additionally, to calculate J-F human capital in Mainland China, recognizing that students rarely take part-time jobs in Mainland China, we exclude the school-work stage. We also adjust estimated earnings with each province-specific living-cost index to compare the monetary values of estimated J-F human capital across provinces.

7.6.3 Total Human Capital

We first estimate the J-F total human capital stock for each region. The results for selected years are shown in Table 7.7 and Fig. 7.4.[ad] Note that due to the different labor force ages, education systems, and living costs between the Mainland China, Hong Kong, and Taiwan, the absolute values of estimated J-F human capital are not directly comparable across places. Therefore, our discussions mostly focus on their relative values and trends by time for each place. For cities/provinces within Mainland China, the J-F estimates are generally comparable because we adjust the impact of living cost on earnings.

We see that the total human capital of Mainland China in 2018 is 7.6 times of that in 1997, while the comparable ratios are only 2.9 and 0.6 for Hong Kong and Taiwan (Table 7.7), respectively. Total J-F human capital increased steadily in both Mainland China and Hong Kong from 1997 to 2018, but it has been declining in Taiwan. The decline in Taiwan is partially related to population aging. Another reason is the fluctuation of exchange rates between RMB currency and the New Taiwan Dollar (NT). For example, from 1997 to 2002, the J-F human capital of Taiwan decreased by 22%. During the same period, the calculated exchange rates increased 21%, from 3.46 NT to 4.18 per RMB Yuan, causing a large decline of the J-F RMB value of human capital in Taiwan.

[ac]Available from Survey Research Data Archive, Academia Sinica. doi:https://doi.org/10.6141/TW-SRDA-AA170043-1, https://srda.sinica.edu.tw/.

[ad]Human capital is in 1985 real RMB. Human capital in Hong Kong and Taiwan is adjusted with exchange rate. We first convert the human capital values estimated for Hong Kong and Taiwan into US dollars, and then convert their values in US dollars into Chinese currency RMB, with the exchange rates from the International Monetary Fund (period average). Exchange rate data are from: https://data.imf.org/?sk=4c514d48-b6ba-49ed-8ab9-52b0c1a0179b.

TABLE 7.7
J-F total human capital (billion RMB).

	TOTAL HUMAN CAPITAL					TOTAL LABOR FORCE HUMAN CAPITAL				
Year	Mainland	Beijing	Shanghai	Hong Kong	Taiwan	Mainland	Beijing	Shanghai	Hong Kong	Taiwan
1997	67,103	1780	1950	4632	34,474	27,293	576	701	2814	18,665
2002	128,739	3830	4150	6587	26,896	48,933	1170	1450	4039	15,005
2007	202,478	7270	9030	8764	25,913	77,360	2600	3030	5421	15,360
2012	320,214	12,800	13,100	9494	21,528	122,654	5060	5020	6079	13,467
2018	512,873	16,700	15,100	13,348	20,331	185,484	7300	5730	8700	13,328

1) Human Capital estimates are from the 2020 human capital project. (2) Human capital is in real 1985 RMB. Human capital for Beijing and Shanghai is adjusted with Living Cost Index (LCI). To compare Mainland China with Hong Kong and Taiwan, we first convert the human capital values estimated for Hong Kong and Taiwan into US dollars, and then convert their values in US dollars into Chinese currency RMB, with the exchange rates from the International Monetary Fund (period average).

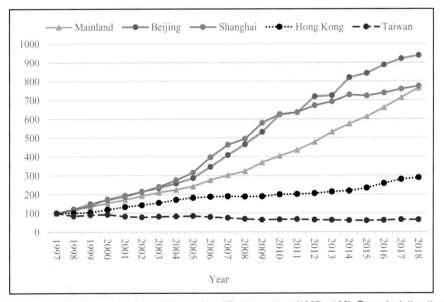

FIG. 7.4 Trends of J-F based total human capital in different regions (1997 = 100). For calculating the cumulative growth rates starting in 1997, we define annual growth rate in year t as gr_t, where $t = 1998, ..., 2018$, the accumulative growth rate is then $g_t = (1 + gr_{1998}) * \cdots * (1 + gr_t) * 100$. This is the same for all cumulative growth rate calculations.

Fig. 7.4 shows the cumulative growth of total human capital, setting the value of 1997 as 100.[ae] We see that between 1997 and 2018, total human capital increased much faster in Beijing and Shanghai than in Hong Kong and Taiwan, with Beijing experiencing the largest

increase 9.4 times higher in 2018 than in 1995 compared to a multiple of 7.7 for Shanghai.

In Table 7.8, we see that the average 1997–2018 annual growth rate of total human capital for Beijing is highest among the four areas, while Taiwan's total human capital actually declined. Moreover, the average annual growth rates in Beijing and Shanghai were much higher before 2010, in the range of 14%–16%, more recently, e.g., in

[ae]The base year for the cumulative growth rate is 1997, and its value is set as 100.

TABLE 7.8
Average annual growth rate of J-F human capital (%).

Year	TOTAL HUMAN CAPITAL				TOTAL LABOR FORCE HUMAN CAPITAL			
	Beijing	Shanghai	Hong Kong	Taiwan	Beijing	Shanghai	Hong Kong	Taiwan
1997–2018	11.2	10.2	5.2	−2.5	12.9	10.5	5.5	−1.6
1997–2003	15.2	15.8	7.5	−3.4	15.3	15.5	7.8	−2.5
2004–2010	15.8	14.7	2.6	−3.8	18.9	16.4	3.0	−2.9
2011–2018	5.7	2.9	5.3	−1.6	7.1	2.8	5.8	−0.8

the period 2011 to 2018, annual growth is 5.7% for Beijing and 2.9% for Shanghai, while Hong Kong and Taiwan experienced relatively stable growth rates.

We use Beijing as the base to compare the dynamics of relative total human-capital gaps among the four locations. Fig. 7.5 demonstrates that the gap of total human capital between the two areas Hong Kong and Taiwan with Beijing has been shrinking over this period, and the gap between Shanghai and Beijing has also declined. In particular, the ratio of Shanghai to Beijing declined from 1.1 to 0.9 between 1997 and 2018. Correspondingly, the ratio of Hong Kong to Beijing declined from 2.6 to 0.8 and that of Taiwan to Beijing declined from 19.4 to 1.2. Overall, the total stock of

human capital converged among the four locations between 1997 and 2018.

Fig. 7.6 shows that the trends of total J-F labor force human capital (hereinafter referred to as "J-F LFHC") among the areas are very similar to that of total human capital. However, the cumulative growth rate of J-F LFHC is lower than that of total human capital in Mainland China, while it is higher in Hong Kong. As discussed above, the average age of the labor force in Mainland China is lower than that either in Hong Kong or Taiwan. However, average schooling years is lower in Mainland China, and the regional gap for the highly educated labor force is even greater.

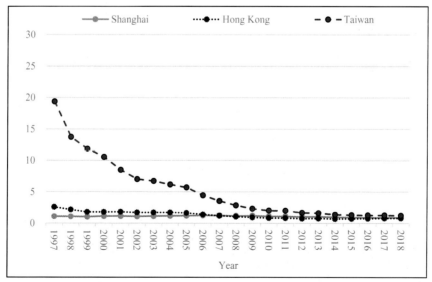

FIG. 7.5 Ratio of J-F based total human capital by geography (Base = Beijing). (1) Human capital estimates are from the 2020 human capital project. (2) Human capital is in real 1985 RMB. Human capital for Beijing and Shanghai is adjusted with Living Cost Index (LCI). To compare Mainland China with Hong Kong and Taiwan, we first convert the human capital values estimated for Hong Kong and Taiwan into US dollars, and then convert their values in US dollars into Chinese currency RMB, with the exchange rates from the International Monetary Fund (period average). This is the same for all graphs.

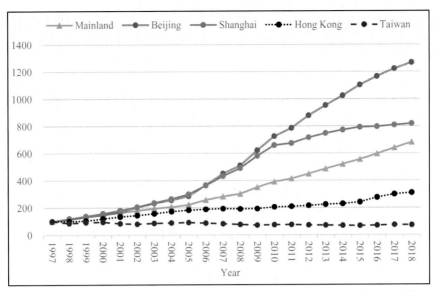

FIG. 7.6 Trends of J-F total labor force human capital in different regions (1997 = 100).

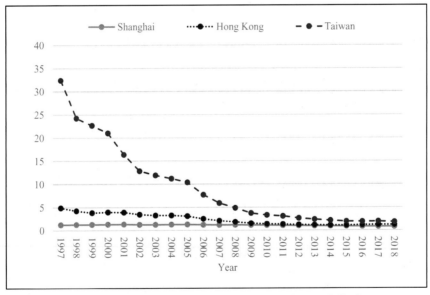

FIG. 7.7 Ratio of J-F labor force human capital (Base = Beijing).

The growth gaps of J-F LFHC in the four locations have been sharply narrowing, as shown in Fig. 7.7. For example, the ratio of Taiwan's J-F LFHC to that of Beijing is 32.4 in 1997, but it declines to only 1.8 in 2018. The gaps in J-F LFHC between Shanghai, Hong Kong and Taiwan with Beijing are larger than that for total human capital. For example, the ratio of total

human capital of Taiwan to Beijing is 19.4 in 1997 and 1.2 in 2018 (Fig. 7.5), much lower than the ratio of J-F LFHC mentioned above. A similar pattern exists for the ratio between Hong Kong and Beijing.

Table 7.8 shows that the J-F LFHC in Beijing and Shanghai converged toward that in Hong Kong and Taiwan between 1997 and 2018. Specifically, the average annual growth rates of J-F LFHC in Beijing and Shanghai from 1997 to 2003 are respectively 15.3% and 15.5%, but the growth rate is only 7.8% in Hong Kong and is declining at −2.5% in Taiwan. Moreover, similar to the growth rate of total human capital, the average annual growth rates of J-F LFHC in Beijing and Shanghai have diminished significantly in recent years.

Table 7.8 also shows that between 1997 and 2018, the average annual growth rate of J-F LFHC is higher than that of total human capital in Beijing, Shanghai, and Hong Kong, the gap being most evident for Beijing. The faster growth of J-F LFHC compared to total human capital is attributable to the population's shrinking below the minimum labor force age (16 years old for Mainland China and 15 years old for Hong Kong and Taiwan).

7.6.4 Human Capital per Capita

Human capital per capita and human capital per worker reflect the average human capital intensity for the total population and labor force, respectively, and they are respective measures of the human capital quality. Note that both the human capital quality of the labor force and that of the population affects current economic activities and that of the population also impacts future economic activities when younger generations enter the labor force.

Table 7.9 shows that although both these two human capital quality indicators have been increasing in Mainland China, they still lag far behind those in Hong Kong and Taiwan. Although the absolute values may not be directly comparable, the diminishing difference is evident. For example, in 1997, Mainland China's per capita

human capital was only 7.3% of that in Hong Kong and 3.7% of that in Taiwan. In 2018, it had grown relatively to 18.7% of that in Hong Kong and 41.2% of that in Taiwan.

Human capital per worker in Mainland China is lower than human capital per capita, which is attributable to the relatively low education of older workers. The gap between human capital per worker of Mainland China and those of other regions is shrinking but remains large. For example, in 1997, Mainland China's human capital per worker was 5.4% of that in Hong Kong, and although it grew almost sixfold by 2018, it remained at only 12.4% of that in Hong Kong.

Human capital per capita in Beijing and Shanghai is much higher than its average value in Mainland China, and it is increasing steadily, although it still lags far behind that in Hong Kong and Taiwan (Table 7.9). Noticeably, although Taiwan has the highest total human capital stock, its human capital per capita has been declining (Fig. 7.8). In 2018, human capital per capita is 2397 thousand RMB in Hong Kong, 1090 thousand RMB in Taiwan, but only 946 thousand RMB and 905 thousand RMB, respectively, in Beijing and Shanghai. The gap between human capital per capita in Shanghai, Hong Kong, and Taiwan with Beijing is smaller than that of total human capital. For example, the ratio of Taiwan's human capital per capita to Beijing is 10.6 in 1997 and 1.2 in 2018 (Fig. 7.9) compared to 19.4 and 1.2 for the ratio of total human capital in 1997 and 2018, respectively.

As shown in Fig. 7.8, the growth rate of human capital per capita between 1997 and 2018 is higher in Beijing and Shanghai than in Hong Kong and Taiwan.

TABLE 7.9
J-F based human capital per unit (thousand RMB).

	HUMAN CAPITAL PER CAPITA					HUMAN CAPITAL PER WORKER				
Year	Mainland	Beijing	Shanghai	Hong Kong	Taiwan	Mainland	Beijing	Shanghai	Hong Kong	Taiwan
1997	62	160	159	851	1696	38	71	77	701	1434
2002	117	308	297	1155	1326	64	122	130	928	1120
2007	179	495	552	1549	1267	97	221	226	1205	1098
2012	273	726	697	1687	1088	147	358	327	1300	958
2018	449	949	849	2397	1090	228	518	404	1840	972

(1) Human capital estimates are from the 2020 human capital project. (2) Human capital is in real 1985 RMB. Human capital for Beijing and Shanghai is adjusted with Living Cost Index (LCI). To compare Mainland China with Hong Kong and Taiwan, we first convert the human capital values estimated for Hong Kong and Taiwan into US dollars, and then convert their values in US dollars into Chinese currency RMB, with the exchange rates from the International Monetary Fund (period average).

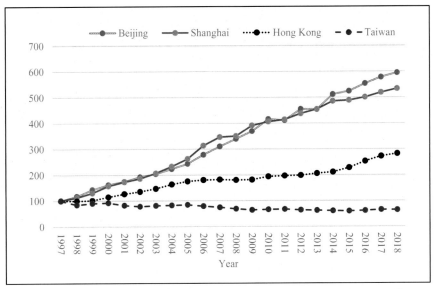

FIG. 7.8 Trends of J-F human capital per capita in different regions (1997 = 100).

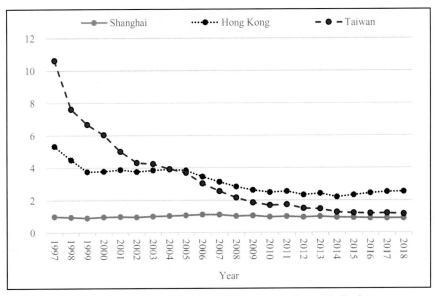

FIG. 7.9 Ratio of J-F human capital per capita (Base = Beijing).

Comparing Table 7.8 with Table 7.10, the average growth rates are smaller for human capital per capita or per worker compared to the comparable total ratios. Similar to total human capital, the growth rate of human capital per capita also declines from the subperiod 2004–10 to that of 2011–18, but more evidently for both Beijing and Shanghai. For example, the average growth rate declined from 10.9% between 2004 and 2010 to 5.4% over the period 2011–18 for Beijing, indicating a slow speed of convergence.

The relationship of human capital per worker among the four areas is shown in Fig. 7.10. Beijing and Shanghai have smaller ratios per worker but are catching up due to their much higher growth rates. In Table 7.10, we see that the average annual growth rate of human capital per worker from 1997 to 2018 is 9.9% and

TABLE 7.10
Average annual growth rate of J-F human capital per unit (%).

Year	HUMAN CAPITAL PER CAPITA				HUMAN CAPITAL PER WORKER			
	Beijing	Shanghai	Hong Kong	Taiwan	Beijing	Shanghai	Hong Kong	Taiwan
1997–2018	8.9	8.3	5.1	−2.1	9.9	8.2	4.7	−1.8
1997–2003	12.6	12.9	6.7	−3.4	11.5	11.3	6.1	−3.0
2004–2010	10.9	9.7	2.8	−3.6	12.9	10.6	2.3	−3.6
2011–2018	5.4	3.7	5.3	−0.6	6.9	4.1	5.3	−0.4

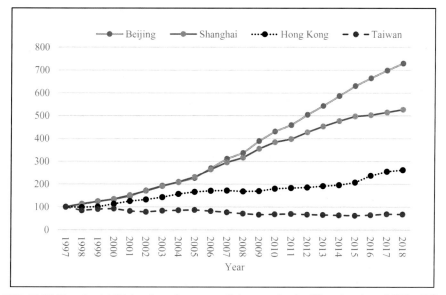

FIG. 7.10 Trends of J-F labor force human capital per worker in different regions (1997 = 100).

8.2% respectively in Beijing and Shanghai, but only 4.7% and −1.8% in Hong Kong and Taiwan. In addition, Fig. 7.11 indicates that the ratio of human capital per worker of Hong Kong and Taiwan to that of Beijing, in general, has substantially declined from 1997 to 2018, indicating a clear pattern of convergence among the four places.

Table 7.11 reports human capital value per capita at various ages for the areas we are comparing. Human capital at age zero is the present value of expected lifetime income for an average individual in a specific region. For Mainland China, the human capital of a newborn boy is much higher than that of a newborn girl, probably because of different lifetime education and employment opportunities. Similar gaps exist for Beijing and Shanghai. The male-female gaps for Hong Kong and Taiwan are much smaller, and in fact, in Hong Kong, the human capital of typical newborn girls is higher than that for boys. Additionally, the newly born in Beijing and Shanghai have much higher human capital values than those born in the rest of Mainland China.

For Mainland China as a whole, as well as for Beijing and Shanghai, human capital at age 6 is lower than that at age 0. However, expected human capital values increase from age 0 to age 6 for Hong Kong and Taiwan.

The patterns of the male-female gaps as noted above persist through age 12, marking completion of primary school, and through age 15, marking completion of middle school, the youngest age at which it is legal to enter the labor market.

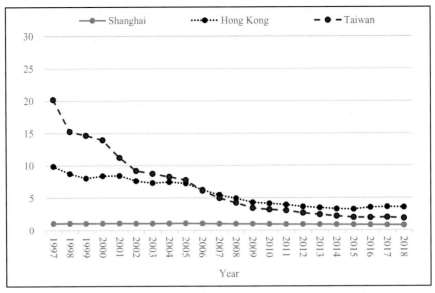

FIG. 7.11 Ratio of J-F human capital per worker (Base = Beijing).

TABLE 7.11
J-F human capital per capita for specific ages, 2018 (1000 RMB).

	MAINLAND		BEIJING		SHANGHAI		HONG KONG		TAIWAN	
Age	Male	Female	Male	Female	Male	Female	Male	Female	Male	Female
0	1612	945	4852	3007	5009	2774	2606	2910	1270	948
6	1126	694	3714	2474	3876	2146	2868	3202	1438	1073
12	1047	633	2982	1964	2988	1654	3150	3519	1620	1209
15	1139	674	2639	1738	2624	1453	2343	2681	1719	1283

(1) Human capital estimates are from the 2020 human capital project. (2) Human capital per capital is in real 1985 RMB. Human capital per capital for Beijing and Shanghai is adjusted with Living Cost Index (LCI). To compare Mainland China with Hong Kong and Taiwan, we first convert the human capital values estimated for Hong Kong and Taiwan into US dollars, and then convert their values in US dollars into Chinese currency RMB, with the exchange rates from the International Monetary Fund (period average).

7.7 HUMAN CAPITAL, GDP AND PHYSICAL CAPITAL

The ratios of J-F human capital to GDP and to physical capital are measures of its contribution to economic growth and the efficiency at which it is utilized.[af]

[af]The GDP data of Mainland China, Beijing, Shanghai, Hong Kong and Taiwan are from the official websites of their statistical bureaus. GDP data source of Beijing, Shanghai and Mainland China: http://humancapital.cufe.edu.cn/ ; GDP data source of Hong Kong: https://www.censtatd.gov.hk ; GDP data source of Taiwan: https://statdb.dgbas.gov.tw. J-F human capital data source: http://humancapital.cufe.edu.cn/.

Fig. 7.12 presents the ratio of GDP per unit of J-F human capital. The ratio in Mainland China is lower than that in Hong Kong and Taiwan. In 1997, the ratio of GDP to J-F human capital in Mainland China was 3.5%, Hong Kong 13.2%, and Taiwan 5.2%. A lower ratio of GDP to human capital may reflect the stage of economic development, as it is affected by the quantity of physical capital and an economy's level of technology. Over time, we see that Hong Kong's GDP per human capital has declined, while that of Taiwan has increased. The ratio is quite stable for Mainland China. Thus, the GDP/human capital gap between Mainland China and Taiwan has expanded, and by 2018, the ratio

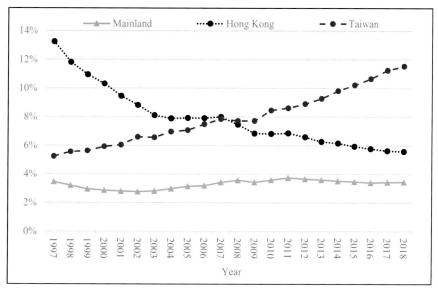

FIG. 7.12 Ratio of GDP to J-F human capital. GDP and human capital are in real 1985 value.

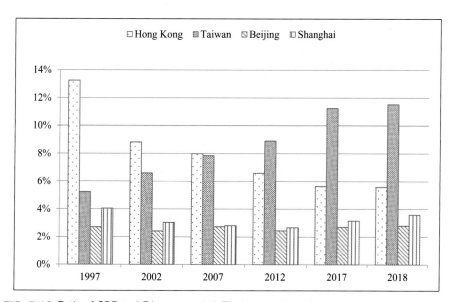

FIG. 7.13 Ratio of GDP to J-F human capital. The data are from the 2020 human capital project.

of GDP to J-F human capital in Mainland China was 3.4%, in Hong Kong 5.6%, and in Taiwan 11.5%.

Fig. 7.13 illustrates the GDP-to-human capital ratios of Beijing, Shanghai, Hong Kong, and Taiwan. In 2018, the ratio of GDP to J-F human capital in Beijing was 2.8%, Shanghai 3.6%, Hong Kong 5.6%, and Taiwan 11.5%. The GDP-to-human capital ratios of Beijing

and Shanghai do not diverge much from the ratio in the remainder of Mainland China. Table 7.12 shows that the ratio of GDP to J-F human capital in Beijing and Shanghai has been very stable between 1997 and 2018, while that in Shanghai fluctuates considerably. For Hong Kong and Taiwan, the ratios display steadily decreasing and increasing trend, respectively.

TABLE 7.12
Ratio of GDP to J-F human capital (%).

Year	Mainland	Beijing	Shanghai	Hong Kong	Taiwan
1997	3.5	2.7	4.0	13.2	5.2
2002	2.8	2.4	3.0	8.8	6.6
2007	3.4	2.7	2.8	8.0	7.8
2012	3.7	2.5	2.7	6.6	8.9
2018	3.4	2.8	3.6	5.6	11.5

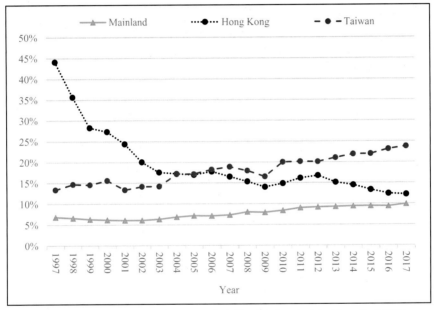

FIG. 7.14 Ratio of physical capital to J-F human capital. The data is calculated from the 2020 human capital project. Physical capital and human capital are in real 1985 value.

Physical capital[ag] and human capital are parallel inputs to production and economic growth and their relative growth is a marker of structural change. As can be seen in Fig. 7.14 the ratio of physical capital to J-F human capital in Mainland China is lower than that in Hong Kong and Taiwan, especially in early years. The higher ratio in Hong Kong and Taiwan indicates that Hong Kong and Taiwan are generally physical-capital richer than the Mainland. For example, in 1997, the ratio of physical capital to J-F human capital in Mainland China was 6.9%, Hong Kong 44.1%, and Taiwan 13.4%. Over time, the physical capital intensity of Mainland China has risen steadily, reflecting growing physical capital investment. The same trend is seen in Taiwan. For Hong Kong, however, physical capital intensity declined continuously from 1997 to 2017. The decline is likely to be the result of Hong Kong's becoming a more service-oriented economy. As shown in Table 7.13, in 2017, the ratios of physical capital to J-F human capital in Mainland China were 9.9%, Hong Kong 12.2%, and Taiwan 23.8%, respectively.

Fig. 7.15 displays the ratio of physical capital to J-F human capital for Beijing, Shanghai, Hong Kong and Taiwan. Before 2002, the measures of physical capital

[ag]Physical capital data source of Beijing, Shanghai and Mainland China source: http://humancapital.cufe.edu.cn/. Physical capital data source of Hong Kong: https://www.censtatd.gov.hk. Physical capital data source of Taiwan: https://statdb.dgbas.gov.tw.

TABLE 7.13 Ratio of physical capital to J-F human capital (%).					
Year	Mainland	Beijing	Shanghai	Hong Kong	Taiwan
1997	6.9	7.4	10.3	44.1	13.4
2002	6.1	6.0	7.9	20.0	14.2
2007	7.3	6.4	6.7	16.5	18.9
2012	9.2	6.0	7.1	16.7	20.1
2017	9.9	6.6	8.5	12.2	23.8

The 2018 result is not available due to the availability of physical capital.

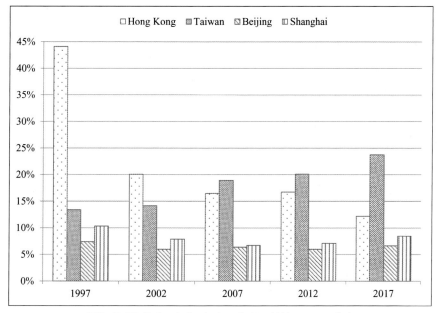

FIG. 7.15 Ratio of physical capital to J-F human capital.

intensity in Beijing and Shanghai are generally higher than for the rest of Mainland China. After 2002, however, the ratios became much lower. One explanation is that Beijing and Shanghai have been moving to a higher degree of service-oriented economies. Nevertheless, their ratios are still much lower than those in Hong Kong and Taiwan. For example, in 2017, the ratio of physical capital to J-F human capital in the Beijing is 6.6%, Shanghai 8.5%, Hong Kong 12.2%, and in Taiwan it is 23.8%.

7.8 HUMAN CAPITAL DEVELOPMENT AND POPULATION DIVIDENDS

Population aging leads to a smaller share of young people in the labor force, thus reducing the population dividend (Bloom and Williamson, 1998). China has experienced more rapid population aging than other countries due to the impact of its One-Child policy. A negative population dividend associated with an aging population can be offset by an increase in the population's average level of education (Zhong et al., 2016).

The demographic dividend, as defined by the United Nations Population Fund (UNFPA), is "the economic growth potential that can result from shifts in a population's age structure, mainly when the share of the working-age population (15 to 64) is larger than the nonworking-age share of the population (14 and younger, and 65 and older)."[ah]

[ah]https://en.wikipedia.org/wiki/Demographic_dividend.

Although population aging reduces the population dividend, if human capital increases fast enough at the individual level, it can offset the negative impact of population aging on the population dividend. In this section, we compare the dynamics of the population age structure with the dynamics of human capital.

A large body of evidence supports the contribution of the population dividend to economic growth in East Asia including China. For example, Bloom and Williamson (1998) report that 25% to 33% of economic growth in East Asia between 1965 and 1990 can be attributed to the population dividend. Wang et al. (2006) claim that the contribution of the population dividend to economic growth between 1982 and 2000 in China is approximately 15%. Researches suggest that China's population dividend is threatened by declining fertility rates and population aging, for example, Yu (2003) predicts that the population dividend in China may disappear around 2030, while Cai (2010) argues that it will disappear as early as 2015.

If the human capital intensity of the labor force increases, the negative impact of a decrease in the ratio of the working-age population becomes smaller. Recent studies suggest that such a human capital dividend has become more important for productivity growth in China than the population dividend (Zhang, 2016; Yang and Yan, 2017).

7.8.1 Education and Age Structure of Labor Force

As Table 7.4 shows, the average years of education of Mainland China's labor force increased from 8.0 years in 1997 to 10.4 years in 2018, Hong Kong's increased from 10.4 to 12.4 years, and Taiwan's increased from 10.4 to 13.7 years.

For Beijing and Shanghai, the increases in years of education are comparable to that of Hong Kong, while in Mainland China, mean education years has increased at a faster rate, close to that of Taiwan. Between 1997 and 2018, the annual mean years of education rose between 2.0 and 3.3 years in Mainland China, Beijing, Shanghai, Hong Kong, and Taiwan, at rates of 1.3%, 1.0%, 0.9%, 0.8%, and 1.3%, respectively.

As the average years of schooling increases, the labor force is also getting older. In Table 7.3, we see that the average age of the labor force increases in the range from 2.1 to 4.5 years among all regions, with Taiwan the fastest and Shanghai the slowest. From 1997 to 2018, the annual growth rates of average age of labor force of Mainland China, Beijing, Shanghai, Hong Kong, and Taiwan are 0.54%, 0.31%, 0.20%, 0.36%, and 0.58%, respectively. However, the annual growth of years of

schooling is higher than that for average age in all places, indicating that human capital growth measured by traditional education is partially offsetting the effect of population aging.

7.8.2 Labor Force Composition and Human Capital Stock

We further explore J-F human capital growth associated with population aging in Fig. 7.16. The cumulative growth of the size of the labor force gets faster for all places since 1997 but slows down around 2010. For the Mainland as a whole, Hong Kong, and Taiwan, it grew by 12.0%, 9.8%, and 1.6% from 1997 to 2018, respectively. However, it declines from the peak period of 2009–13 by approximately 3%, 2% and 5% for the three areas above, respectively.

As Fig. 7.6 shows, J-F LFHC in China has grown much faster than a simple measure of the labor force. During the period 1997 to 2018, total J-F LFHC of Mainland China increased 5.8-fold while that of Hong Kong 2.1-fold. Over the same period, Taiwan's J-F LFHC declined. For Beijing and Shanghai, the growth of J-F LFHC exceeds that of the Mainland as a whole as well as that of Hong Kong, which rose by 11.7- and 7.2-fold, respectively, during the same period.

As shown in Fig. 7.10, human capital per worker increased rapidly between 1997 and 2018, with Beijing reaching 730% of that in 1997, Shanghai 527%, and Hong Kong 262%. However, Tables 7.8 and 7.10 indicate that the growth rates for total J-F LFHC and human capital per worker for Beijing and Shanghai dropped significantly after 2011.

When we examine the ratios of J-F LFHC to total human capital, we see that in Beijing and Shanghai (54.5% and 47.2%, respectively), they fall short of those in Hong Kong (67.9%) and Taiwan (69.5%), implying that human capital in use is a smaller proportion of the total human capital in Beijing and Shanghai.

As shown in Fig. 7.17, the growth pattern of the prime age labor force (ages 25–54), differs from that of the total labor force, exhibiting a general declining trend since 1997 for Hong Kong (a decline of 7.5%) and Taiwan (a decline of 2.0%). In contrast, the prime-age labor force of Mainland China increased by 3.7%, still much slower than that of the overall labor force. For Beijing and Shanghai, the prime age labor force grew much faster, with an increasing trend, although it slowed significantly around 2010. From 1997 to 2018, the total growth of the prime age labor force is roughly in line with total labor force growth.

We see in Fig. 7.18, that similarly to the patterns described above, the J-F human capital of the prime

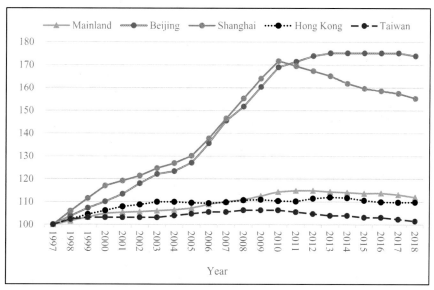

FIG. 7.16 Trends of the labor force in different regions (1997 = 100). Shanghai's growth becomes negative after 2010. One possible reason is the sampling rate in the 2015 census. It is likely that the official sampling rate of 3.0% for 2015 is overestimated, because some evidence shows the actual sampling rate of 2.8%. Overestimated sampling rate will reduce the size of the total population and thus result in lower human capital.

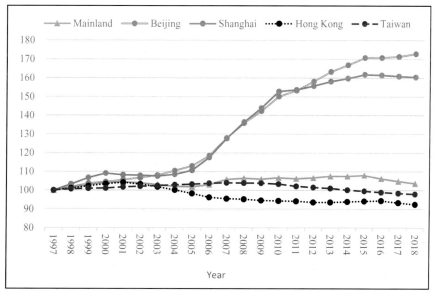

FIG. 7.17 Trends of prime age labor force in different regions (1997 = 100). The prime age labor force is defined as ages from 25 to 45. The results are calculated based on the data from the 2020 human capital project.

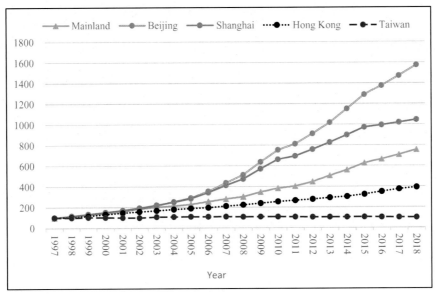

FIG. 7.18 Trends of the J-F human capital of the prime age labor force in different regions (1997 = 100). The 1997 base year is set equal to 100. The data are from the 2020 human capital project. Human capital is in real 1985 value. The prime age labor force is defined as ages of 25–45.

age labor force has grown much more rapidly than that of the labor force itself. From 1997 to 2018, for Mainland China, this part of J-F LFHC increased 755%, and even faster in Beijing and Shanghai. Hong Kong's J-F prime age human capital grew 391%.

7.8.3 Human Capital Reserve and Population Dividend Sustainability

The education-based measure of human capital discussed above does not count the human capital of young individuals outside the labor force age range. The J-F measure includes it as human capital reserve, defined as the value of human capital for those individuals below the legal working age or still enrolled in school. It varies with the age structure of the population and school enrollment and is based on expected lifetime earnings.

From 1997 to 2018, the reserve population of the Mainland, Hong Kong, and Taiwan all show a declining trend, with that in the Mainland decreasing by approximately 20%, Hong Kong by 25% and Taiwan by 42 indicating disappearing population dividends in the future. Moreover, Fig. 7.19 and Table 7.14 display the cumulative growth of the proportion of reserve population in the active population, defined as all nonretired population. The ratio reflects the potential sustainability of the population dividend, and that the reserve

population shares have been declining in all areas. In 2018, the proportions of reserve population are lower than 30%, 28.2% in Mainland China, 26.2% in Hong Kong, and 28.2% in Taiwan, possibly due to declining fertility rates.

The proportion of reserve population has also declined in both Beijing and Shanghai, and at rates faster than the average rate in Mainland, indicating more serious impacts. Between 1997 and 2018, the reserve proportion declined from 27.2% to 19.9% in Beijing, and from 25.0% to 19.7% in Shanghai.

In contrast to the declining trends of the reserve population describe above, when we calculate the cumulative growth of the J-F human capital reserve as shown Fig. 7.20, we see that the human capital reserve grows much faster than the population. From 1997 to 2018, for both Beijing and Shanghai, the stock of human capital reserve increased more than sevenfold, and Hong Kong's human capital reserve also more than doubled during the same period. We see in Fig. 7.21 that the ratio of human capital reserve in Hong Kong and Taiwan to that in Beijing have both declined, and the decline is especially dramatic in Taiwan.

We see in Table 7.14 that the share of human capital reserve in Mainland China has not changed noticeably over the period 1997 to 2018, fluctuating in the range of 47%–54%. Moreover, Fig. 7.22 shows that the shares

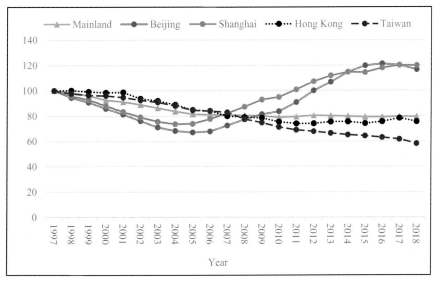

FIG. 7.19 Trends of reserve population in different regions (1997 = 100). The reserve population is defined as individuals below the legal age for entering labor market and those above the minimum legal age of the labor market but still in school. The 1997 value is set equal to 100. The results are calculated based on data from the 2020 human capital project.

TABLE 7.14
Human capital reserve in active population (%).

	RAITO OF RESERVE POPULATION TO TOTAL ACTIVE POPULATION					RATIO OF J-F BASED HUMAN CAPITAL RESERVE TO TOTAL J-F HUMAN CAPITAL				
Year	Mainland	Beijing	Shanghai	Hong Kong	Taiwan	Mainland	Beijing	Shanghai	Hong Kong	Taiwan
1997	32.6	27.2	25.0	31.2	36.4	53.5	53.4	52.4	28.4	32.2
2002	30.3	22.9	20.3	28.5	34.4	52.2	50.4	49.0	27.6	30.3
2007	29.2	19.7	17.9	27.1	32.4	47.1	46.1	52.8	24.1	26.4
2012	28.6	19.2	18.0	25.6	29.7	47.1	45.9	50.7	22.0	22.3
2018	28.2	19.9	19.7	26.2	28.2	51.0	45.6	52.8	21.6	20.4

Active population is defined as labor force age population excluding students.

of human capital reserve in both Beijing and Shanghai have also remained quite stable over the period 1997–2018, varying between 44% and 56%. In contrast, in Hong Kong and Taiwan, the share of human capital reserve has been continuously falling, from 28.4% to 21.6% in Hong Kong and from 32.2% to 20.4% in Taiwan.

We have seen that the younger population's share of the total population in Mainland China, is offset by its much larger share in human capital—around 50%. In contrast, these shares are much more nearly equal to each other in Hong Kong and Taiwan.

The differences between the shares of reserve population and the shares of human capital reserve among Mainland China, Hong Kong, and Taiwan are probably attributable to the rising education opportunities for Mainland China's younger generation, as well as by its increased survival rates and the positive impacts of the 9-years compulsory education law and expanded college enrollment.

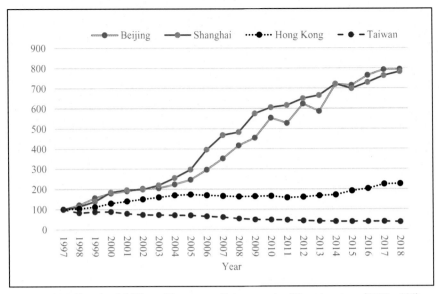

FIG. 7.20 Trends of J-F based human capital reserve in different regions (1997＝100).

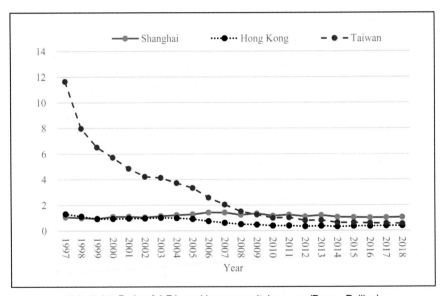

FIG. 7.21 Ratio of J-F based human capital reserve (Base＝Beijing).

7.9 CONCLUSION

This chapter presents estimates of various human capital measures across Mainland China, Hong Kong, and Taiwan, and within the Mainland, a focus on Beijing and Shanghai, which are more closely comparable to Hong Kong and Taiwan in their economic development. The human capital measures reflect labor force age, education attainments of the labor force, and the comprehensive human capital measure is based on the Jorgenson-Fraumeni lifetime income framework.

In general, the importance of human capital in economic development has been shown to be quite robust

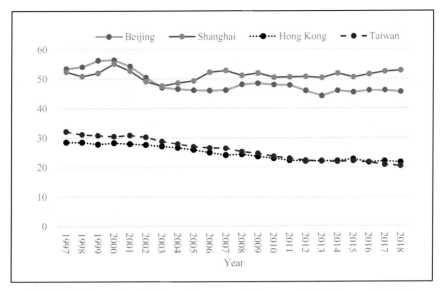

FIG. 7.22 Proportion of J-F based human capital reserve in total human capital (%).

over the areas studied. Traditional human capital indicators, such as education attainment, reflect the rapid development of the education system in Mainland China, particularly in Beijing and Shanghai. From 1997 to 2018, along with economic and education system development, the J-F based total human capital and total labor force human capital in Mainland China, Beijing, and Shanghai have been growing faster than those in Hong Kong and Taiwan.

The comparison of J-F human capital and physical capital with GDP indicates that Mainland China's investment in human capital has contributed a relatively important force to economic growth. Moreover, human-capital growth in Mainland China has notably counteracted the negative impacts of declining population dividend arising from rising shares of the elderly population.

It is clear that human capital investment can offset the effects of population aging, as is the case for Mainland China, especially for Beijing and Shanghai. Our results support the crucial importance of policies to sustain and increase human capital investments.

ACKNOWLEDGMENTS

Partial financial support was provided by the National Natural Science Foundation of China (Grant #71773151). We are grateful for the graduate students at the China Center for Human Capital and Labor Market Research of the Central University of Finance and Economics for assistance. We thank Barbara Fraumeni and Gang Liu for their comments.

REFERENCES

Barro, R.J., Lee, J.W., 1993. International comparisons of educational attainment. J. Monet. Econ. 32, 363–394.

Barro, R.J., Lee, J.W., 2013. A new data set of educational attainment in the world, 1950–2010. J. Dev. Econ. 104, 184–198.

Bloom, D.E., Williamson, J.G., 1998. Demographic transitions and economic miracles in emerging Asia. World Bank Econ. Rev. 12 (3), 419–455.

Cai, F., 2010. Demographic transition, demographic dividend, and Lewis turning point in China. Econ. Res. J. 4, 1–13 (in Chinese).

Cohen, D., Soto, M., 2001. Growth and Human Capital: Good Data, Good Results. OECD Development Centre Technical Papers No. 179, OECD, Paris, France.

Eisner, R., 1985. The total incomes system of accounts. Surv. Curr. Bus. 65 (1), 24–48.

Fleisher, B., et al., 2010. Human capital, economic growth, and regional inequality in China. J. Dev. Econ. 92 (2), 215–231.

Fraumeni, B.M., et al., 2019. Regional distribution and dynamics of human capital in mainland 1985–2014. J. Comp. Econ. 47 (4), 853–866.

Hanushek, E.A., Ludger, W., 2012. Do better schools lead to more growth? Cognitive skills, economic outcomes and causation. J. Econ. Growth 17 (4), 267–321.

Heckman, J.J., et al., 2006. Earnings functions, rates of return and treatment effects: the Mincer equation and beyond. In: Heckman, J.J., Welch, F. (Eds.), Handbook of the

Economics of Education. vol. 1. North-Holland, Amsterdam, Netherlands, pp. 307–458.

Jorgenson, D.W., Fraumeni, B.M., 1989. The accumulation of human and non-human capital, 1948–1984. In: Lipsey, R., Tice, H. (Eds.), The measurement of saving, investment and wealth. University of Chicago Press, NBER, Chicago.

Jorgenson, D.W., Fraumeni, B.M., 1992a. Investment in education and U.S. economic growth. Scand. J. Econ. 94 (Supplement), 51–70.

Jorgenson, D.W., Fraumeni, B.M., 1992b. The output of the education sector. In: Griliches, Z., et al. (Eds.), The Output of the Service Sector. NBER, University of Chicago Press, Chicago, pp. 303–341.

Kendrick, J., 1976. The Formation and Stocks of Total Capital. NBER, Columbia University Press, New York, NY.

Lange, G., et al. (Eds.), 2018. The Changing Wealth of Nations 2018: Building a Sustainable Future. The World Bank, Washington, DC.

Li, H., et al., 2010. China's human capital measurement and index construction. Econ. Res. J. 8, 43–55 (in Chinese).

Li, H., et al., 2013a. Regional distribution and dynamics of human capital in China. Econ. Res. J. 7, 50–63 (in Chinese).

Li, H., et al., 2013b. Human capital in China 1985–2008. Rev. Income Wealth 59 (2), 1–23.

Li, H., et al., 2014. Human capital estimates in China: new panel data 1985–2010. China Econ. Rev. 30, 397–418.

Liu, Z., et al., 2018. Human capital structure upgrading and economic growth: a reconsideration of disparities among China's eastern, central and western regions. Econ. Res. J. 606 (3), 52–65 (in Chinese).

Managi, S., Kumar, P. (Eds.), 2018. Inclusive Wealth Report 2018: Measuring Progress Towards Sustainability. UNEP and Kyushu University Urban Institute, Routledge, London, England and New York, NY.

Mincer, J., 1974. Schooling, Experience and Earning. Columbia University Press, New York, NY.

Mira, M., Liu, G., 2010. The OECD human capital project. In: Progress Report, Paper Prepared for the 31st General Conference of the International Association for Research in Income and Wealth, St. Gallen, Switzerland, August 22–28.

Mulligan, C.B., Sala-i-Martin, X., 1997. A labor income-based measure of the value of human capital: an application to the states of the United States. Jpn. World Econ. 9 (2), 159–191.

OECD, 2010. Statistics Directorate, Committee on Statistics, the OECD Human Capital Project: Progress Report, STD/CSTST/RD (2010) 3, Meeting of the Committee on Statistics, June 7–8. OECD, Paris, France.

Wang, F., Mason, A., Ke, S., 2006. The demographic factor in China's transition. Chin. J. Popul. Sci. 3, 2–18 (in Chinese).

Yang, C., Yan, D., 2017. Analysis on the change trend of China's demographic dividend economic effect from the perspective of population quantity and population quantity. Popul. J. 5, 25–35 (in Chinese).

Ying, Y., 2007. Hong Kong vocational education mode, quality assurance mechanism and its enlightenment. Vocat. Edu. 28 (25), 30–32 (in Chinese).

Yu, X., 2003. The demographic transition of China and strategic opportunities. Chin. J. Popul. Sci. 1, 9–14 (in Chinese).

Zhang, T., 2016. From demographic quantity dividend to human capital quality dividend: a discussion of Chinese economic growth engine transition. Econ. Sci. 5, 5–17 (in Chinese).

Zhong, S., et al., 2016. Research on the substitution effect of education dividend on demographic dividend. China Popul. Sci. 2, 26–34 (in Chinese).

CHAPTER 8

Accumulation of Human and Market Capital in the United States: The Long View, 1948–2013 ☆

BARBARA M. FRAUMENI[a,b,c,d,e,*] • MICHAEL S. CHRISTIAN[f] • JON D. SAMUELS[g,h]
[a]Central University of Finance and Economics, Beijing, China, [b]University of Southern Maine, Portland, ME, United States, [c]National Bureau of Economic Research, Cambridge, MA, United States, [d]IZA Institute for Labor Economics, Bonn, Germany, [e]Hunan University, Changsha, Hunan, China, [f]Education Analytics, Madison, WI, United States, [g]Bureau of Economic Analysis, U.S. Department of Commerce, Suitland, MD, United States, [h]Institute of Quantitative Social Science, Harvard University, Cambridge, MA, United States
*Corresponding author: Barbara_Fraumeni@hotmail.com

Over the 1948–2013 period, many factors significantly impacted on human capital. In 1948, the post-World War II baby boom was well underway. The G.I. Bill (Servicemen's Readjustment Act of 1944) provided stipends for tuition and expenses for veterans attending colleges and trade schools, facilitating matriculation. The average educational attainment by both men and women increased by over 55% between 1950 and 2010. By 2010, women were on average slightly more educated than men, and those aged 25–34 were almost seven percentage points more likely than men to complete tertiary education. Most of the labor force changes came from increasing participation by women. Civilian labor force participation for prime age (35–44 year old) women rose from about 35% in 1950 to 77% in 2000, before declining slightly to 75% in 2010. Only about 23% of married women were part of the civilian labor force in 1948, but by 1970, this number had increased to 41%. By 1980, the "V" drop in civilian female labor force participation during child-bearing ages had disappeared. Male prime age civilian labor force participation by decade peaked in 1970 at about 97%, and then declined over the subsequent decades to less than 92% in 2010. Just over halfway through the covered period, in the mid-eighties, the so-called "Great Moderation" began. In this "moderation,"

business cycles were less volatile, which tends to increase employment stability and therefore the potential pay-off from further education.[a] Toward the end of the covered period, the 2007–2009 Great Recession ended this moderation and reduced employment significantly.

This chapter is the fourth in a series of human capital accounting papers using Jorgenson-Fraumeni methodology. The first in this series established the methodology and emphasis used in subsequent papers (Jorgenson and Fraumeni, 1989). The second, published 28 years later, updated the accounts to reflect many changes in the U.S. national accounts over that time period. The period covered in the second paper includes a gap as human capital estimates from 1985 through 1997 were not available (Fraumeni et al., 2017). The third is the only one in the series that breaks out human capital by gender (Fraumeni and Christian, 2019). As gender-specific estimates are not available in Jorgenson and Fraumeni (1989), the coverage of the 2019 paper begins in 1975. This chapter includes a much longer time period—65 years—than in the previous three papers, accordingly the term "long view" is part of the chapter title.[b] The human capital estimates

---

☆The views expressed in this chapter are solely those of the authors and not necessarily those of the Bureau of Economic Analysis, U.S. Department of Commerce. We thank Mary-Lynne Neil of the Bureau of Economic Analysis for copy-editing a draft version of this chapter.

[a]Bernanke (2004).

[b]Two other papers by Jorgenson and Fraumeni are frequently cited: Jorgenson and Fraumeni, 1992a,b. 1992a is cited because it imbeds an education and human capital sector within an aggregate GDP account. The 1992b paper is cited because for the first time it includes the equations underlying the methodology.

Measuring Human Capital. https://doi.org/10.1016/B978-0-12-819057-9.00002-0
2021 Published by Elsevier Inc.

from 1948 through 1975 are from Jorgenson and Fraumeni (1989); those from 1976 are constructed by Christian (2017) and modified to more closely conform to the Jorgenson-Fraumeni methodology.

An important continuing contribution of this paper series is to integrate human capital estimates with the system of national accounts (SNA). The Bureau of Economic Analysis (BEA) National Income and Product Accounts (NIPA) data for this paper were collected subsequent to the 14th comprehensive revision of the NIPAs.[c] Comprehensive revisions typically occur every 5 years (BEA, 2013, pp. 13–39), accordingly many have occurred since 1948. The NIPAs are the basis for almost all of the core accounts data in this chapter except for human capital data. There have been many definitional, classification, source data, methodological, and presentation changes as a result of the revisions, and it is important to integrate the human capital estimates with the latest definitions used in the U.S. national accounts. It was not until 1951 that constant dollar estimates of Gross National Product (GNP) were released (Jaszi and Kendrick, 1951).[d] Many methodological or statistical improvements have been made since then. Boskin (2000) counted 160 revisions to nominal dollar Gross Domestic Product (GDP) in six comprehensive revisions beginning in 1976 and ending in 1999; certainly, many revisions occurred in the comprehensive revisions before and after the revisions he analyzed. A number of the revisions were concerned with prices or quality change, such as hedonic price indexes for computers and implementation of chained Fisher ideal indexes. Other changes include the classification of software, research and development, and entertainment and literary artistic originals as investment, separation of government expenditures into consumption versus investment, measurement of implicit services provided by property and casualty insurance and by commercial banks, and a complete revamping of the table presentation of the accounts.[e] In addition, the NIPAs changed over time to be in greater conformity with the SNA.[f]

This chapter is organized into six sections: Human capital methodology (Section 8.1), Factors impacting on human and market capital (Section 8.2), Overview of the accounts (Section 8.3), Analysis of the accounts in nominal dollars (Section 8.4), Analysis of contributions and rates of growth (Section 8.5), and Conclusion (Section 8.6).

8.1 HUMAN CAPITAL METHODOLOGY

The measures of human capital employed in this account are based on the methodology of Jorgenson and Fraumeni (1989). The Jorgenson-Fraumeni approach measures human capital as nominal lifetime earnings, in present discounted value, of all living people—adults and children—in an economy. Most aggregate quantities are measured using Törnqvist indexes with the exception of quantities such as net investment, which can include negative components; prices are implicitly determined from the nominal values and the quantities.[g] The Jorgenson-Fraumeni approach includes both a market component, which is measured using nominal lifetime market labor compensation, and a nonmarket component, which is measured using lifetime value of time spent in nonmarket activities other than schooling and personal maintenance. Including nonmarket activities during the 1948–2013 period is particularly important as notably women changed time spent in various activities. Time spent in nonmarket work decreased as time spent in market work increased.

The Jorgenson-Fraumeni approach measures nominal lifetime earnings, using the following equation:

$$i_{y,a,s,e} = \gamma i_{y,a,s,e} + \left[(1+\rho)^{-1}(1+g)sr_{y,a,s}\right]senr_{y,a+1,s,e}i_{y,a+1,s,e+1} + \left[(1+\rho)^{-1}(1+g)sr_{y,a,s}\right](1-senr_{y,a+1,s,e})i_{y,a+1,s,e}$$

(8.1)

where ρ is the discount rate (set to 0.04); g is the earnings growth rate (set to 0.02); and, for a person in year y of age a, sex s, and level of education e:

- $i_{y,a,s,e}$ is average nominal lifetime earnings, in present discounted value;
- $\gamma i_{y,a,s,e}$ is average nominal yearly earnings;

---

[c]The NIPA data is dated July 28, see Bureau of Economic Analysis (2017).

[d]Gross National Product originally was the featured measure of the state of the economy.

[e]See Boskin (2000) and Bureau of Economic Analysis, U.S. Department of Commerce, Various Issues.

[f]For example, the term operating surplus was introduced during the 2003 comprehensive revision.

[g]Quantities such as net investment, which can include negative components, are created using additive aggregation.

- $sr_{y,a,s}$, which is assumed to not vary by education, is the survival rate from year y to year $y+1$; and
- $senr_{y,a,s,e}$ is the school attendance rate.

It is assumed that nominal lifetime earnings at a maximum age (in this application, age 75) are equal to zero among men and women in all years at all levels of education. With this assumption, it is possible to work backward by age, using Eq. (8.1), to compute average nominal lifetime earnings for all combinations of year, sex, age, and education, given measures of average nominal yearly earnings, school enrollment rates, and survival rates by year, age, sex, and education.

The Jorgenson-Fraumeni model divides the life cycle into five stages (Jorgenson and Fraumeni, 1992b). In the first stage, people neither earn income ($yi_{y,a,s,e} = 0$) nor do they attend school ($senr_{y,a,s,e} = 0$). This period covers all ages up to age 4. In the second stage, people do not earn income ($yi_{y,a,s,e} = 0$), but they may attend school ($senr_{y,a,s,e} \geq 0$). This period lasts from age 5 to either age 13 (up to 1975) or 14 (1976 and after); the post-1976 accounts constructed by Christian (2017) ends this phase at age 14 following a change in 1980 to the minimum age for recording work experience and income in the March Current Population Survey (CPS). In the third stage, people may earn income ($yi_{y,a,s,e} \geq 0$) or attend school ($senr_{y,a,s,e} \geq 0$). This period lasts from age 14 (up to 1975) or 15 (1976 and after) and ends at age 34. In the fourth stage, people may earn income ($yi_{y,a,s,e} \geq 0$) but do not attend school ($senr_{y,a,s,e} = 0$). This period lasts from age 35 to age 74. In the fifth stage, which covers ages 75 and up, people do not earn income ($yi_{y,a,s,e} = 0$) or attend school ($senr_{y,a,s,e} = 0$).

The approach of Jorgenson and Fraumeni (1989) includes not only market earnings, but also the value of nonmarket time outside of work, school, and personal maintenance as part of yearly (and, consequently, lifetime) earnings. Jorgenson and Fraumeni (1989) assume that time in school is assumed to be 1300 hours per person among persons enrolled in school; time in personal maintenance is assumed to be 10 hours per day for all persons. The time per year that remains after subtracting time spent in work, school, and personal maintenance is valued at an opportunity cost equal to the wage rate multiplied by the difference between one and the marginal tax rate. The value of nonmarket time is set to zero among persons who are younger than or older than working age. Note that lifetime earnings— and all components of human capital stock and investment—can be computed in a way that includes its market component only, its nonmarket component only, or both.

The nominal stock of human capital in a given year is measured by computing the weighted sum of the population by age, sex, and education, using nominal lifetime income by age, sex, and education as a weight:

$$hc_y = \sum_a \sum_s \sum_e \left(p_{y,a,s,e} \times i_{y,a,s,e} \right) \tag{8.2}$$

This is equal, as mentioned above, to the expected nominal lifetime income, in present discounted value, of all individuals in an economy. The change in the nominal stock of human capital from one year to the next can be split into two components, nominal revaluation and nominal net investment:

$$hc_y - hc_{y-1} = \sum_a \sum_s \sum_e \left[p_{y-1,a,s,e} \times \left(i_{y,a,s,e} - i_{y-1,a,s,e} \right) \right]$$
$$+ \sum_a \sum_s \sum_e \left[\left(p_{y,a,s,e} - p_{y-1,a,s,e} \right) \times i_{y,a,s,e} \right] \tag{8.3}$$

where the left-hand-side term in Eq. (8.3) is the change in the nominal human capital stock from year $y-1$ to y; the first term on the right-hand-side of Eq. (8.3) is nominal revaluation of the human capital stock; and the second term on the right-hand-side of Eq. (8.3) is nominal net investment in human capital. While Eq. (8.3) presents an approach in which revaluation is measured before net investment (so that human capital in year $y-1$ is revaluated using lifetime earnings in year y, as in Jorgenson and Fraumeni, 1989), it can be cast in such a way in which net investment is measured before revaluation.

Note that net investment is driven by changes in the size of the population and in the distribution of the population by age, sex, and education. Net investment can be divided into components associated with the different factors that change the size and distribution of the population: births, deaths, education, aging, and migration. These specific aspects of net investment are grouped more broadly in Jorgenson and Fraumeni (1989) into the component of net investment that increases the human capital stock (births, education, and immigration), which is denoted investment, and the component of net investment that reduces the human capital stock (deaths, aging, and emigration), which is denoted as depreciation.

As noted above, the human capital estimates up to 1975 are from Jorgenson and Fraumeni (1989), while those for 1976 and after are from a modified version of the estimates in Christian (2017), with the modifications made to more closely confirm to the Jorgenson-Fraumeni methodology. Yearly earnings are measured up to 1975 using Gollop and Jorgenson's (1980, 1983) data base of market activities (Jorgenson and Fraumeni, 1989), and in 1976 and after from estimates produced from the March demographic supplements to the CPS (Census Bureau, U.S. Department of Commerce, 2015). Population and school enrollment is measured up to 1975 using a demographic data base produced using Census data for Jorgenson and Fraumeni (1989). For 1976 and after, school enrollment is measured using estimates produced from the October school enrollment supplements to the CPS. The October CPS is also used to measure the distribution of population by age, sex, and education for 1976 and after, but the level of population is measured using Census estimates. Survival data are drawn from life tables published by the National Center for Health Statistics.

The human capital estimates in Christian (2017) differ in substantive ways from those in Jorgenson and Fraumeni (1989). One substantive difference is that net investment is decomposed into five components: investment from births, investment from education, depreciation from deaths, depreciation of aging, and residual net investment, which includes immigration and emigration, as well as any population discrepancies over time that results from using multiple sources of data that do not necessarily agree. We have included residual net investment as part of investment. There are many other differences between the approach in Christian (2017) and that in Jorgenson and Fraumeni (1989), but we have modified the measures in Christian (2017) to reduce these differences. These modifications include the following:

- Results incorporate both market and nonmarket human capital stock and investment, with nonmarket time valued as in Jorgenson and Fraumeni (1989).
- The stock of human capital is measured after investment during that year, rather than before as in Christian (2017).
- Investment in education, which is measured net of depreciation from aging while enrolled in school in Christian (2017), is measured as gross investment in education separate from depreciation of aging while in school.
- Yearly market earnings, which were measured using pretax wage, salary, and self-employment income in Christian (2017), are measured instead using analogous post-tax earnings measures, and adjusted using a multiplier derived from the NIPA tables to better approximate labor compensation.
- The same multiplier is applied to nonmarket earnings, so that the opportunity cost reflects labor compensation rather than only wage, salary, and self-employment earnings.
- Earnings are set to zero after age 74.

- Depreciation from aging is measured before investment in education, rather than after as in Christian (2017).
- The highest level of education is set to 17 years of education, as in Jorgenson and Fraumeni (1989), rather than 18 as in Christian (2017).
- The quantities underlying the contributions shown in this chapter are constructed with Törnqvist indexes as in Jorgenson and Fraumeni (1989), with the exception of the quantities underlying human saving and wealth contributions after 1975, which are constructed with Fisher indexes as in Christian (2017).[h]

8.2 FACTORS IMPACTING ON HUMAN AND MARKET CAPITAL

Among the factors impacting on human and market capital are labor force participation, the state of the economy, education, and the level of income.

Significant changes in labor force participation were highlighted in the introduction; pertinent details of labor force changes are shown in Figs. 8.1–8.3.[i]

There is little variation in the civilian male labor force participation rates for the 10-year periods shown in Fig. 8.1. The rates in the first 3 years—1950, 1960, and 1970—and the next 3 years—1980, 1990, and 2000—are very similar. For the peak working ages of 25 through 54, the male civilian labor force participation rate declines monotonically starting from 1960 for all subsequent years shown. For males aged 55 and over, the rates almost monotonically decline over the 7 years shown. The uptick in 2010 for older individuals and the drop for younger individuals perhaps reflected delayed retirement or difficulty finding jobs subsequent to the Great Recession, which occurred from late 2007 through mid-2009 (see Table 8.1 for a list of recessions). The high civilian labor force participation rate in 1950 for those over 64 might reflect a shortage of male workers in the initial post-World War II era.

There are important changes in the female civilian labor force participation rate (Fig. 8.2). In 1950, 1960, and 1970 the rates decline in a classic "V" shape for those of child-bearing age. In 1950, 1960, and 1970, the "V" shape for those of child-bearing age is centered around ages 25–34; at the same time, the average

---

[h]The rates of growth of NIPA GDP shown in Table 8A.1 are calculated from NIPA GDP quantity levels constructed with Fisher indexes.

[i]Fraumeni and Christian (2019) highlighted gender differences to a greater degree.

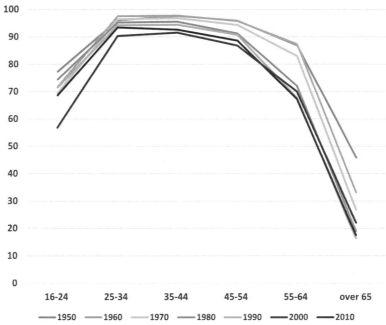

FIG. 8.1 Civilian male labor force participation rate 1950, 1960, 1970, 1980, 1990, 2000, 2010. (Source: Toosi, 2002, 2012.)

TABLE 8.1
List of U.S. recessions between 1940 and 2013 by month, year, and quarter.

November 1948 (IV)	October 1949 (IV)
July 1953 (II)	May 1954 (II)
August 1957 (III)	April 1958 (II)
April 1960 (II)	February 1961 (I)
December 1969 (IV)	November 1970 (IV)
November 1973 (IV)	March 1975 (I)
January 1980 (I)	July 1980 (III)
July 1981 (III)	November 1982 (IV)
July 1990 (III)	March 1991 (I)
March 2001 (I)	November 2001 (IV)
December 2007 (IV)	June 2009 (II)

Source: http://wwwdev.nber.org/cycles/cyclesmain.html, accessed 7/23/2019, see National Bureau of Economic Research, 2019.

civilian labor force participation rate rose for females under the age of 65. The labor force participation rate among married women rose from 23% in 1948 to 41% in 1970 (Fig. 8.3). As the labor force participation rate for widowed or divorced females stayed relatively constant over the same time period (varying from 35 to at most 39%), the increase in labor force participation comes from married women with husbands present. As previously mentioned, the child-bearing "V" disappeared in 1980. In 1990, 2000, and 2010, increases in civilian labor force participation for prime age workers, i.e., ages 25–54, largely no longer occur, although participation among older individuals continued to increase in most cases. The uptick in participation in 2010 among women 65 or older, as is the case with males, may have been due to delayed retirements because of the Great Recession. Females aged 25 to 64 approximately double their civilian labor force participation rates between 1950 and 2010.

Over the period 1950–2010, average educational attainment substantially increases, by over 50% for both males and females. At the beginning of the period, average educational attainment for the younger individuals, aged 25–34, is almost 50% higher than older individuals aged 55–64 (Fig. 8.4). By 2010, there is not much difference between educational attainment of those younger and older cohorts, and all individuals aged 15–74. These trends are very similar for males and females. However, there is a notable difference nearer to the end of the period in the tertiary education enrollment and completion rates for younger males versus

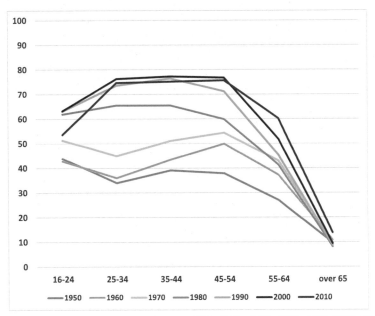

FIG. 8.2 Civilian female labor force participation rate 1950, 1960, 1970, 1980, 1990, 2000, 2010. (Source: Toosi, 2002, 2012.)

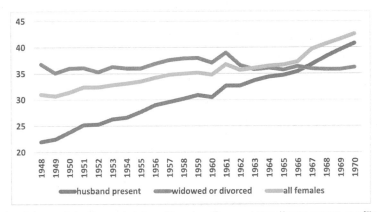

FIG. 8.3 Labor force participation and status of females. (Source: https://www.census.gov/library/publications/1975/compendia/hist_stats_colonial-1970.html, Accessed July 22, 2019, see Census Bureau, 1975.)

females for those aged 25–34 (Fig. 8.5).[j] By 2000, the male percentage of younger individuals who enrolled in tertiary education who complete, which started to

decline in 1995, is less than the female percentage of younger individuals who enrolled in tertiary education who complete, i.e., graduate. By 2010, the female percent of those who enrolled in tertiary education who complete is 6.6 percentage points higher than the same figure for males (37.5% of females complete compared to 30.9% of males).

Another factor impacting human capital and the health of the economy is the level of earnings received. In 2013, mean female earnings in 2018 dollars are more

---

[j]Individuals who have not been in tertiary education long enough clearly have not completed their degree. The percent of individuals who have at least some years of tertiary education compared to the number who have completed is still relevant as the notable trend which begins in 1995 persists long enough for individuals to have had the time to complete.

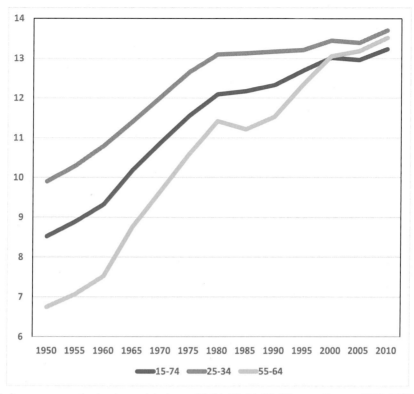

FIG. 8.4 Average years of school completed ages 15–74, 25–34, 55–64, every 5 years, 1950–2010. (Source: Barro and Lee, 2013b, see Barro and Lee, 2013a for a description of the data set.)

than twice that in 1967; mean male earnings in 2018 dollars are just over 40% higher than that in 1967. Between 1967 and 2013, mean female earnings in 2018 dollars on average grew at more than double the rate of male earnings (Fig. 8.6). One factor contributing to this difference is that mean male earnings in 2018 dollars declines during every recession that occurred after 1967; mean female earnings in 2018 dollars declines in only three of the seven recessions during that time period.[k] In addition, the change in the mean female earnings exceeds that of males in two thirds of the covered years. Due in large part to the impact of the Great Recession, the mean income in 2018 dollars of both females and males is lower in 2013 than in 2006.

The mean earnings of females in 2018 dollars increase as a percentage of that of males between 1967 and 2013. Female mean income in 2018 dollars is less than 50% of that of males until 1982; this percentage does not stay consistently above 60% until after 2000, reaching 67% in 2013. However, as Fig. 8.6 shows, sometimes the female percent of mean male earnings in 2018 dollars does not always rise, for example, the highest figure at 67% is attained in 2009.[1]

8.3 OVERVIEW OF THE ACCOUNTS

The backbone of the accounts is the five accounts summarized in Fig. 8.7. Each is outlined in detailed accounting tables with nominal values for 1948 or 1949 and for

---

[1]If the percent that mean female earnings is of mean male earnings is computed with median earnings of full-time, year-round workers as in Table P-40 Women's Earnings as a Percentage of Men's Earnings by Race and Hispanic Origin: 1960 to 2018 (Census Bureau, U.S. Department of Commerce, 2019), the percents are much higher. Table P-40 %s are the percents typically cited, however, in this chapter table P-42 is the basis for the discussion as all earnings impact on human capital.

---

[k]See Table 8.1 for a list of recessions.

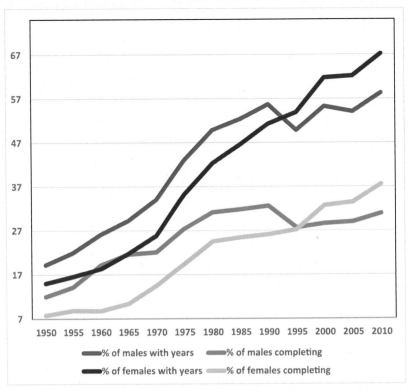

FIG. 8.5 Average tertiary years of school age 25–34, every 5 years, 1950–2010. *Note*: The label term "with years" refers to the percent having completed at least some years of tertiary education without necessarily completing a tertiary degree. (Source: Barro and Lee, 2013b, see Barro and Lee, 2013a for a description of the data set.)

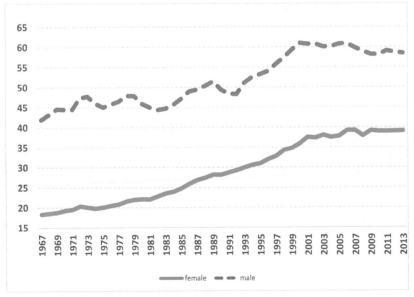

FIG. 8.6 Mean earnings 1967–2013 in 2018 dollars (thousands). (Source: https://www.census.gov/data/tables/time-series/demo/income-poverty/historical-income-people.html, table P-42 Work Experience–All Workers by Mean Earnings and Sex: 1967 to 2018, Accessed 11/15/2019. Includes those 15 years old and over beginning with March 1980, and people 14 years old and over as of March of the following year for previous years. Before 1989 earnings are for civilian workers only. Earnings in 2018 CPI-U-RS (Consumer Price Index, for all urban consumers, research series) adjusted dollars.)

1. EXPANDED PRODUCTION	**2. EXPANDED PRIVATE NATIONAL LABOR & GROSS NATIONAL PROPERTY INCOME**
Expanded Gross Private Domestic Product equals Expanded Gross Private Domestic Factor Outlay	Expanded Private National Labor Income Gross Private National Property Income

3. EXPANDED GROSS PRIVATE NATIONAL RECEIPTS & EXPENDITURES

Expanded Gross Private National Income

Expanded Private National Consumer Outlays plus Expanded Gross Private National Saving

equals Expanded Private National Consumer Expenditures

Expanded Gross Private National Consumer Receipts equals Expanded Private National Consumer Expenditures

4. EXPANDED GROSS PRIVATE NATIONAL CAPITAL ACCUMULATION

Expanded Gross Private National Saving equals

Expanded Gross Private National Capital Formation

5. EXPANDED PRIVATE NATIONAL WEALTH

Private National Market Wealth equals

Private Domestic Tangible Assets plus

Net Claims on Governments and the Rest-Of-The-World

Private National Market Wealth plus Human Wealth equals Expanded Private National Wealth

FIG. 8.7 Overview of the five accounts.

2013.[m] Together they form an expanded, complete, and integrated system for the private economy by combining human capital and NIPA estimates.[n] The expanded accounts include a production account, incorporating data on output and input; an income and expenditures account, giving data on income, consumer expenditures and outlays, and saving; a capital accumulation and saving account, allocating saving to various types of capital formation, and a balance sheet, containing data on national wealth. The accumulation accounts are related to the wealth accounts through the accounting identity between period-to-period changes in wealth and the sum of net saving and the revaluation of assets. Of the five accounts, the expanded production account is most familiar to users as it contains a private version of GDP augmented to include the production of human capital.

---

[m]The first year available from Jorgenson and Fraumeni (1989) for some components of the expanded gross private national capital accumulation and wealth accounts is 1949.

[n]In the previous three Fraumeni co-authored papers cited earlier, the term "full" was used instead of "expanded." Since not all possible components are included in these accounts, notably those related to the environment, terminology was changed.

The production account is for the private domestic economy; the other accounts use private national economy as the conceptual basis. Government measures are included or excluded depending on which concept is being used. The private domestic concept excludes the output and inputs of the government sector.[o] Compensation of government employees appears on the receipts side of the income and expenditure account as this account is based on the accounting identity that the value of consumer receipts equals the value of outlays plus saving. In general, the private national concept includes account-relevant activities that occur in the United States, but it restricts included relevant activities to those made by (such as expenditures), received by (such as income), or held by (such as wealth) private entities. To be consistent with Jorgenson-Fraumeni human capital, the accounts take the recipients' point of view.

Human capital appears in all five accounts in some form as human capital is fully integrated into the accounts. Each human capital component is attributed to the appropriate account construct. All human capital components in the production account are allocated to labor as part of labor services. The value of labor services provided by human capital that are not part of the value of services provided in the market are imputed. Market labor factor outlay includes an imputation for entrepreneurial labor income. In the receipts and expenditures account, the labor income arising from human capital is included as a receipt to be consistent with the inclusion of market labor compensation as a receipt; the labor income arising from human capital is identical to that which appears in the income account. On the expenditures side, the sum of all human capital components is identified as either consumption or savings. Time in household production and leisure is recorded as consumption, while the other human capital components are included in savings.[p] Investment in human capital (education, births, and residual, the latter from 1976) is entered into the savings and capital accumulation parts of the account.[q] The final account is the

wealth account, which includes the sum of market wealth and human lifetime labor earnings.

In the analysis which follows, nominal value shares are shown in figures for selected boundary years, and contributions are shown for selected periods.[r]

Expanded account measures from the accounting tables appear in other tables and in figures. In the first accounting table (Table 8.2), factor outlay inputs to production are shown, where in that table labor outlay equals factor outlay minus property outlay. In that same table, expanded production (output) is built up from GNP, in other tables and figures the expanded production building blocks are consumption and investment. Tables and figures using production constructs include accounting Table 8.2, nominal share Fig. 8.8, contribution Figs. 8.14 and 8.15 and rates of growth Tables 8A.1 and 8A.2. The second and third accounting tables (Tables 8.3 and 8.4) use income, consumer expenditures, and consumer outlays constructs. Tables and figures using these constructs include accounting Tables 8.3 and 8.4, nominal share Figs. 8.9 and 8.10, contribution Fig. 8.17, and rates of growth Tables 8A.3 and 8A.4. These feed into saving (accounting Table 8.5, nominal share Figs. 8.11 and 8.12, contribution Fig. 8.16, and rates of growth Table 8A.5) and wealth (accounting Table 8.6, nominal share Fig. 8.13, contribution Fig. 8.18, and rates of growth Table 8A.6).[s]

8.4 ANALYSIS OF THE ACCOUNTS IN NOMINAL DOLLARS

8.4.1 Expanded Production and Factor Outlay

In the first account, the production account (Table 8.2), production and factor outlay is increased by the sum of investment in education and births and time in

---

[o]The original accumulation paper excluded the government sector because of the complications, data requirements, and overall difficulty of including the government sector.

[p]Time in household production and leisure is recorded as both income and consumption as the individual implicitly receives income from himself because of the value of his time and uses this income to finance consumption.

[q]Human capital saving is equal to human capital investment in the accounts.

[r]The selected boundary years are 1948 (1949), 1973, 1995, 2000, 2007, 2009, and 2013. The selected periods are 1949–2013, 1949–2000, 1949 (1950)–1973, 1973–1995, 1995–2000, 2000–2013, 2000–2007, 2007–2009, and 2009–2013, in that order. The entire period is broken up into a period ending in 2000 and the subsequent 14 years as frequently these major subperiods look quite different; smaller subperiods are chosen for similar reasons. If the first year available from Jorgenson and Fraumeni (1989) is 1949, then nominal shares begin in 1949 and the contributions begin in 1950 (listed as 1949–1950) as contributions depend on a growth rate from the previous year to the current year.

[s]All rates of growth in the appendix tables are computed using logarithms.

TABLE 8.2
Expanded production, United States 1948 and 2013 (billions of dollars).

			1948	2013
Product				
1		Gross national product (table 1.7.5, line 4)	276.3	16,935.8
2	−	Rest-of-world gross national product (table 1.7.5, line 2 minus line 3)	1.4	244.2
3	−	Compensation of government employees (table 6.2B, line 76 for 1948–97; table 6.2D, line 86 for 1998–2016)	22.9	1761.6
4	−	Government consumption of fixed capital (table 5.1, line 17)	10.6	506.5
5	=	Gross private domestic product (NIPA definition)	241.4	14,423.5
6	−	Federal taxes on production and imports (table 3.5, line 2)	7.8	124.8
7	−	Federal current transfer receipts from business (table 3.2, line 19)	0.3	41.3
8	+	Capital stock tax (table 3.5, line 15)	0.0	0.0
9	−	State and local taxes on production and imports (table 3.5, line 16)	11.9	1050.1
10	−	State and local current transfer receipts from business (table 3.3, line 18)	0.1	49.5
11	+	Business property taxes (table 3.5, line 30)	5.9	448.8
12	+	Business motor vehicle licenses (table 3.5, line 31)	0.3	10.2
13	+	Business other taxes (table 3.5, sum of lines 32–34)	1.3	86.0
14	+	Subsidies less current surplus of federal government enterprises (table 3.2, line 35 minus line 22)	0.8	69.9
15	+	Subsidies less current surplus of state and local government enterprises (table 3.3, line 30 minus line 21)	−0.3	10.3
16	+	Imputations for market capital services	19.8	713.4
17	=	Gross private domestic product	249.2	14,496.4
18	+	Time in household production and leisure	333.1	16,472.8
19	+	Investment in human capital, births[a]	346.6	10,714.1
20	+	Investment in human capital, education[a]	349.7	22,864.9
21	+	Investment in human capital, residual	0.0	1461.9
22	=	Expanded gross private domestic product	1278.5	66,010.1
Factor outlay				
1		Compensation of employees, all private industries (table 6.2B for 1982 and table 6.2D for 2009, both line 3)	121.5	7090.3
2	+	Entrepreneurial labor income (imputation)	28.5	957.8
3	+	Full property outlay (line 17 from the Product account, minus lines 1 and 2 from the Factor Outlay account)	99.1	6448.3
4	=	Gross private domestic factor outlay	249.2	14,496.4
5	+	Imputations for human capital from Product account above (lines 18–21)	1029.3	51,513.7
6	=	Expanded gross private domestic factor outlay	1278.5	66,010.1

Note: Totals may differ slightly from the sums due to rounding. Table numbers refer to the National Income and Product Accounts (Bureau of Economic Analysis, U.S. Department of Commerce, Various Issues).
[a]The split between birth and education before 1976 is imputed from a somewhat later version of the accounts presented in Jorgenson and Fraumeni (1989). Accordingly, here and in the associated graph is the only place in this paper where this split is shown.

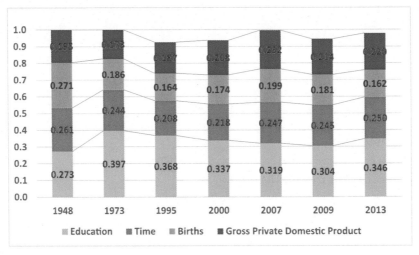

FIG. 8.8 Nominal share in expanded gross private domestic product, selected years.

household production and leisure.[t,u] As in the "new architecture" accounts (Jorgenson and Landefeld, 2006, 2009; Jorgenson, 2010), the core NIPAs are modified in several ways. In the product section of the production account, to allow for integration with productivity accounts, property-type taxes are included, but some other types of taxes, such as primarily sales taxes, are excluded. Several capital services that are not in NIPA GDP are added into gross private domestic product (GPDP). These imputations, which appear in line 16 of the product section, include those for consumer durables and real estate held by institutions and producer durable equipment held by institutions. The other imputation included in line 16 of the product section is an addition to household real estate capital services as this component is estimated differently in NIPA. These modifications are relatively minor in magnitude compared to NIPA GPDP.

Fig. 8.8 gives a sense of the relative size of the nominal dollar expanded components for the boundary years. Education investment in human capital is always the largest component, followed typically by time in household production and leisure. The nominal value of investment in human capital comes from higher levels of education attainment (Fig. 8.4) and the higher levels of female labor force participation, particularly by

1970 by married women (Figs. 8.2 and 8.3). Nominal birth investment in human capital is larger than nominal GPDP as defined in Table 8.2 only in the first 2 years shown. This reflects the post-World War II baby boom in 1948 and the recession in 1973 (Table 8.1). The value of time in household production and leisure follow the trends in births until wages paid to females rose sufficiently to counteract the decrease in time as time in household production and leisure is evaluated at the opportunity cost market wage (Fraumeni and Christian, 2019, p. 524). After 2007, the nominal births share decreases and the nominal time share stays relatively constant. Beginning in 1996, a new component of expanded production exists, the residual investment in human capital, which is the impact of measured changes in the size and distribution of the population by sex, age, and education that cannot be attributed to measured births, deaths, or schooling as previously described. Nominal shares do not always sum to 1.0 because of the residual. In 2007, this residual is such a small percent of expanded production, just 0.4%, that it cannot be seen in the figure.

8.4.2 Expanded Private National Labor and Gross Private National Property Income

The account shown in Table 8.3 separates income into labor and property income. Property income includes only market components; only labor income has nonmarket (human capital related) expanded components. The nonmarket components are by far the largest of nominal income components (Fig. 8.9). Looking at Fig. 8.8, it is the trends in the nominal shares of

---

[t]The residual, as previously described, is included in investment from 1976.

[u]All table numbers in the account tables refer to U.S. Bureau of Economic Analysis NIPA table numbers unless otherwise specified and are data published July 28, 2017.

TABLE 8.3
Expanded private national labor and gross private national property income, United States, 1948 and 2013 (billions of dollars).

			1948	2013
Labor income				
1		Private domestic outlay for labor services (line 1 plus line 2 of the Factor Outlay account in table 8.2)	150.0	8048.1
2	+	Compensation of employees in general government (table 1.13, line 57)	20.3	1608.5
3	+	Compensation of employees in government enterprises (table 1.13, line 37)	2.5	153.1
4	+	Compensation of employees, rest-of-world (table 1.13, line 61)	0.1	−9.4
5	−	Personal income taxes attributed to labor income (imputation)	14.1	1241.8
6	=	Private national market labor income	158.8	8558.4
7	+	Nonmarket labor income (sum of lines 18–21 of the Product account in table 8.2)	1029.3	51,513.7
8	=	Expanded private national labor income	1188.1	60,072.1
Property income				
1		Gross domestic private outlay for capital services (imputation)	99.5	6448.3
2	+	Capital income originating in the rest-of-world (table 1.7.5 line 2 minus line 3 minus table 1.13 line 61)	1.3	253.6
3	+	Personal interest income (table 2.1, line 14)	9.8	1261.6
4	−	Net interest and miscellaneous payments on assets (table 1.7.5, line 20)	2.6	504.6
5	−	Personal interest payments to business (table 2.1, line 30)	1.3	243.9
6	+	Investment income of social insurance funds less transfers to general government (table 3.14, line 8 plus line 22, minus lines 11 and 24)	0.4	94.1
7	+	Rest-of-world contributions to government social insurance (table 3.6, line 32)	0.0	5.2
8	−	Corporate profits tax liability (table 3.2 line 7 plus table 3.3 line 10)	12.5	433.6
9	−	Personal property taxes (table 3.4, sum of lines 10–12)	0.6	33.1
10	−	Business property taxes (sum of lines 11–13 from the Product account in table 8.2)	7.5	545.0
11	−	Personal income taxes attributed to property income (imputation)	4.6	403.0
12	−	Federal estate and gift taxes (table 5.11, line 19)	0.9	20.9
13	−	State and local estate and gift taxes (table 5.11, line 20)	0.2	5.3
14	−	Net business transfer payments to foreigners (table 4.1, line 32 minus line 15)	0.0	20.6
15	−	Dividends received by government (table 3.1, line 14)	0.0	134.9
16	=	Gross private national market property income	80.9	5717.9

Note: Totals may differ slightly from the sums due to rounding. Table numbers, except those referring to Table 8.2, refer to the National Income and Product Accounts (Bureau of Economic Analysis, U.S. Department of Commerce, Various Issues).

education and births investment that underlie the nonmarket labor trend between 1948 and 1973, with the birth share in expanded GPDP dropping by 31% and the corresponding education share increasing by 45%. The nominal share of nonmarket labor drops below 80% by 2000 (Fig. 8.9). The nominal share of market labor rose between 1995 and 2007; the share of nominal property income rose significantly between 1973 and 2009. The nominal share of residential property income in total property income fell to 31% in 2013 after reaching a 1948–2013 period high of 40% in 2009, the 2013 figure as a result of the housing crisis.

FIG. 8.9 Nominal share in expanded income selected years.

The nominal share of gross private national market labor income as a share of gross private national market income is at its highest at 66% in 1948 and 1973 and at its lowest at 59% in 2009. The nominal share is 60% in 2013, very close to the 61% figure in 1995 and 2007.

8.4.3 Expanded Gross Private National Consumer Expenditures

The main interest in the third account listed in Table 8.4 is in the expenditure section of this account. Expanded gross private national consumer receipts are only very slightly larger than expanded gross private national income, accounting for more than 1% of it for only 3 years. Since expanded gross private national income is split into its two component parts—property income and expanded labor income in Table 8.3—only the expenditure section of the third account is shown in Table 8.4. This expenditure section splits expenditures into market consumer outlays (lines 4 plus 7 plus 8) versus saving (line 10). The fourth accounting table, Table 8.5, further splits saving into gross private

national saving and human capital saving; this split is incorporated into Fig. 8.10. After falling between 1948 and 1995, the nominal share of consumption outlays in total outlays including nonmarket outlays rose 7.5 percentage points between 1995 and 2007, amounting to about 40% of the total for the last 3 years shown. Nominal gross private national (market) saving is a small percentage of expanded private national expenditures and varies by at most 0.6 percentage points. The percentage of nominal market saving increases between 1948 and 1973, subsequently declining between 1973 and 2000, increasing again between 2000 and 2007 before settling to about 6.4% in subsequent years shown. As the percentage of nominal market saving is very small compared to human capital saving, the fluctuations in total saving and total consumption arise mainly from fluctuations in the nominal share of human capital saving in expanded private national saving. Nominal human capital saving is about 90% of total saving for all years shown; accordingly, when the total nominal saving share of total private national

TABLE 8.4
Expanded gross private national consumer expenditures, United States, 1948 and 2013 (billions of dollars).

		EXPENDITURES	1948	2013
1		Personal consumption expenditures (table 1.1.5, line 2)	175.0	11,361.2
2	−	Personal consumption expenditures, durable goods (table 1.1.5, line 4)	24.5	1241.7
3	+	Imputation for market capital services (line 16 from the Product account of table 8.2)	19.8	713.4
4	=	Private national consumption expenditure	170.3	10,832.9
5	+	Consumption of nonmarket goods and services (line 18 from the Product account of table 8.2)	333.1	16,472.8
6	=	Expanded private national consumption expenditure	503.4	27,305.7
7	+	Personal transfer payments to foreigners (table 2.1, line 33)	0.7	77.3
8	+	Current transfer receipts from persons (table 3.1, line 17)	0.3	93.4
9	=	Expanded private national consumer outlays	504.4	27,476.4
10	+	Expanded gross private national saving (1948 authors' calculations, 2013, line 15 from the Saving account of table 8.5)	771.9	39,228.6
11	=	Expanded gross private national expenditures	1276.4	66,705.0

Note: Totals may differ slightly from the sums due to rounding. Table numbers, except those referring to Tables 8.2 and 8.5, refer to the National Income and Product Accounts (Bureau of Economic Analysis, U.S. Department of Commerce, Various Issues).

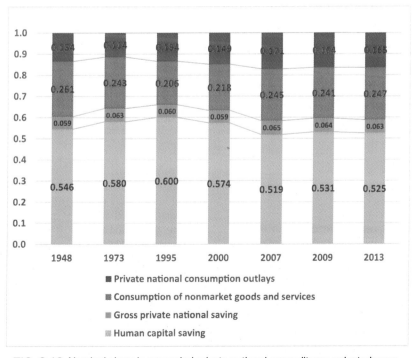

FIG. 8.10 Nominal share in expanded private national expenditures, selected years.

TABLE 8.5
Expanded gross private national saving, United States, 1949 and 2013 (billions of dollars).

		SAVING		
			1949	2013
1		Gross private saving NIPA (table 5.1, line 43)	47.9	3378.3
2	+	Personal consumption expenditures, durable goods (table 1.1.5, line 4)	26.6	1241.7
3	+	Surplus, social insurance funds (table 3.14, line 1 plus line 16 minus lines 10 and 23)	1.5	−286.7
4	+	Statistical discrepancy (table 5.1, line 42)	1.7	−137.9
5	−	Taxes on wealth (Estate and gift taxes, table 5.11, line 18)	0.9	26.1
6	+	Capital transfer payments to persons and financial stabilization payments (table 5.11, sum of lines 12–14)	0.0	6.1
7	+	Other capital transfers paid to business (table 5.11, line 13)	0.0	5.7
8	+	Capital transfers paid, Federal disaster-related insurance benefits (table 5.11, line 11)	0.0	0.0
9	+	Capital transfers paid, State and local disaster-related insurance benefits (table 5.11, line 17)	0.0	0.0
10	−	Capital transfers received, State and local disaster-related insurance benefits (table 5.11, line 39)	0.0	0.0
11	+	Federal net purchases of nonproduced assets (table 3.2, line 46)	0.0	−2.4
12	+	State and local net purchases of nonproduced assets (table 3.3, line 41)	0.2	9.0
13	=	Gross private national saving	77.0	4187.7
14	+	Human capital saving (1949 authors' calculations, 2013 sum of lines 19–21 of the Product account in table 8.2)	742.1	35,040.9
15	=	Expanded gross private national saving	819.1	39,228.6
16	−	Depreciation[a]	625.9	34,899.3
17	=	Net private national saving	193.1	4329.3
18	+	Revaluation[a]	823.6	18,709.6
19	=	Change in expanded private national wealth	1016.7	23,038.9

Note: Totals may differ slightly from the sums due to rounding. Table numbers, except those referring to Tables 8.2 and 8.4, refer to the National Income and Product Accounts (Bureau of Economic Analysis, U.S. Department of Commerce, Various Issues).
[a]A split between market and human capital depreciation, and market and human capital revaluation, is not available until 1976, so these components are not shown separately in this table.

expenditures increases (decreases), the total nominal consumption share of total private national expenditures decreases (increases).

8.4.4 Expanded Gross Private National Capital Saving

The saving section of this accounting table (Table 8.5) shows how change in expanded private national wealth is derived from expanded gross private national saving. Since expanded private national capital accumulation is always equal to private national saving, only the saving section of the account is shown.[v] There is a great deal of

---

[v]Similarly, human capital accumulation is always equal to human capital saving.

variation in the nominal shares of gross private national saving, human capital saving, private national saving, revaluation, and depreciation in change in expanded private national wealth (Fig. 8.11). In this table and in the associated figures, 1949 is the first year shown instead of 1948 because Jorgenson and Fraumeni (1989) published estimates for saving and wealth starting in 1949. Recall that between 1949 and 1973, the nominal share of births in GPDP decreases and the nominal share of education investment in GPDP increases by enough to offset the decrease in the nominal birth share (refer back to Fig. 8.8), reflecting the end of the post-World War II baby boom and the continuing increase in the average number of years of school completed, particularly for younger females

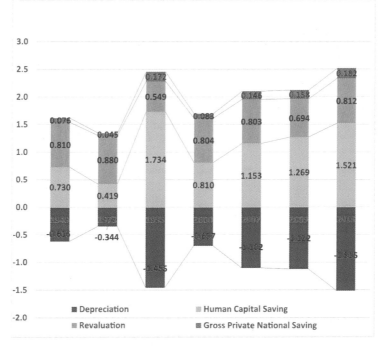

FIG. 8.11 Nominal share in change in expanded private national wealth, selected years.

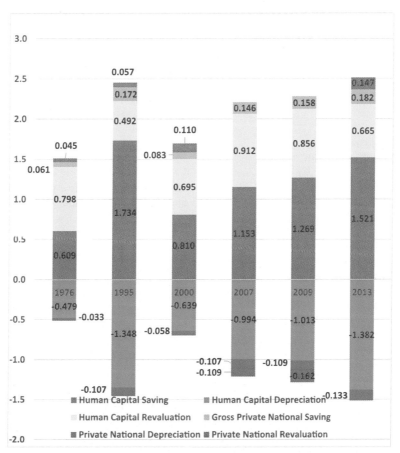

FIG. 8.12 Nominal share in change in expanded private national wealth human and market components, selected years.

(Figs. 8.4 and 8.5). In 1973, the nominal share of human capital saving in change in expanded private wealth decreases in spite of this fact because the increase in the nominal value of the change in private national wealth is more than a third greater than the increase in education investment between 1948 and 1973; this is due to the significant size of revaluation. The nominal value of revaluation increases tenfold between 1949 and 1973, twice the rate of education investment, and the nominal value of depreciation is substantially less negative (Fig. 8.11).

Since revaluation and depreciation can be broken out into human capital and market components beginning in 1976, further analysis refers to Fig. 8.12. In this figure for years in which there is data, the sum of the nominal share of human capital revaluation and private national (market) revaluation and the sum of the nominal share of human capital depreciation and private national (market) depreciation are identical to the total revaluation and depreciation shares shown in Fig. 8.11.[w] In all years, the absolute value magnitude of the nominal share of human capital depreciation is around three-quarters or more of the nominal share of human capital saving. In 2010 and 2013, the ratios of the absolute values of the nominal shares of human capital depreciation to human capital saving are somewhat higher than in other years. In 1995 and 2013, human capital saving and human capital depreciation play a larger role in change in expanded private national wealth than in other years as Fig. 8.12 shows; however, in 1995, compared to 2013 human capital, saving plays a larger role and revaluation a smaller role in change in expanded national wealth. By 2000, the pace of increase in average number of years completed and the difference between the average years of school completed by younger individuals, those 25–34, and older individuals, those aged 55–64, had narrowed considerably (Fig. 8.4). Subsequent to 1995, the absolute value magnitude of both the nominal share of human capital saving and depreciation in change in expanded private national wealth begin to increase. In 2007 and 2009, the nominal share of private national revaluation is negative, reflecting the state of the economy (Table 8.1).

8.4.5 Expanded Wealth

The final set of accounts is the wealth account (Table 8.6). The nominal share of human wealth in expanded private national wealth is always at least 90%, while the nominal share of net claims on government and the rest-of-world is always very small (Fig. 8.13). Human wealth, a stock, fluctuates less than human capital investment as the latter is an annual change. As previously shown in Fig. 8.8, as nominal shares of birth and education investment in GPDP decline between 1973 and 1995, it is not surprising to see a smaller decline in the share of human wealth in expanded private national wealth between the same 2 years. The bigger decline in the nominal human wealth share between 2000 and 2007 reflects the slower pace of education investment noted earlier, as well as the continuing drop in the percentage of males with years of tertiary education who completed (Fig. 8.5). The temporary recovery of the nominal share of human wealth in 2009 is due to the percentages of individuals aged 18–24 enrolled in a postsecondary degree-granting institution increasing substantially from 2006 to 2009 (Fraumeni and Christian, 2019, p. 509), a temporary trend.

8.5 ANALYSIS OF CONTRIBUTIONS AND RATES OF GROWTHS

Contributions are weighted rates of growth, where the weights are average nominal shares and the rates of growth are the rates of growth of the quantities.[x]

8.5.1 Contributions to Expanded Gross Private Domestic Product and Economic Growth and Rates of Growth

This contribution figure is presented without (Fig. 8.14) and with human capital (Fig. 8.15) components for

---

[w]Human capital depreciation includes the change in the present discounted value of lifetime earnings as people age. When an individual ages as retirement is closer, the present discounted value of lifetime earnings normally decreases as there are fewer years left to earn. When an individual retires, reaches 75, or dies, the present discounted value becomes zero.

---

[x]In Figs. 8.14–8.18 and Appendix Tables 8A.1–8A6, the following growth rates..

1949–2013	1949–1950…2012–2013
1949–2000	1949–1950…1999–2000
1949–1973	1949–1950…1972–1973
1973–1995	1973–1974…1994–1995
1995–2000	1995–1996…1999–2000
2000–2013	2000–2001…2012–2013
2000–2007	2000–2001…2006–2007
2007–2009	2007–2008…2008–2009
2009–2013	2009–2010…2012–2013

TABLE 8.6

Expanded private national wealth, United States, 1949 and 2013 (billions of current dollars).

					1949	2013	
1			Private domestic tangible assets		907	63,336	
			Net claims on federal, state, and local governments		233	12,962	
2	+	a.	Federal, monetary		46	3375	
			(i)	+	Vault cash of commercial banks[a]	2	74
			(ii)	+	Member bank reserves[a]	17	2249
			(iii)	+	Currency outside banks[a]	26	1168
			(iv)	+	Par to market value adjustment (imputation)	2	−115
3	+	b.	Federal, nonmonetary		181	7472	
			(i)	+	U.S. government total liabilities[a]	236	16,100
			(ii)	−	U.S. government financial assets[a]	33	1717
			(iii)	+	Net liabilities, federally-sponsored credit agencies[a]	0	−46
			(iv)	+	Assets of social insurance funds[b]	20	3073
			(v)	−	U.S. government liabilities to rest-of-world[c]	0	6420
			(vi)	+	U.S. government credits and claims abroad[c]	−2	227
			(vii)	−	Monetary liabilities[a]	44	3490
			(viii)	+	Par to market value adjustment (imputation)	6	−254
4	+	c.	State and local		6	2114	
			(i)	+	State and local total liabilities[a]	23	5287
			(ii)	−	State and local financial assets[a]	16	2928
			(iii)	+	Par to market value adjustment (imputation)	0	−244
5	+		Net claims on the rest-of-world		18	1829	
		a.		Private U.S. assets and investments abroad[c]		28	16,647
		b.	−	Private U.S. liabilities to foreigners[c]		10	14,818
6	=		Private national nonhuman wealth		1392	91,088	
7	+		Private national human wealth		18,249	785,905	
8	=		Full private national wealth		19,641	876,993	

[a]Board of Governors of the Federal Reserve System, *Flow of Funds Accounts*, various issues.
[b]U.S. Department of Treasury, Treasury Bulletin, February issues and December Monthly Treasury Statement Table 6, Schedule D.
[c]"The International Investment Position of the United States," Survey of Current Business, various issues and the Integrated Macro Accounts for the United States, at https://www.bea.gov/data/special-topics/integrated-macroeconomic-accounts.
Note: Totals may differ slightly from the sums due to rounding.

comparison purposes. The total growth rate with human capital is always less than the total growth rate without human capital. As Fig. 8.8 shows, nominal human capital components are always very large relative to GPDP. Growth in human capital components depends upon population and wage or income growth and increasing levels of education, as reflected in lifetime income weights. These all grow slowly relative to NIPA GDP

(see Table 8A.1). GDP grows at an average rate of 3.2% per year between 1949 and 2013. The progress in raising the average number of years in school for the population aged 15 to 74 (Fig. 8.4) is notable, but the average increase per year between 1950 and 2010 is 0.7%. The average population increase per year between 1949 and 2013 is 1.2% per year (Table 8A.1). Female mean earnings in 2018 dollars grow at an average annual rate of

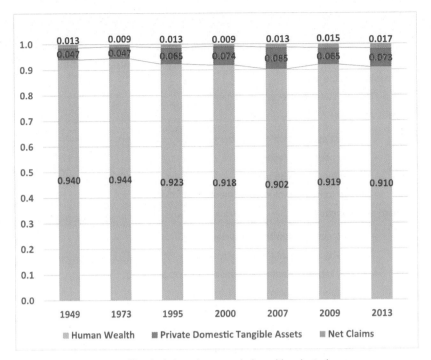

FIG. 8.13 Nominal share in expanded wealth selected years.

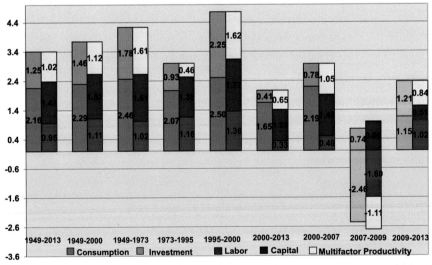

FIG. 8.14 Contributions to expanded gross private domestic product and economic growth without human capital, 1949–2013.

1.6% per year between 1967 and 2013; the corresponding figure for males is 0.7% per year (Fig. 8.6). Lifetime earnings, which directly impact on human capital, are assumed to grow at a real rate of 2% per year across the demographic groups following Jorgenson and Fraumeni (1989), which is fairly high, but the impact of this on human capital growth is tempered as future earnings are discounted to the present value. Accordingly, for the first major subperiod, 1949–2000, the total growth rate without human capital is double that of the version with human capital, although in 1995–2000, it is almost three times as large.

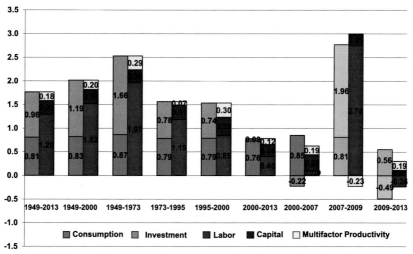

FIG. 8.15 Contributions to expanded gross private domestic product and economic growth with human capital, 1949–2013.

In addition, the absolute value magnitude of multifactor productivity change is always substantially less in the version with human capital than in the version without human capital as it is implicitly assumed that there is no multifactor productivity associated with any of the human capital components. The human capital components quantities on the output side are identical to those on the input side of the accounts. The absolute value magnitude of multifactor productivity change without human capital is usually around five times or more that of the version with human capital.

The two most unusual subperiods in this comparison, aside from the differences between the two major subperiods, 1949–2000 and 2000–2013, are the 1995–2000 and 2007–2009 subperiods, and to some extent the recession recovery subperiod 2009–2013. Note that time in household production and leisure are added to expanded consumption, human capital investment is added to expanded investment and both human capital components—time and investment—are added to expanded labor input. Property outlay, labeled capital in the figures, is only a market concept.[y] The share of expanded investment contribution in total output is always larger in the version with human capital than in the version without human capital in the first major subperiod, 1949–2000. In 1973–1995 and 1995–2000 in the version without human capital and in 1995–2000 in the version with human capital the expanded investment share is 47 to 50%, not much

different from the share of expanded consumption in total output. The typical share relationship is due to time in household production and leisure being substantially less than nominal human capital investment in most cases. The share of expanded labor contribution in total input is always larger in the version with human capital than in the version without human capital in the first major subperiod, 1949–2000. This is a result of the size of human capital components. With respect to the shares of expanded output and input, in the other major subperiod, 2000–2013, the relationships are complicated because of a negative contribution in one or the other version. As expected, in both versions, multifactor productivity growth falls beginning in the 1973–1995 subperiod, recovers strongly in 1995–2000, but falls in 2007–2009 during the Great Recession and recovers in the subperiod 2009–2013. In all subperiods starting with 1995 or later, there are notable differences in the contributions with and without human capital, as well changes in the relative growth rate of GPDP across subperiods.[z] Between 1995 and 2000 and 2000 and 2007, the quantity of human capital investment either rose slightly or fell. By 2000, the difference between the average years of school completed by younger individuals, those 25–34, and older individuals, those aged 55–64,

---

[y]Titles in the figures are truncated because of space considerations.

[z]Contributions are calculated as a weighted rate of growth of quantities in logs, where the weights are the average share of the nominal values for this period and last period's nominal values. The multifactor productivity change contribution is the exception as it is the rate of growth of the quantity of output minus the contributions of all inputs.

narrows considerably (Fig. 8.4). In addition, by 1995, tertiary education completion by males aged 25–34 dropped (Fig. 8.5). The subperiod 1995–2000 is a remarkable time for the impact of computers on economic growth, but not for human capital investment.[aa] When human capital is included, the 1973–1995 and 1995–2000 contributions look much more similar.

During the Great Recession years of 2007 through 2009, tertiary education enrollment differs compared to other subperiods, as previously noted, and in time use. Changes in tertiary enrollment percentages and time use shares by either gender are small or nonexistent in the prior period and the later subperiod. From 2006 to 2009, the percentage of individuals aged 18 to 24 enrolled in a postsecondary degree-granting institution increased substantially. From 2006 to 2009, the percent of 18–24 year-old males enrolled in a postsecondary degree-granting institution increased by 4.3 percentage points, from 34.1 to 38.4%; for females the comparable figure is 3.6 percentage points, from 40.6 to 44.2%. In addition, time use in household production and leisure increased. The share of time devoted to work drops by almost the identical amount that the share of time in household production changes (Fraumeni and Christian, 2019, p. 522). Except for multifactor productivity change, all contributions are positive in 2007–2009 in the version with human capital; in the version without human capital, only two contributions are positive. In 2009–2013, given the trends in human capital investment (years of school and tertiary education completion by males), the economy remained weak in the version with human capital.

Table 8A.1 breaks out changes in nominal dollars of major aggregates into quantity and price changes and includes quantity per capita changes, as well as NIPA GDP rates of growth.[ab,ac,ad] Looking at expanded product, the subperiod rates of growth before the 1995–2000 subperiod look different than those after the 1973–1995 subperiod (Table 8.7), except for the 2007–2009 subperiod. Growth rates for subperiods after the

TABLE 8.7
Average rates of growth in expanded production by major subperiods.

Expanded product	APPROXIMATE % RANGE OF GROWTH RATES	
	Before 1995–2000 subperiod	After 1973–1995 subperiod, except for 2007–2009
Nominal dollar	6.1–7.4	2.0–3.7
Quantity	1.6–2.5	0.1–1.5
Quantity per capita	0.6–1.1	−0.7–0.1
Price	4.3–5.8	1.9–2.6

1973–1995 subperiod almost all drop. Since 1995–2000 is a subperiod of relatively high GDP growth, this may seem surprising. NIPA GDP quantity growth rates are high in the 1949–1973 subperiod, drop in the 1973–1995 subperiod, then return to their previous 1949–1973 level in the 1995–2000 subperiod (see Table 8A.1). Similar growth rate trends comparing before the 1995–2000 subperiod and after, except for in the 2007–2009 subperiod, can be seen in the components of output and input Tables 8A.1 and 8A.2. The explanation for the differences beginning in the 1995–2000 subperiod, sometimes called the "New Economy" time period, is human capital and multifactor productivity.[ad] Although this chapter breaks out time into two major subperiods, the last beginning in 2000, once human capital is included arguably perhaps the last should begin in 1995.

8.5.2 Contributions to Expanded Gross Private National Saving and Rates of Growth

Fig. 8.16 divides gross human and market saving contributions into the contributions of depreciation and net saving. Here, although depreciation reduces net saving, depreciation is shown as an additive component rather than a subtraction from gross saving. For the subperiods 1995–2000, 2000–2007, and 2009–2013, the changes between the previous subperiods 1949–1973 and 1973–1995 show reductions in expanded components growth similar to those shown in Table 8.7 (Table 8A.5). The 2007–2009 subperiod again is an exception. All contributions are positive and higher than in previous subperiods. The contribution of human saving is a result of the impact of school enrollment, as previously noted, and the contribution of depreciation is a

---

[aa]Human capital investment in education occurs when individuals are in school.

[ab]National population estimates are the basis for per capita figures. See two entries in the bibliography for the Census Bureau, accessed August 23, 2019.

[ac]The sum of the growth rate of quantity and price always equals the growth rate of nominal dollars, as it must. Growth rates begin in 1949 as quantity figures for 1948 are not always available, as previously noted.

[ad]Landefeld and Fraumeni (2001).

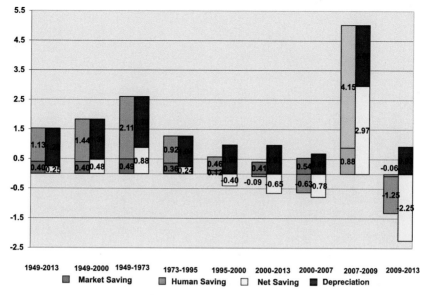

FIG. 8.16 Contributions to expanded gross private national saving.

result of the aging of the work force, as well as retirements and deaths, and possibly lower earnings per hour as a result of the Great Recession. The negative contribution of human saving in 2009–2013 is a return to pre-2007–2009 trends; the negative contribution of market saving is a sign of the weak recovery from the Great Recession. With negative market and human saving contributions, accordingly the contribution of net saving is negative.

8.5.3 Contributions to Expanded Private National Expenditure and Income and Rates of Growth

Most of the major subperiod patterns can be seen in Fig. 8.17. The contributions of all the components, except that for property income, decline between 1949 and 1973 and 1973–1995. In 1995–2000, the contributions of labor income, property income, nonmarket consumption, and net saving are lower than in

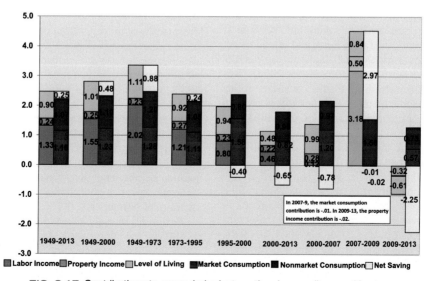

FIG. 8.17 Contributions to expanded private national expenditure and income.

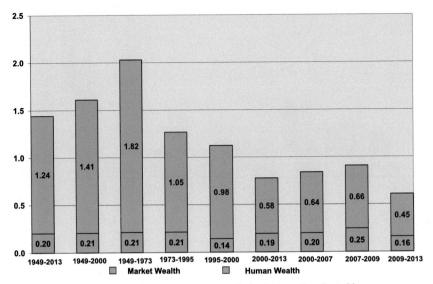

FIG. 8.18 Contributions to expanded private national wealth.

the previous subperiod. In this figure, the contribution of the level of living is defined as the difference between the contribution of income and expenditures (Samuels, 2018). The contribution of net saving is negative as the contribution of total income is decreasing and the contribution of total consumption is increasing. The contribution of the level of living increases slightly as the negative contribution of net saving offsets to a large extent (and is a result of) the difference between the contribution of total income and the contribution of total consumption. The 2000–2007 subperiod component looks somewhat similar to 1995–2000 subperiod components, although the contribution of labor income, market consumption, and net saving fall. Looking at the rates of growth in Tables 8A.4 and 8A.5, which underlie contributions, they fall between the periods before 1995–2000 and the 1995–2000 and 2000–2007 subperiods except for the consumer outlay and property income quantity and quantity per capita. In 2007–2009, primarily because of the impact of investment in education on the contribution of labor income along with the contribution of market consumption being close to zero during the Great Recession, the contribution of net saving becomes a large positive. The probability of 18- to 24-year olds enrolling in postsecondary degree-granting institutions rose significantly as previously described, before declining substantially between 2009 and 2013.[ae] By 2009–2013, the housing crisis had a significant impact on both

quantities and prices of residential units, including those that are owner-occupied.[af] Accordingly, in the 2009–2013 subperiod, the quantity of property income fell and the price of property income rose slightly. In 2009–2013, the contribution of both property income and expanded labor income are negative.

8.5.4 Contributions to Expanded Private National Wealth and Rates of Growth

The creation of two major subperiods, 1949–1995 and 1995–2013, is supported by the decrease in rates of growth between the earlier and the later subperiods shown in Table 8A.6. Except for all price changes and the quantity of market wealth per capita, the downward trend began as early as the 1973–1995 subperiod. The largest drop for a wealth subcomponent is for market wealth quantity and quantity per capita between 1995–2000 and 1973–1995. As national population growth slowed in the later subperiods beginning in 2000–2007, it is not surprising that human wealth accretion slows (see Table 8A.1 for population rates of growth). The quantity per capita of human wealth rate of growth is negative in 1995–2000 and all later subperiods as the rate of national population growth, although low, is higher than the rate of growth of the quantity of human capital.

Beginning in the 1973–1995 subperiod, growth in wealth is less than in 1949–1973 (Fig. 8.18). In 1995–2000, this is equally due to a reduction in the contribution of human and market wealth. The

---

[ae]Table 302.60, National Center for Educational Statistics (2018).

[af]Property income from owner-occupied housing is imputed.

contribution of both forms of wealth recovers in 2000–2007 and 2007–2009, finally feeling the impact of the Great Recession by the 2009–2013 subperiod. As previously noted, increases in enrollments in postsecondary degree institutions by those 18–24 bolstered the 2007–2009 subperiod. The share of human wealth contributions in contributions in total wealth is lower in the second major subperiod, 2000–2012, than in the first major subperiod, 1949–2000, as advancements in the average number of years of school slowed (Fig. 8.4).

8.6 CONCLUSION

The accounts that we have presented in this paper demonstrate how to integrate GDP and human capital accounting to assess the sources of economic growth. Including human capital in any analysis of growth is important to understand the drivers of economic growth for any period of time, but particularly so beginning with the 1995–2000 subperiod in the United States. Before 1995–2000, increasing educational attainment is a dependable source of growth, benefitting both the country and individuals. The 1995–2000 "New Economy" subperiod stands out as a subperiod in which

market economic growth recovered after the post-1973 slowdown. However, increases in educational attainment noticeably slowed, human capital depreciation from an aging work force became a larger factor, and net saving actually decreased from the previous subperiod. In 2007–2009, total market and human capital growth is less than in 1995–2000. A bright spot in the 2007–2009 Great Recession subperiod is that human capital investment increased, as the probability that younger individuals would enroll at the postsecondary level went up. This development, which did not continue into the 2009–2013 subperiod, would be missed if human capital was not included in the analysis. In 2009–2013, the contributions of human capital components to economic growth fell. In the future, a positive net contribution of human capital components to economic growth is in doubt given trends with the workforce continuing to age and average educational attainment through higher enrollments no longer surging. Researchers and policymakers should include human capital components in their analysis to understand the prospects for future growth, as well as how human capital development has interacted with the market sources of growth in the past.

APPENDIX
See Tables 8A.1–8A.6.

TABLE 8A.1
NIPA gross domestic product and expanded gross private domestic product, rates of growth, 1949–2013.

	1949–2013	1949–2000	1949–1973	1973–1995	1995–2000	2000–2013	2000–2007	2007–2009	2009–2013
National population	0.0117	0.0125	0.0146	0.0098	0.0142	0.0087	0.0093	0.0091	0.0075
NIPA GDP quantity	0.0320	0.0359	0.0414	0.0286	0.0421	0.0167	0.0242	−0.0155	0.0199
Expanded product:									
Nominal dollar	0.0607	0.0682	0.0696	0.0737	0.0371	0.0316	0.0324	0.0521	0.0199
Quantity	0.0177	0.0202	0.0253	0.0156	0.0154	0.0079	0.0063	0.0277	0.0007
Quantity per capita	0.0059	0.0077	0.0107	0.0059	0.0012	−0.0009	−0.0030	0.0186	−0.0068
Price	0.0431	0.0480	0.0443	0.0580	0.0217	0.0237	0.0261	0.0243	0.0192
Expanded investment:									
Nominal dollar	0.0603	0.0693	0.0722	0.0749	0.0308	0.0252	0.0210	0.0532	0.0187
Quantity	0.0149	0.0185	0.0259	0.0121	0.0115	0.0006	−0.0035	0.0329	−0.0083
Quantity per capita	0.0032	0.0060	0.0113	0.0023	−0.0027	−0.0081	−0.0129	0.0238	−0.0158
Price	0.0455	0.0508	0.0463	0.0628	0.0193	0.0246	0.0245	0.0203	0.0270
Expanded consumption:									
Nominal dollar	0.0613	0.0663	0.0652	0.0714	0.0490	0.0418	0.0509	0.0504	0.0216
Quantity	0.0223	0.0231	0.0245	0.0217	0.0225	0.0192	0.0222	0.0201	0.0135
Quantity per capita	0.0106	0.0106	0.0099	0.0119	0.0083	0.0105	0.0128	0.0110	0.0061
Price	0.0390	0.0432	0.0407	0.0498	0.0265	0.0226	0.0287	0.0303	0.0081

Sources: NIPA GDP rates of growth are computed from NIPA table 1.1.1, which lists data published July 28, 2017.
Other rates of growth are from the authors' estimates.

TABLE 8A.2
Expanded gross private domestic factor outlay, rates of growth, 1949–2013.

	1949–2013	1949–2000	1949–1973	1973–1995	1995–2000	2000–2013	2000–2007	2007–2009	2009–2013
Expanded factor outlay:									
Nominal dollar	0.0607	0.0682	0.0696	0.0737	0.0371	0.0316	0.0324	0.0521	0.0199
Quantity	0.0158	0.0181	0.0225	0.0147	0.0121	0.0065	0.0041	0.0302	−0.0012

Continued

TABLE 8A.2
Expanded gross private domestic factor outlay, rates of growth, 1949–2013—cont'd

	1949–2013	1949–2000	1949–1973	1973–1995	1995–2000	2000–2013	2000–2007	2007–2009	2009–2013
Quantity per capita	0.0040	0.0056	0.0078	0.0050	−0.0021	−0.0022	−0.0053	0.0211	−0.0086
Price	0.0450	0.0501	0.0471	0.0589	0.0250	0.0251	0.0284	0.0219	0.0211
Expanded labor outlay:									
Nominal dollar	0.0603	0.0679	0.0697	0.0732	0.0362	0.0305	0.0299	0.0530	0.0205
Quantity	0.0141	0.0165	0.0212	0.0132	0.0094	0.0046	0.0011	0.0310	−0.0025
Quantity per capita	0.0024	0.0041	0.0065	0.0034	−0.0049	−0.0041	−0.0082	0.0219	−0.0100
Price	0.0462	0.0514	0.0486	0.0600	0.0268	0.0259	0.0287	0.0220	0.0230
Property outlay:									
Nominal dollar	0.0651	0.0709	0.0676	0.0799	0.0474	0.0423	0.0576	0.0436	0.0149
Quantity	0.0339	0.0361	0.0387	0.0322	0.0411	0.0251	0.0338	0.0226	0.0112
Quantity per capita	0.0222	0.0236	0.0241	0.0224	0.0269	0.0164	0.0244	0.0135	0.0038
Price	0.0312	0.0348	0.0289	0.0477	0.0063	0.0172	0.0238	0.0210	0.0037

TABLE 8A.3
Expanded private national income, rates of growth, 1949–2013.

	1949–2013	1949–2000	1949–1973	1973–1995	1995–2000	2000–2013	2000–2007	2007–2009	2009–2013
Expanded national income:									
Nominal dollar	0.0607	0.0680	0.0697	0.0737	0.0352	0.0320	0.0329	0.0580	0.0174
Quantity	0.0159	0.0182	0.0227	0.0149	0.0106	0.0069	0.0040	0.0369	−0.0033
Quantity per capita	0.0041	0.0057	0.0081	0.0051	−0.0036	−0.0019	−0.0053	0.0278	−0.0107
Price index	0.0449	0.0499	0.0469	0.0588	0.0246	0.0252	0.0289	0.0211	0.0207
Expanded labor income:									
Nominal dollar	0.0603	0.0678	0.0698	0.0730	0.0351	0.0309	0.0306	0.0560	0.0189
Quantity	0.0142	0.0166	0.0214	0.0131	0.0087	0.0050	0.0013	0.0349	−0.0036
Quantity per capita	0.0025	0.0041	0.0068	0.0033	−0.0055	−0.0037	−0.0080	0.0258	−0.0110
Price index	0.0461	0.0512	0.0484	0.0599	0.0264	0.0259	0.0293	0.0211	0.0225

Continued

TABLE 8A.3
Expanded private national income, rates of growth, 1949–2013—cont'd

	1949–2013	1949–2000	1949–1973	1973–1995	1995–2000	2000–2013	2000–2007	2007–2009	2009–2013
Property income:									
Nominal dollar	0.0660	0.0715	0.0671	0.0842	0.0364	0.0444	0.0588	0.0779	0.0024
Quantity	0.0347	0.0367	0.0382	0.0365	0.0300	0.0268	0.0349	0.0567	−0.0025
Quantity per capita	0.0229	0.0242	0.0235	0.0268	0.0157	0.0180	0.0256	0.0476	−0.0099
Price	0.0313	0.0348	0.0290	0.0477	0.0064	0.0176	0.0239	0.0212	0.0049

TABLE 8A.4
Expanded private national expenditures, rates of growth, 1949–2013.

	1949–2013	1949–2000	1949–1973	1973–1995	1995–2000	2000–2013	2000–2007	2007–2009	2009–2013
Expanded expenditures:									
Nominal dollar	0.0609	0.0681	0.0697	0.0739	0.0353	0.0324	0.0334	0.0595	0.0172
Quantity	0.0179	0.0201	0.0255	0.0161	0.0122	0.0091	0.0079	0.0362	−0.0025
Quantity per capita	0.0062	0.0076	0.0109	0.0063	−0.0020	0.0003	−0.0014	0.0271	−0.0099
Price index	0.0430	0.0480	0.0442	0.0578	0.0231	0.0233	0.0255	0.0233	0.0197
Expanded consumer outlays:									
Nominal dollar	0.0615	0.0666	0.0653	0.0717	0.0505	0.0413	0.0511	0.0458	0.0219
Quantity	0.0222	0.0233	0.0248	0.0216	0.0238	0.0181	0.0217	0.0155	0.0129
Quantity per capita	0.0105	0.0108	0.0101	0.0118	0.0096	0.0093	0.0124	0.0064	0.0055
Price index	0.0392	0.0433	0.0406	0.0501	0.0266	0.0232	0.0293	0.0303	0.0090
Expanded gross saving:									
Nominal dollar	0.0605	0.0690	0.0723	0.0750	0.0270	0.0268	0.0220	0.0690	0.0140
Quantity	0.0153	0.0183	0.0261	0.0128	0.0058	0.0032	−0.0009	0.0503	−0.0132
Quantity per capita	0.0035	0.0058	0.0115	0.0030	−0.0085	−0.0055	−0.0103	0.0412	−0.0206
Price	0.0452	0.0507	0.0462	0.0623	0.0213	0.0236	0.0229	0.0187	0.0271

TABLE 8A.5
Expanded gross private national saving, rates of growth, 1949–2013.

	1949–2013	1949–2000	1949–1973	1973–1995	1995–2000	2000–2013	2000–2007	2007–2009	2009–2013
Expanded gross saving:									
Nominal dollar	0.0605	0.0690	0.0723	0.0750	0.0270	0.0268	0.0220	0.0690	0.0140
Quantity	0.0153	0.0183	0.0261	0.0128	0.0058	0.0032	−0.0009	0.0503	−0.0132
Quantity per capita	0.0035	0.0058	0.0115	0.0030	−0.0085	−0.0055	−0.0103	0.0412	−0.0206
Price index	0.0452	0.0507	0.0462	0.0623	0.0213	0.0236	0.0229	0.0187	0.0271
Expanded depreciation:									
Nominal dollar	0.0628	0.0695	0.0710	0.0764	0.0315	0.0368	0.0338	0.0308	0.0450
Quantity	0.0172	0.0187	0.0246	0.0136	0.0126	0.0116	0.0084	0.0243	0.0109
Quantity per capita	0.0055	0.0062	0.0099	0.0039	−0.0016	0.0029	−0.0009	0.0152	0.0034
Price index	0.0456	0.0508	0.0464	0.0628	0.0189	0.0252	0.0254	0.0064	0.0341
Expanded net saving:									
Nominal dollar	0.0486	0.0676	0.0762	0.0709	0.0117	−0.0260	−0.0304	0.2412	−0.1519
Quantity	0.0060	0.0177	0.0318	0.0101	−0.0162	−0.0396	−0.0419	0.1615	−0.1363
Quantity per capita	−0.0057	0.0052	0.0171	0.0003	−0.0304	−0.0484	−0.0513	0.1524	−0.1437
Price	0.0425	0.0499	0.0445	0.0608	0.0280	0.0136	0.0115	0.0797	−0.0156

TABLE 8A.6
Expanded private national wealth, rates of growth, 1949–2013.

	1949–2013	1949–2000	1949–1973	1973–1995	1995–2000	2000–2013	2000–2007	2007–2009	2009–2013
Expanded wealth:									
Nominal dollar	0.0593	0.0654	0.0685	0.0658	0.0486	0.0355	0.0482	0.0270	0.0176
Quantity	0.0144	0.0161	0.0203	0.0127	0.0112	0.0078	0.0084	0.0091	0.0061
Quantity per capita	0.0027	0.0036	0.0057	0.0029	−0.0030	−0.0009	−0.0009	0.0000	−0.0014
Price index	0.0449	0.0493	0.0482	0.0532	0.0373	0.0277	0.0398	0.0179	0.0115
Human wealth:									
Nominal dollar	0.0588	0.0649	0.0686	0.0648	0.0475	0.0348	0.0457	0.0364	0.0149

Continued

TABLE 8A.6
Expanded private national wealth, rates of growth, 1949–2013—cont'd

	1949–2013	1949–2000	1949–1973	1973–1995	1995–2000	2000–2013	2000–2007	2007–2009	2009–2013
Quantity	0.0133	0.0150	0.0193	0.0113	0.0106	0.0064	0.0071	0.0072	0.0049
Quantity per capita	0.0015	0.0025	0.0047	0.0015	−0.0036	−0.0023	−0.0023	−0.0019	−0.0026
Price index	0.0455	0.0499	0.0493	0.0535	0.0369	0.0284	0.0387	0.0292	0.0100
Market wealth:									
Nominal dollar	0.0658	0.0717	0.0657	0.0805	0.0610	0.0428	0.0728	−0.0697	0.0465
Quantity	0.0296	0.0316	0.0359	0.0300	0.0184	0.0219	0.0219	0.0277	0.0190
Quantity per capita	0.0179	0.0191	0.0212	0.0202	0.0042	0.0132	0.0126	0.0186	0.0115
Price	0.0362	0.0401	0.0299	0.0506	0.0426	0.0209	0.0509	−0.0974	0.0275

REFERENCES

Barro, R., Lee, J., 2013a. A new data set of educational attainment in the world, 1950-2010. J. Dev. Econ. 104 (C), 184–198.

Barro, R., Lee, J., 2013b. Barro-Lee educational attainment data set. Last updated April 9, 2013. http://www.barrolee.com/. (Accessed October 2013).

Bernanke, B., 2004. The great moderation. In: Remarks by Governor Ben S. Bernanke, at the meetings of the Eastern Economic Association, Washington, DC, February 20. https://www.federalreserve.gov/boarddocs/speeches/2004/20040220/default.htm. Accessed November 17, 2019.

Boskin, M.J., 2000. Getting the 21st-century GDP right, economic measurement: progress and challenges. Am. Econ. Rev. Pap. Proc. 90 (2), 247–252.

Bureau of Economic Analysis, U.S. Department of Commerce, 2013. Preview of the 2013 Comprehensive Revision of the National Income and Product Accounts, Changes in Definitions and Presentations. Survey of Current Business. U.S. Government Printing Office, Washington, DC, pp. 13–39.

Bureau of Economic Analysis, U.S. Department of Commerce, 2017. National Income and Product Accounts. July 28.

Bureau of Economic Analysis, U.S. Department of Commerce, Various Issues. Survey of Current Business. U.S. Government Printing Office, Washington, DC.

Census Bureau, U.S. Department of Commerce, 1975. Bicentennial Edition: Historical Statistics of the United States, Colonial Times to the Present. U.S. Government Printing Office, Washington, DC.

Census Bureau, U.S. Department of Commerce, 2015. Current Population Survey, Annual Social and Economic Supplements. U.S. Government Printing Office, Washington, DC.

Census Bureau, U.S. Department of Commerce, 2019. Table P-40 Women's Earnings as a Percentage of Men's Earnings by Race and Hispanic Origin: 1960 to 2018. https://www.census.gov/data/tables/time-series/demo/income-poverty/historical-income-people.html. (Accessed 19 November 2019).

Christian, M.S., 2017. Net investment and stocks of human capital in the United States, 1975–2013. Int. Prod. Monit. 33 (Fall), 128–149.

Fraumeni, B.M., Christian, M.S., 2019. Accumulation of human and market capital in the United States, 1975–2012: an analysis by gender. In: Fraumeni, B.M. (Ed.), Measuring Economic Growth and Productivity, Foundations, KLEM Production Models, and Extensions. Academic Press, Cambridge, MA, pp. 509–529.

Fraumeni, B.M., Christian, M.S., Samuels, J.D., 2017. The accumulation of human and nonhuman capital, revisited. Rev. Income Wealth 63 (supplement 2), S381–S410.

Gollop, F.M., Jorgenson, D.W., 1980. U.S. productivity growth by industry, 1947–73. In: Kendrick, J.W., Vaccara, B.N. (Eds.), New Developments in Productivity Measurement and Analysis. University of Chicago Press, NBER, Chicago, pp. 17–136.

Gollop, F.M., Jorgenson, D.W., 1983. Sectoral measures of labor cost of the United States, 1948–1979. In: Triplett, J. E. (Ed.), The Measurement of Labor Cost. University of Chicago Press, NBER, Chicago, pp. 185–235.

Jaszi, G., Kendrick, J.W., 1951. Estimate of Gross National Product in constant dollars, 1929–49. Survey of Current Business. Office of Business Economics, Bureau of Domestic and Foreign Commerce, U.S. Department of Commerce, U.S. Government Printing Office, Washington, DC, pp. 6–11.

Jorgenson, D.W., 2010. Designing a new architecture for the U. S. national accounts. Ann. Amer. Acad. Polit. Social Sci. 631 (1), 63–74.

Jorgenson, D.W., Fraumeni, B.M., 1989. The accumulation of human and nonhuman capital, 1948–1984. In: Lipsey, R., Tice, H. (Eds.), The Measurement of Saving, Investment and Wealth. University of Chicago Press, NBER, Chicago, pp. 227–282.

Jorgenson, D.W., Fraumeni, B.M., 1992a. Investment in education and U.S. economic growth. Scand. J. Econ. 94 (supplement), S51–S70.

Jorgenson, D.W., Fraumeni, B.M., 1992b. The output of the education sector. In: Griliches, Z., Breshnahan, T., Manser, M., Berndt, E. (Eds.), The Output of the Service Sector. University of Chicago Press, NBER, Chicago, pp. 303–341.

Jorgenson, D.W., Landefeld, J.S., 2006. Blueprint for expanded and integrated U.S. accounts: review, assessment, and next steps. In: Jorgenson, D.W., Landefeld, J.S., Nordhaus, W.D. (Eds.), A New Architecture for the U.S. National Accounts. University of Chicago Press, NBER, Chicago, pp. 13–112.

Jorgenson, D.W., Landefeld, J.S., 2009. Implementation of a new architecture for the U.S. national accounts. Am. Econ. Rev. Pap. Proc. 99 (2), 64–68.

Landefeld, J.S., Fraumeni, B.M., 2001. Measuring the New Economy. Survey of Current Business, March, pp. 23–40.

National Bureau of Economic Research, 2019. US business cycle expansions and contractions. http://wwwdev.nber.org/cycles/cyclesmain.html. (Accessed 23 July 2019).

National Center for Education Statistics, 2018. Digest of Education Statistics: 2016. NCES. http://nces.ed.gov/programs/digest/d15/tables/dt15_302.60.asp. (Accessed 15 March 2018).

Samuels, J.D., 2018. Aggregate productivity and the level of living, and estimates for 1948–2016, unpublished manuscript. In: Presented at the International Association for Research in Income and Wealth Conference, Copenhagen, Denmark, August 20. http://www.iariw.org/c2018copenhagen.php.

Toosi, M., 2002. A century of change: the U.S. labor force, 1950–2050: With slower growth, aging, and increasing diversity, the profile of the U.S. labor force is undergoing a gradual, but significant, change. Monthly Labor Review. Bureau of Labor Statistics, U.S. Department of Labor, Washington, DC, pp. 15–28. May.

Toosi, M., 2012. Labor force projections to 2020: A more slowly growing workforce. Monthly Labor Review. Bureau of Labor Statistics, U.S. Department of Labor, Washington, DC, pp. 43–64. January.

Index

Note: Page numbers followed by *f* indicate figures and *t* indicate tables.

A

Accounts in nominal dollars
  education investment, 178
  expanded private national
    consumer expenditures, 180–182,
     181*t*
    labor and property income,
     178–180, 179*t*
    saving, 182–184, 182*t*
    wealth, 184, 185*t*
  expanded production, 177*t*, 188*t*
  list of U.S. recessions, 171*t*
  production account, 176–178
Adult survival rates, 61
Aggregation methodology, 57–59,
  105–106
Air pollution, 4–8, 17–21
  effect of, 7–8
  impact of, 7–8
  mortality, 8–17, 38

B

Better employment rate (BER), 77
Bureau of Economic Analysis (BEA),
  168

C

Capabilities approach, 86
Caribbean region, 131–132
Central Asia region, 131
Composite indices, 106
Conditional cash transfers (CCTs),
  79
Contributions and rates of growths
  expanded gross private domestic
    product and economic growth,
    184–188
  expanded gross private national
    saving, 188–189
  expanded private national
    expenditure
    and income, 189–190
  expanded private national wealth,
    190–191
Cost-based approach, 140
COVID-19 pandemic, 64–65
Cross-country rankings, 71–72
Cyber-physical systems, 125

D

Demographic and Health Surveys
  (DHS), 75
Development component, 128
Divisia decomposition method, 141

E

Early Grade Reading Assessments
  (EGRAs), 61
East Asia, 131
Eastern Europe, 131
Economic development, 69–71
Economic growth, 184–188
Education, 39
  gender gaps, 68–71
  and health, 58–59
  indicators, 92–93
  investment, 178
Educational attainment, 118–119, 126,
  145, 171–172
Education based approach, 140
EGRAs. *See* Early Grade Reading
  Assessments
  (EGRAs)
Executive Opinion Survey (EOS), 126
Expanded account, 176
Expanded factor outlay, 192–193*t*
Expanded gross private domestic
  product, 184–188
Expected years of school (EYS), 60–61

F

Fourth Industrial Revolution, 125
Functional transformation, income,
  95–97

G

Gaussian process regression, 118
Geometric mean, 106–108
Global analysis, 41
Global Burden of Disease (GBD), 92,
  117
Global Competitiveness Report 2019,
  134
Global economic system, 125
Global Gender Gap Report 2020,
  136–137, 134
Global wealth accounts, 22–24
Gross domestic product (GDP), 47*f*,
  168
Gross national income (GNI), 94
Gross national product (GNP), 168
Growth, 59–60

H

Harmonized test scores (HTS), 56–57,
  61–62
HCP. *See* Human Capital Project (HCP)
HDCA. *See* Human Development and
  Capability Association (HDCA)

HDI. *See* Human Development Index
  (HDI)
Health adjusted life expectancy (HALE),
  92
Health indicator, 92
Household surveys, 5–7
HTS. *See* Harmonized test scores
  (HTS)
Human capital, 17–21, 85
  accumulation, 69
  age and impact, 7–8
  air pollution (*see* Air pollution)
  annual growth rates, 139–140
  average year of schooling, 43*f*
  child labor, 51*f*
  data sources and assumptions, 41*t*
  discount rate, 6
  education-based measure, 145–147
  education systems
    in china, 143–144
    in Hong Kong, 144
    in Taiwan, 144–145
  gap filling, 6–7
  genuine savings, 50*f*
  vs. gross domestic product (GDP),
    47*f*
  happiness index, 49*f*
  vs. Human Development Index
    (HDI), 48*f*
  intensity of labor force, 160
  Jorgensen-Fraumeni measure
    individual labor earnings, 148–149
    lifetime income, 139, 149
    per capita, 153–155
    total human capital, 149–153
  labor force
    age structure, 160
    aging, 142–143
    composition, 160–162
    definition and size, 141–142
    education, 160
    human capital stock, 160–162
  literature, 40*t*
  measurement of, 140–141
  methodology, 40–41
  national wealth accounts, 2–3
  vs. natural capital, 45*f*
  percentage growth of, 46*f*
  physical capital, 156–159
  policy recommendation, 52
  population aging, 159
  population dividend sustainability,
    162–163
  reserve, 162–163, 164*f*
  self-employed, 6

Human capital (*Continued*)
total wealth of nations, 44*f*
wealth, 24–38
World Economic Forum (*see* World Economic Forum (WEF))
Human Capital Index (HCI)
aggregation methodology, 57–59
components of, 56–57
development, 72–75
future income, 59–60
growth, 59–60
indicators, 127
limitations, 71
poverty reduction, 59–60
subnational disaggregation, 75–76
Human Capital Index (HCI) 2020
adult survival rates, 61
child survival, 60
expected years of school, 60–61
fraction of children under 5 not stunted, 61
gender gaps, 68–71
harmonized test scores, 61
index components, 62–63
results, 64–67
Human capital methodology
accounts in nominal dollars (*see* Accounts in nominal dollars)
contributions and rates of growths (*see* Contributions and rates of growths)
expanded account, 176
expanded factor outlay, 192–193*t*
expanded private national
expenditures, 194*t*
income, 193–194*t*
saving, 195*t*
wealth, 195–196*t*
factors
educational attainment, 171–172
labor force participation, 170–171
level of earnings, 172–173
five accounts, 173–176
Great Moderation, 167
Jorgenson-Fraumeni methodology, 167–169
life cycle, 169
measures of, 168
modifications, 170
net investment, 169
nominal lifetime income, 169
nominal share, 180–181*f*
nominal stock, 169
production account, 176
system of national accounts, 168
Human capital per capita, 153–155
Human capital per worker, 153
Human Capital Project (HCP), 77
Human development
capabilities approach, 84–86
means and ends, 85–86
measurement framework, 86–88

Human Development and Capability Association (HDCA), 87
Human Development Index (HDI), 48*f*
country ranking, 108–109
criticisms, 88–89
data issues and perspectives, 109–110
functional form, 94–106
indicators, 89–94

I

IGME. *See* Interagency Group for Child Mortality Estimation (IGME)
Inclusive wealth, 40
Income-based approach, 140–141
Inequality, 84–85
Information, communications and technology skills, 129–130
Institute for Health Metrics and Evaluation (IHME)
advantages of, 122–123
annual measurement, 122
educational attainment, 118–119
expected human capital
index of, 119
level of, 120–122, 121*t*
expected human capital *vs.* gross domestic product, 119
expected years lived, 117, 119–120, 122
functional health status measures, 118
Gaussian process regression, 118
Global Burden of Disease, 117
human capital index, 117
learning, 118
limitations of, 123
survival, 118
uncertainty analysis, 118
Interagency Group for Child Mortality Estimation (IGME), 60
International Association for the Evaluation of Educational Achievement (IEA), 118
Interquartile range (IQR), 119

J

Joint Malnutrition Estimates (JME), 61
Jordan's unemployment rate, 127–128
Jorgensen-Fraumeni framework, 148, 167–169
Jorgenson-Fraumeni (J-F) lifetime income, 139

K

Know-how component, 130

L

Labor force
aging, 142–143
composition, 160–162
definitions, 141–142

participation, 127–128, 170–171
Latin American Laboratory for Assessment of the Quality of Education (LLECE), 61
Learning, 118
Level of earnings, 172–173
LinkedIn membership, 126–127
LLECE. *See* Latin American Laboratory for Assessment of the Quality of Education (LLECE)

M

Mean years of schooling (MYS), 93
Measurement agenda, 77–79
Middle East, 132
Mincer equation, 148
Mincer model, 141
Mortality rate, 60
Multiple Indicator Cluster Surveys (MICS), 75
MYS. *See* Mean years of schooling (MYS)

N

National accounts data, 5–6
National Income and Product Accounts (NIPA), 168
National population data, 6
National wealth, 1–2
National wealth accounts, 2–3
Nations' human capital, 41–42
Net investment, 169
Nominal lifetime income, 169
Nominal share, 180–181*f*
Nominal stock, 169
North Africa region, 132
North America, 132

O

Ordinary least squares (OLS), 148
Organisation for Economic Cooperation and Development (OECD), 118

P

Pacific Island Learning and Numeracy Assessment (PILNA), 61
Pacific region, 131
Principal components analysis (PCA), 118
Production account, 176–178
Productivity, 57
Programme for International Student Assessment (PISA), 61, 118
Programme for the Analysis of Education Systems (PASEC), 61
Progress in International Reading Literacy Study (PIRLS), 61, 118
Public-private cooperation organization, 125

S

Scaling of indicators, 97–103
SNA. *See* System of national accounts (SNA)
South Asia, 132
Southern and Eastern Africa Consortium for Monitoring Educational Quality (SACMEQ), 61
Standard of living, 94
Stunting rate, 58
Sub-Saharan Africa, 132–133
Sustainable development, 39–40
System of national accounts (SNA), 168

T

Test score harmonization, 71
Trends in International Mathematics and Science Study (TIMSS), 56–57, 118
Tuition-based system, 147

U

Underemployment rate, 127
Utilization-Adjusted Human Capital Index (UHCI), 76–77

W

Wealth, 24–38
    estimates of, 38
    nations, 5–7
Weighting, 103–105
Western Europe, 133
World Bank. *See* Human Capital Index (HCI)
World Economic Forum (WEF)
    components
        capacity, 126–127
        deployment score, 127–128
        development, 128–130
        know-how, 130
    country indicator, 125
    executive opinion survey, 126
    Fourth Industrial Revolution, 125

The Global Competitiveness Report 2019, 134–137
The Global Gender Gap Report 2020, 134–137
    gross national income per capita, 133–134
    human capital index
        Caribbean region, 131–132
        Central Asia region, 131
        East Asia, 131
        Eastern Europe, 131
        Latin America, 131–132
        Middle East, 132
        North Africa region, 132
        North America, 132
        Pacific region, 131
        South Asia, 132
        Sub-Saharan Africa, 132–133
        Western Europe, 133
    knowledge skills people, 125
    public-private cooperation organization, 125
World Health Organization (WHO), 61